TRANSPORT AND CHILDREN'S WELLBEING

TRANSPORT AND CHILDREN'S WELLBEING

Edited by

E. OWEN D. WAYGOOD
MARGARETA FRIMAN
LARS E. OLSSON
RAKTIM MITRA

ELSEVIER

Elsevier
Radarweg 29, PO Box 211, 1000 AE Amsterdam, Netherlands
The Boulevard, Langford Lane, Kidlington, Oxford OX5 1GB, United Kingdom
50 Hampshire Street, 5th Floor, Cambridge, MA 02139, United States

Library of Congress Cataloging-in-Publication Data
A catalog record for this book is available from the Library of Congress

British Library Cataloguing-in-Publication Data
A catalogue record for this book is available from the British Library

ISBN: 978-0-12-814694-1

For information on all Elsevier publications visit our
website at https://www.elsevier.com/books-and-journals

Publisher: Joe Hayton
Acquisition Editor: Brian Romer
Editorial Project Manager: Andrae Akeh
Production Project Manager: Kamesh Ramajogi
Cover Designer: Matthew Limbert

Typeset by SPi Global, India

Contents

Contributors

Zainab Abbasi
School of Urban and Regional Planning, Ryerson University, Toronto, ON, Canada

Richard W. Baldauf
United States Environmental Protection Agency, Research Triangle Park, NC, United States

Vickie L. Boothe
Centers for Disease Control and Prevention, Atlanta, GA, United States

Marie-Soleil Cloutier
Centre Urbanisation Culture Société, Institut National de la Recherche Scientifique, Montreal, QC, Canada

Adrian Field
Director of Dovetail Consulting Ltd., Auckland, New Zealand

Liraz Fridman
Child Health Evaluative Sciences, The Hospital for Sick Children, Toronto, ON, Canada

Margareta Friman
Service Research Center and Department of Social and Psychological Studies, Karlstad University, Karlstad, Sweden

Lingling He
Beijing Zhishu Consulting, Beijing, China

Andrew Howard
Child Health Evaluative Sciences, The Hospital for Sick Children, Toronto, ON, Canada

Märit Jansson
Dept of Landscape Architecture, Planning and Management, Swedish University of Agricultural Sciences, Alnarp, Sweden

Maria Johansson
Environmental Psychology, Dept of Architecture and Built Environment, Lund University, Lund, Sweden

Astrid Kemperman
Built Environment, Eindhoven University of Technology, Eindhoven, Netherlands

Richard Larouche
Public Health, Faculty of Health Sciences, University of Lethbridge, Lethbridge, AB, Canada

Lin Lin
Xi'an Jiaotong—Liverpool University, Suzhou, China

Kevin Manaugh
Department of Geography, McGill School of Environment, McGill University, Montreal, QC, Canada

Fredrika Mårtensson
Dept of Work Science, Business Economics and Environmental Psychology, Swedish
University of Agricultural Sciences, Alnarp, Sweden

Noreen C. McDonald
Department of City & Regional Planning, University of North Carolina at Chapel Hill,
Chapel Hill, NC, United States

Raktim Mitra
School of Urban and Regional Planning, Ryerson University, Toronto, ON, Canada

Lars E. Olsson
Service Research Center and Department of Social and Psychological Studies, Karlstad
University, Karlstad, Sweden

W. Mathew Palmer
Durham Public Schools, Durham, NC, United States

David Rojas-Rueda
Environmental and Radiological Health Sciences, Colorado State University, Fort Collins,
CO, United States; Barcelona Institute for Global Health, Barcelona, Spain

Timothy Ross
Department of Geography and Planning, University of Toronto, Toronto, ON, Canada

Linda Rothman
Child Health Evaluative Sciences, The Hospital for Sick Children, Toronto,
ON, Canada

Ben Shaw
Department of Sociology, University of Surrey, Guildford, United Kingdom

Ruth L. Steiner
Department of Urban and Regional Planning, University of Florida, Gainesville, FL,
United States

Catharina Sternudd
Dept of Architecture and Built Environment, Lund University, Lund, Sweden

Ayako Taniguchi
Risk Engineering, University of Tsukuba, Tsukuba, Japan

Iris van de Craats
Built Environment, Eindhoven University of Technology, Eindhoven, Netherlands

Pauline van den Berg
Built Environment, Eindhoven University of Technology, Eindhoven, Netherlands

E. Owen D. Waygood
Department of Civil, Geological, and Mining Engineering, Polytechnique Montréal,
Montreal, QC, Canada

Jessica Westman
Service Research Center and Department of Social and Psychological Studies, Karlstad University, Karlstad, Sweden

Karen Witten
SHORE & Whariki Research Centre, Massey University, Auckland, New Zealand

About the editors

E. Owen D. Waygood graduated in 2009 with a PhD in Civil Engineering from Kyoto University (Kyoto, Japan). After a position as a research associate and then research fellow at the Centre for Transport and Society at the University of the West of England (Bristol, United Kingdom), he held first a position of Assistant and then Associate Professor of Transport Planning at Laval University (Quebec, Canada). In 2018 he was recruited by Polytechnique Montréal as an Associate Professor of Transport Engineering. He has published research on children's transport, physical activity, and social connections, sustainable transport, and transport behavior change. He has been a co-guest editor for special issues on transport and child wellbeing, and transport and wellbeing published with the journal *Travel Behaviour and Society*. He conducts research on sustainable transport modes and how to increase their use.

Margareta Friman graduated in 2000 with a PhD from University of Gothenburg (Göteborg, Sweden). After having held positions as Assistant and Associate Professor at Karlstad University (Sweden), she was in 2010 appointed as Professor of Psychology at Karlstad University. For the last 10 years she has been director of an excellent center in service and market oriented public transport research (SAMOT) at Karlstad University. In 2014, she received the Håkan Frisinger Foundation for Transportation Research Award by the Volvo Research and Educational Foundations. She is co-editor of the book "Quality of life and daily travel".

Lars E. Olsson graduated from Göteborg University with a PhD in Psychology of decision making. After a position as researcher at the Center for Consumer Research at the School of Business, Economics, and Law in Gothenburg, he was recruited in 2009 to the Service and Market Oriented Transport Research Group (SAMOT). He is now Professor of Psychology at Karlstad University. Lars E. Olsson has published research in the areas of sustainability, environmental behavior, consumer experiences, travel behavior and wellbeing. His articles have been published in international journals in psychology, environmental studies, economics, and transportation. He is co-editor of the book "Quality of life and daily travel".

Raktim Mitra is an Associate Professor of Urban and Regional Planning at Ryerson University (Toronto, Canada), where his research focuses on the intersection between the neighborhood built environment and transport behavior, and the impact on health outcomes such as physical activity and the quality of life. Raktim is the co-director of TransForm research laboratory of transport and land use planning at Ryerson University, co-chair of a paper review subcommittee (Bicycle Transportation) at the Transportation Research Board, and a member of the editorial board for the international journal—*Urban Planning*. His previous contributions include co-editing a special issue on the topic of transport and land use in childhood for the *Journal of Transport and Land Use*.

CHAPTER ONE

Introduction to transport and children's wellbeing

E. Owen D. Waygood[a], Margareta Friman[b], Lars E. Olsson[b], and Raktim Mitra[c]

[a]Department of Civil, Geological, and Mining Engineering, Polytechnique Montréal, Montreal, QC, Canada
[b]Service Research Center and Department of Social and Psychological Studies, Karlstad University, Karlstad, Sweden
[c]School of Urban and Regional Planning, Ryerson University, Toronto, ON, Canada

Contents

1 Introduction

The aim of this book is to bring together current evidence of the myriad ways in which transport influences children's wellbeing. Many of these influences have previously been hypothesized or argued from a theoretical perspective. As new evidence emerges from empirical research, the nature and direction of the relationship between transport and the various domains of a child's wellbeing are becoming clearer. However, much remains to be learned, and the breadth of knowledge to be introduced and discussed in this book is a step in that direction.

This book has two key concepts, namely "transport" and "wellbeing". For the purposes of this book, we limit the definition of transport to the land-based movement of people and goods from one place to another, in order to facilitate participation in various economic, educational, social and recreational activities on a day-to-day basis. Most citizens, adults and children alike, have to make trips—with some of these happening on a regular basis (e.g., trips to and from school) and some more occasionally (e.g., trips to/from leisure destinations). In making these trips, people make various modal choices, with the common transport modes including privately-owned automobiles (i.e., cars), public transport/mass transit, bicycle, and walking. Some of these transport modes require light to moderate bodily movement and are hence called "active" transport modes (e.g., walking, cycling, and, to some extent, public transport). Others involve less physical activity and are commonly known as "passive" or "inactive" modes of transport (Tudor-Locke, Ainsworth, & Popkin, 2001). In addition, children's travel can occur in the company of adult caregivers (known as escorted trips) or without adult supervision (known as children's independent mobility, or CIM) (Hillman, Adams, & Whitelegg, 1990; Tranter & Whitelegg, 1994).

In comparison with the concepts relating to transport, the definition of wellbeing is somewhat elusive and often poorly conceptualized. The World Health Organization has been defining health as "a state of complete physical, mental, and social wellbeing and not merely the absence of disease or infirmity" since 1948.[a] Within this context, the term wellbeing encompasses aspects of health that include, but are not limited to, illness or other physiological deficiencies. In common parlance, wellbeing is often understood as a perception of life-satisfaction or "happiness" and more broadly, quality of life. However, some researchers emphasized the need for a more inclusive definition of the concept (Dodge, Daly, Huyton, & Sanders, 2012).

While scholarly efforts to identify a unified definition continue, it is possible to define, and therefore operationalize, wellbeing on the basis of an individual's positive state in relation to characteristics pertaining to specific domains. Pollard and Lee (2003) defined wellbeing as a multidimensional construct that for children incorporates mental/psychological, physical, social, cognitive (a sub-domain of the psychological domain) and economic dimensions. They furthermore discuss the differences between psychological and cognitive domains—"The psychological domain includes indicators that pertain to emotions, mental health, or mental illness, while the cognitive domain includes indicators that are considered intellectual or school-related in nature." (p. 64) Physical wellbeing evaluates physical health, e.g., physical activity, collisions, and asthma. The social domain pertains to sociological phenomena such as social interactions and social capital. Lastly, the

---

[a] http://www.who.int/about/mission/en/.

economic domain relates to household income, which has been found to relate to certain wellbeing outcomes (but not all, and not always in a linear manner). For the purposes of this book, we define wellbeing as a child's characteristic positive state with regard to his/her *physical, psychological, cognitive, social* and *economic* health.

A recent review demonstrated that consistent research findings globally demonstrate the links between transport and child wellbeing (Waygood, Friman, Olsson, & Taniguchi, 2017). Unfortunately, the predominant approach to transport planning practice in many Western countries, including the planning of transport infrastructure and the land uses facilitating and creating the demand for transport, has focused largely on the needs and transport patterns of able-bodied working-age adults. The impact of such planning decisions on children often remains overlooked in policy (Freeman & Tranter, 2011). For example, the typical approach to determining the level-of-service (LOS) of roadways focuses primarily on space-time convergence (i.e., speed and related time needs) for cars on the roads. This approach almost entirely ignores the safety of vulnerable users; but more importantly, it also ignores the role of streets as public spaces (Jones & Boujenko, 2009). The more recent introduction of the multi-modal LOS approach also puts its focus on adults' travel. At the same time, contemporary Western urban development policy and practice often feature low-density development at the urban edges, a lack of mixed land use, and "magnet" facilities with larger service areas instead of neighborhood-level amenities (e.g., schools). The result of this can be an urban form where distances between destinations (e.g., between home and school) can be unreasonably large for a child, whereby the perceived level of safety is diminished due to fewer eyes on the street and the lack of pedestrian/cycling infrastructure can encourage automobile-dependency.

The current transport practices of many Western societies limit children's mobility in many ways. Most daily trips made by children relate to local destinations, e.g., schools and local parks, which may be accessed via active modes. However, transport infrastructure or patterns can impact children's travel by creating physical barrier or by elevating parental fear of traffic danger. As children and most adolescents do not drive, their daily mobility in an automobile-dependent urban environment can become excessively dependent on their parents, thus reducing opportunities for physical activity through active travel or play, and at the same time affecting their potential for social interaction. What are the direct and indirect impacts of these transport outcomes on children's physical, psychological, cognitive, social and economic wellbeing? What can be done by policymakers, practitioners and community-organizations to improve transport-related wellbeing? In neighborhoods and societies where the use of active, safe and environmentally-sustainable transport modes is encouraged, do children enjoy better health and wellbeing? In this book, we seek to address these questions.

The book *Transport and Children's Wellbeing* provides a broad overview useful to both academics and practitioners. To this end, we have brought together distinguished scholars from a variety of fields to provide reviews and evidence of current thinking on the links between transport and children's wellbeing. Research on children's wellbeing integrates several fields, including the environment, traffic and transport psychology; transport planning and engineering; transport geography; health geography; transport economics; consumer services; and environmental sociology. We hope that this book will provide a comprehensive understanding of the different domains of children's wellbeing, explored through these different lenses. In this introductory chapter, we provide a brief background to *Transport and Children's Wellbeing* and an overview of the chapters, arranged into five different parts: *Overview of transport and children's wellbeing* (Part I), *Transport externalities and children's wellbeing* (Part II), *Solutions for transport and children's wellbeing* (Part III), *Examples from different cultures* (Part IV), and *Future directions* (Part V).

2 Transport and various domains of wellbeing

The existing literature has reported on consistent findings linking transport to children's wellbeing. We present a summary of this literature as an introduction to the discussion on this topic, and in order to set the context for the upcoming chapters. We acknowledge that the summary presented here is not an exhaustive list of such influences.

2.1 Physical

Indicators from the physical domain include health-compromising behaviors, exercise, or safety-related behavior (Pollard & Lee, 2003). Transport can facilitate access to destinations allowing for exercise; it can also include exercise and cause health problems through externalities to others. Much recent attention has focused on active transport, which is any mode of travel that requires physical activity, with collisions having been a concern since the dawn of the car age. With increasing car use, other externalities have come into focus, e.g., emissions and vibrations/noise pollution. Chapter 2 will examine many of these relationships, with Chapters 6, 7, and 8 focusing respectively on speed and traffic danger, emissions, and health impact assessments.

2.2 Psychological

The psychological domain includes indicators pertaining to emotions, mental health, and mental illness. Measures include anxiety, depression, anger, stress, autonomy, life satisfaction, happiness, positive/negative affect, self-esteem and stress management (Pollard & Lee, 2003). The link between transport and psychological measures of wellbeing is still in its infancy. Here, some relationships have been examined, e.g., self-confidence, and recent research has looked at how transport relates to concepts such as life satisfaction. Psychological measures have been developed for researching travel satisfaction; in the past few years, these have been adjusted and tested on children. Chapter 3 goes into detail about these relationships, with the Chapters 16 and 17 also using measures from this domain.

2.3 Cognitive

The cognitive domain is a sub-domain of the psychological domain, which includes indicators considered intellectual or school-related in nature. Childhood is an important stage of life that is critical for learning and obtaining the skills necessary to thrive as an independent adult, which is why cognitive wellbeing was suggested as a distinct domain (Pollard & Lee, 2003). Examples include concentration, school behavioral problems, cognitive ability, and academic achievement (Pollard & Lee, 2003). Independent travel by children allows for the exploration and development of knowledge of one's living environment. Parents may often be in a hurry, and are uninterested in what they have seen before, but children learn about and explore their environments, and this seems to be most relevant to trips that are not made by car (Carroll, Witten, Kearns, & Donovan, 2015; Hosoda & Nichide, 2009; Kullman, 2010). Chapter 3 will also examine this domain; as with the psychological domain, research on these relationships is limited.

2.4 Social

The social domain includes indicators such as anti-social behavior, peer problems, participation in cultural activities, relationships with others, social skills, and socioeconomic status (Pollard & Lee, 2003). Social interactions and relationships are strong explanatory factors as regards life satisfaction (Huebner & Diener, 2008), but they also relate to mortality (Holt-Lunstad, Smith, & Layton, 2010). Transport can help children reach their friends, but it can also hinder them from spontaneously visiting these friends by creating barriers (e.g., traffic danger) to independent travel. How children travel can also affect whether or not they have any incidental connections with their communities, which can help to build or maintain social capital. These relationships and others are explored in Chapter 4, and in the chapters on Japan and Play Streets.

2.5 Economic

Pollard and Lee (2003) examined the payment of child support as an indicator of children's economic wellbeing. Transport may have a wider economic effect on children, and can include the transport costs directly borne by the household, parental time consumed by serve-passenger trips (trips that are made solely for the passenger's benefit/activity), or costs borne by society due to transport decisions (be they infrastructure, collisions, etc.). The issue of parental time loss was raised by Hillman et al. (1990) in their seminal work on children's independent travel. The argument being that if a child is independent, then the parent is not sacrificing their time. However, escorting and children's CIM are not mutually exclusive as a highly-autonomous child may still need to be escorted (no matter the mode) for certain trips. CIM is on the decline in many countries (Mitra, 2013; Shaw, Bicket, & Elliott, 2015), while the chauffeuring (i.e., escorting by car) of children is increasing. One review (Mitra, 2013) found that chauffeuring increased when parents viewed driving as convenient and socially acceptable, but that reduced distances to destinations were positively associated with increased CIM. Traffic and safety concerns are often found to decrease this kind of travel (Mitra, 2013). CIM is an important measure of many of the wellbeing-related concepts being dealt with in this book, and as a result, several chapters have discussed this topic from various perspectives. In Chapter 10, the economic case for Safe Routes to Schools is made.

3 Transport's three means of impact on child wellbeing

We propose that transport affects wellbeing via at least three means of influence (Fig. 1), namely—access, intrinsic (i.e., during travel), and external (i.e., transport by others) means. Perhaps the most common research approach is to examine transport as a means of access (e.g., to school).

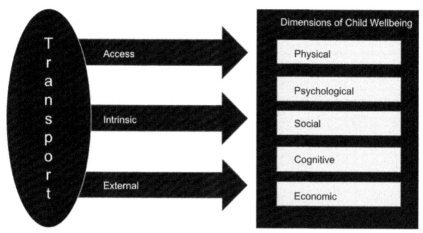

Fig. 1 Conceptual framework of child wellbeing and the three means of impact through which transport can affect children. *(Adapted from Waygood, E. O. D., Friman, M., Olsson, L. E., & Taniguchi, A. (2017). Transport and child well-being: An integrative review.* Travel Behaviour and Society, 9 *(Supplement C), 32–49.)*

Transport effects can also be examined by exploring the experiences during transport; these effects can be intrinsic (e.g., active travel) or potential (e.g., a traffic-related injury or fatality that is not caused by others[b]). The third type is when the society's transport behavior affects a child's wellbeing (e.g., noise and air pollution; injury or fatality caused by others[b]).

The primary purpose of transport as *access* (see Fig. 1) is to get to activities, whether this is for educational and social or for other needs and wants. As children may not have the same mobility resources (e.g., access to cars; parental permission to cycle to destinations, etc.) as adults, their access to their desired destinations will be more limited. Parents and caregivers will often go to great lengths to accommodate their children's travel needs/wants, but this may not always be possible. Matthews and Limb (1999) outline six major distinctions between children and adults with respect to travel: (1) their rhythms of time and space are different; (2) their use of land and facilities is different; (3) CIM is restricted by money, physical capabilities, caretaking conventions, etc.; (4) the threats they face are different

[b]To help explain our approach to the difference between a crash that is not caused by others and a crash that is caused by others, we take the example of a bicycle crash in two different situations. When a child crashes his/her bike when trying to do a jump, this would be a crash not caused by others; this would be intrinsic danger. A child on a bicycle who is hit by an inattentive driver constitutes a crash caused by others; this would be an extrinsic impact.

(e.g., collision point, air quality); (5) even in the same environment, their interpretations and perceptions are different; and (6) children's inability to influence decision-makers. Thus, it is important to look at children's transport separately from that of adults and to not assume that transport systems that provide for adults are also providing for children (Gilbert & O'Brien, 2005).

The *intrinsic* influences of transport occur during a trip. This aspect is increasingly being studied, with particular attention being paid to active travel as a daily source of physical activity in response to growing concerns over more sedentary lifestyles and obesity. Along with this, more research is looking at other measures relating to different domains of wellbeing, e.g., social interaction during trips (see above), experiences contributing to learning, and emotions (Ramanathan, O'Brien, Faulkner, & Stone, 2014; Westman, Johansson, Olsson, Mårtensson, & Friman, 2013; Westman, Olsson, Gärling, & Friman, 2017).

The *extrinsic* influences of transport result from how others travel. Traffic-related injuries/fatalities have long been discussed in literature and policy; however, recent evidence has started demonstrating other influences, including impacts from noise affecting stress, and air pollution affecting asthma (Beatty & Shimshack, 2014), and childhood leukemia (Boothe, Boehmer, Wendel, & Yip, 2014).

Taken together, we suggest that transport consists of more than just moving quickly from A to B; it has to be understood as a daily activity that can contribute to either an improvement or a decline in a child's wellbeing. It must further be understood that impacts exist which relate not only to the child's actual transport, but also to how the system facilitates or limits the use of other people's transport choices.

4 Contributions to the book

Transport and Children's Wellbeing is divided, in addition to this introductory chapter, into five parts. **Part I** consists of four chapters focusing on the relationships between children's transport behavior and their wellbeing. In Chapter 2, Richard Larouche, Raktim Mitra, and Owen Waygood discuss and provide several useful insights into the impact of transport on physical health and wellbeing. In their chapter, they present consistent evidence showing that children who engage in active transport are significantly more active than those who use motorized travel modes. However, the authors also suggest that the causal relationship between active transport and physical activity is complex and difficult to confirm. A general conclusion, however, is that walking and cycling are important for the formation of long-term healthy habits; as a consequence, the importance of both urban planning approaches and public health/grass-roots level interventions is discussed. Larouche, Mitra, and Waygood call for a balanced approach to community planning and policymaking whereby children's health and wellbeing are not compromised in order to enable faster mobility.

In Chapter 3, on the psychological and cognitive domains, Jessica Westman, Margareta Friman, and Lars E Olsson describe how research is emerging linking children's daily travel with the psychological and cognitive domains of wellbeing. In this chapter, Westman, Friman, and Olsson explore how these domains have been operationalized, and what the empirical findings exist on this topic. The chapter focuses on a number of factors, e.g., age, gender, mode, and independent mobility. The authors conclude that psychological measures include a large palette of measurements, e.g., mood, subjective wellbeing (sometimes operationalized as happiness or life satisfaction), travel satisfaction, independence, and confidence, which are all related to travel. In addition, measures related to the cognitive domain are fewer in number and have mainly been categorized as either academic achievement or cognitive abilities, also being affected by transport. A final conclusion drawn is that, due to a plethora of methods and measures, it is somewhat difficult to generalize previous findings.

In Chapter 4, Owen Waygood focuses on transport and the social domain of children's wellbeing. Social wellbeing relates to the child's social needs, support, and interactions. Waygood argues that transport can facilitate interactions with both peers and the community by allowing children to travel to destinations where they can meet with friends or other community members. Incidental interactions can occur along the way, something which can help to either build or maintain community connections, in turn potentially supporting children in different ways. Such support can help in facilitating children's independent travel (CIM), thus allowing for more interactions. Waygood also discusses how transport can limit social interactions when, for instance, the frequency of chauffeured trips increases and when traffic limits access to, and even the use of, local destinations, including the street. Communication technology allows social interactions at a distance; however, the existing literature has emphasized the importance of physical interactions for a child's social development. Using evidence from a limited body of literature, Waygood also explores the links between the social and the built environment, travel behavior and opportunities/barriers to social wellbeing. Based on his findings, the author reflects on where research has taken us and also presents areas for future research.

In the final piece on pathways of impact (Chapter 5), Raktim Mitra and Kevin Manaugh offer a conceptual framework for understanding children's mobility, using a social-ecological approach. In this chapter, the authors propose that a child's socio-demographic characteristics and household composition, as well as available transport options and parental availability, social and built environments, and other external aspects, e.g., the social-political context and urban policy/regulations, all affect a child's transport outcomes. The authors argue for the importance of taking these factors, as well as the interaction between them, into account in order to fully understand children's mobility and potential transport outcomes. This approach can help policy makers, professionals, and communities to develop targeted interventions with the goal of improving children's health and wellbeing.

Part II of the book examines in more detail, in three chapters, the key externalities of transport affecting children's physical wellbeing. In Chapter 6, Linda Rothman, Liraz Fridman, Marie-Soleil Cloutier, Kevin Manaugh, and Andrew Howard concentrate on traffic speed and road traffic injuries. Vehicle speed is a major risk factor in both the incidence and severity of injuries during road traffic collisions. Pedestrian-motor vehicle collisions are a particularly important issue in this context. However, the authors also argue that, in wealthy countries, the majority of child deaths occur as vehicle occupants; thus, putting children in vehicles in order to protect them from traffic danger may not be a true solution. Children are especially vulnerable due to their small stature and developmental abilities when it comes to negotiating road traffic. In their chapter, the authors discuss different road safety strategies, including environmental countermeasures proven to reduce speed, and strategies related to enforcement and education. This is followed by a discussion on the need to revisit the roadway design principles, creating appropriate regulatory changes and enforcing compliance in order to establish safer roadways and encourage active transport for children.

In Chapter 7, Vickie L. Boothe and Richard W. Baldauf concentrate on the global health burden resulting from exposure to traffic emissions.

The authors explore how traffic-related primary pollutants impact children's health and wellbeing. Consistent and compelling scientific evidence suggests that prenatal and childhood exposure to primary traffic emissions can cause the onset and exacerbation of asthma, delayed lung function development, and such exposure is associated with childhood leukemia. Emerging suggestive evidence links traffic emission exposure to autism spectrum disorders, delayed cognitive development, and childhood obesity. Health risks can accumulate throughout life and lead to the development of adult chronic disease, disability, and premature death. Currently, the specific traffic emission constituents responsible for the observed adverse effects remain unknown. In this chapter, the authors discuss effective evidence-based strategies for reducing children's total exposures.

Chapter 8, by David Rojas-Rueda, summarizes the recent evidence relating to health impact assessments, describing the key factors to be considered when a plan, program or policy focuses on transport and children. Health impact assessment steps are outlined, highlighting the aspects that need to be considered in the context of transport and children. Health determinants (i.e., physical activity, air pollution, traffic incidents, etc.), health outcomes, qualitative and quantitative assessments, participatory processes, monitoring and evaluation approaches, and policy contexts relating to transport and children are all described. The chapter also presents how health impact assessments can be used by stakeholders, especially policymakers, to improve transport and childhood interventions. The future of health impact assessments is discussed, and it is proposed that, in the case of transport and children, a health impact assessment can assess and promote transport policies by introducing health considerations into the decision-making process.

Part III of the book, presented over seven chapters, focuses on understanding and discussing how children's travel might be improved, and the topics are organized in line with the socio-ecological framework (see Chapter 5), starting out from the outer sphere of culture and policy. In the first chapter of this section (Chapter 9), Ben Shaw reviews a range of the policy initiatives that have been implemented in order to address the negative impact of transport on children's health and wellbeing. It is argued that children's needs are often overlooked in transport and other related policy, or seen as only relating to how children travel to school safely. Addressing the wider objective of creating safe and pleasant neighborhoods which meet children's needs for transport, mobility, independence and play requires cross-cutting action from policymakers. Linking transport, planning, health, education, housing, and policing policies with a focus on local matters, but with the support of high level regional and national policies, is thus vital.

In Chapter 10, Noreen McDonald, Mathew Palmer, and Ruth Steiner write about the economics of active school transport in a United States context, where unsafe walking conditions are common and where many parents drive their children, contributing to elevated traffic-related health risks. For some, the school bus is an option, but this is also a costly solution for society. The chapter demonstrates that investment in creating safe environments for active travel to school can result in societal savings. Infrastructure investment that makes active travel safe also creates options for children (and all community members), with reduced costs to families and school districts. Case studies of communities that have been successful at implementing this approach are presented and discussed.

Children are often an underrepresented group in transport planning, and so in Chapter 11, Karen Witten and Adrian Field describe a process of engaging children in the redesigning of streets and greenways in order to support active travel in local neighborhoods. Arguments as to why it is important to include children in the planning process are provided, and a neighborhood-scale controlled intervention study aimed at making it easier and safer to walk and cycle to neighborhood destinations is presented. The human-centered design approach deployed in this project meant that a fundamental first step was understanding how local residents, adults and children, moved around their neighborhoods, but also their aspirations as regards doing so differently. Children took part in school-based focus groups prior to design development, with their concerns and desires for change informing the design negotiation process. The findings showed that children felt safer crossing roads after taking part in design interventions, but their people-related fears had not abated. It is concluded that the focus groups provided a rich source of experiential data on children's neighborhood mobility.

In Chapter 12, Maria Johansson, Fredrika Mårtensson, Märit Jansson, and Catharina Sternudd focus on the role of the neighborhood built environment, particularly hard-paved and green open spaces, including streets, squares, parks, and woodland, in enabling children's independent and active mobility. The authors argue that the complex relationship between a child and his/her surrounding environment needs to be understood by means of exploring his/her experiences with outdoor spaces. To this end, the authors present four theoretical approaches, drawing primarily on research from the field of environmental psychology, that focus on the concepts of place attachment, affordance, wayfinding, and prospect-refuge. The authors argue that these four approaches can help us better understand children's use and experiences, in addition to informing the planning, design, and management of outdoor spaces in ways which can support children's independent mobility and active transport, ultimately impacting population health and sustainable living.

In Chapter 13, Raktim Mitra and Zainab Abbasi discuss the emergence of "play streets" across Western communities. Play streets are a grass-roots-driven response to the loss of the local street as a play destination due to elevated perception of traffic danger, and in some cases due to municipal regulations that discourage such use of street right-of-ways. Mitra and Abbasi discuss examples and the current popularity of play streets in various global locations, before detailing a recent project in Toronto, Canada. Their findings would indicate that the residents primarily saw benefits, with few negative consequences regarding their ability to run errands or to park. Such programs are a good opportunity to build local social networks, with the chapter referring to resources that could help citizens implement this idea in their own neighborhoods.

In Chapter 14, Owen Waygood and Kevin Manaugh take both an individual and a household perspective, focusing on the modes accessible to children (e.g., walking, cycling, public transport), particularly in conjunction with CIM. They argue that the choices children and adults make, with regard to travel behavior (mode, frequency, distance), are a function of a vast array of physical, social, and cultural factors. The options available, in terms of transport infrastructure, e.g., bike lanes and transit routes, are of primary importance; however, individual and household factors play an important role. It is concluded that children are capable of independent travel from a young age, but that both children and parents must be involved in that process. Actions are described, as regards both children and parents, which can facilitate greater CIM, including simply walking, cycling, and taking public transport with children so that they learn how to take advantage of these modes in order to gain freedom for themselves and their parents.

In Chapter 15, Tim Ross discusses the troubling childhood disability gap in school transport research and practice. A review is presented of how disabled children's experiences and perspectives have been approached in this transport subfield, followed by a discussion of the new sociology of child-hood perspective and participatory research methods as a means of supporting greater engagement with disabled children. Three considerations are proposed which may help researchers to craft inclusive research designs which adequately account for disabled children, these being-enabling participants via inclusive technologies; supporting their engagement by creating the opportunity for positive participation experiences; and using researcher reflexivity to help ensure adequate representation in research of disabled children's experiences and viewpoints. An inclusive photovoice research design, used in a recent ethnographic study of how families living with childhood disability experience everyday school travel, is presented and discussed as one means of bridging the gap identified in previous research.

In **Part IV** of the book, consisting of three chapters containing examples of children's travel taken from two countries that have managed to protect children's walking (Japan) and cycling (the Netherlands) are presented, along with an example of a country (China) where transport patterns and experiences have been transforming rapidly during recent decades. In Chapter 16, Owen Waygood and Ayako Taniguchi present and discuss the high level of independent travel (CIM) among children in Japan, travel which is predominantly on foot. A review of the literature on walking and independent travel indicates that these modes are important for incidental social interactions and more broadly social wellbeing, and that such occurrences are particularly frequent in Japan. National travel data is used to paint a general picture of the patterns and trend of children's travel in Japan. In addition, findings from a recent study are used to discuss relationships between what children do during their trips and their satisfaction with their travel, as a measure of their psychological wellbeing. Having set the scene, Waygood and Taniguchi present influences, in line with the socio-ecological model, on what might help explain such enduring levels of active and autonomous travel by children in Japan. This includes planning, regulation, and community solutions in support of walking to school. The explanations proposed could be applied to other countries and cultures; the objective is to stimulate solutions to this modern problem.

In Chapter 17, Iris van de Craats, Pauline van den Berg, Astrid Kemperman, and Owen Waygood present the case of children's travel in the Netherlands. Despite a worldwide decline in active transport among children, the Netherlands has managed to protect high levels of cycling in children, which constitutes the largest modal share of trips to school.

A comparison over time shows that, while cycling remains the most popular mode, walking trips have declined, with many of these trips probably having been replaced by car trips. The chapter then continues to explore the association between school travel modes and the various social and ecological characteristics of the child and his/her household, using data that was collected in the Dutch city of Arnhem. Key findings indicate that cycling is more common at distances of 1–2 km, and among children who are older and come from both high-income households and households with multiple children. Some of their findings are different from those reported on by studies from other parts of the world and which, as the authors argue, may relate to a strong bicycling culture and favorable policy and infrastructure. The authors also explored children's satisfaction with their school travel, as a proxy for subjective wellbeing. Children generally found their travel to school to be fun, easy, and exciting, with positive perceptions overall. Similar to what has been reported elsewhere, users of the active modes were more satisfied with their travel experiences than those who were driven to school.

In Chapter 18, Lin Lin and Lingling He present factors associated with active commuting to/from school by school-age children in Shanghai, China, where walking and cycling rates for school transport has rapidly declined over recent decades. Current patterns of school transport outcomes are explored and discussed in terms of how socioeconomic-, social-, and environmental factors might influence the observed behavior. The results show some similarities as well as some differences in potential influences on the likelihood of walking/cycling, when compared to what has been reported in research conducted in Western countries. The authors furthermore discuss the scarcity of detailed data as a barrier to conducting systematic research in developing countries. In this study, the authors used publicly available APIs obtained from a local mapping platform, to objectively measure in detail the built environment attributes at the neighborhood level in Shanghai, in addition to collecting data through parent/caregiver surveys.

The final part of the book, **Part V**, includes the closing chapter (Chapter 19), dealing with both future research directions and policy implications related to transport and children's wellbeing. In this closing chapter, Margareta Friman, Lars E. Olsson, Owen Waygood, and Raktim Mitra highlights the cross-disciplinary focus of this book that brought together a series of works from a variety of disciplinary orientations. We conclude that this breadth and diversity convey an inclusive view of the complex nature of transport and children's wellbeing. By providing a brief overview and summary of some of the important evidence in this field, we point to knowledge gaps and diagnose difficulties that will provide a roadmap for future research and practice. Overall, the most important point made in this book could be that we have to stop believing that providing for adults necessarily also means that we provide for children. Children's development and physical attributes are different than those of adults, but they are still citizens of our cities and nations. When it comes to transport, advantages and conveniences for adults, who are more capable, should not come at the expense of the wellbeing of a vulnerable and marginalized population group.

References

Beatty, T. K., & Shimshack, J. P. (2014). Air pollution and children's respiratory health: A cohort analysis. *Journal of Environmental Economics and Management, 67*(1), 39–57.

Boothe, V. L., Boehmer, T. K., Wendel, A. M., & Yip, F. Y. (2014). Residential traffic exposure and childhood leukemia: A systematic review and meta-analysis. *American Journal of Preventive Medicine, 46*(4), 413–422.

Carroll, P., Witten, K., Kearns, R., & Donovan, P. (2015). Kids in the city: Children's use and experiences of urban neighbourhoods in Auckland, New Zealand. *Journal of Urban Design, 20*(4), 417–436.

Dodge, R., Daly, A. P., Huyton, J., & Sanders, L. D. (2012). The challenge of defining wellbeing. *International Journal of Wellbeing, 2*(3).

Freeman, C., & Tranter, P. J. (2011). *Children and their urban environment: Changing worlds.* Routledge.

Gilbert, R., & O'Brien, C. (2005). *Child- and youth-friendly land-use and transport planning guidelines.* Winnipeg: Centre for Sustainable Transportation.

Hillman, M., Adams, J., & Whitelegg, J. (1990). *One false move… A study of children's independent mobility.* London: Policy Studies Institute.

Holt-Lunstad, J., Smith, T. B., & Layton, J. B. (2010). Social relationships and mortality risk: A meta-analytic review. *PLoS Medicine, 7*(7). e1000316.

Hosoda, S., & Nichide, K. (2009). GPS tracking of children after school who attend elementary school by public transport (5330) (in Japanese). In *Vol. 2. Summaries of technical papers of annual meeting of the Architectural Institute of Japan* (pp. 683–684).

Huebner, E. S., & Diener, C. (2008). Research on life satisfaction of children and youth. *The Science of Subjective Well-Being,* 376–392.

Jones, P., & Boujenko, N. (2009). 'Link' and 'Place': A new approach to street planning and design. *Road & Transport Research: A Journal of Australian and New Zealand Research and Practice, 18*(4), 38.

Kullman, K. (2010). Transitional geographies: making mobile children. *Social & Cultural Geography, 11*(8), 829–846.

Matthews, H., & Limb, M. (1999). Defining an agenda for the geography of children: review and prospect. *Progress in Human Geography, 23*(1), 61–90.

Mitra, R. (2013). Independent mobility and mode choice for school transportation: A review and framework for future research. *Transport Reviews, 33*(1), 21–43.

Pollard, E., & Lee, P. (2003). Child well-being: A systematic review of the literature. *Social Indicators Research, 61*(1), 59–78.

Ramanathan, S., O'Brien, C., Faulkner, G., & Stone, M. (2014). Happiness in motion: Emotions, well-being, and active school travel. *Journal of School Health, 84*(8), 516–523.

Shaw, B., Bicket, M., & Elliott, B. (2015). *Children's independent mobility: An International Comparison and Recommendations for Action*. London: Policy Studies Institute.

Tranter, P., & Whitelegg, J. (1994). Children's travel behaviours in Canberra: Car-dependent lifestyles in a low-density city. *Journal of Transport Geography*, *2*(4), 265–273.

Tudor-Locke, C., Ainsworth, B., & Popkin, B. (2001). Active commuting to school: An overlooked source of children's physical activity? *Sports Medicines*, *31*, 309–313.

Waygood, E. O. D., Friman, M., Olsson, L. E., & Taniguchi, A. (2017). Transport and child well-being: An integrative review. *Travel Behaviour and Society*, *9*(Supplement C), 32–49.

Westman, J., Johansson, M., Olsson, L. E., Mårtensson, F., & Friman, M. (2013). Children's affective experience of every-day travel. *Journal of Transport Geography*, *29*, 95–102.

Westman, J., Olsson, L. E., Gärling, T., & Friman, M. (2017). Children's travel to school: Satisfaction, current mood, and cognitive performance. *Transportation*, *44*(6), 1365–1382.

PART ONE

Overview of transport and children's wellbeing

CHAPTER TWO

Transport and physical wellbeing

Richard Larouche[a], Raktim Mitra[b] and E. Owen D. Waygood[c]

[a]Public Health, Faculty of Health Sciences, University of Lethbridge, Lethbridge, AB, Canada
[b]School of Urban and Regional Planning, Ryerson University, Toronto, ON, Canada
[c]Department of Civil, Geological, and Mining Engineering, Polytechnique Montréal, Montreal, QC, Canada

Contents

1 Introduction

The definition of health has evolved over the past century to include physical, mental and social wellbeing and not merely the absence of disease or illness (World Health Organization (n.d.)); but when one thinks of health, measures of physical health are probably the first things that come to mind. With respect to children, there is a longer history of research that has explored the impacts of transport externalities on their physical health, particularly those relating to traffic collisions (Toroyan & Peden, 2007). Many researchers have discussed the historical role that automobile traffic had in cutting off access to play (Berg & Medrich, 1980; Gaster, 1991; Lynch & Banerjee, 1976) and reducing opportunities for independent mobility (Hillman, Adams, & Whitelegg, 1990). A limited research has also examined the role of transportation in providing access to recreational activities and facilities (Ravensbergen, Buliung, Wilson, & Faulkner, 2016; Roemmich et al., 2006). However, the potential for physical activity accumulation and related physical health benefits from a child's day-to-day transport remained largely unexplored until the early 2000s (Tudor-Locke, Ainsworth, & Popkin, 2001). As the evidence of an worldwide phenomenon of childhood obesity began to emerge, much attention was placed on physical activity gained through independent and active travel (Larouche, 2018). As a result, an expansive literature now exists that has linked children's transport behavior to physical activity and related physical health indicators. This chapter summarizes current knowledge on the abovementioned topics, and describes many impacts that transport has on children's physical wellbeing.

2 Transport and physical activity

The World Health Organization (n.d.) defines physical activity as "any bodily movement produced by skeletal muscles that requires energy expenditure". Physical activity can be accrued in different ways and in different settings including sport, leisure time, active play, chores, and through transport to and from various daily destinations. It can be argued that all other things being equal, an increase in physical activity in the form of transport should result in an increase in overall physical activity. However, it is also plausible that individuals may compensate for an increase in physical activity in one domain by less activity in other domains, contrary to the ceteris paribus assumption that is often adapted in physical activity interventions. Many interventions that have attempted to increase physical activity have yielded disappointing results and this has led researchers to formulate the 'activitystat' hypothesis (Frémeaux et al., 2011; Metcalf, Henley, & Wilkin, 2012; Wilkin, Mallam, Metcalf, Jeffery, & Voss, 2006). This hypothesis suggests that humans have an integrative center (similar to a thermostat) that ensures that we maintain a relatively stable volume of physical activity. While practitioners and policymakers may frown upon this hypothesis, it is important to ensure that the effects of interventions aiming to increase active transportation would not be neutralized by a decline in physical activity in other domains.

Over the past two decades, there has been a lot of research investigating the relationship between children's transportation behavior and physical activity, focusing particularly on transportation to and from school. Several systematic reviews have summarized the literature on this topic (Faulkner, Buliung, Flora, & Fusco, 2009; Larouche, Faulkner, Fortier, & Tremblay, 2014; Larouche, Saunders, Faulkner, Colley, & Tremblay, 2014; Schoeppe, Duncan, Badland, Oliver, & Curtis, 2013). These reviews have reported consistent evidence showing that children who engage in active transportation are significantly more active than those who used motorized travel modes. For instance, in the review conducted by Larouche, Saunders, et al. (2014), over 80% of included studies found that active travelers were significantly more active. More recently, Voss (2019) have arrived at similar conclusions. Recent literature reviews also provide evidence from randomized controlled trials that have consistently observed that children exposed to school transportation-related interventions, such as walking school bus or bicycle train programs, also experienced a significant increase in physical activity (Larouche, Mammen, Rowe, & Faulkner, 2018; Larouche & Mendoza, 2018). Another important means of improving walking to school are the safe routes to school programs, which have now become exceedingly common across the western world (see Chapter 14; Fig. 1).

Thankfully, this current evidence suggests that children engaging in active transportation to/from school do not do this at the expense of other sources physical activity. In one of the first studies examining the relationship between active transport and objectively measured physical activity,

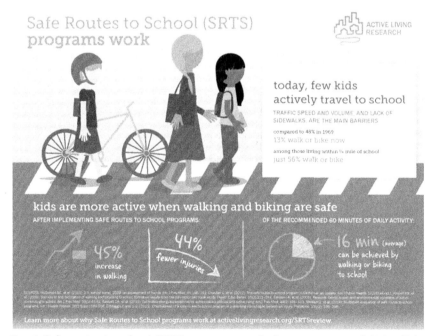

Fig. 1 Safe routes to school (SRTS) programs work. *(Image courtesy of Active Living Research.)*

Cooper, Page, Foster, and Qahwaji (2003) asked children to wear an accelerometer for a week. An accelerometer is a small device similar to a step counter, but it can measure the intensity of physical activity and researchers can tell exactly when physical activity was accrued. Cooper et al. (2003) compared the amount of physical activity accrued in each hour of the day between active and motorized travelers. Not surprisingly, active travelers were more active during the hours that corresponded to school journey times. However, they were also more active during the evening and there was no evidence that they accumulated less activity than motorized travelers in any segment of the day. Other studies have also observed that active travelers were more active during school journey times, with no clear evidence of a compensatory reduction in physical activity in other segments of the day (Mitra, Cantello, Buliung, & Faulkner, 2017; Owen et al., 2012; Sirard, Riner, McIver, & Pate, 2005; van Sluijs et al., 2009). Furthermore, studies of walking school buses and bicycle trains demonstrate that participation in such interventions leads to an increase in physical activity (Larouche & Mendoza, 2018). Collectively, this body of evidence suggests that the relationship between active transportation and physical activity is likely to be causal (Hill, 1965).

2.1 Transport and indicators of physical fitness

Fewer studies have examined the relationship between active transportation and indicators of physical fitness such as cardiovascular fitness, muscle strength and endurance, and flexibility. Cardiovascular fitness is the component of fitness that has been examined most frequently. Irrespective of physical activity level, children who have better cardiovascular fitness have a reduced risk of developing cardiovascular disease risk factors (e.g., high blood glucose, blood pressure, and cholesterol) and they tend to have better mental health and academic performance (Ortega, Ruiz, Castillo, & Sjöström, 2008).

Previous reviews have noted that the relationship between active transport and cardiovascular fitness depends on the actual mode of active transport (Larouche, Saunders, et al., 2014; Voss, 2019). Specifically, there is consistent evidence showing that children and youth who cycle to/from school have greater cardiovascular fitness (Larouche, Saunders, et al., 2014; Voss, 2019). Of particular interest, in two 6-year longitudinal studies conducted in both Denmark and Sweden, children who began to cycle to school experienced a substantial increase in cardiovascular fitness between the ages of 9 and 15 (Andersen et al., 2011; Chillón et al., 2012).

In a different study, Børrestad, Østergaard, Andersen, and Bere (2012) conducted a 12-week randomized controlled trial wherein children were randomly allocated to a cycling group or a control group. The authors observed that compared to participants that did not start cycling during the intervention, those who began cycling experienced an 8% increase in cardiovascular fitness (Børrestad et al., 2012). This represents a clinically meaningful increase in fitness, especially in 10- to 13-year-olds. Inconsistent results were observed between the Danish and Swedish samples, even though study procedures were similar. Danish children who began to cycle to school during the follow-up period had more favorable values for many cardiovascular risk factors including waist circumference, blood glucose and insulin levels, etc. (Andersen et al., 2011). None of these associations were noted in the Swedish sample (Chillón et al., 2012). The reason underlying these differences is unclear, but perhaps the amount of cycling may have differed between the two samples.

In an 8-week intervention by Østergaard, Børrestad, Tarp, and Andersen (2012), children assigned to the cycling group experienced a significant reduction in a composite score representing multiple cardiovascular disease risk factors. Similarly, Ramirez-Velez et al. (2017) reported that, among 9- to 17-year-old girls, cycling to/from school was associated with a 39% reduction in the odds of metabolic syndrome. However, they found no relationship between cycling and cardiometabolic risk in boys. It is plausible that the cardiovascular benefits of cycling are greater in girls because, on average, they are less physically active and have lower cardiovascular fitness compared to boys (Voss, 2019).

Similarly, in an analysis of nationally representative data from the Canadian Health Measures Survey, Larouche, Faulkner, et al. (2014) observed that 12- to 19-year-olds who reported cycling for transport at least 1 h/week had significantly higher moderate- to vigorous-intensity physical activity (MVPA) and cardiovascular fitness, lower body mass index and waist circumference and a better lipid profile compared with those who did not cycle. However, 80.7% of participants reported that they did not cycle for transport in the 3 months preceding the survey while only 10.0% reported cycling at least 1 h/week (Larouche, Faulkner, et al., 2014).

In contrast to the abovementioned findings relating to cycling, studies have generally found no associations between walking to/from school and cardiovascular fitness. In the longitudinal studies mentioned above, no differences in indicators of cardiovascular health were observed between children who walked to/from school and those who traveled by car or bus (Andersen et al., 2011; Chillón et al., 2012). Larouche, Faulkner, et al. (2014) and Larouche, Saunders, et al. (2014) observed some benefits associated with walking at least 5 h/week compared to less than 1 h/week in adolescents, but the results were not as consistent as those observed for cycling. From a physiological standpoint, it has been suggested that the intensity (or speed) at which individuals typically walk is an insufficient stimulus to increase cardiovascular fitness in young people (Shephard, 2008). It is possible that a more vigorous physical activity intensity is needed to improve indicators of cardiovascular health. Nevertheless, habits are a very strong determinant of travel mode choice (de Bruijn & Gardner, 2011; Gardner & Abraham, 2008). Establishing the habit of walking and cycling for transport early in life might increase the likelihood that individuals will walk or cycle regularly later in life. In older adults, walking could be sufficient to maintain or even increase cardiovascular fitness.

2.2 Transport and access to physical activity

Much has been written about the physical activity-related benefits of active transport (e.g., Larouche, 2018). Notwithstanding the contribution of active transport to physical activity, it may not be enough to for some children to accumulate the recommended levels of physical activity on a day-to-day basis. Instead, children should engage in various types of activities. For example, the recent Canadian 24-h Movement Guidelines for Children and Youth (ParticipACTION and Canadian Society for Exercise Psychology, 2016) recommends 60 min of MVPA, including participation in vigorous physical activities and muscle and bone strengthening activities at least 3 days per week. The guideline also emphasizes that children should participate in several hours of various types of structured or unstructured light-intensity physical activities (LPA) on a daily basis. Opportunities to engage in these physical activities and transport to the locations where children can engage in these activities, either independently or in presence of the adults, is important in maintaining a healthy development for children and youth.

The importance of access (i.e., availability of activities to participate) and accessibility (i.e., the ease of accessing locations and activities) are not explicitly discussed in current literature focused on children's transport and physical activity. However, results from current literature implies their significance. For example, distance to school (an important measure of accessibility) has been consistently reported as the most significant barrier to active transport to school and related physical activity among children (Mitra, 2013). In fact, McDonald (2007) noted that nearly half of the decline in active school transport in the US over the past decades can be explained by increased travel distance.

The license to explore neighborhood locations without adult supervision, also known as children's independent mobility (CIM), also creates opportunities for physical activity by offering greater access to places and activities where physical activity can occur. Greater independent mobility allows children to engage in active transport and outdoor play more frequently and longer than when they are accompanied by adult caregivers (Hüttenmoser, 1995; Mahdjoubi, Bates-Brkljac, Ratcliffe-Pacheco, & Mirani, 2011). Not surprisingly, then, the existing literature has consistently reported a statistical association between CIM and their physical activity levels (Schoeppe et al., 2013). In fact, Mitra, Faulkner, Buliung, and Stone (2014) found that independent mobility was associated with up to 19.5% increase in daily MVPA on average, among 11- to 12-year-old children in Toronto, Canada, and the result was consistent across a child's gender. Despite many health and developmental benefits, however, CIM has declined systematically at least over the past half-century in many western countries (Fyhri, Hjorthol, Mackett, Fotel, & Kytta, 2011; Hillman et al., 1990). However, it is not a foregone conclusion as research from some other countries indicate that children still enjoy high levels of independent mobility (Shaw, Bicket, & Elliott, 2015).

Similarly, license to participate in outdoor free play creates opportunities for physical activity, with the intensity depending on the type of play engagement. Current research has confirmed a statistical association between longer periods of outdoor play and higher physical activity levels (Faulkner, Mitra, Buliung, Fusco, & Stone, 2015), but findings relating to the availability and/or accessibility to play opportunities/locations outside of home remain mixed. For example, Bringolf-Isler et al. (2010) reported for primary school children that the lack of access to a garden or park related to less outdoor play. Similarly, Marino, Fletcher, Whitaker, and Anderson (2012) found that access to a yard, park or playground was associated with a greater odds of spending >2h of outdoor play among children. On the contrary, other researchers did not find a correlation between park accessibility and play duration (Cleland et al., 2010; Faulkner et al., 2015). It appears that much of the outdoor play is now taking place in back- or front-yards of homes (Spilsbury, 2005). While this arrangement may deprive children from broader opportunities of playing with others (which may limit the length of play) or to freely choose locations or activities relating to their outdoor play, it also minimizes the need for transport, with or without adults.

Lastly, recreational programs and facilities are often designed to facilitate children's physical activity. Many of these programs are focused on organized sports requiring vigorous physical activity engagement and have financial costs associated to them such a registration and equipment that could limit their access to marginalized populations. Existing literature has consistently reported an association between accessibility to these recreational programs and facilities and physical activity among children (Ding, Sallis, Kerr, Lee, & Rosenberg, 2011; Sallis, Prochaska, & Taylor, 2000). However, previous research has also reported inequalities in how communities may benefit from these programs and facilities. For example, Romero (2005) found that the total number of physical activity facilities available in low-income neighborhoods did not affect the physical activity behavior of the youth living in those communities. Similarly, Ravensbergen et al. (2016) reported that low-income households, on average, had lower accessibility to physical activity facilities and they also used them less frequently.

3 Externalities of transport on children's physical health

Traveling by foot or bicycle has limited external impacts on others, but the use of motorized vehicles has numerous significant negative impacts. Transport, and more specifically motorized road transport, is a primary source of death for children and youth worldwide (Toroyan & Peden, 2007). The burden is especially large in the countries from Global South, but even in western countries it is typically identified as one of the top three sources of death for children. What should be noted is that in wealthy western countries, most of these deaths involve children as passengers in vehicles, which is arguably an intrinsic disadvantage of using privately owned automobiles. For example, in Canada, the per-capita fatality of children in motor vehicles was twice as high when compared to the fatality rate of child pedestrians (Waygood, Taniguchi, Craig-St-Louis, & Xu, 2015). By contrast, in countries where the majority of children walk, such as in Japan, child pedestrians have a higher per-capita fatality rate than those in cars, but the most important point is that their average per-capita fatality is among the lowest in the world (Waygood et al., 2015). In both cases (children as pedestrians, or children as passengers), the source of the danger is often motor vehicle use by other individuals.

Along with use, speed is a crucial component of the extrinsic impact of transport on a child's wellbeing. As will be discussed in Chapter 6, the overall stopping distance increases non-linearly with increased travel speed. Not surprisingly, the amount of energy involved in a crash also increases exponentially with increased vehicle speed. As a result, the likelihood of fatal injuries increases rapidly where the travel speed is above 30 km/h (e.g., WHO, 2004), thus helping to explain why impacts at slightly higher speeds can have much larger probabilities of fatalities. Another key consideration is that with an increase in speed, the distance covered during the driver's reaction time increases, and thus the overall stopping distance also increases non-linearly. For example, given the same reaction time, a vehicle traveling at 30 km/h can come to a complete stop in roughly the same distance that would be covered by a vehicle traveling at 50 km/h during the driver's reaction time. That means that a driver could stop if a child appeared suddenly 20 m down the road, but that a vehicle traveling at 50 km/h would hit the child going at 50 km/h which will likely cause death. Thus, it is for good reason that traffic safety approaches such as Vision Zero (e.g., visionzeronetwork.org) promote vehicle speeds of 30 km/h in urban settings.

The risk (or perceived risk) of traffic-related injuries and death imposes other impacts on children's physical wellbeing by preventing them from using or crossing a street. One such impact is commonly known as the "barrier effect" whereby parents restrict CIM because of traffic. This restriction likely reduces the child's overall physical activity (e.g., Schoeppe et al., 2013), and may result in reduced accessibility to friends and play areas (e.g., Bringolf-Isler et al., 2010; Davison & Lawson, 2006).

The design of streets may also affect children's physical activity. If the roadway is designed for rapid vehicle movement with intersections/stops placed at long distances, large blocks may limit the permeability of the area, reducing accessibility for active modes of transport, especially for children. Such planning approaches also reduce the number of route options for traveling between point A and point B, which has been found to reduce outdoor play by children (Aarts, Wendel-Vos, van Oers, van de Goor, & Schuit, 2010). In contrast, streets that are safe and/or have sidewalks allow children better access to destinations where they can engage in physical activity, whether that be in the street, at a park, or at a school (e.g., Davison & Lawson, 2006; Oliver et al., 2015). While the modern conceptualizations of streets primarily center on the movement of vehicles, historically streets have been used as a public domain where people would socialize and children would interact with one another and play (Cowman, 2017;

Gaster, 1991). More recent studies have reported that where traffic is controlled, children may use streets for diverse activities (Biddulph, 2012;
Ekawati, 2015; Skjœveland, 2001). While most studies have not directly
measured physical activity accumulation, but the types of activities that
are mentioned typically include physical activity including ball games and
practicing with bicycles (Abu-Ghazzeh, 1998). Arguably, communities
can benefit from a balanced approach to street design with an improved public realm that welcomes adults and children alike to use those spaces.
Chapter 11 in this book gives a larger overview of this topic.

In addition to potential health risks relating to injuries and fatalities, fuel
combustion motors emit harmful byproducts that are associated with a number of health issues in children (Perera, 2017). Chapter 7 presents greater
detail and the current state of knowledge on this topic. For instance, increasing evidence suggests that the relationship between vehicle emissions and
childhood asthma is causal. Studies on this topic often examine rates of childhood asthma related to living near highways. There are other studies that
have examined special cases where traffic was restricted for a period of time.
For example, during the Atlanta Olympics, children's visits to hospitals for
acute asthma cases significantly dropped when traffic was restricted and managed (Friedman, Powell, Hutwagner, Graham, & Teague, 2001). Vehicle
emissions are generally reported to be the primary source of air pollution
in modern cities (McNabola, Broderick, & Gill, 2009; Seaton, Godden,
MacNee, & Donaldson, 1995). Perhaps the irony is that many commenta-
tors at the dawn of the automobile era believed that cars were a solution to
air quality problems in cities (Fogelson, 2001).

While health impacts relating to traffic noise remain somewhat less discussed, in a review of epidemiological studies, Paunovic, Stansfeld, Clark,
and Belojevic (2011) found that traffic noise was consistently related to an
increase in children's blood pressure. The difference between sleeping in
a room facing traffic, versus one that does not, has also been found to be
associated with higher blood pressure levels (Liu et al., 2013). A separate
review also found that traffic noise was related to cardiovascular disease,
hypertension and sleep disturbance (Clark & Stansfeld, 2007). Along with
physical measures (e.g., blood pressure levels) of the impact of traffic noise,
cognitive impacts are also found on children (Hygge, 1993; Van Kempen &
Babisch, 2012). Sleep disturbance due to traffic noise (Clark & Stansfeld,
2007) could have cognitive impacts on children. Another study found
that traffic noise negatively impacted reading speed and basic mathematic

exercises (Ljung, Sorqvist, & Hygge, 2009). In that study, irrelevant speech did not affect those measures suggesting that traffic noise is a greater problem than such noise.

4 Transport processes, mobility and physical health implications

A closer look into how, when and where modern-day children and youth are spending time every day reveals that they are largely staying (or are kept) closer to homes, have limited mobility unless accompanied by adult caregivers, and some are getting a large proportion of their physical activity from organized sports or other recreational activities (Loebach & Gilliland, 2014; Mitra et al., 2017). These daily activity behaviors have direct implications for their physical fitness and wellbeing, as discussed earlier in this chapter.

The current role of transport in enabling children's mobility and physical activity participation behavior can be understood better by contextualizing these physical activity outcomes within several social, cultural and institutional processes around children's mobility and caregiving. Historically, streets were common places where children of all ages would play during their leisure time (Berg & Medrich, 1980; Lynch & Banerjee, 1976). The presence of children was accepted as "normal", creating a perception of safety, which also enabled independent mobility (CIM) within the neighborhood. In other words, children were largely free to play on their neighborhood streets and explore their neighborhood alone or with friends without much adult supervision (Wooley & Griffin, 2015). The popularity of the automobiles in the 20th century slowly started to change this. Since the mid-1900s, urban planning-related regulatory mechanisms, such as zoning bylaws in North America, emphasized separation of land uses. Expected users of each types of land use also became more institutionalized, where streets were clearly perceived as spaces for cars (or more broadly mobility) and children's activities were relegated to parks and recreational facilities (Hart, 2002; Read, 2011).

These institutional changes were accompanied by a cultural shift that perceived street or free outdoor play as leading to "inappropriate behavior" (Hart, 2002) and thus deemed undesirable. In England, for example, free play was replaced with 'Free Kindergartens' because it embodied less risk and offered gardens as a safe supervised play space. Free Kindergartens were premised on teaching children appropriate behavior and socialization, as playing on the streets was considered to promote poor behavior (Read, 2011). Around the same time in the US, playgrounds were being used as controlled spaces for children where behavior could be monitored closely and "appropriate" play would occur (Hart, 2002). In recent decades, much emphasis has been placed on organized/structured recreational activities including sports and arts programs, and a modern child is often expected to participate and excel in multiple sports and art skills. When it comes to organized physical activity-related programs, the level of exposure has become somewhat dependent on the ease of access, or accessibility, by means of various transport options. In other words, those with access to automobiles enjoy much greater accessibility to a broader range of activities, compared to others who primarily rely on walking, cycling or transit.

The past five-or-so decades can also be characterized as a period when increased fear around children's traffic safety has significantly affected children's independent mobility outside of their homes. The perception of danger due to traffic has been institutionalized since the 1970s. In their seminal work, Hillman et al. (1990) provided an example by pointing to public campaigns in the UK on themes such as "one false move and you're dead". Hillman and colleagues argued that putting such a onus on children for road safety was eliminating their independent and free travel. Combined with a broader lack of "environmental trust" (Johansson, 2006; Tranter & Whitelegg, 1994), the perceived risks to a child's health and safety has made constant parental surveillance, sometimes known as "helicopter parenting", characteristic of modern childhood experience (Mitra et al., 2014).

These social and institutional processes have had a significant impact on children's physical health, and they have also led to geographical and social inequality with regard to access to locations for physical activity. For example, disaggregated land use planning particularly in the newer suburban locations, school siting requirements, and a more recent focus on large "magnet schools" instead of smaller neighborhood schools have increased school travel distance for many children (Mitra, 2013; Yang, Abbott, & Schlossberg, 2012). But even where the average school travel distance has not changed significantly over time, over-protective parents may often perceive small distances as potentially non-walkable (Grize, Bringolf-Isler, Martin, & Braun-Fahrlander, 2010; Mitra, Papaioannou, & Habib, 2016). For example, Mitra et al. (2016) reported that walking rates for school transportation declined in Toronto, Canada, between 1986 and 2006, even for distances as low as 0.8 km (roughly half-a-mile).

More broadly, a significant and systematic decline in children's 'home range', including the variety of outdoor places that they visit and the range of activities that they participate when unaccompanied by adult caregivers, has been reported in current literature (Fyhri et al., 2011; Hillman et al., 1990; Wooley & Griffin, 2015). Opportunities for physical activity appear to be particularly limited in suburban, automobile-oriented, neighborhoods when compared to inner urban, walkable, neighborhoods (Mitra, 2013), perhaps due to unavailability of nearby facilities and also due to unavailability of adults who could facilitate trips to various recreational activities and locations several times of the week. For example, Mitra et al. (2017) identified four distinct groups of children based on their daily activity-participation profiles in Toronto, Canada, and found that suburban children were more likely to be "homebound"; they had the lowest average levels of participation in sports or arts-related activities, as well as the fewest minutes in active (e.g., walk, cycle) or inactive (i.e., driven) transport. Much of their physical activity likely was accumulated from playing at home (indoor or in the back yards). In contrast, inner-urban children were more likely to be "athletes" who reported the highest level of participation in organized sports, and also a lot of time traveling (actively or inactively) to various locations. Not surprisingly, the "athletes" accumulated the highest MVPA and LPA on an average day, while the "homebound" children accumulated significantly less physical activity.

The socio-economic inequalities in accessibility to recreational facilities have also been documented. Neighborhoods with higher socio-economic status (SES) had better accessibility to physical activity facilities, in addition to parks and youth organizations, when compared to lower SES neighborhoods (Gordon-Larsen, Nelson, Page, & Popkin, 2006). In addition, the mere availability of facilities nearby may not affect children's physical activity participation in a low-income neighborhood (Romero, 2005). Instead, cost of participation and perception of poor quality of facilities were reported as key barriers. More recently, Ravensbergen et al.'s (2016) research based in Toronto, Canada, confirmed these previous observations. While the density of physical activity facilities was similar across high- and low-SES neighborhoods, the overall quality was better in the high-SES locations; the frequency of facility use by children was also higher in high-SES neighborhoods when compared to low-SES neighborhoods in Toronto.

5 Conclusion

This chapter discussed how transport impacts children's physical wellbeing through intrinsic means (i.e., active transport), access to destinations that facilitate physical activity, and through external influences such as collisions, air quality, noise, and barrier effects. With regard to children's active transport, the current literature has largely focused on school journeys, and the evidence consistently indicates that those children who walk or cycle to/from school are more physically active than those who do not. While cycling is likely to provide more immediate benefits such as improved cardiovascular fitness, regular walking is important for the formation of long-term healthy habits. Research has suggested that for adults, moderate-intensity physical activity such as walking and cycling may provide more immediate physical health benefits. In addition, and as discussed in the following chapters, walking has other psychological and social wellbeing-related advantages.

Unfortunately, in many modern western societies, private automobiles have become the most accepted means of transport for children. While automobiles are widely perceived as a faster, safer and more mobility efficient mode of transport, these perceptions are not necessarily always true. While cars do enable access to far-away schools and open up opportunities to participate in a wider diversity of recreational activities including physical activity-related facilities, a closer examination begins to identify multiple negative physical wellbeing-related impacts of this dominant culture of automobility. In-vehicle deaths are more common, and active modes are threatened by vehicles, making them the source of safety problems which increases with greater speeds. Further, over-dependence on automobiles for everyday mobility may reduce opportunities for active transport, independent mobility and free play. An increased number of cars is also associated to problems of air quality (linked to asthma among others), noise (stress, problems of concentration), and prevents the use of streets as public space for play and CIM. In addition, as children's play has largely been replaced by more organized recreational activities, physical wellbeing of those children with limited access to automobiles and with lower financial capacity are disproportionately affected.

The findings from this chapter, then, reemphasize the importance of urban planning approaches and public health/grass-roots level interventions aimed at enabling active transport among children. But more broadly, our observations call for a more balanced approach to community planning and policy-making where children's health and wellbeing are not compromised to enable faster mobility. Chapters 9–15 of this book discuss several approaches relating to improved policy, culture, and neighborhood planning that may be necessary to address this critical problem.

References

Aarts, M. -J., Wendel-Vos, W., van Oers, H. A., van de Goor, I. A., & Schuit, A. J. (2010). Environmental determinants of outdoor play in children: A large-scale cross-sectional study. *American Journal of Preventive Medicine, 39*(3), 212–219.

Abu-Ghazzeh, T. M. (1998). Children's use of the street as a playground in Abu-Nuseir, Jordan. *Environment and Behavior, 30*(6), 799–831.

Andersen, L. B., Wedderkopp, N., Kristensen, P. L., Moller, N. C., Froberg, K., & Cooper, A. R. (2011). Cycling to school and cardiovascular risk factors: A longitudinal study. *Journal of Physical Activity and Health, 8*(8), 1025–1033.

Berg, M., & Medrich, E. A. (1980). Children in four neighborhoods: The physical environment and its effect on play and play patterns. *Environment and Behavior, 12*(3), 320–348.

Biddulph, M. (2012). Street design and street use: Comparing traffic calmed and home zone streets. *Journal of Urban Design, 17*(2), 213–232.

Børrestad, L. A. B., Østergaard, L., Andersen, L. B., & Bere, E. (2012). Experiences from a randomised, controlled trial on cycling to school: Does cycling increase cardiorespiratory fitness? *Scandinavian Journal of Public Health, 40*(3), 245–252.

Bringolf-Isler, B., Grize, L., Mäder, U., Ruch, N., Sennhauser, F., Braun-Fahrländer, C., et al. (2010). Built environment, parents' perception, and children's vigorous outdoor play. *Preventive Medicine, 50*, 251–256.

Chillón, P., Ortega, F. B., Ruiz, J. R., Evenson, K. R., Labayen, I., Martínez-Vizcaino, V., et al. (2012). Bicycling to school is associated with improvements in physical fitness over a 6-year follow-up period in Swedish children. *Preventive Medicine, 55*(2), 108–112.

Clark, C., & Stansfeld, S. A. (2007). The effect of transportation noise on health and cognitive development: A review of recent evidence. *International Journal of Comparative Psychology, 20*(2–3), 145–158.

Cleland, V., Timperio, A., Salmon, J., Hume, C., Baur, L., & Crawford, D. (2010). Predictors of time spent outdoors among children: 5-year longitudinal findings. *Journal of Epidemiology and Community Health, 64*, 400–406.

Cooper, A. R., Page, A. S., Foster, L. J., & Qahwaji, D. (2003). Commuting to school: Are children who walk more physically active? *American Journal of Preventive Medicine, 25*(4), 273–276.

Cowman, K. (2017). Play streets: Women, children and the problem of urban traffic, 1930–1970 AU. *Social History, 42*(2), 233–256.

Davison, K. K., & Lawson, C. T. (2006). Do attributes in the physical environment influence children's physical activity? A review of the literature. *International Journal of Behavioral Nutrition and Physical Activity, 3*(1), 19.

de Bruijn, G. J., & Gardner, B. (2011). Active commuting and habit strength: An interactive and discriminant analyses approach. *American Journal of health Promotion, 25*(3), e27–e36.

Ding, D. J., Sallis, F., Kerr, J., Lee, S., & Rosenberg, D. E. (2011). Neighborhood environment and physical activity among youth: A review. *American Journal of Preventive Medicine, 41*(4), 442–455.

Ekawati, S. A. (2015). Children – Friendly streets as urban playgrounds. *Procedia—Social and Behavioral Sciences, 179*, 94–108.

Faulkner, G. E. J., Buliung, R. N., Flora, P. K., & Fusco, C. (2009). Active school transport, physical activity levels and body weight of children and youth: A systematic review. *Preventive Medicine*, *48*(1), 3–8.

Faulkner, G., Mitra, R., Buliung, R., Fusco, C., & Stone, M. (2015). Children's outdoor playtime, physical activity and parental perception of neighbourhood environment. *International Journal of Play*, *4*(1), 84–97.

Fogelson, R. M. (2001). *Downtown: Its rise and fall, 1880–1950*. New York: Yale University Press.

Frémeaux, A. E., Mallam, K. M., Metcalf, B. S., Hosking, G., Voss, L. D., & Wilkin, T. J. (2011). The impact of school-time activity on total physical activity: The activitystat hypothesis (EarlyBird 46). *International Journal of Obesity*, *35*, 1277–1283.

Friedman, M. S., Powell, K. E., Hutwagner, L., Graham, L. M., & Teague, W. G. (2001). Impact of changes in transportation and commuting behaviors during the 1996 Summer Olympic Games in Atlanta on air quality and childhood asthma. *JAMA: The Journal of the American Medical Association*, *285*(7), 897–905.

Fyhri, A., Hjorthol, R., Mackett, R. L., Fotel, T. N., & Kytta, M. (2011). Children's active travel and independent mobility in four countries: Development, social contributing trends and measures. *Transport Policy*, *18*, 703–710.

Gardner, B., & Abraham, C. (2008). Psychological correlates of car use: A meta-analysis. *Transportation Research Part F*, *11*(4), 300–311.

Gaster, S. (1991). Urban children's access to their neighborhood: Changes over three generations. *Environment and behavior*, *23*(1), 70–85.

Gordon-Larsen, P., Nelson, M. C., Page, P., & Popkin, B. M. (2006). Inequality in the built environment underlies key health disparities in physical activity and obesity. *Pediatrics*, *117*(2), 417–424.

Grize, L., Bringolf-Isler, B., Martin, E., & Braun-Fahrlander, C. (2010). Trend in active transportation to school among Swiss schoolchildren and its associated factors: Three cross-sectional surveys 1994, 2004, and 2005. *International Journal of Behavioral Nutrition and Physical Activity*, *7*, 28. http://www.ijbnpa.org/content/7/1/28.

Hart, R. (2002). Containing children: Some lesson on planning for play from New York City. *Environment & Urbanization*, *14*(2), 135–148.

Hill, A. B. (1965). The environment and disease: Association or causation? *Proceedings of the Royal Society of Medicine*, *58*, 295–300.

Hillman, M., Adams, J., & Whitelegg, J. (1990). *One false move: A study of children's independent mobility*. London: PSI Press.

Hüttenmoser, M. (1995). Children and their living surroundings: Empirical investigations into the significance of living surroundings for the everyday life and development of children. *Children's Environments*, *12*(4), 403–413.

Hygge, S. (1993). A comparison between the impact of noise from aircraft, road traffic and trains on long-term recall and recognition of a text in children aged 12–14 years. *Schriftenreihe des Vereins für Wasser-, Boden- und Lufthygiene*, *88*, 416–427.

Johansson, M. (2006). Environmental and parental factors as determinants of mode for children's leisure travel. *Journal of Environmental Psychology*, *26*, 156–169.

Larouche, R. (2018). *Children's active transportation*. Amsterdam: Elsevier.

Larouche, R., Faulkner, G. E. J., Fortier, M., & Tremblay, M. S. (2014). Active transportation and adolescent's health: The Canadian Health Measures Survey. *American Journal of Preventive Medicine*, *46*(5), 507–515.

Larouche, R., Mammen, G., Rowe, D. A., & Faulkner, G. (2018). Effectiveness of active school transport interventions: A systematic review and update. *BMC Public Health*, *18*, 206.

Larouche, R., & Mendoza, J. A. (2018). Walking school buses and bicycle trains. In R. Larouche (Ed.), *Children's active transportation* (pp. 217–227). Cambridge, MA: Elsevier.

Larouche, R., Saunders, T. J., Faulkner, G. E. J., Colley, R. C., & Tremblay, M. S. (2014). Associations between active school transport and physical activity, body composition and cardiovascular fitness: A systematic review of 68 studies. *Journal of Physical Activity and Health*, *11*(1), 206–227.

Liu, C., Fuertes, E., Tiesler, C. M., Birk, M., Babisch, W., Bauer, C. P., et al. (2013). The association between road traffic noise exposure and blood pressure among children in Germany: The GINIplus and LISAplus studies. *Noise & health*, *15*(64), 165–172.

Ljung, R., Sorqvist, P., & Hygge, S. (2009). Effects of road traffic noise and irrelevant speech on children's reading and mathematical performance. *Noise & Health*, *11*(45), 194–198.

Loebach, J. E., & Gilliland, J. (2014). Free range kids? Using GPS-derieved activity spaces to examine children's neighbourhood activity and mobility. *Environment and Behavior*, *48*, 421–453.

Lynch, K., & Banerjee, T. (1976). Growing up in cities. *New Society*, *37*(722), 281–284.

Mahdjoubi, L., Bates-Brkljac, N., Ratcliffe-Pacheco, T., & Mirani, B. (2011). *Evaluation of bristol play pathfinder programme*. Bristol, UK: Bristol City Council.

Marino, A., Fletcher, E., Whitaker, R., & Anderson, S. (2012). Amount and environmental predictors of outdoor playtime at home and school: A cross-sectional analysis of a national sample of preschoolaged children attending Head Start. *Health & Place*, *18*, 1224–1230.

McDonald, N. C. (2007). Active transportation to school: Trends among US schoolchildren, 1969–2001. *American Journal of Preventive Medicine*, *32*(6), 509–516.

McNabola, A., Broderick, B., & Gill, L. (2009). The impacts of inter-vehicle spacing on in-vehicle air pollution concentrations in idling urban traffic conditions. *Transportation Research Part D: Transport and Environment*, *14*(8), 567–575.

Metcalf, B., Henley, W., & Wilkin, T. J. (2012). Effectiveness of intervention on physical activity of children: Systematic review and meta-analysis of controlled trials with objectively measured outcomes (EarlyBird 54). *BMJ*, *345*, e5888.

Mitra, R. (2013). Independent mobility and mode choice for school transportation: A review and framework for future research. *Transportation Reviews*, *33*(1), 21–43.

Mitra, R., Cantello, I., Buliung, R., & Faulkner, G. (2017). Children's activity-transportation lifestyles, physical activity levels and social-ecological correlates in Toronto, Canada. *Journal of Transport and Health*, *6*, 289–298.

Mitra, R., Faulkner, G. E. J., Buliung, R. N., & Stone, M. R. (2014). Do parental perceptions of the neighbourhood environment influence children's independent mobility? Evidence from Toronto, Canada. *Urban Studies*, *51*(16), 3401–3419.

Mitra, R., Papaioannou, E., & Habib, K. M. N. (2016). Past and present of active school transportation: An exploration of the built environment effects in Toronto, Canada from 1986 to 2006. *Journal of Transport and Land Use*, *9*(2), 1–17.

Oliver, M., Mavoa, S., Badland, H., Parker, K., Donovan, P., Kearns, R. A., et al. (2015). Associations between the neighbourhood built environment and out of school physical activity and active travel: An examination from the Kids in the City study. *Health & Place*, *36*, 57–64.

Ortega, F. B., Ruiz, J. R., Castillo, M. J., & Sjöström, M. (2008). Physical fitness in childhood and adolescence: A powerful marker of health. *International Journal of Obesity*, *32*(1), 1–11.

Østergaard, L., Børrestad, L. A. B., Tarp, J., & Andersen, L. B. (2012). Bicycling to school improves the cardiometabolic risk factor profile: A randomised controlled trial. *BMJ Open*, *2*, e001307.

Owen, C. G., Nightingale, C. M., Rudnicka, A. R., van Sluijs, E. M. F., Ekelund, U., Cook, D. G., et al. (2012). Travel to school and physical activity levels in 9–10 year-old UK children of different ethnic origin; Child Heart and Health Study in England (CHASE). *PLoS ONE*, *7*(2) e30932.

ParticipACTION and Canadian Society for Exercise Psychology (2016). *Canadian 24-hour movement guidelines for children and youth: An integration of physical activity, sedentary behaviour and sleep*. https://participaction.cdn.prismic.io/participaction%2F0f8fcc77-1162-4e8b-867e-85bcd4e12c93_participaction-24hguidelines-05-17en.pdf.

Paunovic, K., Stansfeld, S., Clark, C., & Belojevic, G. (2011). Epidemiological studies on noise and blood pressure in children: Observations and suggestions. *Environment International, 37*(5), 1030–1041.

Perera, F. (2017). Pollution from fossil-fuel combustion is the leading environmental threat to global pediatric health and equity: Solutions exist. *International Journal of Environmental Research and Public Health, 15*(1), 16.

Ramirez-Velez, R., Garcia-Hermoso, A., Agostinis-Sobrinho, C., Mota, J., Santos, R., Correa-Bautista, J. E., et al. (2017). Cycling to school and body composition, physical fitness, and metabolic syndrome in children and adolescents. *Journal of Pediatrics, 188*, 57–63.

Ravensbergen, L., Buliung, R. N., Wilson, K., & Faulkner, G. (2016). Socioeconomic discrepancies in children's access to physical activity facilities: Activity space analysis. *Transportation Research Record, 2598*, 11–18.

Read, J. (2011). Gutter to garden: Historical discourses of risk in interventions in working class children's street play. *Children & Society, 25*(1), 421–434.

Roemmich, J. N., Epstein, L. H., Raja, S., Yin, L., Robinson, J., & Winiewicz, D. (2006). Association of access to parks and recreational facilities with the physical activity of young children. *Preventive Medicine, 43*, 437–441.

Romero, A. J. (2005). Low-income neighborhood barriers and resources for adolescents' physical activity. *Journal of Adolescent Health, 36*, 253–259.

Sallis, J. F., Prochaska, J. J., & Taylor, W. C. (2000). A review of correlates of physical activity of children and adolescents. *Medicine Science Sports Exercise, 32*(5). 963, 975.

Schoeppe, S., Duncan, M. J., Badland, H., Oliver, M., & Curtis, C. (2013). Associations of children's independent mobility and active travel with physical activity, sedentary behaviour and weight status: A systematic review. *Journal of Science and Medicine in Sport, 16*(4), 312–319.

Seaton, A., Godden, D., MacNee, W., & Donaldson, K. (1995). Particulate air pollution and acute health effects. *The Lancet, 345*(8943), 176–178.

Shaw, B., Bicket, M., & Elliott, B. (2015). *Children's independent mobility: An International Comparison and Recommendations for Action*. London: Policy Studies Institute.

Shephard, R. J. (2008). Is active commuting the answer to population health? *Sports Medicine, 38*(9), 751–758.

Sirard, J. R., Riner, W. F., McIver, K. L., & Pate, R. R. (2005). Physical activity and active commuting to elementary school. *Medicine & Science in Sports & Exercise, 37*(12), 2062–2069.

Skjœveland, O. (2001). Effects of street parks on social interactions among neighbors: A place perspective. *Journal of Architectural and Planning Research*, 131–147.

Spilsbury, J. C. (2005). 'We don't really get to go out in the frontyard'—Children's home range and neighborhood violence. *Children's Geographies, 3*, 79–99.

Toroyan, T., & Peden, M. (2007). *Youth and Road Safety*. Geneva: World Health Organization.

Tranter, P., & Whitelegg, J. (1994). Children's travel behaviours in Canberra: Car-dependent lifestyles in a low-density city. *Journal of Transport Geography, 2*(4), 265–273.

Tudor-Locke, C., Ainsworth, B. E., & Popkin, B. M. (2001). Active commuting to school: An overlooked source of children's physical activity? *Sports Medicine, 31*(5), 309–313.

Van Kempen, E., & Babisch, W. (2012). The quantitative relationship between road traffic noise and hypertension: A meta-analysis. *Journal of Hypertension, 30*(6), 1075–1086.

van Sluijs, E. M. F., Fearne, V. A., Mattocks, C., Riddoch, C., Griffin, S. J., & Ness, A. (2009). The contribution of active travel to children's physical activity levels: Cross-sectional results from the ALSPAC study. *Preventive Medicine, 48*(6), 519–524.

Voss, C. (2019). Public health benefits of active transportation. In R. Larouche (Ed.), *Children's active transportation* (1st ed., pp. 1–20). Cambridge, MA: Elsevier.

Waygood, E. O. D., Taniguchi, A., Craig-St-Louis, C., & Xu, X. (2015). International origins of walking school buses and child fatalities in Japan and Canada. *Traffic Science Society of Osaka, 46*(2), 30–42.

Wilkin, T. J., Mallam, K. M., Metcalf, B. S., Jeffery, A. N., & Voss, L. D. (2006). Variation in physical activity lies with the child, not his environment: Evidence for an 'activitystat' in young children (EarlyBird 16). *International Journal of Obesity, 30*, 1050–1055.

Wooley, H. E., & Griffin, E. (2015). Decreasing experiences of home range, outdoor spaces, activities and companions: Changes across three generations in Sheffield in north England. *Children's Geographies, 13*(6), 677–691.

World Health Organization (n.d.). Physical activity. Geneva: World Health Organization. Available from: https://www.who.int/dietphysicalactivity/pa/en/.

World health Organization—WHO (2004). *World report on road traffic injury prevention.* Geneva: Switzerland.

Yang, Y., Abbott, A., & Schlossberg, M. (2012). The influence of school choice policy on active school commuting: A case study of a middle-sized school district in Oregon. *Environment and Planning A, 44*, 1856–1874.

Further reading

Aarts, M. -J., de Vries, S. I., Van Oers, H. A., & Schuit, A. J. (2012). Outdoor play among children in relation to neighborhood characteristics: A cross-sectional neighborhood observation study. *International Journal of Behavioral Nutrition and Physical Activity, 9*(1), 98.

Christian, H., Zubrick, S. R., Foster, S., Giles-Corti, B., Bull, F., Wood, L., et al. (2015). The influence of the neighborhood physical environment on early child health and development: A review and call for research. *Health & Place, 33*, 25–36.

Engwicht, D. (1992). *Towards an eco-city: Calming the traffic.* Sydney (Australia): Envirobook.

Fusco, C., Moola, F., Faulkner, G. E. J., Buliung, R., & Richichi, V. (2012). Toward an understanding of children's perceptions of their transport geographies: (Non)active school travel and visual representations of the built environment. *Journal of Transport Geography, 20*(12), 62–70.

King, N. A., Caudwell, P., Hopkins, M., Byrne, N. M., Colley, R., Hills, A. P., et al. (2007). Metabolic and behavioral compensatory responses to exercise interventions: Barriers to weight loss. *Obesity, 15*(6), 1373–1383.

Marks, D. F. (2015). Homeostatic theory of obesity. *Health Psychology Open, 2*(1), 1–30.

Mendoza, J. A., Haaland, W., Jacobs, M., Abbey-Lambertz, M., Miller, J., Salls, D., et al. (2017). Bicycle trains, cycling, and physical activity: A pilot cluster RCT. *American Journal of Preventive Medicine, 53*(4), 481–489.

Sayers, S. P., LeMaster, J. W., Thomas, I. M., Petroski, G. F., & Ge, B. (2012). A walking school bus program: Impact on physical activity in elementary school children in Columbia, Missouri. *American Journal of Preventive Medicine, 43*(5S4), S384–S389.

World Health Organization (2010). *Global recommendations on physical activity for health.* Geneva (Switzerland): World Health Organization. Available from: http://apps.who.int/iris/bitstream/10665/44399/1/9789241599979_eng.pdf.

CHAPTER THREE

Travel and child wellbeing: The psychological and cognitive domains

Jessica Westman, Margareta Friman and Lars E. Olsson
Service Research Center and Department of Social and Psychological Studies, Karlstad University, Karlstad, Sweden

Contents

1 Introduction

The change in children's travel behavior over recent decades can be described as moving away from predominately active modes (e.g., cycling and walking) toward motorized and inactive modes (e.g., private cars) (Ahern et al., 2017; Larsen et al., 2009). This has led to an increase in children living sedentary lifestyles, with attendant negative effects on their physical health (e.g., increasing obesity, type 2 diabetes), something that has been well documented in the literature (King, Parkinson, & Adamson, 2011; Landsberg et al., 2008; Larouche et al., 2014; Schoeppe, Duncan, Badland, Oliver, & Curtis, 2013). Although research linking children's travel with other outcomes is beginning to mature, there is still a need to compile the current state of knowledge and to reflect upon what we know, thus providing future research needs with direction.

In an integrative review, Waygood, Friman, Olsson, and Taniguchi (2017) concluded that daily travel affects children's wellbeing in five different domains, two of which are related to the *psychological* (e.g., wellbeing, travel satisfaction, independence) and *cognitive* (e.g., cognitive ability, academic achievement) domains. Pollard and Lee (2003, p. 64) define the differences between the psychological and cognitive domains thus: "The psychological domain includes indicators that pertain to emotions, mental health, or mental illness, while the cognitive domain includes those indicators that are considered intellectual or school-related in nature." However, further attention is needed since, in the literature, findings are somewhat scarce and reveal inconsistent and anecdotal results. Furthermore, most previous studies have primarily focused on adults' travel and wellbeing (Friman, Ettema, & Olsson, 2018) rather than on children's travel and wellbeing. Earlier research, focusing on children's life and development, has included many important aspects regarding children but has generally omitted the potential effect of everyday travel. As daily travel is extensive, growing, and even changing, for many children all over the world, this is a highly relevant research area. However, current transportation plans primarily focus on moving children between different destinations (e.g., school and leisure activities) in a cost-effective and timely manner, largely ignoring the potential impact on, for instance, the activities undertaken while traveling and at destinations. If children's wellbeing and school performance can be influenced by their method of travel, it is important for parents and policymakers to learn about this relationship in order to motivate and guide children as regards choosing a travel mode that best matches and enhances their abilities. Additionally, if children (re)adapt to healthy travel behaviors, this will most likely influence how they choose to travel as grown-ups since travel behaviors often accompany children into adulthood (Haustein, Klöckner, & Blöbaum, 2009).

This book chapter provides an overview of how children's travel relates to the psychological and cognitive domains, being structured as follows. First, we briefly go through the literature on children's travel, focusing on how it has changed and on which factors affect travel mode choice. This is followed by two sections on children's travel which focus on the psychological and cognitive domains, respectively. In the closing section, we discuss some future challenges.

2 Children's travel

Children's independent travel, which can be described as the freedom to travel to places without adult supervision (Hillman, Adams, & Whitelegg, 1990), has dramatically decreased over recent decades. This change can be seen in terms of an increase in car use, but also in terms of longer travel distances and more frequent journeys (Carver, Timperio, & Crawford, 2013; McDonald et al., 2014). This change is particularly noticeable in schoolchildren; in Sweden, in 2013, 24% of all schoolchildren between the ages of 6 and 16 were driven to school in cars, whereas only 3 years earlier, the corresponding number was 21%. Children between the ages of seven and fifteen (grades 1–9) in the Nordic countries still have a relatively high level of travel independency since parental fears and mobility restrictions are less significant than in many other countries (Chillon et al., 2010; Fyhri & Hjortol, 2009; Fyhri, Hjorthol, Mackett, Nordgaard Fotel, & Kyttä, 2011; Horelli, 2001; Johansson, 2006; Kyttä, Hirvonen, Rudner, Pirjola, & Laatikainen, 2015). Finnish children living in rural areas have more travel freedom than their peers in cities and small towns (Kyttä, 1997)—a pattern similar to the other Nordic countries (Fyhri, Bjørnskau, & Ulleberg, 2004). Icelandic children are expected to be travel-autonomous at an earlier age than children in the other Nordic countries, but they also face higher levels of traffic-related injuries (Fyhri et al., 2004). Parents of primary school children report that their children often face difficulties in traffic, while parents of older children do not list this as a barrier as frequently (Dellinger & Staunton, 2002). This is a pattern to be found in most of the developed countries, where older children have more travel independence than younger ones—a natural result of the increasing level of traffic awareness in older children (Chillon et al., 2010; Gustat et al., 2015).

Age affects children's school travel inasmuch as children over eleven are more likely to use an active mode, and the school bus, and less likely to be escorted by their parents (Wilson, Clark, & Gilliard, 2018), which is a notable trend in many countries, for example, Sweden, Finland, Norway, the Netherlands, and the UK (Schoeppe et al., 2013). Boys are more likely to travel actively than girls, but the school bus is used equally by both sexes (McMillan, 2006). Also, boys aged between six and eleven are more frequently allowed to travel to school alone, or with a friend, while girls are more often escorted by their parents (Hillman et al., 1990; McDonald, 2005). These gender differences in travel behavior may possibly be the result of the social construction that girls' identities are more endangered or in need of protection, which seems to inhibits girls' travel independence (Marzi, Demetriou, & Reimers, 2018). The children of high-income, car-owning, and well-educated parents are driven to school more frequently than the children of families with more modest incomes (Rothman et al., 2015; Wilson et al., 2018). Children living in densely built-up areas use non-motorized modes more, being generally less likely to travel on the school bus (McDonald, 2005). Clearly, the difference in the travel mode choice of children of different socioeconomic backgrounds and genders creates a lack of balance in travel mode choice whereby the girls and children of less financially fortunate families are less exposed to the health benefits associated with active travel.

3 Psychological and cognitive domains of wellbeing in children's travel

Research shows that travel is related to children's wellbeing; however, exactly how and to what extent is far from established. The specific aim of this chapter is to discuss research looking into the psychological and cognitive domains of wellbeing in order to present a clearer image of the relationship between wellbeing and children's experiences of everyday travel. This knowledge is important for parents and for scholars in various fields. It is also important for policymakers with the power to influence children so that they adopt healthy travel habits, with the power to enable the use of healthy travel modes, and with the power to protect children from the potentially negative effects of everyday travel.

In Table 1, we summarize the selected studies that will be discussed in this chapter. In addition to the population identified in these studies, the studies are categorized according to a number of measures linked to the psychological and cognitive domains of wellbeing. As can be seen in the table, most of the children participating in these studies attend elementary school, while younger children (<7) and older teens (>14) are less noticeable.

With regard to transport measures, we focus on children's independent mobility, their mode use and their travel distances. The measurements included in Table 1 are based on the findings from the studies. One interesting observation here is that the studies often focus on one choice of mode, for example, car or active mode, rather than on comparing several modes. The type of mode is recorded in almost all the studies included in Table 1. Another interesting observation is that distance is used as a variable in studies conducted in the cognitive domain, while not being as visible in the psychological domain. The opposite applies to independent mobility.

With regard to the psychological measures included, we notice a larger palette of measurements. As an example, children's travel is linked to mood, wellbeing (sometimes operationalized as life satisfaction or happiness), travel satisfaction, independency, and confidence. Thus, a range of psychological

Table 1 Selected studies of the psychological and cognitive domains of child wellbeing and travel

Study	Population/ age group	Transport measures			Cognitive measures		Psychological measures				
		Independent mobility	Mode use	Distance	Academic achievement	Cognitive abilities	Mood	Wellbeing	Travel satisfaction	Independency	Confidence
The psychological domain											
Barker, 2009	6–12		✓				✓				
Fusco, Moola, Faulkner, Buliung, & Richichi, 2011	9–12	✓	✓				✓				
Hillman et al., 1990	7–15	✓	✓							✓	✓
Jones, Steinbach, Roberts, Goodman, & Green, 2012	12–18	✓	✓					✓			
Lambaise, Barry, & Roemmich, 2010	10–14		✓	✓						✓	✓
Leung & Loo, 2017	6–12	✓	✓				✓	✓			
Mackett, Lucas, Paskins, & Turbin, 2005	9–11		✓				✓				
	5–15		✓				✓	✓			

Continued

Table 1 Selected studies of the psychological and cognitive domains of child wellbeing and travel—cont'd

		Transport measures			Cognitive measures		Psychological measures				
Study	Population/ age group	Independent mobility	Mode use	Distance	Academic achievement	Cognitive abilities	Mood	Wellbeing	Travel satisfaction	Independency	Confidence
Ramanathan, O'Brien, Faulkner, & Stone, 2014											
Romero, 2015	9–11	✓	✓				✓			✓	
Tranter & Pawson, 2001	9–11	✓	✓							✓	
Waygood, Friman, Taniguchi, & Olsson, 2018	10–12	✓	✓	✓				✓	✓		
Westman, Johansson, Olsson, Mårtensson, & Friman, 2013	11–12		✓				✓				
The cognitive domain											
Domazet et al., 2016	12–14		✓			✓					
Fang & Lin, 2017	7–12		✓	✓	✓	✓					
Hillman et al., 2009	9–10		✓			✓					

Study	Age							
Joshi, MacLean, & Carter, 1999	7–12	✓	✓		✓			
Martínez-Gómez et al., 2011	13–18	✓		✓	✓			
Paskins, 2005	8–11	✓	✓		✓			
Rissotto & Tonucci, 2002	8–11	✓	✓		✓	✓		
Van Dijk, De Groot, Van Acker, Savelberg, & Kirschner, 2014	7–9	✓		✓	✓			
The psychological and cognitive domains								
Ahmadi & Taniguchi, 2007	9–13	✓	✓		✓			✓
Jamme, Bahl, & Banerjee, 2018	10–11	✓		✓	✓		✓	
Westman, Olsson, Gärling, & Friman, 2016	10–15	✓		✓	✓	✓		

measurements relates to travel. As noted, we have only identified three studies that include both the psychological and cognitive domains.

As regards the cognitive measures included, we identified academic achievement and cognitive abilities. Academic achievement is related to children's school grades, while cognitive abilities is a broader term that includes, for example, spatial abilities, concentration, and reading comprehension. Academic achievement is much less in focus than cognitive abilities.

3.1 Wellbeing: The psychological domain

Different key elements are included in the psychological domain of wellbeing. Early work by Ryff (1989) identified six elements: self-acceptance, relations with others, environmental mastery, purpose in life, autonomy, and personal growth. More recent research has emphasized happiness (Pollard & Lee, 2003) and life satisfaction (Diener & Suh, 1997). Research focusing on both children's daily travel and the psychological domain of wellbeing identifies travel as a contributor by means of increasing or decreasing happiness, stress, developing confidence and social skills, and a sense of social inclusion (Hillman et al., 1990; Mackett et al., 2005). Thus, in the context of children's travel, the psychological domain of wellbeing has previously been defined as an umbrella term encompassing the underlying elements of positive psychological functioning and human development (e.g., Ryff, 1989), rather than positive/negative affect and satisfaction with life (e.g., Kahneman, Diener, & Schwarz, N. (Eds.)., 1999). As research into children's psychological domain of wellbeing grows, there is a greater necessity for clarifying the concept wellbeing, and what is being measured, in order to reach valid conclusions.

In Table 1, we have categorized the identified observable and measurable indicators of the psychological domain relating to children's travel. As can be seen, five different measures were identified, relating to independency, confidence, mood, wellbeing, and children's satisfaction with travel. Independency is related to a sense of being independent and less to the instrumental aspect of having a parental license to travel without adult company. Confidence relates to the child's sense of having the ability to travel by different means. Mood is related to feelings and emotions in general (as a consequence of travel), while travel satisfaction captures the very same aspects but specifically in relation to the journey, using indicators such as stress, excitement, and the standard of travel. The final psychological measure is labeled wellbeing and includes measures of life satisfaction and happiness.

Although there is both limited and concordant knowledge of the relationship between children's everyday travel and the psychological domain of wellbeing, research suggests that a decrease in active and independent travel results in children losing the freedom to explore their local environment and to achieve mastery of their physical and social environments (Hillman et al., 1990). Children who are not allowed to move around independently are exposed to fewer opportunities to spontaneously socialize with others, negatively affecting their independence and wellbeing (Westman et al., 2013). This additionally deprives them of opportunities to acquire a sense of community and familiarity, something which builds confidence and self-esteem through increased independence and responsibility (Hillman et al., 1990).

An Australian study, conducted on 200 children aged 9 and 10, reported that, by walking to school or taking the school bus, children, more than anything else, appreciated the possibilities of meeting, talking, and interacting with their friends (Romero, 2015). Another factor that children appreciate when taking the school bus is a greater sense of independence, with car travel depriving them of these cherished social opportunities. Independence and social support are both factors related to wellbeing (Park & Huebner, 2005; Siedlecki, Salthouse, Oishi, & Jeswani, 2014; Waygood et al., 2018). The importance of friendships cannot be overestimated during childhood and adolescence as these are a source of social inclusion and belonging. When children travel to school together with their friends, they have a natural opportunity to engage with one another, which is one important factor as regards feeling socially included (Wentzel, McNamara-Barry, & Caldwell, 2004). Social interaction with friends is additionally important when it comes to experiencing journeys positively; when interviewed, 9-year-old children said that, if a friend joined them in the car, they would enjoy the journey. In contrast, children who traveled by car with other family members said they would rather travel independently. The same children also expressed the positive aspects of traveling by car in that this can provide the space and opportunity for both play and conversation; but again, preferably with friends (Barker, 2009). As indicated by children's self-reports, those who are able to walk to different destinations display independence, happiness, and the positive social aspects of wellbeing, things that are not attained during car travel (Romero, 2015). Another study, on a sample of 5400 children aged between 5 and 15, using both questionnaires and interviews, revealed that there are emotional benefits associated with active travel to school. Children who traveled to school by active mode reported emotions of happiness, excitement, and relaxation, while those traveling by passive motorized modes experienced emotions such as feeling rushed or tired (Ramanathan et al., 2014). One study (Leung & Loo, 2017) additionally found that younger children (<9 years of age) had reported higher momentary wellbeing (i.e., mood) when accompanied by their parents to school, thus challenging how we value independent travel as a contributor to other dimensions of wellbeing (e.g., curiosity; confidence, and social skills). However, this was a study of elementary school children in the major city of Hong Kong, where independent travel is not always possible due to distances and traffic dangers. A cross-cultural study of 9–12-year-olds in Canada, Japan, and Sweden yielded almost identical results in these three countries, with a significantly positive relationship between independent mobility, travel satisfaction and life satisfaction. One unexpected result was the negative relationship between increased travel frequency and travel satisfaction and life satisfaction, suggesting that children may not enjoy frequent travel (Waygood et al., 2018).

Research shows how independent travel is important for children's curiosity, independence, and confidence (Fusco et al., 2011; Mackett et al., 2005; Rissotto & Tonucci, 2002; Tranter & Pawson, 2001). Children who walk to school generally have a more positive attitude toward their local environment, something which increases certain aspects of wellbeing (Jamme et al., 2018). When children independently orient themselves in their neighborhoods, they gain opportunities to broaden their social networks and their sense of community. Of course, many of these positive effects can also be obtained by using public transport and the school bus, encouraging children to move from one place to another and providing opportunities for valuable socialization—all without adult supervision (Jones et al., 2012). However, the potential effects of the different motorized transport modes on children's psychological wellbeing are not well established as yet since research mainly focuses on the relationship between active travel and increased wellbeing.

3.2 Wellbeing: The cognitive domain

Part of the World Health Organization (2002) definition of wellbeing is the cognitive domain of function, which involves memory, executive functioning, attention, language and communication, as well as sensory and motor functioning. Thus, the cognitive domain of function is broadly defined. However, the measures used in the context of children's travel have so far been rather limited. Research has primarily focused on the possible effects of travel on children's cognitive functioning and has identified factors that are considered intellectual, such as cognitive abilities (e.g., risk aversion, spatial skills, traffic awareness). Although many studies of school-related travel have been published, only three could be categorized in terms of measuring academic achievement (Ahmadi & Taniguchi, 2007; Jamme et al., 2018; Westman et al., 2016). In Table 1, the identified studies are marked as measures of academic achievement and cognitive abilities.

The link between physical activity and cognitive functioning has been well established in research (Kramer et al., 1999). As an example, physical exercise is beneficial to executive functioning (e.g., working memory, attention, volitional inhibition) and can increase synaptic plasticity and flexibility in certain areas of the brain (Davis et al., 2011; Guiney & Machado, 2013). The notion that a journey can influence children's academic achievement has only quite recently been targeted in research; specifically, how school journeys (i.e., car versus active mode) correlate with student achievement (Martínez-Gómez et al., 2011; Westman et al., 2016). The Programme for International Student Assessment (PISA) evaluates education systems worldwide by means of, for example, testing the skills and knowledge of 15-year-old students. The results of these assessments reveal that, in some countries, there is a decline in academic achievement in subjects such as mathematics, reading skills, and science. On some level, this may be related to children's school journeys. This is, of course, a rather daring statement, supported by anecdotal findings such as the study of Martínez-Gómez et al. (2011), which found that actively commuting girls, aged 13–18, performed better at multiple cognitive tasks than girls traveling to school by motorized transport, independent of potential confounders, including extra-curricular physical activities and weight status. These results contribute to a growing body of evidence indicating that physical activity may have a beneficial influence on cognition during youth (Martínez-Gómez et al., 2011; Trudeau & Shephard, 2008). In relation to these findings, children and adolescents who travel to school by active mode experience less stress when confronting cognitive challenges during their school day. This may be the result of a reduction in stress and increased positive emotions among active travelers (Hillman et al., 2009; Lambaise et al., 2010). Since physical activity helps to reduce stress, the link between active commuting and cognitive performance does not seem very farfetched. Active commuting additionally facilitates environmental engagement, which improves attention, memory, and energy, and also reduces levels of stress, anxiety, and fatigue (Bowler, Buyung, Knight, & Pullin, 2010; Eysenck, 1992).

One field of research investigates how children's active and independent travel is related to their spatial skills. Spatial cognition is defined as the acquisition, organization, utilization and revision of knowledge regarding the spatial properties of objects and events in the world (Montello, 2001). For example, by exploring and experiencing environments, children develop their spatial cognition (Paskins, 2005). Joshi et al. (1999), with Rissotto and Tonucci (2002) arguing that children who travel to school without an adult draw more neighborhood landmarks in their cognitive maps than children who are accompanied by an adult. Furthermore, Ahmadi and Taniguchi (2007) also concluded that children who walk or take buses on their own to school are able to present more accurate sketch maps than those who are driven by car or take school buses, a finding that is in line with research suggesting that independent travel affects spatial skills in a positive way (Fang & Lin, 2017).

There are some contradictory findings regarding active commuting and cognitive performance. One study, which investigated the relationship between active commuting and student achievement, found no link between the two (Van Dijk et al., 2014). It did, however, find a gender difference whereby girls (aged 15–16) who were active travelers scored better in an attention test, indicating that their results might have been moderated by gender (Van Dijk et al., 2014). Literature reviews, however, conclude that physical activity is positively related to cognitive functioning (Bielak, Cherbuin, Bunce, & Anstey, 2014; Burkhalter & Hillman, 2011; Stea & Torstveit, 2014). As an example, Westman et al. (2016) found that children who were active during their journey to school, and engaged in social activities, performed better in a cognitive test. Additionally, Domazet et al. (2016) found that children's cycling to school was positively associated with their performance in mathematics. All in all, there is scant knowledge of the link between children's daily travel and their academic performance; the research that does exist provides inconclusive results. This could partly be explained by the fact that, while some studies investigate children's cognitive performance in laboratory settings (e.g., after treadmill walks) (i.e., Hillman et al., 2009), other studies only compare different travel modes with academic results (Martínez-Gómez et al., 2011). This variance in research methods may provide differences in results, whereby academic results depend on many factors over a full school year while experiments may fail to mirror all the different elements of a journey.

4 Conclusion

Few would argue that the current trend, when it comes to children's travel behavior, is sustainable. Children's travel behavior has changed from being predominantly active and independent to being inactive and motorized, a trend that is negative for both children and the environment. This chapter has reviewed research assessing the consequences of travel for children's cognitive and psychological domains. One conclusion we draw is that researchers have indeed acknowledged the importance of examining the psychological and cognitive domains of wellbeing as regards studying children's everyday travel; however, findings from this emerging literature are still somewhat anecdotal and in need of replication.

From our vantage point, we can discern some significant gaps and future challenges regarding research on travel and wellbeing. The first relates to how children's travel can affect their psychological wellbeing. The positive effects of different travel modes, for example, active modes, have been shown to improve children's mood and long-term wellbeing. Not being allowed to travel independently may, furthermore, contribute negatively to children's life satisfaction. One research question to follow up in future studies is how particular characteristics of travel (e.g., travel activities, critical incidents, social interactions, travel time, travel mode) affect psychological wellbeing. Additionally, how do these characteristics affect children of different age groups and development stages? The latter is especially important as some age groups have been underrepresented in previous research. A plethora of methods has been used to capture the effect of a journey, which may explain some of the diverse results found in the research. Surveys, diaries, interviews, and experiments are all very different techniques, yet sometimes used to investigate similar phenomenon and relationships (e.g., effects of mode use on wellbeing or physical activity). Children of different ages may interpret questions differently and be susceptible, to varying degrees, to memory distortion or pre- and post-experiences. As an example, older children are more easily affected by social influences and can change their statements in order to be attuned to their peers, whereas younger children can face more difficulties when providing free recall statements about their travel experiences. Thus, when providing children with questionnaires, or when conducting interviews, questions should be adapted to match the age of the child; for example, younger children should receive more focused and open-ended questions while older children could be encouraged to sit alone rather than with their peers to avoid social influences (Brown & Lamb, 2015). Research suggests that, when asking a child about his or her journey experiences, he or she should be encouraged to travel back in time by drawing a mental picture (e.g., what did the scenery look like, how did it smell, how was the temperature), in order to recall as many accurate memories as possible (Paulo, Albuquerque, & Bull, 2016). Also, asking questions at a point in time as close as possible to the actual journey is recommended in order to avoid distortion from post-experiences, that is, experiences unrelated to travel. The type of question asked affects the number, accuracy, and organization of children's responses, which is something researchers should take into account in order to obtain statements from children that are as correct as possible.

The second challenge concerns the relationship between travel and the cognitive domain of function. Research evidence indicates that travel influences children's general cognitive functioning, with active travel seeming to have a positive effect on various abilities, for example, academic achievement, spatial skills, and risk assessment. We note, however, the absence of long-term studies. It would be of great importance to gain a better understanding of the relationship between children's cognitive abilities and their travel behavior over time. There are, furthermore, new "digital activities" to use during travel which are reshaping children's interactions with their friends. A related question, here, is whether or not travel activities can be integrated into children's schoolwork as an important part of it; something worth studying in relation to, among other things, children's cognitive abilities at school. It has furthermore been shown, in research, that children and adolescents who travel to school by active mode experience less stress when confronted with cognitive challenges during their school day.

It should also be mentioned that some children lack access to different travel modes, because their families are unable, or unwilling, to provide this or because there is no secure infrastructure that these children can safely use. Thus, equality may be an important issue when it comes to school travel, raising questions about how to encourage, and even change, children's travel behavior with or without the involvement of their parents during the change process.

One fundamental issue concerns whether or not transport policies should aim to improve certain aspects of travel which positively affect the psychological and cognitive domains of wellbeing. Research on adult's travel behavior suggests that only weakly positive correlations exist between travel and different measures related to the psychological domain of wellbeing, and that there may be many other domains in life that are of greater importance (Mokhtarian, 2018). Similar criticism may be leveled at measures concerning, for instance, academic achievement where travel may only have limited explanatory power compared to the other dimensions of a child's life. More empirical studies are needed to disentangle the strengths of these relationships; to find out whether or not they are stable across contexts and geographical settings, for children of different ages, and over time. As an accompaniment to this, we also need an ongoing debate on the validity of the different measures used, where some may be important and valid for short-term effects (e.g., mood, cognitive performance) and others for long-term effects (e.g., grades, life satisfaction). We constantly need to be asking ourselves if we are measuring the relevant factors, and if we are measuring them in a valid way.

Many studies have focused solely on the psychological and cognitive domains of wellbeing (sometimes not even explicitly measuring these factors). In future studies, we would encourage researchers to specifically integrate the psychological and cognitive domains of wellbeing in order to fully capture the links between children's travel, their cognitive abilities, and the different dimensions of psychological wellbeing. Once a more comprehensive picture of children's travel and wellbeing has been established, more detailed policy recommendations can be made with the aim of improving the travel and wellbeing of children and adolescents. This book makes the attempt to establish such a comprehensive picture.

References

Ahern, S. M., Arnott, B., Chatterton, T., de Nazelle, A., Kellar, I., & McEachan, R. R. C. (2017). Understanding parents' school travel choices: A qualitative study using the theoretical domains framework. *Journal of Transport and Health*, 4, 278–293.

Ahmadi, E., & Taniguchi, G. (2007). Influential factors on children's spatial knowledge and mobility in home–school travel. A case study in the city of Tehran. *Journal of Asian Architecture*, 6(2), 275–282.

Barker, J. (2009). Driven to distraction?: Children's experiences of car travel. *Mobilities*, 4(1), 59–76. https://doi.org/10.1080/17450100802657962.

Bielak, A. A. M., Cherbuin, N., Bunce, D., & Anstey, K. J. (2014). Preserved differentiation between physical activity and cognitive performance across young, middle, and older adulthood over 8 years. *Journals of Gerontology. Series B, Psychological Sciences and Social Sciences*, 69(4), 523–532. https://doi.org/10.1093/geronb/gbu016.

Bowler, D. E., Buyung, L. M., Knight, T. M., & Pullin, A. S. (2010). A systematic review of evidence for the added benefits to health of exposure to natural environments. *BMC Public Health*, 10, 456–556.

Brown, D. A., & Lamb, M. E. (2015). Can children be useful witnesses? It depends how they are questioned. *Child Development Perspectives*, 9(4), 250–255.

Burkhalter, T. M., & Hillman, C. H. (2011). A narrative review of physical activity, nutrition, and obesity to cognition and scholastic performance across the human lifespan. *Advances in Nutrition, 2*(2), 2015–2065.

Carver, A., Timperio, A., & Crawford, D. (2013). Parental chauffeurs: What drives their transport choice? *Journal of Transport Geography, 26*, 72–77.

Chillon, P., Ortega, F. B., Ruiz, J. R., Veidebaum, T., Oja, L., Mäestu, J., et al. (2010). Active commuting to school in children and adolescents: An opportunity to increase physical activity and fitness. *Scandinavian Journal of Public Health, 38*, 873–879.

Davis, C. L., Tomprowski, P. D., McDowell, J. E., Austin, B. P., Miller, P. H., & Naglieri, J. A. (2011). Exercise improves executive function and alters neural activation in overweight children: A randomized controlled trial. *Health Psychology, 30*(1), 91–98.

Dellinger, A., & Staunton, C. E. (2002). Barriers to children walking and biking to school— United States 1999. *Morbidity and Mortality Weekly Report, 51*, 701–704.

Diener, E., & Suh, E. (1997). Measuring quality of life: Economic, social, and subjective indicators. *Social Indicators Research, 40*(1–2), 189–216.

Domazet, S. L., Tarp, J., Huang, T., Geil, A. K., Andersen, L. B., Froberg, K., et al. (2016). Associations of physical activity, sports participation and active commuting on mathematic performance and inhibitory control in adolescents. *PLoS ONE, 11*(1).

Eysenck, M. W. (1992). *Anxiety: The cognitive perspective.* Hove, UK: Erlbaum.

Fang, J. T., & Lin, J. J. (2017). School travel modes and children's spatial cognition. *Urban Studies, 54*(7), 1578–1600.

Friman, M., Ettema, D., & Olsson, L. E. (2018). *Quality of life and daily travel.* Cham, Switzerland: Springer Nature.

Fusco, C., Moola, F., Faulkner, G. E. J., Buliung, R. N., & Richichi, V. (2011). Toward an understanding of children's perceptions of their transport geographies: (Non)active school travel and visual representations of the built environment. *Journal of Transport Geography, 20*(12), 62–70.

Fyhri, A., Bjørnskau, T., & Ulleberg, P. (2004). Traffic education for children with a tabletop model. *Transportation Research Part F, 7*, 197–207.

Fyhri, A., Hjorthol, R., Mackett, R., Nordgaard Fotel, T., & Kyttä, M. (2011). Children's active travel and independent mobility in four countries: Development, social contributing trends and measures. *Transport Policy, 18*(5), 703–710.

Fyhri, A., & Hjortol, R. (2009). Children's independent mobility to school, friends, and leisure activities. *Journal of Transport Geography, 17*(5), 377–384.

Guiney, H., & Machado, L. (2013). Benefits of regular aerobic exercise for executive functioning in healthy populations. *Psychonomic Bulletin & Review, 20*(1), 73–86.

Gustat, J., Richard, K., Rice, J., Andersen, L., Parker, K., & Cole, S. (2015). Youth walking and biking rates vary by environments around 5 Louisiana schools. *Journal of School Health, 85*, 36–42.

Haustein, S., Klöckner, C. A., & Blöbaum, A. (2009). Car use of young adults: The role of travel socialization. *Transportation Research Part F, 12*, 168–178.

Hillman, M., Adams, J., & Whitelegg, J. (1990). *One false move…: A study of children's independent mobility.* London: PSI.

Hillman, C. H., Pontifex, M. B., Raine, L. B., Castelli, D. M., Hall, E. E., & Kramer, A. F. (2009). The effect of acute treadmill walking on cognitive control and academic achievement in preadolescent children. *Neuroscience, 159*, 1044–1054.

Horelli, L. A. (2001). Comparison of children's autonomous mobility and environmental participation in northern and southern Europe—The case of Finland and Italy. *Journal of Community & Applied Social Psychology, 11*, 451–455.

Jamme, A. -T., Bahl, D., & Banerjee, T. (2018). Between "broken windows" and the "eyes on the street:" Walking to school in inner city San Diego. *Journal of Environmental Psychology, 55*, 121–128.

Johansson, M. (2006). Environment and parental factors as determinants of mode for children's leisure travel. *Journal of Environmental Psychology, 26*(2), 156–169.

Jones, A., Steinbach, R., Roberts, H., Goodman, A., & Green, J. (2012). Re-thinking passive transport: Bus fare exemptions and young people's wellbeing. *Health & Place, 18*(3), 605–612.

Joshi, M. S., MacLean, M., & Carter, W. (1999). Children's journey to school: Spatial skills, knowledge and perceptions of the environment. *British Journal of Developmental Psychology, 17,* 125–139.

Kahneman, D., Diener, E., & Schwarz, N. (Eds.), (1999). *Well-being: Foundations of hedonic psychology*. Russell Sage Foundation.

King, A. C., Parkinson, K. N., & Adamson, A. J. (2011). Correlates of objectively measured physical activity and sedentary behaviour in English children. *European Journal of Public Health, 21*(4), 424–443.

Kramer, A. F., Hahn, S., Cohen, N. J., Banich, M. T., McAuley, E., & Harrison, C. R. (1999). Ageing, fitness and neurocognitive function. *Nature, 400,* 418–419.

Kyttä, M. (1997). Children's independent mobility in urban, small town, and rural environments. In R. Camstra (Ed.), *Growing up in a changing urban landscape* (pp. 41–52). Assen: Van Gorcum.

Kyttä, M., Hirvonen, J., Rudner, J., Pirjola, I., & Laatikainen, T. (2015). The last free-range children? Children's independent mobility in Finland in the 1990s and 2010s. *Journal of Transport Geography, 47,* 1–12. https://doi.org/10.1016/j.jtrangeo.2015.07.004.

Lambaise, M., Barry, H., & Roemmich, J. (2010). Effect of a simulated active commute to school on cardiovascular stress reactivity. *Medicine & Science in Sports & Exercise, 42,* 1609–1616.

Landsberg, B., Plachta-Danielzik, S., Much, D., Johannsen, M., Lange, D., & Muller, M. J. (2008). Associations between active commuting to school, fat mass and lifestyle factors in adolescents: The Kiel obesity prevention study (KOPS). *European Journal of Clinical Nutrition, 62,* 739–747.

Larouche, R., Saunders, T. J., Edward, G., Faulkner, E. J., Colley, R., & Tremblay, M. (2014). Associations between active school transport and physical activity, body composition, and cardiovascular fitness: A systematic review of 68 studies. *Journal of Physical Activity and Health, 11,* 206–227.

Larsen, K., Gilliland, J., Hess, P., Tucker, P., Irwin, J., & He, M. (2009). The influence of the physical environment and socio-demographic characteristics on children's mode of travel to and from school. *American Journal of Public Health, 99*(3), 520–526.

Leung, K. Y. K., & Loo, B. P. Y. (2017). Association of children's mobility and wellbeing: A case study in Hong Kong. *Travel Behavior and Society, 9,* 95–104.

Mackett, R. L., Lucas, L., Paskins, J., & Turbin, L. (2005). The therapeutic value of children's everyday travel. *Transportation Research Part A, 39,* 205–219.

Martínez-Gómez, D., Ruiz, J. R., Martínez-Gómez, S., Chillo, P., L'opez, P. R., Díaz, L. E., et al. (2011). Active commuting to school and cognitive performance in adolescents. The AVENA study. *Archives of Pediatrics & Adolescent Medicine, 165*(4), 300–305.

Marzi, I., Demetriou, Y., & Reimers, A. K. (2018). Social and physical environmental correlates of independent mobility in children: A systematic review taking sex/gender differences into account. *International Journal of Health Geographics, 17,* 27.

McDonald, N. C. (2005). *Children's travel: Patterns and influences*. [Doctoral dissertation] Berkeley: University of California. Retrieved from: http://www.uctc.net/research/diss118.pdf.

McDonald, N. C., Steiner, R. L., Lee, C., Smith, T. R., Zhu, X., & Yang, Y. (2014). Impact of the safe routes to school program on walking and bicycling. *Journal of the American Planning Association, 80*(2), 153–167.

McMillan, T. (2006). Johnny walks to school—Does Jane? Sex differences in children's active travel to school. *Children, Youth and Environments*, *16*(1), 75–89.

Mokhtarian, P. L. (2018). Subjective well-being and travel: Retrospect and prospect. *Transportation*, *46*(2), 493–513.

Montello, D. R. (2001). Spatial cognition. In N. J. Smelser & P. B. Baltes (Eds.), *International encyclopedia of the social and behavioral sciences* (pp. 14771–14775). Pergamon Press: Oxford.

Park, N. E., & Huebner, S. (2005). A cross-cultural study of the levels and correlates of life satisfaction among adolescents. *Journal of Cross-Cultural Psychology*, *36*(4), 444–456.

Paskins, J. (2005). *Are differences in children's travel reflected in their cognitive maps?* (pp. 49–62) Traffic and Transport Psychology: Theory and Application.

Paulo, R. M., Albuquerque, P. B., & Bull, R. (2016). Improving the enhanced cognitive interview with a new interview strategy: Category clustering recall. *Applied Cognitive Psychology*, *30*, 775–784.

Pollard, E., & Lee, P. (2003). Child well-being: A systematic review of the literature. *Social Indicators Research*, *61*(1), 59–78.

Ramanathan, S., O'Brien, C., Faulkner, G., & Stone, M. (2014). Happiness in motion; emotions, well-being, and active school travel. *Journal of School Health*, *84*(8), 516–523.

Rissotto, A., & Tonucci, F. (2002). Freedom of movement and environmental knowledge in elementary school children. *Journal of Environmental Psychology*, *22*, 65–77.

Romero, V. (2015). Children's experiences: Enjoyment and fun as additional encouragement for walking to school. *Journal of Transport and Health*, *2*(2), 230–237.

Rothman, L., Buliung, R., To, T., Macarthur, C., Macpherson, A., & Howard, A. (2015). Associations between parents' perception of traffic danger, the built environment and walking to school. *Journal of Transport and Health*, *2*(3), 327–335. https://doi.org/10.1016/j.jth.2015.05.004.

Ryff, C. D. (1989). Happiness is everything, or is it? Explorations on the meaning of psychological well-being. *Journal of Personality and Social Psychology*, *57*(6), 1069.

Schoeppe, S., Duncan, M. J., Badland, H., Oliver, M., & Curtis, C. (2013). Associations of children's independent mobility and active travel with physical activity, sedentary behavior and weight status: A systematic review. *Journal of Science and Medicine in Sport*, *16*(4), 312–319.

Siedlecki, K. L., Salthouse, T. A., Oishi, S., & Jeswani, S. (2014). The relationship between social support and subjective well-being across age. *Social Indicators Research*, *117*(2), 561–576.

Stea, T. J., & Torstveit, M. K. (2014). Association of lifestyle habits and academic achievement in Norwegian adolescents: A cross-sectional study. *BMC Public Health*, *14*, 829.

Tranter, P., & Pawson, E. (2001). Children's access to local environments: A case-study of Christchurch, New Zealand. *Local Environment*, *6*(1), 27–48. https://doi.org/10.1080/13549830120024233.

Trudeau, F., & Shephard, R. J. (2008). Physical education, school physical activity, school sports and academic performance. *International Journal of Behavioral Nutrition and Physical Activity*, *5*(10).

Van Dijk, M. L., De Groot, R. H., Van Acker, F., Savelberg, H. H., & Kirschner, P. A. (2014). Active commuting to school, cognitive performance, and academic achievement: An observational study in Dutch adolescents using accelerometers. *BMC Public Health*, *14*, 799. https://doi.org/10.1186/1471-2458-14-799.

Waygood, O., Friman, M., Olsson, L. E., & Taniguchi, A. (2017). Transport and child well-being: An integrative review. *Travel Behaviour and Society*, *9*, 32–49.

Waygood, O., Friman, M., Taniguchi, A., & Olsson, L. E. (2018). Children's life satisfaction and travel satisfaction: Evidence from Canada, Japan, and Sweden. *Travel Behaviour and Society*, *16*, 215–223.

Wentzel, K. R., McNamara-Barry, C., & Caldwell, K. A. (2004). Friendships in middle school: Influences on motivation and school adjustment. *Journal of Educational Psychology*, *96*, 195–203.

Westman, J., Johansson, M., Olsson, L. E., Mårtensson, F., & Friman, M. (2013). Children's affective experience of every-day travel. *Transport Geography*, *29*, 95–102.

Westman, J., Olsson, L. E., Gärling, T., & Friman, M. (2016). Children's travel to school: Satisfaction, current mood, and cognitive performance. *Transportation*, 1–18. https://doi. org/10.1007/s11116-016-9705-7.

Wilson, K., Clark, A. F., & Gilliard, J. A. (2018). Understanding child and parent perceptions of barriers influencing children's active school travel. *BMC Public Health*, *18*, 1053.

World Health Organization (2002). *Quantifying selected major risks to health. World Health Report: Reducing Risks Promoting Healthy Life* (pp. 57–61). Geneva: WHO.

CHAPTER FOUR

Transport and social wellbeing

E. Owen D. Waygood

Department of Civil, Geological, and Mining Engineering, Polytechnique Montréal, Montreal, QC, Canada

Contents

1 Introduction

This chapter will focus largely on published evidence that relates transport with social wellbeing as one of the three main domains of wellbeing (Dodge, Daly, Huton, & Sanders, 2012). Its definition is somewhat elusive, but researchers in the field of wellbeing (e.g., Pollard & Lee, 2003) use indicators such as anti-social behavior, peer problems, participation in cultural activities, relationships with others, social skills, and socioeconomic status to help define this term. One can imagine the different ways that transport might relate to such measures, but for the most part, this chapter will report on published evidence. This chapter will focus on social relationships, as they are found to have higher impacts on mortality than the commonly discussed health impacts such as physical activity, BMI (obesity), and air quality. Furthermore, the impacts from social relationships are not age-dependent (Holt-Lunstad, Smith, & Layton, 2010) and are typically found to be key explanatory factors in personal assessments of quality of life. For children, this can be seen in their subjective wellbeing and life satisfaction

(Park, 2004; Park & Huebner, 2005) (see Chapter 3 for more on these latter points).

Transport can influence social wellbeing through different means-of-influence (Waygood, Friman, Olsson, & Taniguchi, 2017b). Transport can influence one's ability to reach a destination and thus meet with others, it can influence whether social connections are made during a trip, and it can create barriers to social interaction at the street level or by limiting children's independent mobility. This chapter will discuss various links to social wellbeing with respect to these three means-of-influence.

1.1 Social relationships and children's lives

The advantages of social wellbeing can often be seen through its contribution to measures such as subjective wellbeing and life satisfaction (see Chapter 3). Having social interactions and a sense of belonging greatly contribute to the wellbeing of adolescents and young children (Park, 2004; Pretty, Conroy, Dugay, Fowler, & Williams, 1996). Although based on studies of adults, Helliwell and Putnam (2004) found that neighborhood and community ties support both physical and subjective wellbeing. They go on to mention that greater social networks are associated with better child welfare outcomes. Having social support is positively linked with the life satisfaction of children and adolescents (Park, 2004). Loneliness, a measure of negative social wellbeing, was found to be lower in adolescents who experience a better sense of community (Prezza & Pacilli, 2007). Chipuer (2001) argues that the need to belong is one of the most basic human needs; individuals need close, personal contact and connections to larger groups or communities. Establishing local relationships can also help diminish the perceptions of danger in one's environment (Prezza & Pacilli, 2007). This is important, as the mental health of youths with higher perceptions of danger are negatively affected (Leventhal & Brooks-Gunn, 2000). These local networks can improve their collective efficacy (Bandura, 1986 in Leventhal & Brooks-Gunn, 2000) through communities observing and enforcing socially accepted practices with the goal of supervising children. Thus, there are many reasons why it is important to develop social wellbeing.

The findings detailed above relate to Putnam et al.'s definition of social capital (Putnam, Leonardi, & Nanetti, 1994) which includes social networks, reciprocal support, civic engagement, community identity, and trust. Having the perception of higher social capital is associated with better mental health outcomes (Renalds, Smith, & Hale, 2010). However, Putnam et al.'s definition is related to the social capital of adults, and Morrow (2000) critiques that this definition does not necessarily pertain directly to children. She writes that it is perhaps better to see social capital as "a set of processes and practices that are integral to the acquisition of other forms of 'capital' such as human capital and cultural capital (i.e., qualifications, skills, group memberships, etc.)." In a separate critique of the "theoretical fathers" of capital (here including Putnam, Coleman, and Bourdieu), Holland, Reynolds, and Weller (2007) wrote that children are seen as passive consumers of their parents' social capital, as opposed to *active agents in the development and use of it.* Whether taking Putnam's definition, or the revised conceptualization by Morrow, it is important to understand the way that transport is related to those measures as it influences their social wellbeing.

Research also highlights that different relationships perform different functions. Putnam (2001) describes how there are bonding and bridging social capitals. Bonding social capital refers to inward-looking bonds that focus on relationships and networks of trust and reciprocity that reinforce the ties within close groups, such as family. Bridging social capital refers to outward-looking connections among heterogeneous groups. For children, these heterogeneous groups could be adults or other children. It has been argued that bonding social capital permits people to 'get by', whilst bridging social capital enables people to 'get ahead' (Holland et al., 2007). Those same authors refer to the study by Scales et al. (2001 in Holland et al., 2007) where it was found that apart from parental support, children need support from other adults in their neighborhood. How might transport relate to building those relationships?

Thus, it is important to see how transport affects and is affected by the diverse social relationships because they impact children's health and wellbeing. Are children developing their social capital and does how they travel affect this? Does the community's social context impact how children travel? Does transport facilitate or limit children seeking out friends for activities? These are a few of the questions that this chapter will shed some light on. The evidence in this chapter will be organized by transport's three main means-of-influence on wellbeing: intrinsic (i.e., during travel), as access, and external (i.e., transport by others) (Waygood et al., 2017b).

2 The trip is half the fun

Transport research and development often focuses on getting to a location, but what happens during the trip can also be important.

Two key people who began the *International Making Cities Livable Council* argue that the human dimension of children's travel is often forgotten, writing, "to walk down the street and be recognized and greeted... conversations and encounters and special events that give meaning to the urban environment" (Lennard & Lennard, 2000). Other authors write that adults and children use the streets as a place to socialize and that it affords places to "wander" (Ker & Tranter, 1997). Children also desire what is termed "ambient companionship" (Nansen et al., 2015). Ambient companionship is defined as natural surveillance, where children speak about the social and visible presence of other known or unknown children and adults along the routes they travel. Evidence has shown that walking and children's independent travel are by far the most strongly associated with these incidental interactions while traveling from A to B. However, travel by car is strongly negatively correlated with incidental interactions (Waygood & Friman, 2015; Waygood, Friman, Olsson, & Taniguchi, 2017a). As Grannis (2011) argues, incidental interactions are important for establishing and maintaining neighborhood networks. His research finds that the majority (roughly 80%) of neighborhood networks relate to local travel with children. In fact, it seems having children at home increases neighborhood connections (Kamruzzaman et al., 2014; Leyden, 2003). As written above, these social networks help support children's wellbeing. Independent children and their parents are found to have more social connections (Hüttenmoser, 1995; Prezza et al., 2001). This gives evidence to children building social capital, as opposed to only being recipients of their parents'.

It is highly desirable for children to have companionship during trips. The travel companions are typically friends and siblings rather than parents (Romero, 2011). Children desire companionship for social interaction, but also for safety (Mikkelsen & Christensen, 2009). Walking with friends is often mentioned by children as the desirable or preferred way to travel (Curtis, Babb, & Olaru, 2015; Kirby & Inchley, 2013; Murray & Mand, 2013; Romero, 2011; Yatiman, Aziz, & Said, 2012), whereas children felt that travel by car was isolating from friends (Barker, 2006; Barker, Kraftl, Horton, & Tucker, 2009). A study from Denmark for both boys and girls found that children enjoyed cycling with friends as a social activity in of itself (Mikkelsen & Christensen, 2009). In the UK, children talked of selecting public buses based on the preferred mix of friends (this may be dependent on living in an urban area where service levels are sufficient), as opposed to school buses where they have no choice and where there can be "emotional battlegrounds" (Murray & Mand, 2013). Companionship can also facilitate greater freedom as children are motivated to go explore and experience things with a friend (Milne, 2009; Morrow, 2000). Traveling with a companion can also give children greater freedom by increasing their parents' sense of safety in letting them travel unsupervised (Mikkelsen & Christensen, 2009). Related to the mode of travel, children who walked to school felt that talking with friends and getting physical activity were important. However, children who traveled by car talked of being safe from strangers, which may be a reflection of their parents' views (Romero, 2011). In social psychology, it was found that parents with social phobias also had children with social phobias, including the fear of strangers (Lieb et al., 2000). Thus, it can be seen here that active and public transport are more associated with social interactions, and the trips themselves can be considered social activities.

Although many children want to travel with friends, others also mention traveling alone (typically walking or cycling) as desirable (Curtis et al., 2015; Mikkelsen & Christensen, 2009). This preference may relate to children's personalities, though this has yet to be investigated. It may be that extraverted children seek out social interactions, while introverts desire more time for reflection. Children wish for different things depending on the modes they typically use. For example, walking alone may be positively seen as a way to get out and be independent (Witten, Kearns, & Carroll, 2015) or as a way to control the duration of the trip (not to rush) and have time to think (Romero, 2010). Companionship can also vary within active modes. Active commuters (those who go by modes such as walking and cycling) preferred cycling alone to school, followed by walking or taking public transport with friends (Curtis et al., 2015).

The social knowledge of public places can be developed through walking, either to get around or to access public transport (Milne, 2009). However, traveling independently can lead to interactions that come in direct conflict with the phrase many are raised with: "don't talk to strangers." This is due to that fact that one needs to interact with unknown adults such as bus drivers or employees at destinations (Milne, 2009) while traveling independently. Kidsmartz, which is an educational branch of the American "National Center for Missing & Exploited Children" recommends against the term "stranger danger"(Kidsmartz, 2019). They suggest that rather than teaching children to avoid all strangers, it is better to teach children that most adults are helpful and help them recognize which adults are best to approach if they need help.

It is not always possible to live in a good social environment. Studies of children in low socio-economic conditions report that these children may be constrained due to their poor conditions. However, at the same time, Witten et al. (2015) suggest that these children may in fact appreciate being able to see the "real life" conditions of their society. Despite poor urban conditions, the children in that study still valued being out and exploring alone. The children explained that it gave them a chance to be away from their parents and hang out with friends (Witten et al., 2015).

Finally, Morrow (2000) argues that children are unlikely to have civic engagement (one of the components of Putnam's social capital concept). This may relate to their lack of power in such situations, to the fact that they are not invited to participate, or to their views not being taken seriously (e.g., Matthews & Limb, 1999). They may also feel that their inputs are not even wanted (Stark et al., 2018). However, research has found that children can be stewards of the local environment by cleaning up garbage and petting bored animals. Kullman (2014) referred to children as "skilled urban carers", a term first coined by Jacobs (1993), which may represent their independent civic engagement.

2.1 Summary—Social wellbeing during the trip

This section examined how transport affects children's social wellbeing during the trip. It is not an exhaustive discussion of how transport might affect this, but rather an overview of the existing evidence. It has been shown that children who walk not only contribute to building their own social capital, but also to that of their parents, which supports the theories presented above. Active modes give children the freedom to not only access their friends on their own time, but are also seen as social activities themselves. At other times, the freedom of walking allows the child to reflect on things and manage their time. Although situations (e.g., social environment) are not always ideal, this is a real aspect of life for these children and they may appreciate the diversity of society as well as the opportunity to learn how to cope with these life experiences.

3 We're finally there

Reaching a destination is often the primary goal of travel. However, the destination may not be known at the outset of a child's trip. Children venture out to explore or seek out friends without knowing for certain where their friends may be. Their final destination may be a home, a public square, a park, or the street just in front of their home. Through these trips, children will likely develop a sense of belonging and even a sense of control over their environment.

Lynch (1981) wrote that children gain a sense of control over their environment through four means: presence, use and action, appropriation, and disposition. *Presence* is the child having some means of access (i.e., travel), but traffic can limit their range (e.g., Berg & Medrich, 1980). *Use and action* means the children must be able to play freely (e.g., Min & Lee, 2006), which can again be limited by traffic in the case of streets as playgrounds (e.g., Abu-Ghazzeh, 1998; Berg & Medrich, 1980; Moore, 1987; see also Chapter 10), or by parked cars taking up open space or restricting the type of play. *Appropriation* requires that the children feel that the space belongs to them, and as Matthews and Limb (1999) argue, children are often pushed from their immediate environments into designated "areas for children" such as parks. Finally, *disposition* is allowing other children to join in and participate in activities (which is of course limited to whether or not other children are able to reach the same location) (Abu-Ghazzeh, 1998). Playing together is essential for social and cognitive development. For example, games requiring collaboration develop the child's ability to handle emotions or manage interpersonal conflicts (Prezza & Pacilli, 2007). However, if children are constantly escorted and supervised, they seem less likely to develop these skills (Hüttenmoser, 1995). These neighborhood activities allow children to practice and develop their social skills, which is linked with lower levels of loneliness (Chipuer, 2001). The greater use of public spaces and CIM are associated with a lower sense of crime and a higher sense of community (Prezza & Pacilli, 2007).

Although incidental interactions likely help start or maintain social networks, it is the quality of social interactions and not the quantity that is more related to subjective wellbeing (Makino & Tagami, 1998), thus being with friends is important. Certainly, children meet friends at school, but it can also be a place of conflicts, fights, and harassment (Morrow, 2000). Children who had more independent mobility were found to be more confident about knowing where they could find friends outside of school (Lim & Barton, 2010). Having greater CIM was positively associated with playing more with friends both outdoors and indoors (Prezza et al., 2001). While children with lower independent mobility were found to have greater feelings of loneliness, related to a weaker sense of community (related to belonging, influence, integration and fulfillment of needs, and emotional connection), along with a lower sense of safety and less frequent activities with friends

(Pacilli, Giovannelli, Prezza, & Augimeri, 2013). For loneliness, dyadic attachments with friends is more important than with parents for children's experiences of loneliness. Whereas, attachments with parents was not associated with any of the measures of loneliness (Chipuer, 2001). In other situations, the parents themselves complain about the constraints of traffic and transport on their children's social inclusion (Davies, Davis, Cook, & Waters, 2008). Thus, children being able to travel freely is again associated with more frequent social interactions, contributing positively to their social wellbeing.

Although parents may seek out parks for their children, it is not necessarily true that all children prefer parks. A park is likely more exciting if there are friends or at least other children (who are potential friends). This can be seen in a study of children in South Korea where the majority of important places for the children were outdoors, with most of these places related to play areas, and about one-fifth related to parks (Min & Lee, 2006). The children in this study preferred places that were close to their homes where they had a high likelihood of meeting a friend, but that also contained some physical or social risks which might be stimulating. Some research does find that boys have favorite places such as hills and football (soccer) fields (which itself is likely linked to social interactions), but it also finds that they name shopping areas as preferred locations (Mikkelsen & Christensen, 2009). Findings show that children may prefer public social locations such as commercial establishments or other convivial places where they can find social interactions (Banerjee, Uhm, & Bahl, 2014; Morrow, 2000). Such places are desirable as they allow for the chance to "bump into friends" (Banerjee et al., 2014). The separation of these types of destinations from residential areas is seen as problematic by children, though it may be sought out by parents (Berg & Medrich, 1980). Again, this illustrates the problem of cutting children off from public gathering points where they can interact, have unstructured play, and observe social life. Children found streets themselves to be more desirable than parks and playgrounds, which were seen to be dull in comparison (Berg & Medrich, 1980). Streets are places where children may pass a lot of time (Abu-Ghazzeh, 1998; Morrow, 2000). Many children seek out play and social interaction at various settings such as playgrounds, street fairs, on the street, or on a staircase of a building (Lim & Barton, 2010). Children may also prefer such locations due to the passive observation and presence of adults (even unknown adults) in case the children need assistance (Depeau, 2001). In other words, these places offer the children spaces to interact, while at the same time allowing children to keep adults within reach if the need arises. These local places matter to children as it affords them personal identity through attachment, personal development through effective use of local resources, and civic and social belongingness through participation (Matthews & Limb, 1999). All of these aspects relate to children building and using social capital, as was argued by Holland et al. (2007). Thus, the presence children in parks may be more a result of having pushed them into these "child-oriented" locations as their local areas, such as streets, were taken away from them (Matthews & Limb, 1999).

Children being able to independently reach certain locations is strongly related to distance, especially as children's independent mobility is highly dependent on active modes (Pont, Ziviani, Wadley, Bennett, & Abbott, 2009). Distance can also affect children's appraisal of destinations (Depeau, 2001). A study on places that were important to children highlighted that the vast majority were outdoors, and that being at a distance that allowed them frequent and easy access was a key feature (Min & Lee, 2006).

Although local destinations are important for the children, research also finds that with their independence, they also seek to connect to the world beyond their neighborhood (Milne, 2009). Children often seek this extended mobility in order to reach destinations such as cinemas, swimming pools, and shops in the city center where they can find a concentration of public social life (Milne, 2009). Through this type of independent travel, they gain experience with their community which is then linked to a lower fear of crime and a higher sense of community (Prezza & Pacilli, 2007).

The places where children want to go will change as they age, as their desires may shift from exploring their immediate surroundings to simply "hanging out". This change can be seen across generations of children suggesting that it is not just a current behavior (Gaster, 1991). Children operate within the world that adults have created, but want places to "hang out" in order to socialize, be seen, and to add to their sense of belonging, identification, and place ownership (Matthews & Limb, 1999). The adolescents who are "hanging out" may be seen as a source of fear by adults whose "hectic, mobile lifestyle" results in them being between places rather than in places, which may result in a lack of understanding about how adolescents use public spaces (Prezza & Pacilli, 2007). Even the way one gets around can impact the impression that one has about youths hanging out. A study that documented people's impressions of youth in a park showed that people in cars believed that the adolescents were "up to no good". However, the slower the mode (cycling, walking) of the traveler, the more accurate their impressions of the youths were; they observed that the youths were laughing, playing and just having fun with each other (Gatersleben, Murtagh, & White, 2013). Thus, parents that travel primarily by car may have a distorted view of public life that may make them more likely to restrict their children's independence, thus reducing the likelihood of their children going to seek out friends when they want.

3.1 Summary of trip destination and social wellbeing

This section discusses literature related to how the destination of a trip can impact a child's social wellbeing. The majority of the research is related to social connections, but other links may also exist. A key point is that CIM is associated with finding friends, building social bonds and strengthening a child's sense of belonging. Children often seek out social interactions with their peers and their community, and need places to gather that are local and diverse. Parks are not necessarily the destinations that children prefer, but they are one of the few places left where they are allowed to gather. Finally, the way that adults travel can affect their impressions of the social environment, so it is important for them to walk to better understand these young residents.

4 External impacts

Much less research has directly studied how the transport system affects children's social interactions. Studies on adults have demonstrated in numerous countries that as traffic increases, social connections and interactions diminish along with what is considered to be the individual's living space (e.g., Appleyard, 1980; Hart & Parkhurst, 2011; Sauter & Huettenmoser, 2008). For children, it was found that the lowest frequency of incidental social interactions during travel occurred in the area with the highest recorded traffic (Waygood & Friman, 2015).

In Sweden, parents' perceptions of the traffic environment (amount, control, etc.) was positively related to foot and cycle paths, a sense of community, and environmental trust. However, when their perceptions of the traffic environment were lower, parents felt a greater need to protect children and perceived their children as less mature (Johansson, 2006). When traffic environments were positive, parents held more negative attitudes towards chauffeuring and car trips, but felt positively about independent trips. However, in that study, a sense of community was positively related to chauffeuring attitudes and car journeys, with no relationship to attitudes towards CIM nor actual independent trips. The measures related to environmental trust (i.e., it is safe for the child to be out alone at night, to walk along alley-ways, etc.) and trust in strangers were not significant in relation to chauffeuring, car trips, or independent trips. Nevertheless, environmental trust did increase the parent's attitudes towards CIM. Taken as a whole, these results might suggest that traffic is more important than the social context for CIM.

There are numerous ways to reduce the impacts of traffic on neighborhoods, and this often involves designing streets that restrain the movement of cars (lower speeds to reduce danger, make it less attractive as a through street, etc.). Children living in "Smart Growth" neighborhoods (where controls over traffic are put in place), were found to play with friends more frequently than those in conventional low-to-medium density neighborhoods in the USA (Dunton, Intille, Wolch, & Pentz, 2012). Another study examined how the use of a street differed according to the type of traffic restriction applied (Biddulph, 2012). The study compared a traffic calmed street and a *home zone* street. The characteristics of the traffic calmed street included: lower speeds of 18 mph (29 kmh) on average, tightened corner radii junctions, raised roads creating plateaus that are level with sidewalks, and added trees and planters. The *home zone* street had these features: closed to through traffic but open to pedestrians, shares space with a mix of all modes, had entrance posts, among other elements. Observation through hidden cameras found that on the traffic calmed street, people walked and stopped to chat. On the shared street (home zone), children actively played using the entire area, people stopped and socialized, and simply stopped to watch and observe others. Thus, this suggests that stronger restrictions on through traffic and taking away the delineation of the space (i.e., shared open space as opposed to sidewalks and roads) allowed children to appropriate the space and interact with their friends and neighbors. This relates back to Lynch's theory (Lynch, 1981) on children exercising control over their environment. The same was also argued by Depeau (2001), who wrote that the functional separation of traffic and pedestrian infrastructure may be perceived as improving the safety for children (though it generally facilitates higher speeds which are more dangerous if there is a collision), but it reduces children's socio-visibility.

Often, traffic can be a barrier to reaching friends as it limits children's independent travel. For example, children in rural areas were isolated as a result of the low density and high speed traffic of the rural roads (Mikkelsen & Christensen, 2009). Due to long distances and traffic dangers, children took trips to socialize much less frequently, and these trips needed to be arranged ahead of time as they depended on access to cars (Mikkelsen & Christensen, 2009). Traffic safety along with personal safety are often mentioned as the primary constraints to children's independent mobility (e.g., Berg & Medrich, 1980), though this is moderated by distance meaning that for shorter distances, such concerns are generally lower. Depending on the context, traffic can prevent children from using facilities that are intended for them, keep children from using streets and sidewalks, or simply keep them in their homes (Berg & Medrich, 1980). Modern designs such as transit-oriented development is found to increase people's connectedness and trust with their neighbors (Kamruzzaman et al., 2014), likely supporting children's independent mobility.

Traffic impacts children's independent travel by occupying space that could otherwise be used by children and affecting parents' perceptions of safety. Traffic was found to prevent children at the age of five from being independent, which limited the development of their social and motor skills by limiting the variety and duration of their play (Hüttenmoser, 1995). The study examined five-year-old children without older siblings in Zurich, Switzerland. Children who lived where traffic did not limit their independent play with other children were able to list a greater variety of things to do with friends, and to offer conflict resolutions (Hüttenmoser, 1995). The parents in the study who felt that children should be escorted naturally tried their best to provide play opportunities for them by making efforts, such as organizing play dates and taking the children to parks. However, due to the parents' limitations of available time, the children's play times were considerably lower than those of the independent children. Further, there was less variety in the games played at the park than those played in the street. One explanation that was given for this difference was that children could develop games and stories over time when playing with the same group of children. They could also easily return home to get objects that facilitate or enhance their play. The study found that parents who thought that it was irresponsible to let children out alone were those that lived in "unfavorable environments" that related to higher levels of traffic. The author suggested that parents developed this belief as a result of the higher level of traffic, due to the fact that this group of parents was the only one to express this opinion. The author argued that protecting their child from the dangerous traffic caused parents to naturally develop the belief that it would be irresponsible to let children out alone. Thus, traffic was found to create the parents' negative views towards children's independent mobility, which then limited the children's social and physical development. This could be related to the findings by Johansson (2006). Here, having positive perceptions of traffic led to increased perceptions of a child's maturity. If traffic conditions are worse, it would only be natural for the parent to believe the child lacks maturity. As well, Curtis et al. (2015) found that children whose parents "bubble wrapped" them (i.e., did not allow them any travel freedoms or risks) were more likely to believe it was irresponsible to let children out alone, but also that others would consider them irresponsible parents if they were to let their children out alone. Like the relationship found in Johansson's study, these parents also had less confidence in their children to negotiate the traffic environment.

Numerous authors lament the consequences of putting cars before people, and in this case, children. Lennard and Lennard (2000) wrote, "development of city modern does not include child needs; to accommodate the car, children's autonomy has been sacrificed". One study examined how children's travel evolved over generations in the same location (Gaster, 1991). The respondents' childhoods dated from 1915 to the mid 1970s. The general findings were that the obstacles and barriers to independent travel grew over time, and that the age at which children were allowed to roam freely increased. This change was linked to increasing levels of traffic. Along with increasing traffic, children started getting ticketed for playing and cycling in the street, getting told not to play in courtyards, and even older children experienced being told that they couldn't play in parks (by park employees). Local places being taken away and the restrictions on CIM resulted in children being mostly involved in structured and organized play that increasingly required trips out of their neighborhoods. This trend of taking children out of their immediate environment and putting them into designated areas is also critiqued by Jacobs (1993) and Matthews and Limb (1999). One author (Abu-Ghazzeh, 1998) articulated that "planners need… to elevate the street in the residential neighborhood from a mere traffic channel to a social institution for children."

4.1 Summary of transport as an extrinsic impact on child social wellbeing

This section highlighted a number of external impacts that transport has on a child's social wellbeing. As with the other sections, the arguments that were expressed are limited to existing research, and other relationships may exist. Traffic is the key external impact of transport on child social wellbeing. It limits children's social wellbeing by occupying space, creating danger in areas with traffic, creating unwelcoming environments, and manifesting in parental perceptions that it is too dangerous to allow CIM, which further limits the social interactions of children.

5 Diagram of interactions

This last section presents two syntheses of the preceding discussions. Many of the relationships between transport and children's social wellbeing seem to be two-way relationships. This means that each affects the other, and not necessarily that the direction of influence is in one direction only (Fig. 1). For example, children who walk and are independent see and interact with people in their neighborhoods more often, both while they travel and at their destinations. The fact that they will see other people, particularly those that they know, reduces parents' anxieties about letting their children go out.

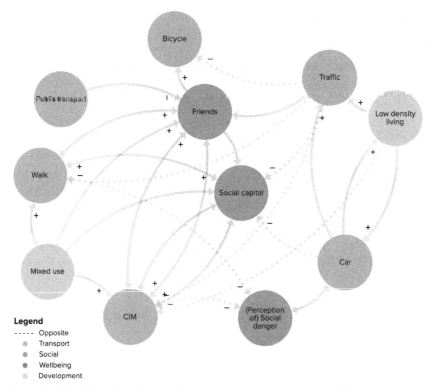

Fig. 1 Relationships found in the literature relating transport and different measures related to social wellbeing (connecting with friends, social capital, (perception of) social danger). *(Image produced using www.kumu.io.)*

A synthesis of such relationships is shown in Fig. 1 with references given in Table 1. It should be noted that this is not an extensive list of all possible inter-actions, but the relationships that were found in the literature.

Table 1 Relationships between transport and different measures of social wellbeing

From	To	Direction	References
Car	Traffic	+	(Johansson, 2006)
Car	(Perception of) Social danger	+	(Gatersleben et al., 2013)
Car	Social capital	−	(Barker, 2006, 2009; Waygood & Friman, 2015)
CIM	(Perception of) Social danger	−	(Alparone & Pacilli, 2012; Banerjee et al., 2014; Milne, 2009)
CIM	Friends	+	(Berg & Medrich, 1980; Hüttenmoser, 1995; Pacilli et al., 2013; Prezza et al., 2001; Witten et al., 2015; Yatiman et al., 2012)
CIM	Social capital	+	(Pacilli et al., 2013; Prezza & Pacilli, 2007; Witten et al., 2015)
CIM	Life satisfaction; SWB	+	(Waygood, 2018)
Friends	Life satisfaction; SWB	+	(Park, 2004)
Friends	Bicycle	+	(Mikkelsen & Christensen, 2009; Morrow, 2000)
Mixed use	Walk	+	(Pont et al., 2009)
Mixed use	CIM	+	(Cervesato & Waygood,2019; Waygood & Kitamura, 2009)
Low density living	Car	+	(Cervesato & Waygood, 2019; Mikkelsen & Christensen, 2009; Pont et al., 2009; Waygood & Kitamura, 2009)
Low density living	CIM	−	(Cervesato & Waygood, 2019; Waygood & Kitamura, 2009)
Mixed use	Walk	+	(Pont et al., 2009)
Mixed use	CIM	+	(Cervesato & Waygood, 2019; Waygood & Kitamura, 2009)
Public transport	Friends	+	(Murray & Mand, 2013)

Continued

Table 1 Relationships between transport and different measures of social wellbeing—cont'd

From	To	Direction	References
Social capital	Life satisfaction; SWB	+	(Park, 2004)
(Perception of) Social danger	CIM	−	(Alparone & Pacilli, 2012)
Traffic	Social capital	−	(Appleyard, 1980; Biddulph, 2012; Hart & Parkhurst, 2011; Sauter & Huettenmoser, 2008)
Traffic	Friends	−	(Davies et al., 2008; Hüttenmoser, 1995; Waygood & Friman, 2015)
Walk	Friends	+	(Curtis et al., 2015; Kirby & Inchley, 2013; Murray & Mand, 2013; Romero, 2011; Yatiman et al., 2012)
Walk	Social capital	+	(Grannis, 2011; Waygood et al., 2017a; Waygood & Friman, 2015)
Walk	(Perception of) Social danger	−	(Romero, 2011; Witten et al., 2015)

6 Conclusion

Children's social wellbeing is affected by transport through all three means-of-influence. Children who are independent and walk or cycle in their neighborhoods connect with their neighbors and friends more often, building the social capital that further supports their independence. Through exploration, these children develop knowledge of where to find friends and observe how society interacts. Children with the ability to go see friends when they have free time have more frequent and longer sessions of play and interaction. Unfortunately, traffic planning typically seeks to promote dangerous speeds and high traffic flows without consideration to the negative impacts on health and wellbeing. This results in a situation that severely limits children's freedom and play. This decreases leisure activities out of the home for not only the child but also the parent, as it increases their chauffeuring burden. Traffic physically occupies space, and also takes away local open spaces where children can interact with their neighbors through the threat of physical harm.

To support greater social wellbeing for children a fundamental point appears to be supporting walking. In later chapters, more details on how this can be accomplished are described, but a few points are given here. As parents, simply walking with your child to destinations and through your neighborhood will help build connections to neighbors and shop owners, along with developing the skills and confidence for a child to make independent trips. Developing these skills and connections then allows the child the opportunity to make local trips themselves. Many cities have realized the unreasonable safety burden that traffic imposes, and are lowering speeds and changing street design. Supporting and encouraging such measures will help facilitate children to make connections with their community. Street parties and other such events can also help develop social relations, and allow children the opportunity for play.

This chapter focused primarily on existing literature, but many interactions between transport and child social wellbeing have yet to be investigated. Modern life includes technology that allows a greater range of social interactions such as video calls and texting. How these relate to children's travel, whether they facilitate social interactions or substitute for meeting up in person, is not well studied. Important characteristics of the child such as being an extrovert and how that relates to transport and social wellbeing should also be investigated. Although this chapter focused on social relationships, there are other indicators of social wellbeing that may also link to transport, including children's participation in cultural activities and peer problems. The literature concerning these aspects is still limited compared to the attention paid to physical activity, and much has yet to be learned about how transport can hinder or facilitate greater social wellbeing for children.

References

Abu-Ghazzeh, T. M. (1998). Children's use of the street as a playground in Abu-Nuseir, Jordan. *Environment and Behavior, 30*(6), 799–831.

Alparone, F. R., & Pacilli, M. G. (2012). On children's independent mobility: The interplay of demographic, environmental, and psychosocial factors. *Children's Geographies, 10*(1), 109–122.

Appleyard, D. (1980). Livable streets: Protected neighborhoods? *The ANNALS of the American Academy of Political and Social Science, 451*(1), 106–117.

Banerjee, T., Uhm, J., & Bahl, D. (2014). Walking to school: The experience of children in inner city Los Angeles and implications for policy. *Journal of Planning Education and Research, 34*(2), 123–140.

Barker, J. (2006). "Are we there yet?": Exploring aspects of automobility in children's lives. In *Faculty of Geography and Earth Sciences*: Brunel University.

Barker, J. (2009). 'Driven to distraction?': Children's experiences of car travel. *Mobilities, 4*(1), 59–76.

Barker, J., Kraftl, P., Horton, J., & Tucker, F. (2009). The road less travelled – New directions in children's and young people's mobility. *Mobilities, 4*(1), 1–10.

Berg, M., & Medrich, E. A. (1980). Children in four neighborhoods: The physical environment and its effect on play and play patterns. *Environment and Behavior, 12*(3), 320–348.

Biddulph, M. (2012). Street design and street use: Comparing traffic calmed and home zone streets. *Journal of Urban Design, 17*(2), 213–232.

Cervesato, A., & Waygood, E. O. D. (2019). Children's independent trips on weekdays and weekends: Case study of Quebec City. *Transportation Research Record, 2673*(4), 907–916. https://doi.org/10.1177/0361198119837225.

Chipuer, H. M. (2001). Dyadic attachments and community connectedness: Links with youths' loneliness experiences. *Journal of Community Psychology, 29*(4), 429–446.

Curtis, C., Babb, C., & Olaru, D. (2015). Built environment and children's travel to school. *Transport Policy, 42*, 21–33.

Davies, B., Davis, E., Cook, K., & Waters, E. (2008). Getting the complete picture: Combining parental and child data to identify the barriers to social inclusion for children living in low socio-economic areas. *Child Care Health and Development, 34*(2), 214–222.

Depeau, S. (2001). Urban Identities and Social Interaction: A cross-cultural analysis of young people's spatial mobility in Paris, France, and Frankston, Australia. *Local Environment, 6*(1), 81–86.

Dodge, R., Daly, A., Huyton, J., & Sanders, L. (2012). The challenge of defining wellbeing. *International Journal of Wellbeing, 2*(3), 222–235. https://doi.org/10.5502/ijw.v2i3.4

Dunton, G. F., Intille, S. S., Wolch, J., & Pentz, M. A. (2012). Investigating the impact of a smart growth community on the contexts of children's physical activity using Ecological Momentary Assessment. *Health & Place, 18*(1), 76–84.

Gaster, S. (1991). Urban children's access to their neighborhood: Changes over three generations. *Environment and behavior, 23*(1), 70–85.

Gatersleben, B., Murtagh, N., & White, E. (2013). Hoody, goody or buddy? How travel mode affects social perceptions in urban neighbourhoods. *Transportation Research Part F: Traffic Psychology and Behaviour, 21*, 219–230.

Grannis, R. (2011). *From the ground up: Translating geography into community through neighbor networks*. Princeton University Press.

Hart, J., & Parkhurst, G. (2011). Driven to excess: Impacts of motor vehicles on the quality of life of residents of three streets in Bristol UK. *World Transport Policy & Practice, 17*(2), 12–30.

Helliwell, J. F., & Putnam, R. D. (2004). The social context of well-being. *Philosophical Transactions-Royal Society of London Series B Biological Sciences*, 1435–1446.

Holland, J., Reynolds, T., & Weller, S. (2007). Transitions, networks and communities: The significance of social capital in the lives of children and young people. *Journal of Youth Studies, 10*(1), 97–116.

Holt-Lunstad, J., Smith, T. B., & Layton, J. B. (2010). Social relationships and mortality risk: A meta-analytic review. *PLoS Medicine, 7*(7). e1000316.

Hüttenmoser, M. (1995). Children and their living surroundings: Empirical investigations into the significance of living surroundings for the everyday life and development of children. *Children's Environments, 12*(4), 403–413.

Jacobs, J. (1993). *The death and life of Great American cities*. New York: Random House.

Johansson, M. (2006). Environment and parental factors as determinants of mode for children's leisure travel. *Journal of Environmental Psychology, 26*(2), 156–169.

Kamruzzaman, M., Wood, L., Hine, J., Currie, G., Giles-Corti, B., & Turrell, G. (2014). Patterns of social capital associated with transit oriented development. *Journal of Transport Geography, 35*, 144–155.

Ker, I., & Tranter, P. (1997). A wish called wander: Reclaiming automobility from the motor car. *World Transport Policy and Practice, 3,* 11–16.

Kidsmartz (2019). *Rethinking "stranger danger"* .

Kirby, J., & Inchley, J. (2013). Walking behaviours among adolescent girls in Scotland: A pilot study. *Health Education & Behavior, 113*(1), 28–51.

Kullman, K. (2014). Children, urban care, and everyday pavements. *Environment and Planning A, 46*(12), 2864–2880.

Lennard, H. L., & Lennard, S. H. C. (2000). *The forgotten child: Cities for the well-being of children.* Gondolier Press.

Leventhal, T., & Brooks-Gunn, J. (2000). The neighborhoods they live in: The effects of neighborhood residence on child and adolescent outcomes. *Psychological Bulletin, 126* (2), 309.

Leyden, K. M. (2003). Social capital and the built environment: The importance of walkable neighborhoods. *American Journal of Public Health, 93*(9), 1546–1551.

Lieb, R., Wittchen, H. -U., Höfler, M., Fuetsch, M., Stein, M. B., & Merikangas, K. R. (2000). Parental psychopathology, parenting styles, and the risk of social phobia in offspring: A prospective-longitudinal community study. *Archives of General Psychiatry, 57*(9), 859–866.

Lim, M., & Barton, A. C. (2010). Exploring insideness in urban children's sense of place. *Journal of Environmental Psychology, 30*(3), 328–337.

Lynch, K. (1981). *A theory of good city form.* Cambridge, MA: MIT Press.

Makino, Y., & Tagami, F. (1998). Relations of social interactions to subjective well-being. *J-STAGE, 46*(1), 52–57.

Matthews, H., & Limb, M. (1999). Defining an agenda for the geography of children: Review and prospect. *Progress in Human Geography, 23*(1), 61–90.

Mikkelsen, M. R., & Christensen, P. (2009). Is children's independent mobility really independent? A study of children's mobility combining ethnography and GPS/mobile phone technologies. *Mobilities, 4*(1), 37–58.

Milne, S. (2009). Moving into and through the public world: Children's perspectives on their encounters with adults. *Mobilities, 4*(1), 103–118.

Min, B., & Lee, J. (2006). Children's neighborhood place as a psychological and behavioral domain. *Journal of Environmental Psychology, 26*(1), 51–71.

Moore, R. (1987). Streets as playgrounds. In A. V. Moudon (Ed.), *Public streets for public use, Van Nostrand Reinhold* (pp. 45–62).

Morrow, V. M. (2000). 'Dirty looks' and 'trampy places' in young people's accounts of community and neighbourhood: Implications for health inequalities. *Critical Public Health, 10* (2), 141–152.

Murray, L., & Mand, K. (2013). Travelling near and far: Placing children's mobile emotions. *Emotion Space and Society, 9,* 72–79.

Nansen, B., Gibbs, L., MacDougall, C., Vetere, F., Ross, N. J., & McKendrick, J. (2015). Children's interdependent mobility: Compositions, collaborations and compromises. *Childrens Geographies, 13*(4), 467–481.

Pacilli, M. G., Giovannelli, I., Prezza, M., & Augimeri, M. L. (2013). Children and the public realm: Antecedents and consequences of independent mobility in a group of 11–13-year-old Italian children. *Children's Geographies, 11*(4), 377–393.

Park, N. (2004). The role of subjective well-being in positive youth development. *Annals of the American Academy of Political and Social Science, 591,* 14.

Park, N., & Huebner, E. S. (2005). A cross-cultural study of the levels and correlates of life satisfaction among adolescents. *Journal of Cross-Cultural Psychology, 36*(4), 444–456.

Pollard, E., & Lee, P. (2003). Child well-being: A systematic review of the literature. *Social Indicators Research, 61*(1), 59–78.

Pont, K., Ziviani, J., Wadley, D., Bennett, S., & Abbott, R. (2009). Environmental correlates of children's active transportation: A systematic literature review. *Health & place, 15*(3), 849–862.

Pretty, G. M., Conroy, C., Dugay, J., Fowler, K., & Williams, D. (1996). Sense of community and its relevance to adolescents of all ages. *Journal of Community Psychology, 24*(4), 365–379.

Prezza, M., & Pacilli, M. G. (2007). Current fear of crime, sense of community, and loneliness in italian adolescents: The role of autonomous mobility and play during childhood. *Journal of Community Psychology, 35*(2), 151–170.

Prezza, M., Pilloni, S., Morabito, C., Sersante, C., Alparone, F. R., & Giuliani, M. V. (2001). The influence of psychosocial and environmental factors on children's independent mobility and relationship to peer frequentation. *Journal of Community & Applied Social Psychology, 11*(6), 435–450.

Putnam, R. D. (2001). *Bowling alone: The collapse and revival of American community.* Simon and Schuster.

Putnam, R. D., Leonardi, R., & Nanetti, R. Y. (1994). *Making democracy work: Civic traditions in modern Italy.* Princeton University Press.

Renalds, A., Smith, T. H., & Hale, P. J. (2010). A systematic review of built environment and health. *Family & Community Health, 33*(1), 68–78.

Romero, V. M. (2010). Children's views of independent mobility during their school travels. *Children Youth and Environments, 20*(2), 46–66.

Romero, V. M. (2011). Children's thoughts about what makes walking fun: Advancing our understanding of school travel. In *Faculty of the built environment*: The University of New South Wales.

Sauter, D., & Huettenmoser, M. (2008). Liveable streets and social inclusion. *Urban Design International, 13*(2), 67–79.

Stark, J., Uhlmann, T., Fanninger, C., Schützhofer, B., Berger, W., & Kirchner, M. (2018). Seeing the world through the eyes of a child—A smartphone application to visualize children's perceptions of their transport geographies. In J. Zvobgo & K. de Vos (Eds.), *9th child in the city world conference, Vienna, Austria.* .

Waygood, E. O. D. (2018). Transport and child well-being: Case study of Quebec City. In M. Friman, D. Ettema, & L. E. Olsson (Eds.), *Quality of life and daily travel* (pp. 199–218). Springer.

Waygood, E. O. D., & Friman, M. (2015). Children's travel and incidental community connections. *Travel Behaviour and Society, 2*(3), 174–181.

Waygood, E. O. D., Friman, M., Olsson, L. E., & Taniguchi, A. (2017a). Children's incidental social interaction during travel international case studies from Canada, Japan, and Sweden. *Journal of Transport Geography, 63*, 22–29.

Waygood, E. O. D., Friman, M., Olsson, L. E., & Taniguchi, A. (2017b). Transport and child well-being: An integrative review. *Travel Behaviour and Society, 9*(Suppl. C), 32–49.

Waygood, E. O. D., & Kitamura, R. (2009). Children in a rail-based developed area of Japan travel patterns, independence, and exercise. *Transportation Research Record*, (2125), 36–43.

Witten, K., Kearns, R., & Carroll, P. (2015). Urban inclusion as wellbeing: Exploring children's accounts of confronting diversity on inner city streets. *Social Science & Medicine, 133*, 349–357.

Yatiman, N. A., Aziz, N. F., & Said, I. (2012). Affordances of homeschool journey in rural environment for children's performances. *Aice-Bs 2012 Cairo (Asia Pacific International Conference on Environment-Behaviour Studies), 68*, 395–405.

CHAPTER FIVE

A social-ecological conceptualization of children's mobility

Raktim Mitra[a] and Kevin Manaugh[b]
[a]School of Urban and Regional Planning, Ryerson University, Toronto, ON, Canada
[b]Department of Geography, McGill School of Environment, McGill University, Montreal, QC, Canada

Contents

1 Introduction

In 2007, a British national newspaper reported on an intergenerational study that highlighted a major decline in children's independent mobility (CIM), or the ability and license for children to explore their neighborhood on their own, over the past century (Derbyshire, 2007). The story featured a family living in Sheffield, England. The oldest member of the family, Mr. Thomas, walked regularly as an 8-year old in the 1920s, up to six miles without adult supervision. By the 1970s, children in Sheffield, England, were already experiencing reduced independence. When Mr. Thomas's grand-daughter Vicky Grant was 8, she was still allowed to play with friends in the park and walk to school and swimming pool. In contrast, Vicky's son Edward had little independence outside of their house when he was 8-years old in 2007. He was driven to his school that was a

Transport and Children's Wellbeing
https://doi.org/10.1016/B978-0-12-814694-1.00005-1

few minutes away and also driven to a "safe place" where he could ride his bike. None of his friends were allowed to go beyond their home or garden unsupervised. A further systematic study on other families in Sheffield confirmed a reduction in CIM with regard to their home range, the variety of outdoor places that they visited, the range of activities that they participated, as well as the number of friends who accompanied them when exploring places without adult supervision (Wooley & Griffin, 2015).

The abovementioned observations from Sheffield, although somewhat anecdotal, draw the picture of a broader change that we have observed with regard to children's everyday mobility. Several studies have provided evidence of a systematic and consistent decline in children's independence and a corresponding increase in chauffeuring and adult surveillance over at least the past five decades (Fyhri, Hjorthol, Mackett, Fotel, & Kyttä, 2011; Gaster, 1991; Hillman, Adams, & Whitelegg, 1990; Mackett, Brown, Gong, Kitazawa, & Paskins, 2007; Shaw et al., 2015; Tranter & Whitelegg, 1994). Research on children's home range (i.e., the spatial extent within which children are allowed to explore unsupervised) and activity-space (i.e., out-of-home places where children are allowed to spend time frequently) has also shown very limited independent mobility, as well as a decline over time (Loebach & Gilliland, 2014; Villanueva et al., 2013; Wooley & Griffin, 2015).

A license to go to places without constantly being supervised is a necessary condition that enables active transportation (defined as transportation using human powered options, including foot and bicycle) and other daily activities that involve physical activity. Our recent research in Toronto, Canada showed that an average 9–12 year-old child is spending 29 min daily being driven by adults to different places (including school), and a full 87 min a day in front of television, computer, phone or video–gaming screens (Mitra, Cantello, Buliung, & Faulkner, 2017). Limited independent mobility and an overdependence on automobiles may have significant implications for a child's physical, psychological, cognitive and social health, and an emerging literature has provided evidence of such impacts. Some of this evidence is summarized in Chapters 2–4 in this book. In addition, childhood is an important time for habit formation. Active and independent children can develop skills to become active, confident and socially engaged adults and reap related benefits throughout their lives.

For these reasons, academics, professionals and community groups alike have widely acknowledged and emphasized, both in literature and policy, the need for promoting and enabling active transportation and independent mobility among children. Why then, despite many advantages, are today's children walking and biking less? What explains the constant adult supervision that characterizes modern childhood? It is critically important to address these questions before we can develop effective policies and programs that focus on the mobility, health and wellbeing of today's children and the next generation of young adults.

The answers, however, are not straightforward, as there are multiple factors that may influence household decisions regarding a child's outdoor mobility, and these factors might operate at different levels and interact with each other in complex ways. For example, distance to school is often mentioned by caregivers as the primary reason for chauffeuring a child to/from school. McDonald (2007) concluded that nearly half of the decline in walking to school can be explained by increased distance to school that resulted due to suburbanization and/or school closure. However, research conducted in Canada and Europe showed that between 1980s and early 2000s, average school travel distance generally remained similar, and yet, fewer children are walking or bicycling to and from schools (Grize, Bringolf-Isler, Martin, & Braun-Fahrlander, 2010; Mitra, Papaioannou, & Habib, 2016). On the other hand, adult surveillance has become an important part of the "good parenting" model (Fotel & Thomsen, 2004; Mitra, Faulkner, Buliung, & Stone, 2014; Valentine, 1997a, 1997b; Waygood, 2009), and parents' schedules also have become busier with less time to walk/cycle with their children to school and other destinations (Fyhri et al., 2011). To understand the nature of children's mobility and the factors that may influence household decisions, we also have to understand the social and environmental contexts within which a child spends their everyday life and travels to various locations.

In this chapter, we discuss these factors and present a conceptual framework using a social-ecological approach. The conceptual model is a tool that may help scholars, policy makers and community-based organizations in systematically understanding children's independent mobility and other travel outcomes, including the use of transportation modes, and in developing targeted programs and policy to produce behavioral change.

2 Key approaches to understanding transportation behavior

There is a long history of exploring a household's transportation outcomes using econometric approaches. Researchers have hypothesized that travel outcomes are determined based on a 'rational' evaluation of costs involved, travel time, convenience and other perceived benefits

(Ben-akiva & Lerman, 1985), and that a household's activity space, or the geographical extent within which they can or would be mobile during a day, is constrained by time and access to mobility options (Hägerstrand, 1970; Jones, 1979).

Further advancements within this theoretical approach emphasized the importance of the neighborhood environment within which a household lives and travels, and hypothesized that the neighborhood's natural and built environment characteristics may influence the 'utility' of a trip and therefore the likelihood of choosing a particular trip and the mode used (Boarnet & Crane, 2001; Cervero, 2002; Cervero & Kockelman, 1997). Since the 1990s, numerous studies have empirically tested this hypothesis and provided evidence of such a relationship (see Ewing & Cervero, 2010, 2017 for a review).

The relationship between attitudes/preferences, cognitive processes and transportation demand is also widely recognized (Boarnet & Crane, 2001; Cao, Mokhtarian, & Handy, 2009; Ewing & Cervero, 2010; Kitamura, Mokhtarian, & Laidet, 1997). A household, when they can afford to do so, may self-select themselves into a neighborhood that fits its transportation preferences. To address this possibility, existing research on travel behavior have often explored attitudes/preferences as confounding or latent factors that may moderate the observed association between neighborhood environment and transportation outcomes (Cao et al., 2009; Kitamura, 2009; Willis, Manaugh, & El-Geneidy, 2015). Some researchers have taken a more behavioral approach to understand these travel attitudes and preferences, drawing on the Theory of Planned Behavior (TPB) that focuses on the intention or motivation (of traveling) as a function of attitudes, subjective norms and perceived capability of undertaking a trip (Ajzen, 1991; Bagley & Mokhtarian, 2002; Cao et al., 2009; Handy, Cao, & Mokhtarian, 2006). Questioning the 'rationality' of decision-making processes, other scholarship has engaged with debates on 'subjective' versus 'objective' factors (Scheiner & Holz-Rau, 2007).

These factors, however, do not work in isolation, and may influence one another. For example, the cost of travel and available transportation options (e.g., car, transit) may be influenced by national and municipal policy; individuals with different socio-economic and employment characteristics may also assess these factors very differently with regard to their importance. A household's travel attitudes may change over time and become stronger/ weaker through repeated exposure to the neighborhood context or repeated use of a transportation mode (Kroesen, Hancy, & Chorus, 2017). A growing number of researchers have also been exploring variances in travel behavior through the concept of 'mobility cultures' and linking wider cultural beliefs and values about transportation at a large-scale (national, provincial, city) level (Alfred & Jungnickel, 2014; Klinger, Kenworthy, & Lanzendorf, 2013). Some researchers have tried to understand these relationships within the contexts of the social-ecological models (Lee & Moudon, 2004; Transportation Research Board, 2005). This theoretical approach highlights the importance of interactions between psychological, social and environmental influences in explaining human behavior or a behavioral change (Sallis, Owen, & Fisher, 2008; Stokols, 1992). An emerging body of research has adopted this theoretical approach in the contexts where the economic rationalization is often insufficient in explaining transportation outcomes (such as the decision to walk or cycle for transportation or recreational purposes) (Lee & Moudon, 2006; Nahal & Mitra, 2018). We examine this theoretical concept later in this chapter.

3 What about children's mobility?

While the foundational works on children's mobility in the 1970's and 80's explored how travel related to children's overall experience, perception of their surroundings and overall quality of life, a new body of literature emerged in the early 2000s that focused specifically on children's transportation and mode choice outcomes (e.g., walking versus being driven) (Ewing, Schroeer, & Greene, 2004; McDonald, 2008). This current research focuses largely on trips to and from school, where cost of travel (such as distance to school) and access to alternatives (such as automobile ownership) have been emphasized as major determinants of travel. Some researchers also emphasized caregiver availability to facilitate an escorted trip to or from school (Vovsha & Petersen, 2005; Yarlagadda & Srinivasan, 2008), which would, in turn, influence the choice of travel modes. Within the same line of inquiry, a smaller body of literature has explored children's daily time use, as they relate to various activities and locations (e.g., Copperman & Bhat, 2010; Vovsha & Petersen, 2005). These studies were primarily aimed at incorporating children's transportation into predictive transportation demand modeling and discussed how children's participation in different activities and the timing of these activities are negotiated within a household, although these conceptualizations are more relevant to the automobile-oriented western culture.

More recent research, however, has pointed out that household decisions around a child's mobility may not be sufficiently explained by the economics of transportation. Instead, the importance of inter-personal, socio-cultural and environmental contexts is paramount. In other words, the evaluation of pros and cons of a transportation outcome is influenced by the circumstances under which the event takes place (Epstein, 1998; Faulkner, Richichi, Buliung, Fusco, & Moola, 2010). Findings from our research based in Toronto, Canada, where we examined school travel behavior of more than 700 children studying in 16 public elementary schools, can be used as an example of such contextual decision making. First, we found that the influence of the neighborhood built environment was much stronger for a child's likelihood of walking to school, compared to a youth for whom travel distance was the main barrier to walking (Mitra & Buliung, 2015). Second, we found that the perceptions of traffic safety and walking infrastructure form somewhat differently based on the gender of the child who is traveling to school; the potential influence of these perceptions on a boy's transportation outcome are also different than a girl's transportation outcome (Guliani, Mitra, Buliung, Larsen, & Faulkner, 2015). Our research also indicated a weaker effect of the neighborhood built environment on a child's school-to-home trip in the afternoon, when compared to a home-to-school trip in the morning (Mitra, Buliung, & Roorda, 2010). These findings emphasized that the perception of environmental barriers may be different depending on parents' availability (or unavailability) to facilitate an escorted automobile trip.

Existing international literature on children's home range, territorial range and activity space, although relatively limited in its breadth and depth compared to the literature focusing on transportation mode choice, has also reported similar observations. For example, in Canada, Loebach and Gilliland (2014) found that 95% children spent their out-of-school time within a very short distance from home, while in Australia, Villanueva et al. (2013) found that for 45% of 10–12 year-old children, their activity space covered less than 25% of their neighborhood (defined by 800 m traveling distance). In addition, qualitative inter-generational studies have reported a decline in home range over time, and have identified safety concerns and a key reason (Wooley & Griffin, 2015).

It is also important to recognize that children's license to explore and to spend time within their neighborhoods may vary significantly depending on socio-cultural and environmental contexts. For example, research indicates that older children and children with less parental restrictions on mobility may explore further and/or spend more outdoor time without adult supervision (Loebach & Gilliland, 2014; Spilsbury, 2005). Parental perception of neighborhood safety has been identified as an important factor that explains variations in children's outdoor activity participation (Loebach and Gilliland, 2014; Valentine, 1997a, 1997b; Villanueva et al., 2013). Our recent research in Toronto also showed significant differences in children's daily activity patterns between inner-urban and suburban neighborhoods and between high- and low-income neighborhoods (Mitra et al., 2017).

This growing body of research has emphasized the importance of examining children's mobility within the political, social, environmental and household-specific contexts within which a child performs their day-to-day activities. To this end, the use of ecological models has become increasingly common in research focusing on active transportation and physical activity outcomes (Sallis et al., 2008; Transportation Research Board, 2005). The core concept acknowledges that human behavior has multiple levels of influence and a reciprocal interaction between these levels. Exploring those influences and their interactions is an effective approach to understand behavior or a behavioral change. A desired behavioral outcome can be maximized within a supportive 'behavior settings' (e.g., supportive policy or enabling social and built environment), given the presence of individual motivations and household support.

4 A social-ecological model of children's mobility

In this chapter, we propose a conceptual model for understanding children's mobility through the lens of a social-ecological framework (Fig. 1). In this context, mobility is defined as the act or license of a child's traveling to destinations within or beyond their neighborhood of residence, and to participate in various obligatory or discretionary activities, which may include, for example, journeys to/from school, organized sports and recreational activities, park/playgrounds or a friend's house. Our proposed conceptualization builds on a previously proposed theoretical model that focused on children's travel behavior specifically relating to school journeys (Mitra, 2013). Empirical research over the past decade has examined many of the hypothesized relationships in the proposed conceptualization, while some other factors remain less studied.

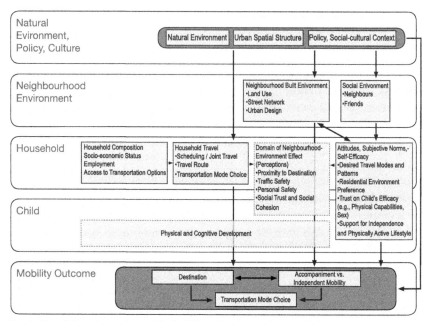

Fig. 1 A social-ecological model of children's independent mobility and transportation outcomes. Note: Construct within dotted boxes represent the "mediators" or the conceptual domains of relationship between different levels.

4.1 The outcome

A child's mobility outcome is negotiated by the household members based on three components: the location where a child is traveling to/from (i.e., the destination), whether or not the child is being accompanied by an adult (i.e., the accompaniment), and the transportation option that is being used to make the trip (i.e., the travel mode). The household members, including adult caregivers and a child evaluate alternative outcomes based on the specific context within which these decisions are being made. After repeated use of the same combination of destination, accompaniment and transportation mode, the choices may become habitual, and a child may continue to demonstrate similar mobility behavior, unless the social, environmental, household or personal circumstances change to require further evaluation (Mitra, 2013).

A child travels to various destinations to participate in regular or occasional activities. Some of these activities are obligatory (such as school) and may be fixed in time and/or space (such as organized sports), and for some, the participation may be discretionary, meaning that it is optional and/or the location or time may be flexible (such as playing in a park or visiting a friend). The destination is often chosen concurrently with the decisions regarding adult accompaniment, particularly so for younger children. Adult household members and children negotiate these outcomes based on: (1) the importance of an activity- obligatory activities receive a higher importance over the discretionary activities, and are decided upon before the other travel decisions (Copperman & Bhat, 2010); (2) A child's ability to participate in an activity and travel to/from that activity; and (3) caregivers' capacity to facilitate a trip with regard to available transportation options, including the availability of adults to accompany a child, as well as a higher order financial influence (i.e., whether the household can afford discretionary activities and trips in the first place). Each household's evaluation of these three factors may be different, and may be influenced by a multitude of social and ecological factors.

Once a decision regarding adult accompaniment has been negotiated, the adult household members and/or the child choose their transportation mode, given the location of the activities and the available and preferred transportation options. For example, parents may walk their children to nearby locations or drive them everywhere, but when adults are not available or are not accompanying a child, the choice set is likely to become limited to using transit or other nonmotorized modes including walk or bicycle. Children's transportation mode choice has been extensively studied in the past decade, and recent studies confirm multi-level influences on mode choice outcomes (Rothman, Macpherson, Ross, & Buliung, 2018).

In the remainder of this section, we discuss these different levels of influences that may interact in influencing household decisions relating to a child's mobility.

4.2 Natural environment, policy and culture of mobility

Children's transportation does not take place in isolation from the broader patterns of policy and culture of mobility. In North American regions for example, economic, urban, and education-related policies reflect and further enhance a social/popular culture of mobility that heavily emphasizes private automobiles. Most North American regions and even urban municipalities are characterized by sprawled land use and large streets that encourage driving and reduce the feasibility of providing or using other alternative modes of transport. School boards have policies regarding the location of schools and the delineation of catchment areas and the trend over the past few decades, particularly in North America, is toward consolidation (e.g., larger "magnet schools" versus smaller neighborhood schools) (Bosetti, Van Pelt, & Allison, 2017). The differences between Western European and North American policy frameworks around automobile taxation and registration as well as fuel taxes have been well-established (see, for example Pucher, 1988 and Jensen, 2008), as well as mobility and land use policy which directly impact travel decisions (Pucher & Buehler, 2008). Japan has had a national walking to school program since the 1950's which pre-dates the concept of the 'walking school bus' that is now becoming popular across the western world (Waygood, Taniguchi, Craig-St-Louis, & Xu, 2015). The prevailing attitude influencing policy in Sweden is that if traffic patterns are too complex or dangerous for children to navigate, it is the system of traffic that must change, not the children (Bjoklid & Gummesson, 2013).

The coexistence of automobile-centric policy and culture is a key barrier to enabling the use of other alternative modes such as transit, walking or bicycling among adults and children alike, particularly in North America but also across much of the western world. The impacts on children are particularly disproportional. Because of their inability to drive due to younger age, adult accompaniment has become perhaps a necessary experience in a child's everyday life and an expected parenting model for adults, significantly limiting children's mobility within and beyond their neighborhoods (Buliung, Larsen, Faulkner, & Ross, 2017; Fotel & Thomsen, 2004; Mitra et al., 2014). However, it is worth noting that some European societies that have historically celebrated their urban policies that facilitate "basic mobility" by enabling walking and cycling have also experienced some decline in independent mobility and active transportation use by children and youth. For example, Buehler and Pucher (2012) reported that walking rates in France and the UK dropped by half between 1975 and 2008, while a UK government document reports that walking among children has decreased in both frequency and distance between 2005 and 2015 (Department for Transport, 2018) likely due to increased concerns relating to traffic and personal safety (Wooley & Griffin, 2015) and other changes in the economic, social or the built environment.

In addition, topographic and climatic conditions are often discussed as key barriers to active modes of transportation including walking and bicycling. For example, steep hills and extreme-weather conditions are known to limit opportunities to walk or bike to school (Timperio et al., 2006; Zwerts, Allaert, Jenssens, Wets, & Witlox, 2010). However, in the presence of other supporting environmental conditions, climatic conditions (i.e., winter versus spring or fall) may not have a significant limiting influence on children's mobility (Mitra & Faulkner, 2012; Robertson-Wilson, Leatherdale, & Wong, 2008).

4.3 Neighborhood environment

A child's level of independence and transportation outcomes are influenced by the characteristics of the neighborhood in which they live. The effects of the neighborhood built environment (which includes the land use, street network and urban design characteristics (Transportation Research Board (2005)) on transportation behavior has been subject to much research over the past decades (Ewing & Cervero, 2010, 2017), primarily because the built environment characteristics are viewed as modifiable through better policy and planning. The social environment of the neighborhood has also received some attention in current research.

But how does the neighborhood environment influence household decisions around a child's mobility? Previous theoretical works have discussed several domains of relationship—these domains are the intervening causal factors or the 'mediators' between the physical or the social environment as we see them, and a child's transportation outcome (McMillan, 2005; Mitra, 2013; Mitra et al., 2010). Put differently, these are the perceptual factors that are influenced by the neighborhood environment, which in turn, affect household decisions relating to a child's transportation.

First, *proximity to destinations* is the primary factor that may enable children's independent mobility and the use of active modes of transportation. The presence of open space/parks near home is important (Villanueva et al., 2013). Proximity to school also makes walking/cycling a feasible option for school transportation (McDonald, 2008; Mitra et al., 2016). However, the perception of proximity (e.g., what is a "walkable distance"?) may vary across households and may also change over time and space (Grize et al., 2010; Mitra et al., 2016; Waygood & Susilo, 2015), influenced by various household-level or environmental factors.

Second, concerns relating to *traffic and personal safety* are a major barrier to children's independent mobility and impediment to the use of transit, cycles or walking (Hsin-ping & Jean-Daniel, 2014; Lee, Zhu, Yoon, & Vami, 2013; McDonald & Aalborg, 2009). Wider streets, fast and high volume of traffic, and busy intersections may produce safety concerns (Giles-Corti et al., 2011; Kaplan, Sick Nielson, & Giacomo Prato, 2016; Larouche,

Chaput, Leduc, Boyer, & Belanger, 2014). By contrast, smaller residential blocks, narrower lanes with slow traffic, traffic calming measures and street-facing residential building that places eyes on street, may increase perceived pedestrian safety (Guliani et al., 2015; Kaplan et al., 2016; Vanwollegham et al., 2016). Concerns around "stranger danger" has also been reported as a major deterrent (Mammen, Faulkner, Buliung, & Lay, 2012; Mitra et al., 2014); the prospect of a child being bullied would discourage walking, cycling or using transit unsupervised (Mammen et al., 2012; Zwerts et al., 2010).

Third, the level of *social trust and social cohesion* has also been identified as an important factor to influence independent mobility and active transport to school and non-school destinations (Carver, Timperio, & Crawford, 2013; Mitra et al., 2014; Pont, Ziviani, Wadley, Bennett, & Abbott, 2009; Schoeppe et al., 2015). A walkable environment with a strong sense of community and social cohesion, produces opportunities to meet and play with other children and adults alike, and facilitates the maintenance and production of social capital. Recent research in Toronto has highlighted the importance of back alleys and neighborhood social trust in facilitating, training, and encouraging children to become more independently mobile (Furneaux & Manaugh, 2018). Previous research has also explored several other domains of the relationship between the neighborhood environment and a children's mobility, including the aesthetics and street connectivity (Mitra, 2013), but the results have been inconclusive.

4.4 Household

Households with lower income may have limited transportation options (e.g., access to private automobiles, ability to use public transit often). The nature of workforce participation may also affect adult availability for escorting a child to various destinations. The effects of these mobility constraints on children's mobility are not entirely clear. Some have argued that limited transportation options and caregiver unavailability may result in increased independent mobility among children and youth, and enable more walking and cycling (Kaplan et al., 2016; Lee et al., 2013), others have reported a decline in overall mobility among children in low-income and suburban communities, perhaps as a result of limited transportation options and/or caregiver unavailability due to longer commute, in addition to poor geographical and financial accessibility to destinations (Mitra et al., 2017).

The adult caregiver(s) may also adjust their travel schedule to facilitate children's obligatory trips, such as journeys to and/or from school, when a supervised trip is perceived to be highly important, in certain situations and cultural settings. This negotiation would introduce new trip-chains in an adult's daily travel pattern (e.g., home-school-work trip), and the transportation mode of an escorted school trip will likely be decided based on the advantages and disadvantages in relation to the overall journey (Copperman & Bhat, 2010; Vovsha & Petersen, 2005; Yarlagadda & Srinivasan, 2008). On the contrary, children with siblings might enjoy more independence from adult supervision with regard to their traveling; some parent may see siblings' traveling together as a form of 'escorted' trip where the elder sibling is perceived as a caregiver (Hsin-ping & Jean-Daniel, 2014; Kaplan et al., 2016).

Research on adults' transportation behavior has long emphasized the importance of transportation-related attitudes, social norms resulting from ethnic/cultural values and peer support (Cao et al., 2009; Handy et al., 2006). These household-level factors may also have significant influence on children's mobility outcomes. Parents or other adult caregivers who view driving as a more convenient and socially desirable option compared to other transportation modes would likely escort their children to daily destinations (Carver et al., 2013; Faulkner et al., 2010). In contrast, parents who are active in their everyday lives may allow more independence to their children, and allow them to walk and/or bike often and from an early age (Curtis, Babb, & Olaru, 2015). A household's transportation-related attitudes may influence their residential location preference, if and when they can afford to do so (Cao et al., 2009; Kitamura, 2009). Once a household has self-selected themselves in a neighborhood of their preference (e.g., a household that prefers to walk and bike whenever possible may choose to live in a "walkable" inner urban neighborhood), the built and social environments of the neighborhoods may further enable their desirable travel behavior.

In addition, parents who acknowledge the importance of a child's social interaction (i.e., meeting and playing with other children) may also allow their child(ren) to walk or cycle more often or spend more time independently (Emond & Handy, 2012; Ramanathan, O'Brien, Faulkner, & Stone, 2014). Cultural norms around mobility (e.g., when adult caregivers are more protective of girls compared to boys), may also produce transportation outcomes where girls enjoy less independence with regard to where and how they travel, though these patterns are not universal (Shaw et al., 2015). For instance, research has shown that social norms concerning gendered expectations of accompanying children on daily trips is less prevalent in Japan, where children often travel alone as young as 10 or 11 years old (Waygood, 2009). While the effect of attitudes and norms on a child's mobility outcomes may be moderate when compared to other intra-household factors (Mitra et al., 2014), it is important to note that unlike a household's socio-economic characteristics, these factors are potentially modifiable through systematic and targeted interventions.

4.5 The child

Lastly, children play an important role in the decisions around their own mobility. While at an early age, the adult caregivers may take most decisions (McMillan, 2005; Copperman & Bhat, 2010), a child develops their own transportation attitudes and behavior as they mature through repeated exposure to the built and social environment over time (Bronfenbrenner, 1989; Mitra, 2013), and may take a more direct role in taking decisions around their mobility as youth. The physical and cognitive development of a child's capabilities to navigate their surroundings can occur as a child grows older, and/or with the length of time spent in the same neighborhood growing up (Mitra et al., 2014). Adult attitudes toward when, where and how children spend their outdoor times and travel also change with a child's perceived maturity (Fang & Lin, 2017; Johansson, 2006).

Existing research confirms that older children and those who are considered more "mature" are likely to enjoy more independence and walk or cycle more often (Johansson, 2006; Johansson, Hesselberg, & Lafflame, 2011; Prezza et al., 2001; Vanwollegham et al., 2016). Those who lived in the same neighborhood for a longer period of time were also found to be allowed more independent mobility (Mitra et al., 2014). However, each child is different and some are more confident about their own capabilities of exploring traveling independently than others (Robertson-Wilson et al., 2008). A child may also adapt, over time, the culture of mobility that is prevalent within the context, both culturally and spatially (at the neighborhood level), where they spend most of their daily time.

5 Conclusion

Children's travel behavior, and in particular their independent mobility or CIM, is influenced by a wide range of physical, policy, and cultural factors. Furthermore, these factors are filtered through individual parents and caregivers, households, neighborhoods, cities, and even countries to result in a variety of transport outcomes. In other words, what behaviors are considered "normal" or desirable can vary from household to household, neighborhood to neighborhood and city to city. Research in recent years has continued to embrace social-ecological approaches that strive to understand travel behavior as a complex interaction among these personal, household, spatial and cultural factors. These approaches can inform policy design as well as determine how policy and infrastructure changes are framed and presented to the public. For example, the Ontario Active School Travel program in Canada is working toward creating a positive culture around children's mobility while addressing safety concerns by supporting and funding grass-roots level initiatives. Municipal efforts (such as Vision Zero policies) are also focusing on safety; a key aspect of these programs lies in challenging the culture of "automobility" as much as changes to policy and infrastructure.

Going forward, a deeper understanding of how parental attitudes and opinions change with regard to the travel behavior of their children will aid researchers on which policy changes and messaging might be most effective in leading to behavioral changes. While physical infrastructure changes are vital for ensuring the safety of children traveling by active modes, an understanding of the multitude of household and cultural factors that influence mode choice will help guide action and policy toward more (and safer) walking and cycling.

References

Ajzen, I. (1991). The theory of planned behavior. *Organizational Behavior and Human Decision Processes, 50*, 179–211.

Alfred, R., & Jungnickel, K. (2014). Why culture matters for transport policy: The case of cycling in the UK. *Journal of Transport Geography, 34*, 78–87.

Bagley, M. N., & Mokhtarian, P. L. (2002). The impact of residential neighborhood type on travel behavior: A structural equations modeling approach. *The Annals of Regional Science, 36*(2), 279–297.

Ben-Akiva, M., & Lerman, S. R. (1985). *Discrete choice analysis: Theory of application to travel demand.* Cambridge, MA: The MIT Press.

Bjoklid, P., & Gummesson, M. (2013). *Children's independent mobility in Sweden.* Swedish National Road and Transport Research Institute.

Boarnet, M. G., & Crane, R. (2001). *Travel by design: The influence of urban form on travel.* New York: Oxford University Press.

Bosetti, L., Van Pelt, D., & Allison, D. (2017). The changing landscape od school choice in Canada: From pluralism to parental preference? *Education Policy Analysis Archives, 25*(38). https://doi.org/10.14507/epaa.25.2685.

Bronfenbrenner, U. (1989). Ecological systems theory. *Annals of Child Development, 6*, 187–249.

Buehler, R., & Pucher, J. (2012). Walking and cycling in Western Europe and the United States: Trends, policies, and lessons. *TR News, 2012*, 34–42. May–June.

Buliung, R., Larsen, K., Faulkner, G., & Ross, T. (2017). Children's independent mobility in the City of Toronto, Canada. *Travel Behavior and Society*, *9*, 58–69.

Cao, X., Mokhtarian, P. L., & Handy, S. L. (2009). The relationship the built environment and nonwork travel: A case study of Northern California. *Transportation Research Part A*, *43*, 548–559.

Carver, A., Timperio, A., & Crawford, D. (2013). Parental chauffeurs: What drives their transport choice? *Journal of Transport Geography*, *23*, 72–77.

Cervero, R. (2002). Built environments and mode choice: Toward a normative framework. *Transportation Research Part D*, 7(4), 265–284.

Cervero, R., & Kockelman, K. (1997). Travel demand and the 3Ds: Density, diversity, and design. *Transportation Research Part D*, *2*(3), 199–219.

Copperman, R. B., & Bhat, C. R. (2010). *An assessment of the state-of-the-research of US children's time-use and activity-travel patterns*. *http://www.ce.utexas.edu/prof/bhat/ABSTRACTS/Assess_of_StateofResearch_of_Childrens_Jan2010.pdf*.

Curtis, C., Babb, C., & Olaru, D. (2015). Built environment and children's travel to school. *Transport Policy*, *42*, 21–33.

Department for Transport (2018). *Walking and cycling statistics, England. 2016*. https://assets. publishing.service.gov.uk/government/uploads/system/uploads/attachment_data/file/674503/walking-and-cycling-statistics-england-2016.pdf.

Derbyshire, D. (2007, June 15). How children lost the right to roam in four generations. *Daily Mail*. https://www.dailymail.co.uk/news/article-462091/How-children-lost-right-roam-generations.html.

Emond, C. R., & Handy, S. L. (2012). Factors associated with bicycling to high school: Insights from Davis, CA. *Journal of Transport Geography*, *20*, 71–79.

Epstein, L. (1998). Integrating theoretical approaches to promote physical activity. *American Journal of Preventive Medicine*, *15*, 257–265.

Ewing, R., & Cervero, R. (2010). Travel and the built environment: A meta analysis. *Journal of the American Planning Association*, *76*(3), 265–294.

Ewing, R., & Cervero, R. (2017). "Does compact development make people drive less?" The answer is yes. *Journal of the American Plannign Association*, *83*, 19–25.

Ewing, R., Schroeer, W., & Greene, W. (2004). School location and student travel: Analysis of factors affecting mode choice. *Transportation Research Record*, *1895*, 55–63.

Fang, J. T., & Lin, J. J. (2017). School travel modes and children's spatial cognition. *Urban Studies*, *54*(7), 1578–1600.

Faulkner, G. E. J., Richichi, V., Buliung, R., Fusco, C., & Moola, F. (2010). What's "Quickest and Easiest?": Parental decision making about school trip mode. *International Journal of Behavioral Nutrition and Physical Activity*, *7*, 62. https://doi.org/10.1186/1479-5868-7-62.

Fotel, T., & Thomsen, T. U. (2004). The surveillance of children's mobility. *Surveillance and Society*, *1*(4), 535–554.

Furneaux, A., & Manaugh, K. (2018). Eyes on the alley: Children's appropriation of alley space in Riverdale, Toronto. *Children's Geographies*, https://doi.org/10.1080/14733285.2018.1482409.

Fyhri, A., Hjorthol, R., Mackett, R. L., Fotel, T. N., & Kyttä, M. (2011). Children's active travel and independent mobility in four countries: Development, social contributing trends and measures. *Transport Policy*, *18*, 703–710.

Gaster, S. (1991). Urban children's access to their neighborhood: Changes over three generations. *Environment and Behavior*, *23*(1), 70–85.

Giles-Corti, B., Wood, G., Pikora, T., Learnihan, V., Bulsara, M., Van Niel, K., et al. (2011). School site and the potential to walk to school: The impact of street connective and traffic exposure in school neighborhoods. *Health & Place*, *17*, 545–550.

Grize, L., Bringolf-Isler, B., Martin, E., & Braun-Fahrlander, C. (2010). Trend in active transportation to school among Swiss school children and its associated factors: Three cross-sectional surveys 1994, 2004 and 2005. *International Journal of Behavioral Nutrition and Physical Activity*, 7, 28.http://www.ijbnpa.org/content/7/1/28.

Guliani, A., Mitra, A., Buliung, R. N., Larsen, K., & Faulkner, G. E. J. (2015). Gender-based differences in school travel mode choice behaviour: Examining the relationship between the neighbourhood environment and perceived traffic safety. *Journal of Transport & Health*, 2(4), 502–511.

Hägerstrand, T. (1970). What about people in regional science? *Papers in Regional Science, 24* (1), 6–21.

Handy, S. L., Cao, X., & Mokhtarian, P. L. (2006). Does self-selection explain the relationship between built environment and walking behavior? Empirical evidence from Northern California. *Journal of the American Planning Association*, 72(1), 55–74.

Hillman, M., Adams, J., & Whitelegg, J. (1990). *One false move: A study of children's independent mobility*. London: PSI Press.

Hsin-ping, H., & Jean-Daniel, S. (2014). Impacts of parental gender and attitudes on children's school travel mode and parental chauffeuring behaviour: Results for California based on the 2009 National Household Travel Survey. *Transportation*, 41(3), 543–565.

Jensen, O. (2008). Biking in the land of the car, clashes of mobility cultures in the USA. In: *Conference Paper. Selected Proceedings from the Annual Transport Conference at Aalborg University*.

Johansson, M. (2006). Environmental and parental factors as determinants of mode for children's leisure travel. *Journal of Environmental Psychology, 26*, 156–169.

Johansson, K., Hesselberg, M., & Lafflame, L. (2011). Active commuting to and from school among Swedish children: A national and regional study. *The European Journal of Public Health*. https://doi.org/10.1093/eurpub/ckr042.

Jones, P. M. (1979). New approach to understanding travel behaviour: The human activity approach. In D. Hensher & R. Stopher (Eds.), *Behavioural travel modelling* (pp. 55–80). London: Groom Helm.

Kaplan, S., Sick Nielson, T. A., & Giacomo Prato, C. (2016). Walking, cycling and the urban form: A Heckman selection model of active travel mode and distance by young adolescents. *Transportation Research Part D, 44*, 55–65.

Kitamura, R. (2009). Life-style and travel demand. *Transportation, 36*, 679–710.

Kitamura, R., Mokhtarian, P. L., & Laidet, L. (1997). A micro-analysis of land use and travel in five neighborhoods in the San Francisco Bay Area. *Transportation, 24*, 125–158.

Klinger, T., Kenworthy, J., & Lanzendorf, M. (2013). Dimensions of urban mobility cultures – a comparison of German cities. *Journal of Transport Geography, 31*, 18–29.

Kroesen, M., Hancy, S., & Chorus, C. (2017). Do attitudes cause behavior or vice versa? An alternative conceptualization to the attitude-behavior relationship in travel behavior modeling. *Transportation Research Part A, 101*, 190–202.

Larouche, R., Chaput, J. R., Leduc, G., Boyer, C., & Belanger, P. (2014). A cross-sectional examination of socio-demographic and school-level correlates of children's school travel mode in Ottawa, Canada. *BMC Public Health. 14*, https://doi.org/10.1186/1471-2458-14-497.

Lee, C., & Moudon, A. V. (2004). Physical activity and environment research in the health field: Implications for urban and transportation planning practice and research. *Journal of Planning Literature, 19*(2), 147–181.

Lee, C., & Moudon, A. V. (2006). The 3Ds + R: Quantifying land use and urban form correlates of walking. *Transportation Research Part D, 11*(3), 204–215.

Lee, C., Zhu, X., Yoon, J., & Vami, J. (2013). Beyond distance: Children's school travel mode choice. *Annual Behavioural Medicine, 45*, s55–s67.

Loebach, J. E., & Gilliland, J. (2014). Free range kids? Using GPS-derieved activity spaces to examine children's neighbourhood activity and mobility. *Environment and Behavior, 48*, 421–453.

Mackett, R., Brown, B., Gong, Y., Kitazawa, K., & Paskins, J. (2007). *Setting children free: Children's independent movement in the local environment, Paper 118, UCL working paper series*. Centre for Advanced Spatial Analysis, University College London.

Mammen, G., Faulkner, G., Buliung, R., & Lay, J. (2012). Understanding the drive to escort: A cross-sectional analysis examining parental attitudes towards children's school travel and independent mobility. *BMC Public Health. 12*, https://doi.org/10.1186/1471-2458-12-862.

McDonald, N. C. (2007). Active transportation to school: Trends among US schoolchildren, 1969–2001. *American Journal of Preventive Medicine, 32*(6), 509–516.

McDonald, N. C. (2008). Household interactions and children's school travel: The effect of parental work patterns on walking and biking to school. *Journal of Transport Geography, 16* (5), 324–331.

McDonald, N. C., & Aalborg, A. E. (2009). Why parents drive children to school? Implications for safe routes to school program. *Journal of the American Planning Association, 75* (3), 331–342.

McMillan, T. E. (2005). Urban form and a child's trip to school: The current literature and a framework for future research. *Journal of Planning Literature, 19*(4), 440–456.

Mitra, R. (2013). Independent mobility and mode choice for school transportation: A review and framework for future research. *Transportation Reviews, 33*(1), 21–43.

Mitra, R., & Buliung, R. (2015). Exploring differences in school travel mode choice behaviour between children and youth. *Transport Policy, 42*, 4–11.

Mitra, R., Buliung, R., & Roorda, M. J. (2010). The built environment and school travel mode choice in Toronto, Canada. *Transportation Research Record, 2156*, 2150–2159.

Mitra, R., Cantello, I., Buliung, R., & Faulkner, G. (2017). Children's activity-transportation lifestyles, physical activity levels and social-ecological correlates in Toronto, Canada. *Journal of Transport and Health, 6*, 289–298.

Mitra, R., & Faulkner, G. E. J. (2012). There's no such thing as bad weather, just the wrong clothing: Climate, weather and active school transportation in Toronto, Canada. *Canadian Journal of Public Health, 103*(3), s35–s41.

Mitra, R., Faulkner, G. E. J., Buliung, R. N., & Stone, M. R. (2014). Do parental perceptions of the neighbourhood environment influence children's independent mobility? Evidence from Toronto, Canada. *Urban Studies, 51*(16), 3401–3419.

Mitra, R., Papaioannou, E., & Habib, K. M. N. (2016). Past and present of active school transportation: An exploration of the built environment effects in Toronto, Canada from 1986 to 2006. *Journal of Transport and Land Use, 9*(2), 1–17.

Nahal, T., & Mitra, R. (2018). Facilitators and barriers to winter cycling: Case study of a downtown university in Toronto, Canada. *Journal of Transport and Health*, https://doi.org/10.1016/j.jth.2018.05.012.

Pont, K., Ziviani, J., Wadley, D., Bennett, S., & Abbott, R. (2009). Environmental correlates of children's active transportation: A systematic literature review. *Health & Place, 15*(3), 849–862. https://doi.org/10.1016/j.healthplace.2009.02.002.

Prezza, M., Pilloni, S., Morabito, C., Sersante, C., Alparone, F. R., & Guiliani, M. V. (2001). The influence of psychological and environmental factors on children's independent mobility and relationship to peer frequentation. *Journal of Community and Applied Social Psychology, 11*, 435–450.

Pucher, J. (1988). Urban travel behavior as the outcome of public policy: The example of modal-split in western Europe and North America. *Journal of the American Planning Association, 54*, 509–520.

Pucher, J., & Buehler, R. (2008). Making cycling irresistible: Lessons from The Netherlands, Denmark and Germany. *Transport Reviews, 28*(4), 495–528.

Ramanathan, S., O'Brien, C., Faulkner, G., & Stone, M. (2014). Happiness in motion: Emotions, well-being, and Active School Travel. *Journal of School Health, 84*(8), 516–523.

Robertson-Wilson, J. E., Leatherdale, S. T., & Wong, S. L. (2008). Social-ecological correlates of active commuting to school among high school students. *Journal of Adolescent Health, 42*(5), 486–495.

Rothman, L., Macpherson, A. K., Ross, T., & Buliung, R. (2018). The decline in active school transportation (AST): A systematic review of the factors related to AST and changes in school transport over time in North America. *Preventive Medicine, 111,* 314–322.

Sallis, J. F., Owen, N., & Fisher, E. B. (2008). Ecological models of health behavior. In K. - Glanz, B. K. Rimer, & K. Viswanath (Eds.), *Health behavior and health education: Theory, research, and practice* (4th ed, pp. 466–485). San Francisco: Jossey-Bass.

Scheiner, J., & Holz-Rau, C. (2007). Travel mode choice: Affected by objective or subjective factors. *Transportation, 34,* 487–511.

Schoeppe, S., Duncan, M. J., Badland, H. M., Alley, S., Williams, S., Rebar, A. L., et al. (2015). Socio-demographic factors and neighbourhood social cohesion influence adults' willingness to grant children greater independent mobility: A cross sectional study. *BMC Public Health, 15.* https://doi.org/10.1186/s12889-015-2053-2.

Shaw, B., Bicket, M., Elliott, B., Fagan-Watson, B., Mocca, E., & Hillman, M. (2015). *Children's independent mobility: An international comparison and recommendations for action.* Policy Studies Institute, University of Westminster.*http://westminsterresearch.wmin.ac.uk/15650/1/PSI_Finalreport_2015.pdf.*

Spilsbury, J. C. (2005). 'we don't really get to go out in the frontyard'—Children's home range and neighborhood violence. *Children's Geographies, 3,* 79–99.

Stokols, D. (1992). Establishing and maintaining healthy environments: Toward a social ecology of health promotion. *American Psychologist, 47,* 6–22.

Timperio, A., Ball, K., Salmon, J., Roberts, R., Giles-Corti, B., Simmons, D., et al. (2006). Personal, family, social, and environmental correlates of active commuting to school. *American Journal of Preventive Medicine, 30*(1), 45–51.

Transportation Research Board (2005). *Does the built environment influence physical activity? Examining the evidence, TRB Special Report Number 282.* Washington, DC: Transportation Research Board of the National Academies.

Tranter, P., & Whitelegg, J. (1994). Children's travel behaviours in Canberra: Car-dependent lifestyles in a low-density city. *Journal of Transport Geography, 2*(4), 265–273.

Valentine, G. (1997a). A safe place to grow up? Parenting, perceptions of children's safety and the rural idyll. *Journal of Rural Studies, 13,* 137–148.

Valentine, G. (1997b). 'My son's a bit dizzy.' 'My wife's a bit soft': Gender, children and cultures of parenting. *Gender, Place and Culture, 4*(1), 37–62.

Vanwollegham, G., Schipperjin, J., Gheyson, F., Cardon, G., De Boureaudhuij, I., & Van Dyck, D. (2016). Children's GPS-determined versus self-reports transport in leisure time and associations with parental perceptions of the neighbourhood environment. *International Journal of Health Geographic's, 15*(16), 1–12.

Villanueva, K., Giles-Corti, B., Bulsara, M., Timperio, A., McCormack, G., Beesley, B., et al. (2013). Where do children travel to and what local opportunities are available? The relationship between neighborhood destinations and children's independent mobility. *Environment and Behavior, 45,* 679–705.

Vovsha, P., & Petersen, E. (2005). Escorting children to school: Statistical analysis and applied modeling approach. *Transportation Research Record, 1921,* 131–140.

Waygood, E. O. D. (2009). What is the role of mothers in transit-oriented development: The case of Osaka-Kyoto-Kobe, Japan. In: *Paper presented at the Women's Issues in Transportation, Irvine, CA.*

Waygood, E. O. D., & Susilo, Y. O. (2015). Walking to school in Scotland: Do perceptions of neighbourhood quality matter? *IATSS Research*, *38*, 125–129.

Waygood, E. O. D., Taniguchi, A., Craig-St-Louis, C., & Xu, X. (2015). International origins of walking school buses and child fatalities in Japan and Canada. *Traffic Science Society of Osaka*, *46*(2), 30–42.

Willis, D. P., Manaugh, K., & El-Geneidy, A. (2015). Cycling under influence: Summarizing the influence of perceptions, attitudes, habits, and social environments on cycling for transportation. *International Journal of Sustainable Transportation*, *9*(8), 565–579.

Wooley, H. E., & Griffin, E. (2015). Decreasing experiences of home range, outdoor spaces, activities and companions: Changes across three generations in Sheffield in north England. *Children's Geographies*, *13*(6), 677–691.

Yarlagadda, A. K., & Srinivasan, S. (2008). Modeling children's school travel mode and parental escort decisions. *Transportation*, *35*(2), 201–218.

Zwerts, E., Allaert, G., Jenssens, D., Wets, G., & Witlox, F. (2010). How children view their travel behaviour: A case study from Flanders (Belgium). *Journal of Transport Geography*, *18*, 702–710.

PART TWO

Transport externalities and children's wellbeing

CHAPTER SIX

Impact of road traffic and speed on children: Injuries, social inequities, and active transport

Linda Rothman[a], Liraz Fridman[a], Marie-Soleil Cloutier[b], Kevin Manaugh[c] and Andrew Howard[a]
[a]Child Health Evaluative Sciences, The Hospital for Sick Children, Toronto, ON, Canada
[b]Centre Urbanisation Culture Société, Institut National de la Recherche Scientifique, Montreal, QC, Canada
[c]Department of Geography, McGill School of Environment, McGill University, Montreal, QC, Canada

Contents

1 Introduction

The presence of automobile traffic in urban areas has a host of well-documented health, environmental, social, and aesthetic impacts. The effects of noise, pollution, and risk of collisions can impact travel choices, possible destinations and activity patterns, and safety of children and other travelers. Urban highways and high-speed arterials generate noise, vibration and pollutants, which can impact the health, well-being, and accessibility of local residents (see Chapters 2 and 7). Furthermore, the populations exposed to these harmful effects often do not reap the benefits (e.g., in the form of faster mobility or convenient accessibility to amenities). In addition to these environmental and health impacts, traffic flow also has an important impact on social connections within neighborhoods whereby the amount and speed of automobile traffic has clear connections to where and when people travel, congregate, and interact with neighbours (Appleyard, 1980) (see also Chapter 4).

Automobiles and automobility as a cultural phenomenon, have been central to the urban revolution of this past century, including the building of low-density suburbs and the resultant car-dependency (Walks, 2014). The relationship between roads and land use has consequences on road injuries: the idea to separate local street networks (around home and schools) from faster moving and much wider arterial roads with higher speed limits (typically 50–60 km/h, ~30–37 mph) have created dangerous situations for pedestrians, who need to make use of the entire network (Dumbaugh & Rae, 2009). Children's greater vulnerability due to their small height and cognitive abilities, put them at great risk of injury and death when vehicle speed is higher. In Canada, where the use of a car to get to work has increased by 28% from 1996 to 2016 and obesity rates continue to rise, stakeholders from public health and provincial and federal transportation agencies argue for an increase in walking as a utilitarian mode (Burigusa, Lavoie, Maurice, Hamel, & Duranceau, 2011; Noxon, 2014; Statistics Canada, 2017; Twells, Gregory, Reddigan, & Midodzi, 2014). This move to increase active modes also for children in their journey to school and other destinations necessitates greater attention to the safety of the neighborhood walking environment.

This chapter presents background on the impact of traffic and speed on children with a focus on pedestrian motor vehicle road traffic injuries as a means to facilitate more active and independent travel. We will first describe the epidemiology of road traffic injuries for children, both globally and in Canada with a focus on pedestrians as they are the most common type of vulnerable road user (compared to cyclists and motorcyclists) in children. Secondly, speed, as the most important contributing factor for motor vehicle collisions, will be discussed followed by a description of the social inequities in child pedestrian injury and fatalities related to income and race. Thirdly, we will discuss active transportation in children, as it is directly related to their exposure to road injury risk. Finally, we examine interventions to reduce the burden of road traffic in children.

2 Child road traffic injuries: A public health concern

According to the 2018 World Health Organization (WHO) Global Status Report on Road Safety, road traffic injuries claim more than 1.35 million lives each year (World Health Organization, 2015). It is the ninth leading cause of death across all ages. Low and middle-income countries have double the fatality rates of high-income countries and account for 90% of global road traffic deaths. Vulnerable road users (i.e., pedestrians, cyclists and motorcyclists) make up half of these fatalities. In addition, up to 50 million people sustain non-fatal injuries each year due to road traffic collisions.

As for children, despite improvements in occupant safety, traffic fatalities are still one of their primary causes of death worldwide, with more than 90% of child road traffic deaths in low-income and middle-income countries (World Health Organization, 2008). According to the Global Burden of Disease (GBD) visualization tool, road injuries represent 8% of all fatalities globally in younger children aged 5–14 years; similar to malaria and intestinal infections (Institute for Health Metrics and Evaluation (IHME), 2016). In high income countries, road traffic injuries are the leading cause of death for 5–14 year olds; representing 15% of all fatalities. Persistent issues related to road traffic fatalities include the continued underuse and misuse of child restraints, issues regarding helmet standards for growing children on motorcycles in many countries, and risky pedestrian environments for children worldwide.

Road traffic injury remains the fourth highest cause of premature death in Canada, with an age-standardized rate of 335.6/100,000. However, the situation has been improving generally, as data from Transport Canada's National Collision Database found a 36% decrease in motor vehicle fatalities overall in the 10 years from 2005 to 2014 (Transport Canada, 2016). Most of this decrease has been in motor vehicle occupants (drivers and passengers), where there has been a 42% decrease in fatalities. Decreases in the number of motor vehicle occupant fatalities have been even more marked in children with a reduction of 62% in ages 0–14 (71–27) from 2005 to 2014, and a decrease of 56% (270–119) in ages 15–19. Much of the success influencing these declining rates for motor vehicle occupant fatalities in Canadian children can be attributed to policies related to the use of child restraints and seatbelts and graduated licensing for teenagers and young adults (World Health Organization, 2015).

2.1 Child pedestrian motor vehicle collisions (PMVC)

As a consequence of increasing motor vehicle use worldwide, walking and cycling has become more dangerous. This poses challenges for vulnerable road users who have to share the road with high-speed vehicles, forcing them to navigate through risky situations that involve fast moving traffic. Children are especially at risk when navigating the roadways as pedestrians. Processing feedback from the road environment can be challenging for children as they are still developing the cognitive skills regarding decision making (Canadian Council of Motor Transport Administrators (CCMTS), 2013). Their ability to make decisions about when to cross a roadway involves deciding on an adequate route, detecting traffic, assessing the speeds and distances of motor vehicles, and integrating that information to make a decision about when to cross (Canadian Council of Motor Transport Administrators (CCMTS), 2013). Additionally, children are smaller in stature, making them less visible within the road environment and their size also makes them more vulnerable to head injuries (Canadian Council of Motor Transport Administrators (CCMTS), 2013). According to the GBD visualization tool, worldwide, there were approximately 72,000 pedestrian fatalities in young people <20 and children ages 0–14 in 2016 (Institute for Health Metrics and Evaluation (IHME), 2016). Although the numbers have decreased substantially in the high (75%) and upper middle income countries (60%), there has actually been an increase by 10% in low income countries from 1990 to 2016, likely due to increased levels of motorization (Institute for Health Metrics and Evaluation (IHME), 2016).

In Canada, although the rates of PMVC in all ages have decreased from 1990 (2.6/100,000) to 2016 (1.8/100,000), the numbers of PMVC have remained quite static at approximately 700 per year (Institute for Health Metrics and Evaluation (IHME), 2016). In 2017, transport injuries including PMVC and motor vehicle occupant injuries were the 2nd leading cause of death for Canadian children ages 5–14 after cancer (26% vs. 19%). PMVC themselves made up 5% of all deaths in this age group (Institute for Health Metrics and Evaluation (IHME), 2016). Although PMVC fatalities have decreased by almost half nationally in ages 0–14 from 21 deaths in 2005 to 11 in 2014, the numbers of fatalities doubled in the 15–19 age group from 13 to 26 during the same period (Transport Canada, 2016). In a city like Toronto, the biggest Canadian city, the situation for child pedestrians has not been improving enough; between 2005 and 2016, 3 children were killed (City of Toronto, 2016). In 2017 and 2018 alone, 3 children have died as a result of a PMVC during school travel. It is a societal responsibility to ensure that the traffic environment for children is safe. The convenience of automobile travel for an individual should not trump the safety overall for child pedestrians. Moreover, it has been speculated that the reduction in PMVC fatalities among younger children is not necessarily the result of safer roadways, but may in fact, be more related to the steady decline in children walking and the increase in car travel, particularly on the trip to/from school.

3 Speed as a risk factor for road traffic injury

Traffic speed is key risk factor for collisions and collision severity. Traffic speed influences both the energy involved in a collision as well as the necessary stopping distance to avoid a collision. According to The World Health Organization, pedestrians have a 60% risk of dying at 80 km/h which is reduced to 20% at 50 km/h. The ability to stop and avoid a crash is substantially decreased at higher speeds; at 80 km/h it takes 58 m to stop, which is reduced to 27 m at 50 km/h (Fig.1). It is estimated that 1 in 3 deaths in high-income countries is due to speed.

With higher average traffic speeds, the severity of injury is increased especially for pedestrians. Although the magnitude of this relationship varies slightly by factors such as age and sex, studies around the world consistently demonstrate a decrease in pedestrian fatality with lower speed limits. An adult pedestrian has less than a 20% chance of dying if struck by a car traveling at speeds lower than 50 km/h and that risk increases 3-fold if they are struck at 80 km/h (World Health Organization, 2015). Moreover, pedestrians struck at 50 km/h are estimated to be eight times more likely to be killed than a pedestrian struck at 30 km/h (Canadian Council of Motor Transport Administrators (CCMTS), 2013). In 1987, Fieldwick and Brown examined the road crash fatality rates of 21 countries (Fieldwick & Brown, 1987). They found that countries that have speed limits of 60 km/h could reduce their fatality rate by 25% by switching to a speed limit of 50 km/h on urban roads. Similarly, Anderson et al. reconstructed over 100 fatal PMVC and demonstrated that reduced speeds would have resulted in a 32% reduction in fatalities (Anderson, McLean, Farmer, Lee, & Brooks, 1997). Rosén et al. summarized 11 studies on car impact speed and pedestrian fatality risk from 1980 to 2010, and found that pedestrian fatality risk is consistently reported to increase monotonically with car impact speed (Rosen, Stigson, & Sander, 2011). Martin and Wu confirmed findings from other studies that report on car impact speed and pedestrian risk and

SPEED
is at the core of the road traffic injury problem.

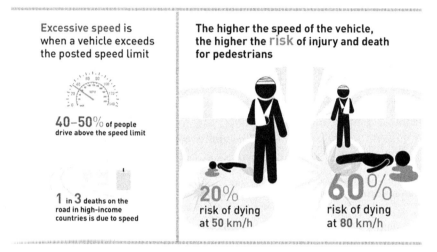

Fig. 1 Pedestrian fatality risk as a function of the impact speed of a car (Pasanen, 1991).

concluded that there is an argument to be made for strict speed limits on roads where pedestrians have greater exposure (Martin & Wu, 2018). Not only do higher speeds increase the likelihood of being fatally injured in a PMVC but they also increase the probability of being involved in a crash.

While lowering speed limits is one method to decrease the severity of PMVC, there is also evidence that narrower roads have fewer pedestrian collisions due to reduced vehicle speeds, as people drive slower on narrower streets (Rothman, 2015).

Fewer studies have examined the relationship between speed and PMVC risk specifically in children. Retting et al. in their review of engineering measures to reduce PMVC stated that slower speeds allow motorists more time to react, as stopping distances are lower and the driver's field of vision is wider as they do not need to focus on points as far in the distance. Slower speeds can therefore, reduce the severity of injuries with a child pedestrian if a collision occurs (Retting, Ferguson, & McCartt, 2003). Roberts et al. published a study from New Zealand that examined the effects of environmental factors on injury risk of child PMVC (Roberts, Norton, Jackson, Dunn, & Hassall, 1995). The authors concluded that children were at increased odds for PMVC on roads with mean speeds over 40 km/h compared to <40 km/h (OR: 2.68, 95% CI: 1.26; 5.69). One study from the United Kingdom (UK) demonstrated that speed limit zones of 20 mph (32 km/h) have shown a 70% reduction in child pedestrian fatalities (Webster & Mackie, 1996). The relationship between child pedestrian injuries and speed has also been examined in Tehran, Iran. A case-control study by Jamshidi et al. found that child PMVC was significantly associated with a 2-fold increase at speeds >50 km/h compared with ≤50 km/h (OR = 2.1, 95% CI: 1.3–3.2) (Jamshidi, Moradi, & Majdzadeh, 2017).

4 Spatial and social inequities in traffic exposure

As previously mentioned, the presence of automobile traffic in urban areas has a host of well-documented health impacts. As pedestrians or cyclists, the exposure of children to cars can be measured in terms of the number of intersections crossed, by the traffic volume in their home neighborhoods or in their school area. An important environmental justice question involves the analysis and understanding of how high-speed traffic is distributed in space and across socio-economic factors (and therefore how the exposure to pollutants, danger of collision, noise and other externalities is distributed). Due to geographic, historical, and political forces the distribution of urban highways and arterials are not evenly distributed in cities (Golub, Marcantonio, & Sanchez, 2013) A large body of work explores the distribution of roadway infrastructure as well as traffic danger. Yiannakoulias & Scott have explored the concept of the 'spatial displacement of risk' in the context of children's road safety, positing that the burden of risk of injuries and death due to traffic is often displaced from a location with high automobile ownership and use to one with fewer local drivers (Yiannakoulias & Scott, 2013). This further reinforces the inequities inherent in road safety and risk (Pabayo et al., 2012). This concept is useful in gaining insights into how the safety of the pedestrian realm is distributed.

In North American cities, there is a greater likelihood of high traffic volumes and multilane major roads in the poorest sectors and around schools in deprived areas (Green, Smorodinsky, Kim, McLaughlin, & Ostro, 2004; Morency, Gauvin, Plante, Fournier, & Morency, 2012). As studied by Routledge 40 years ago in Nottingham (UK), the mean number of roads crossed per day and the average number of cars encountered per day is greater for children living in central city than for those living in the suburbs (Routledge, Repetto-Wright, & Howarth, 1974) For decades, the injury rate for children has been associated with the number of roads or, at the neighborhood level, traffic volume and major roads (Rao, Hawkins, & Guyer, 1997; Routledge et al., 1974; Wier, Weintraub, Humphreys, Seto, & Bhatia, 2009).

5 Children and active transportation: Safe school travel

Also related to exposure is the number of children walking or conversely, being driven to school. There has been an increase in children being driven to school in many countries. In Canada for example, the proportion in the Greater Toronto Hamilton Area (GTHA) of children driven to school more than doubled from 1986 to 2011 for children ages 11–17 (Buliung, Mitra, & Faulkner, 2009). Increased driving is the result of numerous influences including: increased home-school distances (from rapid suburbanization/urban sprawl), increased vehicle access due to recent improvements in vehicle quality-increased quality means cars last longer leading to more used cars on the market- and a proliferation of a car-based culture affecting parent perceptions of safety and convenience. Current perceptions of "good" parenting include greater adult supervision sometimes leading to a decline in active school transportation (Rothman, Macpherson, Ross, & Buliung, 2017). The result is increased traffic congestion around schools and along school routes, creating a dangerous environment for child pedestrians themselves, and a vicious circle where parents drive because of their fear of traffic while actually creating the traffic danger. Worldwide trends in decreasing active transport have also been linked to decreased autonomy and children's independent travel (Furneaux & Manaugh, 2018).

Active school transportation must be encouraged to decrease traffic danger related to congestion and risky driving behaviors around schools (Rothman, Buliung, Howard, Macarthur, & Macpherson, 2017). Previous research demonstrates that more walking to school was not associated with more collisions, as long as the built environment around schools is safe (Rothman, Macarthur, To, Buliung, & Howard, 2014). However, the issue of school trip safety remains a challenge for urban environments that has not yet been adequately addressed. A 2011 study of Toronto elementary schools described 481 police-reported incidents of child PMVC within school attendance boundaries from 2002 to 2011; 45 occurring during pickup and drop off times, with over half resulting in hospital visits (Rothman et al., 2014). Socioeconomic inequities exist as well; higher collision rates occur near disadvantaged schools even after controlling for the numbers of children walking (Rothman et al., 2014). Risky driving behaviors were observed at approximately 90% of schools during drop-off times, and have been associated with a 45% increase in collision rates (Rothman, Howard, Buliung, Macarthur, & Macpherson, 2016). Parent's decisions regarding school travel mode are primarily related to time and convenience associated with work schedules, distance from school and multi-activity trip chains (Faulkner, Richichi, Buliung, Fusco, & Moola, 2010). These time-related pressures create a stressful drop-off period, with pervasive risky driving behaviors that include speeding, illegal parking and disobeying traffic rules that are not easily changed.

6 Keeping children safe on the roads

6.1 Changing the built environment (traffic calming and speed reduction counter-measures)

As vehicle speed is the key variable in terms of determining injury severity, slowing down traffic is the most important variable that can be changed to reduce injuries and fatalities. Traffic calming refers to a suite of design, infrastructure, or policy intervention that has the effect of reducing the number and slowing the speed of vehicles. Reducing roadway speeds can be achieved through a variety of countermeasures including built environment changes (speed humps, raised crosswalks, lane narrowings), regulatory modifications (speed limit changes), and enforcement (automated speed enforcement). There is consistent empirical evidence that environmental roadway modification reduces PMVC and that speed reduction is the most effective way to reduce the number and severity of collisions. In Toronto, speed humps were associated with a 43% reduction in PMVC incidence rates in children (Rothman, Macpherson, Buliung, et al., 2015). Other similar studies have demonstrated the effectiveness of speed humps and traffic calming in reducing vehicle speeds and pedestrian collisions (Ewing, 2001; Jones, Lyons, John, & Palmer, 2005; Tester, Rutherford, Wald, & Rutherford, 2004).

Research has also shown a decrease in the number of pedestrians killed or seriously injured after the implementation of posted speed limit reductions in Europe. A Swiss study demonstrated a 16%, 20%, and 25% reduction in car-pedestrian collisions, pedestrian injuries, and fatalities respectively after speed limit reductions from 60 to 50 km/h (Waiz, Hoefliger, & Fehlmann, 1983). Similarly, in the UK, Grundy et al. (2009) found that 20 mph speed zones are effective at reducing the risk of fatality for individuals involved in a motor vehicle collision in Britain (Grundy et al., 2009). They reported that speed limit reductions to 20 mph were associated with a 41.9% decrease in road traffic casualties. The largest percent reduction was observed in younger children and for killed or seriously injured persons compared to those with minor injuries. Additionally, there was no evidence of increased casualties on adjacent roads without speed limit reductions. Injuries to pedestrians were reduced by approximately one third with greater reductions seen in children ages 0–15 years. A 2011 AAA study in the United States examined speeds and risk of injury or fatality for pedestrians. The study found that the average risk of death for a pedestrian is high at 10% at impact speeds of 23 mph which is typical of residential areas in North America (~37 km/h) this is much lower than 25% at 32 mph (~52 km/h) and 50% at 42 mph (~68 km/h) (National Conference of State Legislatures, 2016). Given the effectiveness of reduced speed limit zones, metropolitan areas with similar road traffic environments should consider implementing 20 mph reductions.

The automated speed enforcement devices including speed display boards and photo-radar are another interesting measures to lower speed on specific roads. Bloch (1998) compared the speed reduction effects for both of these interventions and concluded that both devices while deployed significantly reduce vehicle speeds by approximately 8 km/h and also reduce the speeds of vehicles traveling over the posted speed limit (Bloch, 1998). Both devices produced substantial reductions in speed while in operation; however, only display boards demonstrated carry-over effects. Automated speed enforcement is increasingly effective when display boards are supplemented with intermittent enforcement. In areas with automated speed enforcement such as British Columbia, photo radar programs (PCP) have shown a reduction in speed and improved safety in deployment locations. Chen, Meckle, and Wilson (2002) reported that at times and locations where programs were operating, mean traffic speeds were reduced below the limit. Speeds were also reduced among adjacent stretches of roadway even in the absence of radar devices, suggesting that automated speed enforcement may be an effective intervention in lowering vehicle speeds. A Cochrane Systematic Review (2012), assessed whether the use of speed cameras reduces the incidence of speeding, road traffic collisions, injuries and fatalities (Wilson, Willis, Hendrikz, Brocque, & Bellamy, 2010). Thirty-five studies were included in this review, compared with controls the reduction in average speed ranged from 1% to 15% and the reduction in speeding ranged from 14% to 65%. The pre/post reductions ranged from 8% to 49% for all crashes and 11% to 44% for fatal and serious injury crashes. Although there is variability in the magnitude of this effect across studies, all studies show that speed cameras are a worthwhile intervention for reducing the number of road traffic injuries and deaths.

6.2 The need for a system approach in road safety

The Vision Zero (VZ) framework, which originated in Sweden in 1997, implements many countermeasures using a safe systems approach. The philosophy of this approach is that the transportation system needs to be designed to account for human error to eliminate fatalities and serious injuries (Business Sweden – The Swedish Trade and Invest Council, n.d.). The framework's key concept is to remove the responsibility of road safety off the individual and focusing instead on the transportation system. Vision Zero has proven to be effective in reducing the number of collisions that result in serious injuries and deaths by 50% in Sweden and by 60% in Edmonton, Canada (Business Sweden – The Swedish Trade and Invest Council, n.d.; Vision Zero Edmonton, 2016). Cities such as New York have also begun to see a downward trend in the number of fatally injured road users since the implementation of Vision Zero, with pedestrian deaths dropping 45% since 2013 (New York City Mayor's Office of Operations, 2018).

VZ has also been aligned with other road safety plans in many cities throughout Europe, Australia, New Zealand and the United States, with most prioritizing children as vulnerable road users and schools as key destinations. For example, Toronto adopted its VZ Road Safety Plan in 2017, and VZ principles are currently being incorporated into safety plans in other Canadian cities including Vancouver, Calgary, Edmonton and Montreal. As part of the Vision Zero road safety plan in Toronto, traffic calming, environmental modifications, and enforcement strategies have been implemented in an effort to decrease speed on roadways. These include, speed limit reductions along pedestrian safety corridors from 50 to 40 km/h and in some places from 40 to 30 km/h (City of Toronto, 2019). There have also been 837 speed-limit signs installed which reduced speeds, permanent "Watch your Speed" driver feedbacks signs added at schools, and 186 new speed humps installed at 56 locations. Automated speed enforcement will be implemented in school zones with confirmed speeding issues. Key intersections have been selected to implement a new corner radius design that encourages vehicles to slow down as they make right turns. Police enforcement has also been enhanced particularly with respect to school zone speed limits and aggressive driving. Another important element of equity is concerned with the placement of traffic calming devices and other policy interventions. Recent work in New York City, for example, found higher rates of speed humps in wealthier areas while controlling for length of street network and reported collisions (Rebentisch, Wasfi, Piatkowski, & Manaugh, 2019). Similarly, in Toronto, Canada, it was found that there were higher collision rates and lower densities of speed humps and low-speed local roads in low income versus high income areas, after adjusting for length of street network (Rothman et al., 2017).

7 Conclusions

As motor-vehicle use continues to increase globally, pedestrians are at increased risk of injury. Traffic and vehicle speed are the main risk factor for collisions and collision severity. Although cities that have implemented Vision Zero or similar road safety strategies are making some progress in reducing speeds, currently less than half of the countries surveyed by the WHO allow local authorities to modify national speed limits (World Health Organization, 2015). The smaller stature of children and their developing ability to integrate feedback from the road traffic environment puts them at greater risk for a PMVC. At the same time, active transportation in children is decreasing, and is contributed to by parental fears of traffic safety. Modifying the built environment (i.e. road design), creating appropriate regulatory changes (i.e. speed limit reduction zones), and enforcing compliance through for example, speed cameras, are essential to establish safer roadways and encourage active transportation for our children.

References

Anderson, R. W., McLean, A. J., Farmer, M., Lee, B. -H., & Brooks, C. G. (1997). Vehicle travel speeds and the incidence of fatal pedestrian crashes. *Accident; Analysis and Prevention, 29*(5), 667–674.

Appleyard, D. (1980). Livable streets: Protected neighborhoods? *The ANNALS of the American Academy of Political and Social Science, 451*(1), 106–117.

Bloch, S. (1998). Comparative study of speed reduction effects of photo-radar and speed display boards. *Transportation Research Record: Journal of the Transportation Research Board, 1640*, 27–36.

Buliung, R. N., Mitra, R., & Faulkner, G. (2009). Active school transportation in the Greater Toronto area, Canada: An exploration of trends in space and time (1986–2006). *Preventive Medicine, 48*(6), 507–512.

Burigusa, G., Lavoie, M., Maurice, P., Hamel, D., & Duranceau, A. (2011). *Sécurité des élèves du primaire lors des déplacements à pied et à vélo entre la maison et l'école au Québec.* Quebec, QC: Institut national de santé publique du Québec.

Business Sweden – The Swedish Trade and Invest Council. *Vision zero initiative.* http://www.visionzeroinitiative.com/taking-safety-to-new-levels/. (Accessed 11 April 2018).

Canadian Council of Motor Transport Administrators (CCMTS). (2013). *Countermeasures to improve pedestrian safety in Canada.* http://ccmta.ca/images/publications/pdf//CCMTA_Pedestrian_Report_Eng_FINAL.pdf. (Accessed 6 September 2018).

Chen, G., Meckle, W., & Wilson, J. (2002). Speed and safety effect of photo radar enforcement on a highway corridor in British Columbia. *Accident Analysis & Prevention, 34*(2), 129–138.

City of Toronto (2016). *Road Safety Plan (RSP) 2017–2021.* Available at:https://www.toronto.ca/legdocs/mmis/2016/pw/bgrd/backgroundfile-93990.pdf. (Accessed 9 July 2019).

City of Toronto (2019). *Vision Zero 2.0—Road Safety Plan Update.* Available at:https://www.toronto.ca/legdocs/mmis/2019/ie/bgrd/backgroundfile-134964.pdf. (Accessed 9 July 2019).

Dumbaugh, E., & Rae, R. (2009). Safe urban form: Revisiting the relationship between community design and traffic safety. *Journal of the American Planning Association, 75*(3), 309–329.

Ewing, R. (2001). Impacts of traffic calming. *Transportation Quarterly, 55*(1), 33–46.

Faulkner, G. E., Richichi, V., Buliung, R. N., Fusco, C., & Moola, F. (2010). What's "quickest and easiest?": Parental decision making about school trip mode. *International Journal of Behavioral Nutrition and Physical Activity, 7*, 62.

Fieldwick, R., & Brown, R. (1987). Effect of speed limits on road casualties. *Traffic Engineering and Control, 28*(12), 635–640.

Furneaux, A., & Manaugh, K. (2018). Eyes on the alley: children's appropriation of alley space in Riverdale, Toronto. *Children's Geographies*, 1–13.

Golub, A., Marcantonio, R. A., & Sanchez, T. W. (2013). Race, space, and struggles for mobility: Transportation impacts on African Americans in Oakland and the East Bay. *Urban Geography, 34*(5), 699–728.

Green, R. S., Smorodinsky, S., Kim, J. J., McLaughlin, R., & Ostro, B. (2004). Proximity of California public schools to busy roads. *Environmental Health Perspectives, 112*(1), 61.

Grundy, C., Steinbach, R., Edwards, P., Green, J., Armstrong, B., & Wilkinson, P. (2009). Effect of 20 mph traffic speed zones on road injuries in London, 1986–2006: Controlled interrupted time series analysis. *BMJ, 339*, .

Institute for Health Metrics and Evaluation (IHME). (2016). *Global burden of disease deaths.* https://vizhub.healthdata.org/gbd-compare/. (Accessed 5 September 2018).

Jamshidi, E., Moradi, A., & Majdzadeh, R. (2017). Environmental risk factors contributing to traffic accidents in children: A case-control study. *International Journal of Injury Control and Safety Promotion, 24*(3), 338–344.

Jones, S. J., Lyons, R. A., John, A., & Palmer, S. R. (2005). Traffic calming policy can reduce inequalities in child pedestrian injuries: Database study. *Injury Prevention*, *11*(3), 152–156.

Martin, J. -L., & Wu, D. (2018). Pedestrian fatality and impact speed squared: Cloglog modeling from French national data. *Traffic Injury Prevention*, *19*(1), 94–101.

Morency, P., Gauvin, L., Plante, C., Fournier, M., & Morency, C. (2012). Neighborhood social inequalities in road traffic injuries: The influence of traffic volume and road design. *American Journal of Public Health*, *102*(6), 1112–1119.

National Conference of State Legislatures. (2016). *Transportation review: Trends in state speed legislation.* http://www.ncsl.org/Portals/1/Documents/transportation/speed_limit_rpt2.pdf. (Accessed 11 September 2018).

New York City Mayor's Office of Operations. (2018). *Vision zero: Year four report.* https://www1.nyc.gov/assets/visionzero/downloads/pdf/vision-zero-year-4-report.pdf. (Accessed 5 September 2018).

Noxon, G. (2014). *Mobilizing knowledge on active transportation.* Ottawa, ON: Public Health Agency of Canada.

Pabayo, R. A., Gauvin, L., Barnett, T. A., Morency, P., Nikiema, B., & Seguin, L. (2012). Understanding the determinants of active transportation to school among children: Evidence of environmental injustice from the Quebec longitudinal study of child development. *Health & Place*, *18*(2), 163–171.

Pasanen, E. (1991). *Ajonopeudet ja jalankulkijan turvallisuus [Driving speeds and pedestrian safety].* Espoo, Finland: Teknillinen korkeakoulu, Liikennetekniikka.

Rao, R., Hawkins, M., & Guyer, B. (1997). Children's exposure to traffic and risk of pedestrian injury in an urban setting. *Bulletin of the New York Academy of Medicine*, *74*(1), 65–80.

Rebentisch, H., Wasfi, R., Piatkowski, D. P., & Manaugh, K. (2019). Safe streets for all? Analyzing infrastructural response to pedestrian and cyclist crashes in New York City, 2009–2018. *Transportation Research Record*, *2673*(2), 672–685. 0361198118821672.

Retting, R. A., Ferguson, S. A., & McCartt, A. T. (2003). A review of evidence-based traffic engineering measures designed to reduce pedestrian–motor vehicle crashes. *American Journal of Public Health*, *93*(9).

Roberts, I., Norton, R., Jackson, R., Dunn, R., & Hassall, I. (1995). Effect of environmental factors on risk of injury of child pedestrians by motor vehicles: A case-control study. *BMJ*, *310*(6972), 91–94.

Rosen, E., Stigson, H., & Sander, U. (2011). Literature review of pedestrian fatality risk as a function of car impact speed. *Accident; Analysis and Prevention*, *43*(1), 25–33.

Rothman, L. (2015). Physical and built environments, street design. In I. Pike, S. Richmond, L. Rothman, & A. Macpherson (Eds.), *Canadian injury prevention resource.* Toronto, ON: Parachute.

Rothman, L., Buliung, R., Howard, A., Macarthur, C., & Macpherson, A. (2017). The school environment and student car drop-off at elementary schools. *Travel Behaviour and Society*, *1*(9), 50–57.

Rothman, L., Cloutier, M., Manaugh, K., Howard, A., Macpherson, A., & Macarthur, C. (2017). Child pedestrian risk and social equity: The spatial distribution of roadway environment features in Toronto. In *Canada Transportation Research Board Annual Meeting, Washington DC.*

Rothman, L., Howard, A., Buliung, R., Macarthur, C., & Macpherson, A. (2016). Dangerous student car drop-off behaviours and child pedestrian-motor vehicle collisions: An observational study. *Traffic Injury Prevention*, *7*(5), 454–459. https://doi.org/10.1080/15389588.2015.1116041.

Rothman, L., Macarthur, C., To, T., Buliung, R., & Howard, A. (2014). Motor vehicle-pedestrian collisions and walking to school: The role of the built environment. *Pediatrics*, *133*(5), 776–784.

Rothman, L., Macpherson, A., Buliung, R., et al. (2015). Installation of speed humps and pedestrian-motor vehicle collisions in Toronto, Canada: A quasi-experimental study. *BMC Public Health, 15*(74).

Rothman, L., Macpherson, A. K., Ross, T., & Buliung, R. N. (2017). The decline in active school transportation (AST): A systematic review of the factors related to AST and changes in school transport over time in North America. *Preventive Medicine, 111*, 314–322.

Routledge, D., Repetto-Wright, R., & Howarth, C. (1974). The exposure of young children to accident risk as pedestrians. *Ergonomics, 17*, 457–480.

Statistics Canada. (2017). *Journey to work: Key results from the 2016 census*. https://www150.statcan.gc.ca/n1/daily-quotidien/171129/dq171129c-eng.htm. (Accessed 7 March 2019).

Tester, J. M., Rutherford, G. W., Wald, Z., & Rutherford, M. W. (Apr 2004). A matched case-control study evaluating the effectiveness of speed humps in reducing child pedestrian injuries. *American Journal of Public Health, 94*(4), 646–650.

Transport Canada (2016). *National Collision Database Online*. http://wwwapps2.tc.gc.ca/Saf-Sec-Sur/7/NCDB-BNDC/p.aspx?l=en. (Accessed 29 November 2018).

Twells, L. K., Gregory, D. M., Reddigan, J., & Midodzi, W. K. (2014). Current and predicted prevalence of obesity in Canada: A trend analysis. *CMAJ Open, 2*(1), E18.

Vision Zero Edmonton (2016). *Annual Report 2016. Edmonton, Alberta: City of Edmonton.*

Waiz, F. H., Hoefliger, M., & Fehlmann, W. (1983). *Speed limit reduction from 60 to 50 km/h and pedestrian injuries:* (pp. 0148–7191). SAE Technical Paper.

Walks, A. (2014). *Driving cities, driving inequality, driving politics: The urban political economy and ecology of automobility: Driving cities, driving inequality, driving politics.* Routledge.

Webster, D. C., & Mackie, A. M. (1996). *Review of traffic calming schemes in 20 mph zones. TRL REPORT 215.*

Wier, M., Weintraub, J., Humphreys, E. H., Seto, E., & Bhatia, R. (2009). An area-level model of vehicle-pedestrian injury collisions with implications for land use and transportation planning. *Accident; Analysis and Prevention, 41*(1), 137–145.

Wilson, C., Willis, C., Hendrikz, J. K., Le Brocque, R., & Bellamy, N. (2010). Speed cameras for the prevention of road traffic injuries and deaths. *Cochrane Database of Systematic Reviews, 11.*

World Health Organization (2008). *World report on child injury prevention.* Geneva, Switzerland: World Health Organization.

World Health Organization (2015). *Global status report on road safety 2015.* Geneva, Switzerland: World Health Organization.

Yiannakoulias, N., & Scott, D. M. (2013). The effects of local and non-local traffic on child pedestrian safety: A spatial displacement of risk. *Social Science & Medicine, 80*, 96–104.

CHAPTER SEVEN

Traffic emission impacts on child health and well-being

Vickie L. Boothe[a] and Richard W. Baldauf[b]
[a]Centers for Disease Control and Prevention, Atlanta, GA, United States
[b]United States Environmental Protection Agency, Research Triangle Park, NC, United States

Contents

Transport and Children's Wellbeing
https://doi.org/10.1016/B978-0-12-814694-1.00007-5

1 Problem significance

The global burden of disease resulting from exposure to traffic-related air pollution is an urgent public health threat. According to the World Health Organization, outdoor air pollution contributes to more than 4.2 million deaths annually (WHO, 2016). In urban areas, where more than 50% of the world's population live, traffic emissions are typically the largest outdoor air pollution contributor (Khreis et al., 2016). Without appropriate action, persistent global trends towards urbanization, continued economic growth, and increased motor vehicle dependency and personal vehicle ownership will inevitably lead to increased worldwide exposures to traffic-related air pollution and deaths (HEI, 2010a; Karagulian et al., 2015; Schultz, Litonjua, & Melén, 2017).

Governmental regulations in developed nations have achieved major reductions in ambient air pollution and associated increases in life expectancies (Henneman et al., 2017; Münzel et al., 2017). In the 10 years following passage of the 1990 U.S. Clean Air Act Amendments, emissions of regulated ambient air pollutants (e.g., ozone (O_3), particulate matter (PM), and carbon monoxide (CO)) declined 70% (Samet, Burke, & Goldstein, 2017). Despite these achievements, millions of adults and children are routinely exposed to near-road elevated concentrations of regulated and unregulated pollutants in the form of gases, solids, and liquid aerosols, many of which are toxic to human health (HEI, 2010a). This chapter explores how children's health and well-being is affected by exposures to near-road traffic emissions and describes some effective strategies capable of preventing or mitigating adverse outcomes.

2 Susceptibility of children

Children—from infancy to the age of 14—are especially susceptible to traffic emission-related health effects due to their rapidly developing immune, neurologic, and lung systems and high ventilation rates relative to body mass (Behrentz et al., 2005; Slezakova et al., 2015).

Children with pre-existing health conditions are comparatively more susceptible to traffic emission-related health effects. Living in disadvantaged neighborhoods increases exposures to independent risk factors (e.g., poverty, poor housing, and psychosocial stressors) which can synergistically impact child health. Disadvantaged or racial/ethnic minority children are also more likely to live in close proximity to polluting sources such as high-volume roadways and bus depots (Boehmer et al., 2013; Hooper & Kaufman, 2018; Pratt et al., 2015; Wang et al., 2016).

To fully assess and design mitigation strategies to reduce the impact of near-environment exposures, it is necessary to understand (1) the composition and distribution of pollutant concentrations within the microenvironments where children are exposed, (2) the known and suspected health effects resulting from children's acute short- and long-term exposures, and (3) typical time-activity-location patterns of children (Morawska et al., 2017; Perez et al., 2013).

3 Studies of traffic emission generation, concentrations, and patterns of distributions

Motor vehicles emit thousands of compounds (primary pollutants) through fuel combustion and evaporation, brake and tire wear, and deterioration of engine and exhaust components. Primary pollutants known to impact health include particulate matter (PM) such as highly respirable fine particles ($PM_{2.5}$, diameter $< 2.5\,\mu m$) and ultrafine particles (UFPs, diameter $< 100\,nm$), nitrogen oxides (NOx), carbon monoxide (CO), metals, and volatile organic compounds (VOCs) including benzene and polycyclic aromatic hydrocarbons (PAHs). UFPs can be of particular concern because these size particles can cross biological barriers (blood-brain, placenta cell membranes), and effectively transport absorbed toxics throughout the body (Burgio, Di Ciaula, & Capello, 2018).

Diesel exhaust particles, which were classified as a human carcinogen by the International Agency for Research on Cancer in 2012, also pose significant risks to human health (Hime, Marks, & Cowie, 2018). Diesel PM is a highly complex mixture primarily consisting of an elemental (i.e., black) carbon (EC/BC) core, coated with organic compounds including particle-bound PAHs, and smaller amounts of absorbed metals. Diesel PM also includes aerosols including sulfates and nitrates, which are produced by the intermediate reactions of gases shortly after release in the atmosphere (IARC, 2014).

Concentrations of primary pollutants emitted by vehicle exhaust are significantly higher near the road compared to concentrations across larger areas (Zhang & Wexler, 2004). Motor vehicles also emit and re-suspend PM constituents from brake, tire, and pavement wear. Key factors contributing to observed near-road pollutant concentrations include source strength (e.g., number and types of vehicles and their emission rates); distance from a road to a receptor location (e.g., nearby homes, schools, and other common microenvironments); and meteorological conditions (wind speed and direction and atmospheric stability). These combined influences result in both daily and seasonal variations in near-road pollutant concentrations. Elevated near-road concentrations generally occur on a scale of 100's of meters from the road, which means the timeframe for pollutant transport from the source to the receptor is on the order of seconds to minutes. At these time scales, concentrations are primarily reduced through dispersion by turbulence caused by the atmospheric turbulence, vehicles on the nearby road, or by nearby structures like buildings and noise barriers. Reduced concentrations can also result from chemical and physical transformations (e.g., nucleation, condensation, evaporation). Fig. 1 depicts results of a meta-analysis showing concentrations of key primary pollutants (e.g., UFP and certain VOCs), which can be as much as an order of magnitude higher within the first 100–200 m of a large highway compared to urban background concentrations (Karner, Eisinger, & Niemeier, 2010). (See Table 1.)

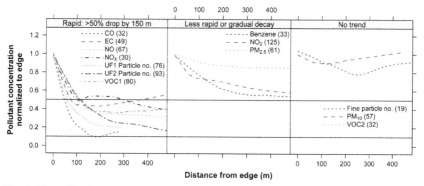

Fig. 1 Normalized concentrations of air pollution reductions with distance from the road based on a meta-analysis. Local regression of edge normalized concentrations on distance. The horizontal black lines show a reduction from the edge-of-road concentration of 90% (at 0.1) and 50% (at 0.5). A loess smoother (alpha = 0.70, degree = 1) was fitted to pollutant data which was placed in one of three groups. The regression sample size, n, is given in parentheses after each pollutant. *(Reprinted with permission from Karner, A., Eisinger, D., & Niemeier, D. (2010). Near-roadway air quality: Synthesizing the findings from real-world data (Vol. 44, pp. 5334–44). Copyright 2010 American Chemical Society).*

Table 1 Pollutant descriptions by group classification (Fig. 1)

Group classification	Pollutant description
Rapid: >50% drop by 150 m	CO: carbon monoxide EC: elemental carbon including black carbon, black smoke, and the reflectance of PM filters NO: nitrogen monoxide NOx: nitrogen oxides UF1 particle no.: ultrafine particles with a diameter ranging from 3 nm (nm) to 14 nm measured in particle numbers (no.) UF2 particle no.: ultrafine particles with a diameter ranging from 15 to 299 nm measured in particle numbers VOC 1: volatile organic compounds that vary with distance including 1,3-butadiene, methyl tert-butyl ether, n-hexane
Less rapid or gradual decay	Benzene NO_2: nitrogen dioxide $PM_{2.5}$: particulate matter with a diameter $< 2.5\,\mu m$ (μm)
No trend	Fine particle no.: fine particles with a diameter ≥ 300 nm PM_{10}: particulate matter with a diameter $< 10\,\mu m$ VOC2: volatile organic compounds that do not vary with distance including ethane, isobutane, n-butane, propane

4 Existing body of evidence on exposures and health effects

Our understanding of the impact of traffic emissions on children's health largely stems from a combination of toxicological studies, controlled human exposure experiments, and epidemiological studies. Toxicological and controlled exposure studies of healthy subjects provide critical knowledge on biological mechanisms of action between pollutant exposures and health effects. Epidemiological (i.e., observational) studies explore health effects resulting from exposures of populations in defined real-world settings (e.g., homes, schools). Epidemiological studies provide the majority of scientific evidence underpinning current air pollution policies and regulations (Brauer et al., 2008).

Generally, well-designed systematic reviews and meta-analyses provide the best scientific evidence because they include all available studies and systematic, objective analyses of the results, strengths, and weaknesses of the entire body of research (Hoffmann, Hopp, & Rittenmeyer, 2010).

Meta-analyses are systematic reviews that mathematically synthesize existing evidence into a single summary measure, which helps quantify and explore observed differences across individual study findings (Berman & Parker, 2002).

5 Summary of evidence for select health effects in children

Information in this chapter reflects the most recent, highest quality, available systematic review evidence on child health effects associated with exposure to direct or surrogate measures of traffic-related air pollution (HEI Panel on the Health Effects of Traffic-Related Air Pollution, 2010). Importantly, not all health outcomes linked to traffic emission exposures are included. Instead, we use a narrative approach in order to focus attention on existing and emerging potential causal evidence on the most prevalent, severe, and currently less recognized health effects including neurodevelopmental outcomes.

5.1 Respiratory effects

In 2010, the Health Effects Institute (HEI) issued a Special Report synthesizing the body of evidence on health effects related to individual traffic emissions including CO, NO_2, EC/BC, PM, benzene, and UFP and measures of traffic density and proximity. The panel reported suggestive evidence of a causal relationship between exposure to traffic-related air pollution and the onset of childhood asthma, non-asthma respiratory symptoms, and impaired lung function and sufficient evidence to support a "causal" association for asthma exacerbations (HEI, 2010b; HEI Panel on the Health Effects of Traffic-Related Air Pollution, 2010). Recent research confirmed and expanded these HEI findings. Authors of a 2017 meta-analysis of 41 studies reported significant associations between the onset of asthma and exposures to traffic-related pollutants including elemental carbon (EC), NO_2, $PM_{2.5}$ and PM_{10} (Khreis et al., 2017). As part of the California Children's Health Study (CHS), researchers conducted a systematic review of 5 CHS cohort studies. Exposures to regional air pollutants and near-road traffic emissions were reported to be independently associated with increased asthma prevalence and new-onset asthma, increased chronic and acute respiratory symptoms among children with asthma, delayed lung function development, and higher airway inflammation (Chen et al., 2015).

5.2 Childhood cancer

Researchers of three recent meta-analyses employing varying exposure assessment methods independently reported post-natal exposure to traffic emissions was associated with childhood leukemia (Whitehead et al., 2016). The strongest associations were reported for residential exposures to traffic proximity measures and all types of childhood leukemia combined (Boothe, Boehmer, Wendel, & Yip, 2014), exposures to modeled benzene concentrations and acute myeloblastic leukemia (AML) (Filippini et al., 2015), and exposures to traffic proximity measures and modeled concentrations of benzene and associations with both AML and acute lymphoblastic leukemia (ALL) (Carlos Wallace et al., 2016).

5.3 Autism

Researchers of a 2016 meta-analysis of primarily U.S. studies assessed associations between autism spectrum disorder (ASD) and ambient concentrations of $PM_{2.5}$ and PM_{10} and traffic-related diesel PM. The strongest associations were reported for diesel PM and ambient $PM_{2.5}$ (Morales-Suárez-Varela et al., 2017). A 2017 meta-analysis of 7 cohort and 5 case-control studies conducted in Taiwan, Europe, and the U.S. found the strongest associations for exposures to $PM_{2.5}$ and NO_2 during the first year after birth (Flores-Pajot et al., 2016). Lam and colleagues reported strongest associations for prenatal exposures to $PM_{2.5}$ and ASD based on meta-analysis results of 23 studies (Lam et al., 2016). More recently, Fu et al. reported significant associations between exposures to $PM_{2.5}$ and multiple neurological disorders including ASD based on results of a 2019 meta-analysis of 80 studies of more than 6.33 million residents of 26 countries across Africa, Asia, Australia, Europe, North America and South America (Fu et al., 2019). Additional evidence is provided from a recently published narrative review on the impact fossil fuel combustion on pediatric health (Perera, 2018) and a scoping review assessing associations between ASD and a wide range of environmental exposures (Ng et al., 2017).

In summary, there is a growing body of compelling evidence suggesting exposure to $PM_{2.5}$ and traffic emissions (diesel PM, NO_2) are risk factors for ASD. Important limitations include the relatively small number of studies and inconsistent results outside of the U.S., which may be due to differences in air pollution concentrations and measures, racial or ethnic susceptibility, or ASD diagnostic methods and inclusion criteria (Flores-Pajot et al., 2016; Lam et al., 2016). More high quality research is needed to address inconsistencies and differentiate between exposures to traffic emissions and ambient $PM_{2.5}$ before causality can be determined (Flores-Pajot et al., 2016; Lam et al., 2016; Ng et al., 2017; Perera, 2018).

5.4 Adverse birth outcomes

Less robust evidence suggests potential links between exposures to traffic-related pollutants and birth outcomes. Authors of a 2017 narrative review of 12 studies primarily using measures of residential traffic proximity reported preterm birth as the most likely impacted outcome (Woods, Gilliland, & Seabrook, 2017). Li and colleagues reported significant associations between interquartile range increase in $PM_{2.5}$ and preterm birth and term low birth weight based on meta-analysis of 23 studies using ambient $PM_{2.5}$ concentrations generated with various modeling techniques (Li et al., 1987).

5.5 Other health effects

Results of multiple systematic reviews suggest prenatal exposure to traffic-related particle-bound polycyclic aromatic hydrocarbons (PAH) contributes to attention-deficit/hyperactivity disorder (ADHD) and delayed cognitive development (Burgio et al., 2018; Sram, 2017). Other systematic review results link chronic exposure to traffic-related pollutants to increased childhood obesity, type II diabetes, and insulin resistance (Burgio et al., 2018; Münzel et al., 2017).

Although the primary focus of this chapter is on adverse health effects occurring during childhood, recent research suggests prenatal and childhood exposure to traffic-related pollutants can significantly affect adult health. Childhood exposures to PAHs and other traffic-related carcinogens can cause genetic mutations leading to elevated risks of adult cancer (Oliveira et al., 2017). Early childhood exposure to $PM_{2.5}$ and UFP can accelerate early aging of the brain and potentially lead to adult neurodegenerative disorders such as Alzheimer's and Parkinson diseases (Burgio et al., 2018; Wang, Xiong, & Tang, 2017).

6 Impact of exposure to greenspace on children's health

Greenspace can be an important mediator of impacts of exposure to traffic emissions. A 2018 systematic review assessed potential causal relationships between urban greenspace and health based on results of 68 studies restricted to experimental, quasi-experimental, or longitudinal designs. The authors reported consistent positive associations for urban greenspace exposures and mood, cognitive function, and physical activity and negative associations for mortality, heart rate, and violence (Kondo et al., 2018).

Other systematic review results suggest childhood exposure to greenspace enhances cognitive development, improves sleep patterns, and reduces behavioral problems including aggressive behavior (Kabisch, van den Bosch, & Lafortezza, 2017; Nieuwenhuijsen, 2016). Reduced exposure to air pollution and increased physical activity are among the hypothesized pathways.

7 Microenvironment contributions to total personal traffic-related pollutant exposure

Total personal exposure is determined by the amount of time spent and the traffic-related pollutant concentrations within typical child microenvironments including homes, day care centers or schools, in transit, and outdoors (Capizzano, 2005; Che, Frey, & Lau, 2015; de Nazelle, Bode, & Orjuela, 2017; Dons et al., 2011).

Depending on the day of the week, school-aged children spend the majority of time, between 60% and 72% at home indoors (Che et al., 2015). Very young children spend an even larger percent of time at home indoors (Morawska et al., 2017). The average weekday amount of time spent in other microenvironments is 5.8 h in day care centers or 6.8 h at school, 1.4 h in transit, and between 0.8 and 2 h outdoors, depending on the season (Che et al., 2015).

Multiple traffic-related air pollutants including gaseous pollutants (CO, NO_2, benzene) can infiltrate indoor microenvironments and combine with pollutant emissions generated from indoor activities and sources. Indoor and total personal PM exposure is of particular interest because it is associated with multiple adverse child health outcomes and $PM_{2.5}$ is the pollutant most closely studied and most commonly used as a proxy for air pollution in general (WHO, 2016).

Important knowledge on the origins of different PM size fractions and average concentrations within typical micro-environments is provided by a 2017 pooled analysis of data from the published studies conducted in multiple urban indoor environments including homes, schools, and day care centers. The goal of the study was to inform prevention strategies by assessing generalizable trends in PM sources, concentrations, and exposure

Fig. 2 Distribution of highway traffic emissions across typical child microenvironments. This figure depicts the relative distribution and concentrations of individual pollutants emitted from the highway, located on the left side of the figure, across typical child microenvironments. *EC*, elemental carbon; *UFP*, ultrafine particles; *NO*, nitrogen monoxide; *NOx*, nitrogen oxides; *CO*, carbon monoxide; *VOC1*, volatile organic compounds; *MTBE*, methyl tert-butyl ether; *NO₂*, nitrogen dioxide; *PM₂.₅*, particulate matter with a diameter < 2.5 μm.

routes (Morawska et al., 2017). Studies of homes with indoor biomass burning and active cigarette smoking were excluded.

Information from the pooled analysis was used to develop Fig. 2, which depicts the relative distribution and concentrations of individual pollutants emitted from the highway, located on the left side of the figure, across typical child microenvironments.

7.1 Homes

Based on pooled data from 58 studies, researchers reported local outdoor air pollution sources (traffic emissions, fossil fuel burning) are the main source of indoor $PM_{2.5}$ and PM_{10} concentrations. In contrast, indoor activities including cooking, cleaning, candle use and incense burning are the primary source of indoor UFP measured by mean particle number (PN). These indoor activities can also be the source of short-term peak $PM_{2.5}$ and PM_{10} concentrations (Morawska et al., 2017).

7.2 Schools

Findings from the pooled data analysis from 50 studies, suggests indoor mean $PM_{2.5}$ and PM_{10} concentrations primarily originate from resuspension of particles by student activity and local traffic emissions. Traffic emissions and other outdoor emission sources were also identified as the predominant contributors to mean indoor PN (Morawska et al., 2017).

Similarly, researchers of a 2017 comparative assessment of exposures of Portuguese students aged 8–10 years in 10 schools, found emissions from diesel and gasoline vehicle traffic were the predominant source of indoor PAHs. The estimated cancer risks of the students were up to 22 times higher than the threshold established by the US Environmental Protection Agency (EPA) and 2–10 times greater than the risk from outdoor exposures, primarily due to the relative amount of time spent in the classrooms (Oliveira et al., 2017).

7.3 Day care centers

Findings from the pooled data analysis from 12 Day Care Center studies were very similar to those for schools, suggesting resuspension combined with outdoor sources, especially traffic-related emissions, are the predominant source of indoor $PM_{2.5}$ and PN concentrations (Morawska et al., 2017).

7.4 Transit microenvironments

Current scientific knowledge on comparative traffic-related emission exposures and associated health impacts based on different travel modes is supported by two 2017 systematic reviews.

Researchers conducted a systematic review of 10 European studies comparing air pollution exposures resulting from various travel modes including cars, public buses, bicycles, and walking. Across all studies, walking represented the least exposed mode to $PM_{2.5}$, UFP, and EC/BC. For $PM_{2.5}$, bicyclists, car and bus passengers were exposed to average concentrations 30%, 40%, and 50% greater than pedestrians. Passengers in cars without controlled ventilation tended to be exposed to the highest concentrations of air pollutants. Bus passengers and cyclists tended to have similar exposure patterns for $PM_{2.5}$ and EC/BC. However, bus passengers' exposure to UFP were significantly lower than those of cyclists (de Nazelle et al., 2017).

Results of a comprehensive systematic review of 39 U.S., European, and Asian studies confirmed these findings and expanded the scientific evidence base by providing comparative inhalation doses associated with commute modes of car, bus, motorcycle, bicycle, and walking. Additionally, these researchers calculated the comparative trade-offs in years of life expectancy based on different commute mode exposure levels to $PM_{2.5}$ (Cepeda et al., 2017).

Passengers in car without ventilation controls followed by bus and motorcycle commuters were consistently exposed to higher concentrations of $PM_{2.5}$, NO_2, and EC/BC compared to active commuters. Car commuters with controlled ventilation were exposed to higher concentrations than active commuters and lower concentrations than other motorized modes. In contrast, active commuters—specifically, bicyclists followed by pedestrians, had the highest uptake doses. Among commuters using motorized transport modes, car commuters (with and without controlled ventilation) had the lowest uptake doses followed by higher doses among motorcyclists and public bus commuters due to relatively higher inhalation rates.

Although active commuters had higher doses, estimated life expectancy benefits of physical activity outweighed those of lower $PM_{2.5}$ doses among motorized commuters. Median losses in life expectancy for motorized commuters were up to 1 year larger than among cyclists. The life expectancy losses for motorized commuters compared to pedestrians were even larger, primarily due to the longer physically active commute times (Cepeda et al., 2017).

These findings are consistent with results of a 2015 systematic review of a separate body of health impact assessment (HIA) literature. Specifically, researchers analyzed 30 peer-reviewed HIA studies of the health risks and benefits associated with a mode shift to active travel. The benefits of increased lifetime physical activity strongly outweighed the increased risks from air pollution exposure and motor vehicle-related pedestrian injuries and fatalities (Mueller et al., 2015).

Although these findings represent the highest quality scientific evidence to date, important identified limitations should be addressed in future studies. Specifically, future research should account for toxicity of other traffic-related pollutants and address additional physical activity- and traffic pollutant-related health endpoints.

8 Estimated exposure magnitudes and disparities

8.1 Residential

Approximately 3.7% of all U.S. residents (11 million people) live within 150 m of a highway, defined as interstates (Class 1) or as other freeways and expressways (Class 2) based on the Federal Highway Administration (FHWA) Functional Classification system. Almost half of these residents are poor or near poor and compared to whites, racial and ethnic minority populations are much more likely to live next to a highway (Boehmer et al., 2013; Carlson, 2018).

The percentage of populations living next to heavily trafficked roads within urban cities are significantly higher than the national estimates. More than a third of the Toronto and Los Angeles residents live within 300 m of a highway or major road (HEI, 2010a). Within 10 European cities, the average percent of populations living within 75 m and 150 m of roads with more than 10,000 vehicles per day is 31% and 53%, respectively (Perez et al., 2013).

8.2 Schools

In the U.S., approximately 7.4% of all schools representing over 4 million students are located within 100 m of a highway or primary road (Kingsley et al., 2014). Similar to residences, the percentages of urban schools located near major roads are significantly higher. In the U.S., an estimated 15% of urban schools are located within 100 m of a highway or major road (Kingsley et al., 2014). Approximately 34% of Prague's public elementary schools are located within 100 m of roads with more than 10,000 vehicles per day (Štych, Šrámková, & Braniš, 2016). A reported 16.2% of elementary schools in 10 Canadian cities are located within 75 m of a major road. However, the percentage of schools in the lowest income neighborhoods located within 75 m of a major road is 22% (Amram et al., 2011). Similarly, U.S. schools in close proximity to major roads typically have significantly higher percentages of low income and minority students compared to reference schools (Tian, Xue, & Barzyk, 2012).

8.3 Travel microenvironments

A large majority of North American students commute to school in motorized vehicles. In the U.S., over 25 million students (>50%) commute on diesel school buses and 42%–47% of students living within one mile of school commute in passenger vehicles (Adar et al., 2015; Beck & Nguyen, 2017). In Canada, between 67% and 80% of girls and 64%–71% of boys commute on school buses or passenger vehicles (Freeman, King, & Pickett, 2016).

The percent of students actively commuting to school in the U.S. is 21.4% (Yang et al., 2016). With few exceptions, most other countries have substantially higher rates. Results from European studies conducted in multiple countries including Denmark, Estonia, the U.K., Sweden, and Switzerland suggest between 50% and 85% of students walk or cycle to school. In Mexico, approximately 68% of students walk and 2% cycle to school (Jáuregui et al., 2015). The estimated percentage of active student commuters in China is 80%–90%. Across all countries, distance to school is the strongest predictor of active commuting and higher percentages of students in urban cities walk or cycle to school compared to rural areas (Johansson, Laflamme, & Hasselberg, 2012).

9 Strategies for reducing exposure and preventing or mitigating children's health effects

9.1 Multi-sector comprehensive community design

Despite the large and rapidly growing body of high-quality research, there is no scientific consensus on the specific traffic-related constituents and mechanisms most responsible for observed adverse effects on children's health (Dias, 2018).

In light of these uncertainties, a systems-based, comprehensive approach to residential, urban, and transportation planning which can reduce near environment exposure to traffic-related pollutants and other environmental risk factors while concurrently increasing exposure to health promoting social and physical environments is likely to result in the most successful, sustainable, and cost-effective strategies for child health improvements (Roy, Riley, Sears, & Rula, 2018; Nieuwenhuijsen, 2016; Vardoulakis et al., 2018; Villanueva et al., 2016).

High-density, mixed-use development, combined with effective strategies for reducing car use including ready access to public transit, active transport options, and green space can reduce exposures to traffic-related pollutants and noise, promote physical activity and social cohesion, and reduce aggravation and stress. Co-benefits would include reduced carbon emissions and mitigated heat island effects (Nieuwenhuijsen, 2016). Through a child health lens, optimum urban neighborhoods consist of high-quality affordable housing, low levels of traffic, safe and attractive places where families and children can socialize and play (e.g., parks, community centers, schools), with clean technology-based public transport options within walking distance (Roy et al., 2018; Villanueva et al., 2016). Results of rigorous economic modeling evaluations suggest such combined interventions can be highly cost effective (Vardoulakis et al., 2018).

In the United Kingdom (U.K.), the National Health Service's Healthy New Homes Program is testing the efficacy of a "place-based, whole systems, approach" in improving population health including physical and psychological well-being. Out of 100 applicants, 10 diverse sites were selected to evaluate measurable outcomes of new "healthier" homes constructed in communities with inclusive public space designed to reduce isolation and promote social cohesion and infrastructures designed to reduce automobile dependence, promote walking and cycling, and increase access to greenspace, healthy food, and sunlight. Evaluation results of this 5-year pilot will guide future broad strategies for creating healthier environments for U.K. residents across the country (Norman & McDonnell, 2017).

Discovery Bay, a residential community located on Hong Kong's largest outlying island, has been a car-free zone for more than 30 years. Characteristics of this "eco-friendly" development include convenient public railway and regular ferry service options for workers commuting to Hong Kong's employment centers, high quality schools catering to diverse educational needs, and 24-h local bus service providing easy retail access to fresh produce, groceries, and fine dining options. Discovery Bay meets the social and physical activity needs of its 12,000 residents through provision of multiple community centers, parks, and recreational facilities (Loo & Loo, 2018).

Designing or retrofitting communities to optimize child health and well-being requires significant broad political and social change, financial investments, long-term commitment, and effective multi-sector planning, monitoring, and evaluation tools. Additionally, effective systems-based community design requires a change in professional and organizational cultures and sector-centric perspectives by multiple governmental agencies and non-profit and private sector organizations including public health, transportation, housing, urban planning, education, land use, and economic development (Giles Corti et al., 2016; Khreis et al., 2016; Villanueva et al., 2016). Recent research suggests such holistic, place-based efforts requires new planning models such as Collective Impact (CI) specifically designed to generate long-term commitments and collective actions from historically siloed disciplines and organizations (Taylor et al., 2018; Villanueva et al., 2016).

In cases where limited resources prohibit comprehensive community redesign, CI can promote coordinated delivery of prioritized single-sector, mutually reinforcing actions and sustainable achievement of measurable child health improvements (Taylor et al., 2018).

9.2 Single sector federal, state, and local governmental actions

Government agency strategies for controlling motor vehicle air pollution generally focus on regulatory emission standards. Beginning in 2007, U.S. EPA standards for heavy-duty diesel engines mandated at least 90% emission reductions and conversion to ultralow-sulfur diesel (ULSD) fuel. Resulting technology advancements are projected to achieve annual reductions of 110,000 tons of PM, 17,000 tons of benzene, and substantially reduced particle toxicity and associated health risks (Baldauf, 2008; Baldauf et al., 1994; Pratt et al., 2015).

9.3 Roadside barriers

Roadside sound walls and vegetation barriers can reduce the concentrations of near-road air pollutants; thus, reducing exposures in nearby homes, schools, and while walking or cycling (Baldauf, 2017; Baldauf et al., 1994). For solid structures like sound walls, the barriers block airflow from the road, forcing the traffic-emitted pollutants to go up and over the structure (Baldauf et al., 1994). This change in air flow increases turbulence and dilution, resulting in lower downwind concentrations (Baldauf et al., 1994). Most studies have shown pollutant concentrations behind a barrier located downwind of a roadway can be reduced by as much as 50% (Baldauf, 2008). Downwind concentration reductions increase with increasing wall height (Hagler et al., 2012). When considering a sound wall, planners should ensure that the structures do not isolate buildings, discourage active transportation, or present a potential safety hazard by hindering visibility for drivers, bicyclists, and pedestrians.

Roadside vegetation can also improve local air quality and provide green space benefits. Trees and bushes along roadways can reduce downwind pollutant concentrations by acting as a physical barrier between roadways and downwind land uses and by filtering some pollutants as they pass through and adsorb onto leaf surfaces (Baldauf, 2017). The amount of adsorption depends on season, plant species, leaf size, and pollutant. Effectiveness of trees and plants as physical barriers depends on the density, width and foliage height and coverage. EPA recommendations to urban planners and developers describe the roadside vegetation characteristics needed to obtain improved air quality and characteristics to avoid that can lead to no reductions or even increase downwind concentrations (US EPA, 2016a). Vegetative barriers can also provide effective roadway buffers from roadways while creating a more aesthetically pleasing space to encourage active transportation.

Use of vegetation and sound walls together can effectively reduce $PM_{2.5}$ and UFP near-road emissions by up to 60% (Lee et al., 1994). Green walls and green roofs can also be cost effective strategies for improving health and psychological well-being by reducing air pollution, energy use, urban temperatures, heat island effects, and storm water runoff (Abhijith et al., 1994; US EPA, 2018).

9.4 Indoor air treatment

For decades, filtration has been used to remove indoor air pollutants from residential and commercial buildings. Filtration systems are generally included as part of a building's heating, ventilation, and air conditioning (HVAC) system, although portable air cleaners are also available. Numerous studies show filtration systems can significantly reduce indoor exposures to traffic-related air pollution, especially indoor particulate concentrations. The degree of improvement varies as a function of the HVAC system's Minimum Efficiency Reporting Value (MERV) rating, with greater improvement achieved by filters with higher MERV ratings providing the HVAC system is designed for the higher-pressure drops associated with higher MERV rated filters and no leaks within the system. A recent pilot study conducted in an Amsterdam school located next to a highway demonstrated a new ventilation system with an MERV14 filter could reduce average EC/BC exposure by 36% and $PM_{2.5}$ exposure by 30% (van der Zee et al., 2017). Portable HEPA air cleaners can reduce near road residential $PM_{2.5}$ concentrations by as much as 60% (Cox et al., 2018). Upgraded residential and occupational building filtration systems across Europe would potentially prevent 27,000 to 100,000 annual premature deaths. Health-related economic benefits of improved filtration are estimated to far exceed total costs (Fisk, 2013).

Penetration of traffic-related pollution can also be minimized by locating HVAC air intakes on rooftops or the side of building farthest from the roadway (Brugge et al., 2015). The intakes should be located away from other pollution sources including school bus and personal vehicle loading and unloading areas, cooking stacks and laboratory vents. Best practices should also prevent draw-in of traffic emissions through open windows and doors in buildings using pressurized HVAC systems (Brugge et al., 2015). Regular maintenance and filter replacement are essential for maintaining high filter performance (US EPA Agency, 2016b).

9.5 Diesel buses and vehicles

U.S. and Canadian students are exposed to elevated diesel bus emissions at bus stops, during bus commutes, and outside and inside of school during times when school buses arrive, idle, and depart. Typically, the highest exposures occur during commutes on diesel buses. In addition to the mandated limits on diesel fuel content and emission standards, the US EPA created a voluntary retrofit initiative to assist states with installing cleaner technologies on school buses including closed crankcase ventilation systems, diesel oxidation catalysts, and diesel particle filters. Researchers of a natural experiment conducted in two large Washington State cities reported the combined strategies reduced $PM_{2.5}$ and UFP concentrations by 10%–50% and reduced airway inflammation (measured as exhaled nitric oxide) and school absenteeism among students (aged 6–12 years), with stronger associations reported for asthmatic children (Adar et al., 2015; Laumbach, 2015). Accelerating fleet turnover and policies prohibiting idling school buses or personal vehicles dropping off and picking up children at school can also greatly reduce exposures around and inside the school building (Adams & Requia, 2017; Morawska et al., 2017).

Although most European students do not commute in diesel school buses, children living or attending school in urban near-road microenvironments are routinely exposed to elevated diesel emissions. In response to European Union-recommended policies designed to reduce greenhouse gas emissions, sales of diesel vehicles—which use fuel more efficiently and emit less CO_2 than gasoline-powered vehicles—increased sharply. Ireland's switch to a CO_2-based automobile taxation scheme resulted in a 28%–71% increase in new diesel car sales from 2007 to 2015. The increased health risks are especially concerning in cities such as Dublin, where the entire bus and commercial vehicle fleets are also diesel powered. Several European cities (e.g., Athens, Madrid, and Paris) are addressing these unintended consequences through proposed bans of new diesel car sales beginning in 2025. London has proposed a ban of all cars 20 years and older. Adoption of the diesel sales and older car bans of in Dublin would reduce $PM_{2.5}$ and NOx emissions by 52% and 47%, respectively and save an estimated 300 disability-adjusted life years (DALYs) and €43.8 million ($51.5 million USD) (Dey, Caulfield, & Ghosh, 2018).

For the future, widespread transitions to electric buses and commercial and private vehicle fleets can essentially eliminate exposures to diesel and other tailpipe emissions and significantly improve the health of urban populations. However, without concurrent transitions to lower emitting or renewable electricity generation systems, much of the health risks will likely shift to suburban and rural populations most affected by power plant emissions (Requia et al., 1994). Detailed life cycle analysis results comparing multiple strategies for reducing risks from U.S. light-duty transport suggested electric vehicles powered by natural gas, wind, water, or solar power would reduce health impacts by 50% or more. Comparatively, electric vehicles powered by coal-based or the current mix of U.S. electric generation would increase the monetized health impacts by 80% (Tessum, Hill, & Marshall, 2014). It is also important to note, electric conversion would not reduce health risks from brake, tire, engine and pavement wear emissions.

10 Conclusions

There is strong evidence prenatal and early life exposures to near-road traffic emissions adversely affect child health and cognitive development. These risks accumulate over the life course and can lead to adult chronic disease, disability, and premature death, especially for children who were concurrently exposed to poverty and other disadvantaged neighborhood conditions.

Continued worldwide urbanization will intensify the already urgent need to transition from car-dependent urban sprawl to more compact, greener cities with high-quality, affordable housing and well-designed public and active transport options. Such sustainable, cost-effective urban design approaches can reduce or eliminate harmful traffic-related exposures, promote physical activity, social inclusion, and psychological well-being, while concurrently reducing greenhouse gas emissions and heat island effects. In areas with strictly constrained resources, validated data-driven models such as Collective Impact can bring together community members and historically siloed public and private sector organizations and guide implementation of prioritized, mutually reinforcing interventions that can most effectively promote child health and well-being.

References

Abhijith, K. V., et al. (1994). Air pollution abatement performances of green infrastructure in open road and built-up street canyon environments—A review. *Atmospheric Environment*, *2017*(162), 71–86.

Adams, M. D., & Requia, W. J. (2017). How private vehicle use increases ambient air pollution concentrations at schools during the morning drop-off of children. *Atmospheric Environment, 165*, 264–273.

Adar, S., et al. (2015). Adopting clean fuels and technologies on school buses. Pollution and health impacts in children. *American Journal of Respiratory & Critical Care Medicine, 191*(12), 1413–1421.

Amram, O., et al. (2011). Proximity of public elementary schools to major roads in Canadian urban areas. *International Journal of Health Geographics, 10*(1), 68.

Baldauf, R. W. (2008). The influence of roadway configuration on near road air quality. Proceedings of the air and waste management association's annual conference and exhibition. *AWMA, 1*, 297–309.

Baldauf, R. (2017). Roadside vegetation design characteristics that can improve local, near-road air quality. *Transportation Research. Part D, Transport and Environment, 52*, 354–361.

Baldauf, R., et al. (1994). Influence of solid noise barriers on near-road and on-road air quality. *Atmospheric Environment, 2016*(129), 265–276.

Beck, L., & Nguyen, D. (2017). School transportation mode, by distance between home and school, United States, ConsumerStyles 2012. *Journal of Safety Research, 62*, 245–251.

Behrentz, E., et al. (2005). Relative importance of school bus-related microenvironments to children's pollutant exposure. *Journal of the Air & Waste Management Association, 55*(10), 1418–1430.

Berman, N., & Parker, R. (2002). Meta-analysis: Neither quick nor easy. *BMC Medical Research Methodology, 2*, 10.

Boehmer, T., et al. (2013). Residential proximity to major highways—United States, 2010. *MMWR Supplements, 62*(3), 46–50.

Boothe, V., Boehmer, T. K., Wendel, A. M., & Yip, F. Y. (2014). Residential traffic exposure and childhood leukemia: A systematic review and meta-analysis. *American Journal of Preventive Medicine, 46*(4), 413–422.

Brauer, M., et al. (2008). *Models of exposure for use in epidemiological studies of air pollution health impacts.* Dordrecht: Springer Netherlands.

Brugge, D., et al. (2015). Developing community-level policy and practice to reduce traffic-related air pollution exposure. *Environmental Justice, 8*(3), 95–104.

Burgio, E., Di Ciaula, A., & Capello, F. (2018). Epigenetic effects of air pollution. In *Clinical handbook of air pollution-related diseases* (pp. 231–252). .

Capizzano, J. (2005). *Many young children spend long hours in child care. Snapshots of America's families III no. 22.* .

Carlos Wallace, F., et al. (2016). Parental, in utero, and early-life exposure to benzene and the risk of childhood leukemia: A meta-analysis. *American Journal of Epidemiology, 183*(1), 1–14.

Carlson, A. E. (2018). The clean air act's blind spot: Microclimates and hotspot pollution. *UCLA Law Review, 65*(5), 1036–1088.

Cepeda, M., et al. (2017). Levels of ambient air pollution according to mode of transport: A systematic review. *The Lancet Public Health, 2*(1), e23–e34.

Che, W. W., Frey, H. C., & Lau, A. K. H. (2015). Comparison of sources of variability in school age children exposure to ambient $PM_{2.5}$. *Environmental Science & Technology, 49*(3), 1511–1520.

Chen, Z., et al. (2015). Chronic effects of air pollution on respiratory health in Southern California children: Findings from the Southern California Children's health study. *Journal of Thoracic Disease, 7*(1), 46–58.

Cox, J., et al. (2018). *Effectiveness of a portable air cleaner in removing aerosol particles in homes close to highways.* .

de Nazelle, A., Bode, O., & Orjuela, J. (2017). Comparison of air pollution exposures in active vs. passive travel modes in European cities: A quantitative review. *Environment International, 99*, 151–160.

Dey, S., Caulfield, B., & Ghosh, B. (2018). Potential health and economic benefits of banning diesel traffic in Dublin, Ireland. *Journal of Transport & Health*.

Dias, D. (2018). Spatial and temporal dynamics in air pollution exposure assessment. *International Journal of Environmental Research and Public Health, 15*(3), 558.

Dons, E., et al. (2011). Impact of time-activity patterns on personal exposure to black carbon. *Atmospheric Environment, 45*, 3594–3602.

Filippini, T., et al. (2015). A review and meta-analysis of outdoor air pollution and risk of childhood leukemia. *Journal of Environmental Science and Health, Part C: Environmental Carcinogenesis and Ecotoxicology Reviews, 33*(1), 36–66.

Fisk, W. J. (2013). Health benefits of particle filtration. *Indoor Air, 23*(5), 357–368.

Flores-Pajot, M. C., et al. (2016). Childhood autism spectrum disorders and exposure to nitrogen dioxide, and particulate matter air pollution: A review and meta-analysis. *Environmental Research (New York, NY), 151*, 763–776.

Freeman, J. G., King, M., & Pickett, W. (2016). *Health behaviour in school-aged children (HBSC) in Canada: Focus on relationships*. Ottawa, ON: P.H.A.o. Canada.

Fu, P., et al. (2019). The association between $PM_{2.5}$ exposure and neurological disorders: A systematic review and meta-analysis. *Science of the Total Environment, 655*, 1240–1248.

Giles Corti, B., et al. (2016). City planning and population health: A global challenge. *Lancet (British edition), 388*(10062), 2912–2924.

Hagler, G. S. W., et al. (2012). Field investigation of roadside vegetative and structural barrier impact on near-road ultrafine particle concentrations under a variety of wind conditions. *Science of the Total Environment, 419*, 7–15.

HEI (Health Effects Institute). (2010a). *HEI panel on the health effects of traffic-related air pollution traffic-related air pollution: A critical review of the literature on emissions, exposure, and health effects. HEI special report. Vol. 17*.

HEI (Health Effects Institute). (2010b). *HEI panel on the health effects of traffic-related air pollution. Traffic-related air pollution: A critical review of the literature on emissions, exposure, and health effects. HEI Special Report* (p. 17).

HEI (Health Effects Institute). (2010). *HEI Panel on the health effects of traffic-related air pollution: Traffic-related air pollution: A critical review of the literature on emissions, exposure, and health effects*. Boston, MA: Health Effects Institute.

Henneman, L. R. F., et al. (2017). Evaluating the effectiveness of air quality regulations: A review of accountability studies and frameworks. *Journal of the Air & Waste Management Association, 67*(2), 144–172.

Hime, N., Marks, G., & Cowie, C. (2018). A comparison of the health effects of ambient particulate matter air pollution from five emission sources. *International Journal of Environmental Research and Public Health, 15*(6), 1206.

Hoffmann, T., Hopp, L., & Rittenmeyer, L. (2010). *Evidence-based practice across the health professions introduction to evidence based practice: A practical guide for nursing* (pp. 16–37).

Hooper, L., & Kaufman, J. (2018). Ambient air pollution and clinical implications for susceptible populations. *Annals of the American Thoracic Society, 15*(Suppl. 2), S64–S68.

IARC. (2014). *Diesel and gasoline engine exhausts and some nitroarenes. IARC monographs on the evaluation of carcinogenic risks to humans. Vol. 105* (pp. 9–699).

Jáuregui, A., et al. (2015). Active commuting to school in Mexican adolescents: Evidence from the Mexican National Nutrition and Health Survey. *Journal of Physical Activity and Health, 12*(8), 1088–1095.

Johansson, K., Laflamme, L., & Hasselberg, M. (2012). Active commuting to and from school among Swedish children—A national and regional study. *European Journal of Public Health, 22*(2), 209–214.

Kabisch, N., van den Bosch, M., & Lafortezza, R. (2017). The health benefits of nature-based solutions to urbanization challenges for children and the elderly—A systematic review. *Environmental research (New York, NY), 159*, 362–373.

Karagulian, F., et al. (2015). Contributions to cities' ambient particulate matter (PM): A systematic review of local source contributions at global level. *Atmospheric Environment, 120*, 475–483.

Karner, A., Eisinger, D., & Niemeier, D. (2010). *Near-roadway air quality: Synthesizing the findings from real-world data. Vol. 44* (pp. 5334–5344).

Khreis, H., Warsow, K. M., Verlinghieri, E., Guzman, A., Pellecuer, L., & Ferreira, A. (2016). The health impacts of traffic-related exposures in urban areas: Understanding real effects, underlying driving forces and co-producing future directions. *Journal of Transport & Health, 3*(3), 249–267.

Khreis, H., Kelly, C., Tate, J., Parslow, R., Lucas, K., & Nieuwenhuijsen, M. (2017). Exposure to traffic-related air pollution and risk of development of childhood asthma: A systematic review and meta-analysis. *Environment International, 100*, 1–31.

Kingsley, S., et al. (2014). Proximity of US schools to major roadways: A nationwide assessment. *Journal of Exposure Science and Environmental Epidemiology, 24*(3), 253–259.

Kondo, M., et al. (2018). Urban green space and its impact on human health. *International Journal of Environmental Research and Public Health, 15*(3), 445.

Lam, J., et al. (2016). A systematic review and meta-analysis of multiple airborne pollutants and autism Spectrum disorder. *PLoS One, 11*(9)e0161851.

Laumbach, R. (2015). The engine on the bus Goes vroom, vroom, vroom! And the fumes on the bus go …? *American Journal of Respiratory & Critical Care Medicine, 191*(12), 1350–1352.

Lee, E., et al. (1994). Field evaluation of vegetation and noise barriers for mitigation of near-freeway air pollution under variable wind conditions. *Atmospheric Environment, 2018*(175), 92–99.

Li, X., et al. (1987). Association between ambient fine particulate matter and preterm birth or term low birth weight: An updated systematic review and meta-analysis. *Environmental Pollution, 2017*(227), 596–605.

Loo, B. P. Y., & Loo, B. P. Y. (2018). Realising car-free developments within compact cities. *Proceedings of the Institution of Civil Engineers. Municipal Engineer, 171*(1), 41–50.

Morales-Suárez-Varela, M., et al. (2017). Systematic review of the association between particulate matter exposure and autism spectrum disorders. *Environmental Research (New York, NY), 153*, 150–160.

Morawska, L., et al. (2017). Airborne particles in indoor environment of homes, schools, offices and aged care facilities: The main routes of exposure. *Environment International, 108*, 75–83.

Mueller, N., et al. (2015). Health impact assessment of active transportation: A systematic review. *Preventive Medicine, 76*, 103–114.

Münzel, T., et al. (2017). Environmental stressors and cardio-metabolic disease: Part I—Epidemiologic evidence supporting a role for noise and air pollution and effects of mitigation strategies. *European Heart Journal, 38*(8), 550–556.

Ng, M., et al. (2017). Environmental factors associated with autism spectrum disorder: A scoping review for the years 2003–2013. *Health Promotion and Chronic Disease Prevention in Canada: Research, Policy and Practice, 37*(1), 1–23.

Nieuwenhuijsen, M. (2016). Urban and transport planning, environmental exposures and health-new concepts, methods and tools to improve health in cities. *Environmental Health, 15*(S1).

Norman, H., & McDonnell, D. (2017). The NHS healthy new towns programme. *Perspectives in Public Health, 137*(1), 29–30.

Oliveira, M., et al. (2017). Polycyclic aromatic hydrocarbons in primary school environments: Levels and potential risks. *Science of the Total Environment, 575*, 1156–1167.

Perera, F. (2018). Pollution from fossil-fuel combustion is the leading environmental threat to global pediatric health and equity: Solutions exist. *International Journal of Environmental Research and Public Health, 15*(1), 16.

Perez, L., et al. (2013). Chronic burden of near-roadway traffic pollution in 10 European cities (APHEKOM network). *European Respiratory Journal, 42*(3), 594–605.

Pratt, G., et al. (2015). Traffic, air pollution, minority and socio-economic status: Addressing inequities in exposure and risk. *International Journal of Environmental Research and Public Health, 12*(5), 5355–5372.

Requia, W., et al. (1994). How clean are electric vehicles? Evidence-based review of the effects of electric mobility on air pollutants, greenhouse gas emissions and human health. *Atmospheric Environment, 2018*(185), 64–77.

Roy, B., Riley, C., Sears, L., & Rula, E. Y. (2018). Collective well-being to improve population health outcomes: An actionable conceptual model and review of the literature. *American Journal of Health Promotion, 32*(8), 1800–1813. https://doi.org/10.1177/0890117118791993.

Samet, J. M., Burke, T. A., & Goldstein, B. D. (2017). The trump administration and the environment—Heed the science. *New England Journal of Medicine, 376*(12), 1182–1188.

Schultz, E. S., Litonjua, A. A., & Melén, E. (2017). Effects of long-term exposure to traffic-related air pollution on lung function in children. *Current Allergy and Asthma Reports, 17*(6), 41.

Slezakova, K., et al. (2015). Children's indoor exposures to (ultra)fine particles in an urban area: Comparison between school and home environments. *Journal of Toxicology and Environmental Health. Part A, 78*(13–14), 886–896.

Sram, R. J. (2017). The impact of air pollution to central nervous system in children and adults. *Neuro-Endocrinology Letters, 38*(6), 389–396.

Štych, P., Šrámková, D., & Braniš, M. (2016). Assessment of exposure of elementary schools to traffic pollution by GIS methods. *Central European Journal of Public Health, 24*(2), 109–114.

Taylor, C., et al. (2018). Systemic approach for injury and violence prevention: What we can learn from the Harlem children's zone and promise neighborhoods. *Injury Prevention, 24*(Suppl 1), i32.

Tessum, C., Hill, J., & Marshall, J. (2014). Life cycle air quality impacts of conventional and alternative light-duty transportation in the United States. *Proceedings of the National Academy of Sciences of the United States of America, 111*(52), 18490–18495.

Tian, N., Xue, J., & Barzyk, T. M. (2012). Evaluating socioeconomic and racial differences in traffic-related metrics in the United States using a GIS approach. *Journal Of Exposure Science And Environmental Epidemiology, 23*, 215.

US EPA (2016a). *Recommendations for constructing roadside vegetation barriers to improve near-road air quality.* Research Triangle Park, NC: O.o.R.a. Development.

US EPA (United States Environmental Protection Agency). (2016b). *Best Practices for Reducing Near-Road Pollution Exposure at Schools.* O.o.C.s.H Protection.

US EPA (United States Environmental Protection Agency). (2018). *Estimating the environmental effects of green roofs: A case study in Kansas City, MO.*

van der Zee, S. C., et al. (2017). The impact of particle filtration on indoor air quality in a classroom near a highway. *Indoor Air, 27*(2), 291–302.

Vardoulakis, S., et al. (2018). Local action on outdoor air pollution to improve public health. *International Journal of Public Health, 63*(5), 557–565.

Villanueva, K., et al. (2016). Can the neighborhood built environment make a difference in children's development? Building the research agenda to create evidence for place-based children's policy. *Academic Pediatrics, 16*(1), 10–19.

Wang, Y., Xiong, L., & Tang, M. (2017). Toxicity of inhaled particulate matter on the central nervous system: Neuroinflammation, neuropsychological effects and neurodegenerative disease. *Journal of Applied Toxicology, 37*(6), 644–667.

Wang, L., et al. (2016). Air quality strategies on public health and health equity in Europe—A systematic review. *International Journal of Environmental Research and Public Health, 13*(12), 1196.

Whitehead, T. P., et al. (2016). Childhood leukemia and primary prevention. *Current Problems in Pediatric and Adolescent Health Care, 46*(10), 317–352.

WHO (World Health Organization). (2016). *Ambient air pollution: A global assessment of exposure and burden of disease.* .

Woods, N., Gilliland, J., & Seabrook, J. A. (2017). The influence of the built environment on adverse birth outcomes. *Journal of Neonatal-Perinatal Medicine, 10*(3), 233–248.

Yang, Y., et al. (2016). Active travel to school: Findings from the survey of US health behavior in school-aged children, 2009–2010. *Journal of School Health, 86*(6), 464–471.

Zhang, K. M., & Wexler, A. (2004). Evolution of particle number distribution near roadways—Part I: Analysis of aerosol dynamics and its implications for engine emission measurement. *Atmospheric Environment (1994), 38*(38), 6643–6653.

CHAPTER EIGHT

Health impact assessment in transport related to children

David Rojas-Rueda

Environmental and Radiological Health Sciences, Colorado State University, Fort Collins, CO, United States
Barcelona Institute for Global Health, Barcelona, Spain

Contents

Health impact assessment is becoming a common approach to promote health in non-health policies and interventions. Multinational organizations (e.g., World Health Organization) and national authorities encourage the use of health impact assessment as a tool for health in all policies. Health impact assessment has been specially used for transport policies to minimize their risks and maximize health benefits. In the case of transport and childhood, health impact assessment can assess and promote transport policies by introducing health in the decision-making process. This chapter summarizes the recent evidence related to health impact assessment in the context of transport and childhood, describing the key factors to be considered when a plan, program or policy focuses on transport and childhood. Health impact assessment steps are outlined in this chapter highlighting the aspects that need to be taken into account in the context of transport and childhood. This chapter describes health determinants (i.e., physical activity, air pollution, traffic incidents, etc.), health outcomes, qualitative and quantitative assessments, participatory processes, monitoring and evaluation approaches and policy contexts related to transport and childhood.

Transport and Children's Wellbeing
https://doi.org/10.1016/B978-0-12-814694-1.00008-7

1 Health impact assessment

Health impact assessment (HIA) is defined as a combination of procedures, methods and tools to systematically judge the potential effects of a policy, plan, program or project on the health of a population, and the distribution of those effects within the population. HIA is an approach to assess the health risks and benefits of future interventions (or policies) in non-health sectors and the distribution of such impacts within the population (Harris, Harris-Roxas, Harris, & Kemp, 2007). HIA has been proposed by multiple governments and international agencies (like the World Health Organization) (Mindell et al., 2010) as a tool to include health in all policies and develop evidence-based policymaking. In the transport sector, HIA has often been used to assess the health risks and benefits of transport infrastructure, and policies, such as the implementation of roadways, public transport networks or walking and cycling policies (de Nazelle et al., 2011; Rojas-Rueda, de Nazelle, Tainio, & Nieuwenhuijsen, 2011; Rojas-Rueda, De Nazelle, Teixidó, & Nieuwenhuijsen, 2012). Most of the available HIA are focused on adult population, due to the lack of robust quantitative evidence from populations different than adults. As a consequence, children have been widely missing in the scope of many transport-related HIA.

A HIA has six steps (1) screening, (2) scoping, (3) appraisal, (4) recommendations, (5) reporting, and (6) monitoring and evaluation (Harris et al., 2007). The screening step examines if an HIA is necessary or appropriate for a specific policy, also including an assessment of the feasibility of the HIA. The scoping step includes a description of how the HIA will be done, the type of HIA, the population, setting, temporality and health determinants. The appraisal step includes the actual assessment of the health impacts (which could be either qualitative or quantitative). In the appraisal step, the health outcomes will be identified. This step also provides an assessment of the distribution of the health impacts on vulnerable populations. The recommendations step develops a list of recommendations for stakeholders and policy-makers. In this step, the identification of relevant stakeholders and policy-makers who will receive the recommendations will also be listed. The reporting step is aimed at developing a report in a language and context for stakeholders and policy-makers. This step is essential as often the results of the assessment are not presented or translated in a language that policy-makers and stakeholders (including citizens) can always understand. Finally, the last HIA step is the monitoring and evaluation process, in this step a list of indicators (of health determinants and health outcomes) will be provided to monitor the impacts of the transport policy. These steps in the context of transport policies and childhood health are described in Table 1.

2 HIA in transport related to children

Transport policies have many implications for children's health. Transport policies often come inside of the transport or urban master plan, which has multiple possible scenarios or policies to be implemented. The understanding of the health implications of those different policies or scenarios is essential to achieve the goal of implementing the most healthy transport policies for children. Methods like health impact assessment (HIA) help to characterize and estimate the health implications of different transport policies and scenarios.

The overall framework of transport policies, health determinants, and health outcomes is presented in Fig. 1. This conceptual framework presents an example of transport policies, plans or programs, their relation with behavioral and environmental health determinants and includes a list of possible health outcomes. This conceptual framework will help to improve understanding of the relationship between transport and health, especially in the context of an HIA.

Table 1 Health impact assessment steps in the context of transport related to children and policy implications

HIA steps	Interpretation in transport and childhood context	Policy implications
Screening	– The transport policy is relevant for children, the community and the region? – Are there any previous HIAs on transport in similar contexts? – Identify stakeholders.	– Policy framework development to assess transport interventions. – Development of a database of transport policies and their assessments. – Development of a network of stakeholders in transport and childhood. – Promote participatory policy making, including children's visions.

Continued

Table 1 Health impact assessment steps in the context of transport related to children and policy implications—cont'd

HIA steps	Interpretation in transport and childhood context	Policy implications
Scoping	- Consult different stake-holders, from different sectors and backgrounds to establish the scope. - Define the transport inter-vention. Where and when will it be implemented? Which modes of transport will be affected? Will it modify the built environ-ment and/or another health determinant? Who will be affected/benefit? Are vulnerable groups implicated? - Identify available databases to define the scope (i.e., mobility and urban plans, travel and health surveys, etc.).	- Promote intersectorality and health in all policies. - Promote open data and governance transparency.
Appraisal	- Identify children's health determinants related to transport interventions. - Give special attention to physical activity, traffic incidents, air pollution, if considering performing a quantitative HIA. - Collect information on health determinants and their distribution with respect to children. - Identify the availability and assess the weight of the evidence related to important children's health determinants and their health outcomes.	- Promote open data and governance transparency; with special attention to collecting and reporting health, environmental, and socioeconomic data related to children. - Promote public health research on children. - Promote participatory policymaking.

Table 1 Health impact assessment steps in the context of transport related to children and policy implications—cont'd

HIA steps	Interpretation in transport and childhood context	Policy implications
	- Consult stakeholders and citizens (including children) to identify preferences in terms of expected outcomes (qualitative, quantitative, economic assessment). - If quantitative, follow a risk assessment approach and if required/possible estimate the economic assessment and compare with the transport intervention costs.	
Recommendations	- Develop recommendations for each transport policy, and stakeholder. - Consider the recommendations also to the different phases of development and implementation of transport policies.	- Provide an open list of the policy plans and description. - Provide a list of the stakeholders, policy-makers and authorities related to the transport policy.
Reporting	- Prepare a stakeholder report and dissemination activities with special attention on transport policy makers and stakeholders. - Design report and dissemination activities with a language that stakeholders can understand and in the context of transport policies.	- Develop mechanisms to integrate HIA recommendations in transport policy frameworks. - Promote participatory policy making.
Monitoring and evaluation	- Develop and collect indicators on children's health determinants, health outcomes and policy processes for monitoring and evaluation.	- Promote open data and governance transparency; with special attention to reporting children's health, environmental, and socioeconomic data).

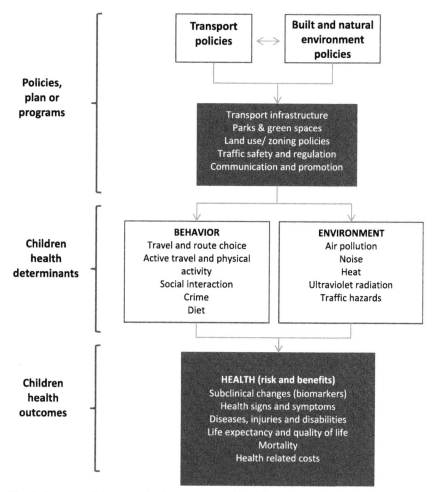

Fig. 1 Conceptual framework of transport and health.

An example of how different transport interventions should be conceptualized concerning the impacts on children health determinants is presented in Fig. 2. When an HIA is considered, the health determinants of different transport scenarios could be available, for this case it is essential to consider how these scenarios could affect multiple health determinants, for example, if those scenarios will increase or reduce traffic safety, or the air quality. We need to consider children not only as a population living in the surroundings of the intervention, but also as travelers themselves. As well, it is important to understand that in some cases the same health determinants could act as risks for certain scenarios or as benefits for other scenarios.

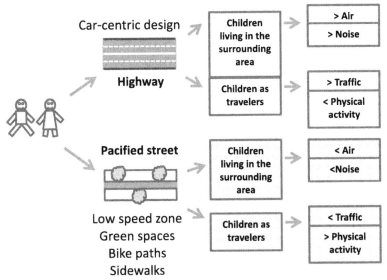

Fig. 2 Example of impacts in health determinants of two different transport interventions on children living in the surrounding area and children as travelers (">" relates to an increase; "<" relates to a decrease).

3 Transport and childhood: Health determinants and health outcomes

Transport has been related to multiple health determinants (de Nazelle et al., 2011). The scoping step of the HIA aims to identify children health determinants related to transport (see Table 1). Most of the health determinants related to transport that have been widely described relate to adults. The main health determinants in adults reported in scientific reviews include: traffic incidents, air pollution, noise, physical activity, social interaction, ultraviolet radiation exposure, diet, heat and cold exposure, among others (de Nazelle et al., 2011; Mueller et al., 2015). In the case of children many of those health determinants have also been reported (air pollution, noise, diet, extreme temperature, physical activity, etc.), although only in a few studies compared with other populations. The precautionary principle suggests that even in the absence of evidence, if the risk to health appears to be plausible, interventions to reduce the risks should be implemented. Applying this precautionary principle to the case of transport and childhood, when transport interventions could imply any risk for children, even with a lack of epidemiological evidence, the health impact assessment should consider these risks and generate recommendations to avoid or attenuate such risks.

The health determinants of transport can be classified based on the population affected. The two main groups are the travelers and the population living in the surrounding areas (see Fig. 2) (Rojas-Rueda, de Nazelle, Teixidó, & Nieuwenhuijsen, 2013). The health determinants that should be considered for travelers during the trip are: increasing physical activity, air pollution inhalation, traffic incidents (crashes and falls), traffic noise exposure, green space exposure, ultraviolet radiation exposure, exposure to heat and cold, increasing social interaction, exposure to crime and finally a change in diet associated with increasing physical activity.

All these health determinants could have multiple health outcomes that should be included in the HIA (appraisal step). The health outcomes can be classified as subclinical changes, signs and symptoms, diseases, injuries, and disabilities, quality of life, life expectancy, and mortality. Table 2 shows

Table 2 Example of health outcomes for children related with transport heath determinants

Health determinant	Health outcomes
Physical activity	Life expectancy, quality of life, cardiovascular and metabolic risk factors, respiratory diseases, neurodevelopment, bone/joint/muscle diseases, among others.
Air pollution	Respiratory diseases, cardiovascular and metabolic risk factors, neurodevelopment, birth outcomes, mortality, among others.
Traffic noise	Cardiovascular risk factors, sleep disturbance and annoyance, among others.
Green spaces	Mental health, stress, life expectancy, quality of life, cardiovascular risk factors, among others.
Ultraviolet radiation	Skin cancer, bone diseases, immunological disorders, among others.
Heat	Dehydration and electrolyte disorders, respiratory diseases, cardiovascular and cerebrovascular diseases, heat stroke, among others.
Cold	Infectious diseases, respiratory diseases, among others.
Social interaction	Mental health, infectious diseases, life expectancy, quality of life, among others.
Crime	Injuries, fatalities, mental disorders, and quality of life, among others.
Diet	Metabolic and digestive disorders, cardiovascular risk factors, life expectancy and quality of life, among others.

some examples of health outcomes for children related with transport heath determinants.

On the other hand, transport also modifies health determinants that affect the children living in the surrounding area (non-travelers), such as air and noise pollution, and the improvement of the built environment and public spaces. The most common health determinants related to transport policies that affect children living in the surrounding area (non-travelers) are the reduction of air pollution, reduction of traffic noise, increasing of green spaces (and possible reduction of the heat island effect), increasing social capital, reduction of crime, reduction of traffic incidents. The health outcomes related to these general population health determinants are similar to those mentioned for travelers.

4 Qualitative HIA in transport related to children

As mentioned above there exist two main types of HIA, qualitative and quantitative. Qualitative HIA is the most common approach to transport. Qualitative HIAs could provide enough information to create recommendations for policy-makers. Qualitative HIA in transport can be applied when sufficient resources (personal and monetary) and/or time is not available. Qualitative HIA is also commonly described as a rapid HIA and should include all the HIA steps (see Table 1). Qualitative HIA can also include a participatory approach (see below) where the stakeholders and citizens can take part in multiple HIA steps.

An example of a qualitative HIA on transport and childhood is shown in Fig. 3 where a cascade of health determinants and health outcomes related to transport intervention are presented. Based on this description and following the HIA steps the qualitative approach will also generate specific indicators (health determinants or health outcome indicators) to monitor and evaluate the health impacts of transport policies. An example of health determinant indicators could be the annual average concentration of air pollution, daily traffic noise levels, the number of active travel trips per day/year, the duration or distance of trips, the amount of green spaces, the number of traffic crashes or falls, or the percentage of modal shift, among others. Examples of health outcome indicators are incidence or prevalence of cardiovascular risk factors (such as cholesterol, blood pressure), asthma, etc., the number of hospital admission for asthma attacks, hypertensive emergencies, etc., the percentage of children reporting annoyance or sleep disturbance, the traffic injuries and fatalities, among others.

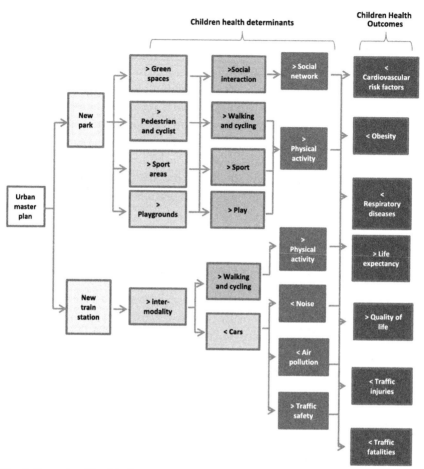

Fig. 3 Example of health determinants and health outcomes reported in a qualitative HIA in transport related to children (">" relates to an increase; "<" relates to a decrease).

HIA recommendations derived from qualitative HIA could be very similar to those obtained from a quantitative HIA (Harris et al., 2007). General recommendations for policymakers will be based on the city context and characteristics (Rojas-Rueda, de Nazelle, Andersen, & Braun, 2016). For example, an HIA comparing six European cities found that the risk of traffic fatalities between active transport modes was higher in cities like Warsaw or Prague (Rojas-Rueda et al., 2016). As such, recommendations were focused more on improving traffic safety. On another hand in the same study other cities like Basel or Copenhagen showed a greater benefit to promote more active transport modes and the recommendations were focused on promoting active modes especially in those populations that are not currently active transport users.

Recommendation for other audiences including citizens, health practitioners, and researchers can also be generated by qualitative HIAs on transport (Nieuwenhuijsen, Khreis, & Verlinghieri, 2017). The importance of including recommendations to audiences beyond policy-makers will improve the acceptability and performance of transport policies. Examples of recommendations for citizens are the integration of active transport into their daily activities, the reduction of the use of cars, increased intermodality, increased healthy behaviors such as physical activity, and support to sustainable development through active transport activities, among others. For health practitioners, some general recommendations are promoting health in all policies, stimulating intersectoriality, providing health data related to health determinants and outcomes of transport interventions, and increasing the use and knowledge of HIA, among others. Finally, HIA recommendations for researchers are increased evidence on transport and health, developing studies on different vulnerable subgroups (children and children with disability) and settings (low income and deprived neighborhoods), include health equity, sustainability, and governance in research, promoting intersectoriality and health in all policies, including responsible research and innovative approaches in transport research, among others. An example of the HIA steps in a decision tree is presented in Fig. 4, where different points should be considered, such as health determinants, vulnerable groups, long or short-term impacts, type of recommendations among others. Considering these questions when an HIA in transport related to children is on the table will help to guide and develop a more comprehensive HIA process.

5 Quantitative HIA in transport related to children

Quantitative HIA refers to those HIAs that include a quantitative assessment of health determinants and health outcomes. A quantitative assessment is a useful complement of an HIA, and should be performed when the possibility exists to measure different health determinants and estimate the health outcomes of different policies. The quantitative HIA is dependent on the availability of resources (monetary and personnel), time to conduct measurements and/or quantitative estimates (quantitative exposure assessment and quantitative risk assessment). It is important to highlight

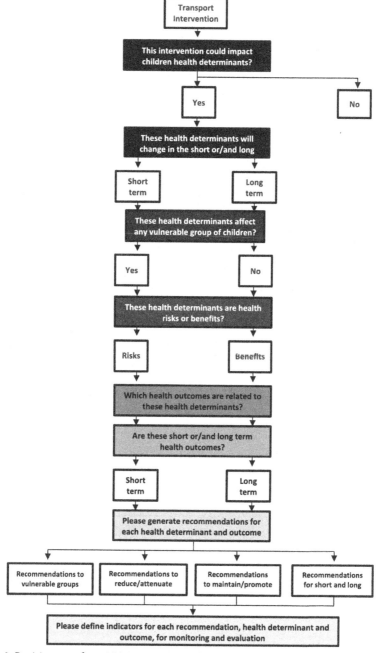

Fig. 4 Decision tree for a HIA in transport related to children.

that *a quantitative HIA is not a necessary step*, and does not necessarily provide more information (or produce different conclusions) than those already provided by a qualitative HIA. However, a quantitative HIA could increase the value, acceptability, support of, and precision of HIA conclusions. The final decision to execute a quantitative HIA in transport related to children will change in each situation and should be based on the assessor's expertise, resources, data availability and stakeholder necessities and expectations.

In transport and childhood, few quantitative HIAs have been performed, mostly due to the lack of epidemiological evidence to quantify health impacts in children. The main quantitative health determinants and outcomes included in transport and childhood HIAs are presented in Table 3. The most common health determinants included in a quantitative HIA for children travelers are physical activity, traffic incidents and the inhalation of air pollution. Other health determinants as presented in Table 2 are lees used due to the lack of robustness in the available evidence. Quantitative HIA can also be performed to quantify the health outcomes in children living in the surrounding areas (non-travelers). In a quantitative HIA, the most common health determinant included for assessing the impact of transport policies on children living in the surrounding areas (non-travelers) is air pollution.

A quantitative approach to estimating the health risks and benefits is known as comparative risk assessment as proposed by the World Health Organization (Ezzati, Lopez, Rodgers, & Murray, 2004). Sometimes the comparative risk assessment approach has also been incorrectly labeled "impact modeling," but this can produce confusion between conventional epidemiological analysis and other impact assessments available. The comparative risk assessment approach proposed by the World Health Organization includes four steps, (a) hazard identification, (b) dose-response assessment, (c) exposure assessment, and (d) risk characterization. Hazard identification consists of the identification of health risk/benefits (health determinants) associated with transport (physical activity, air pollution, and traffic incidents) and their possible health outcomes. Dose-response assessment refers to the identification of the available risk estimates (e.g., relative risk, odds ratios) from epidemiological studies describing the relationship between the magnitude of a dose and a specific biological response (health outcome). The dose-response functions are particular to each exposure and outcome. The third step of a comparative risk assessment is exposure assessment. Exposure assessment focuses on the design and conduct of

Table 3 Quantitative dose-response functions for multiple health determinants and health outcomes used in transport related to children HIA

Health determinant	Health outcome	Population	Unit of exposure	Unit of outcome	DRF	Reference
Physical activity	Systolic blood pressure	6–10 years	Active/no active	mmHg	−1.25 (−2.47 to −0.02)	Cesa et al. (2014)
Physical activity	Diastolic blood pressure	6–10 years	Active/no active	mmHg	−1.34 (−2.57 to −0.11)	Cesa et al. (2014)
Physical activity	Triglycerides	6–10 years	Active/no active	mmol/L	−0.09 (−0.14 to −0.04)	Cesa et al. (2014)
Physical activity	Body mass index	6–10 years	Active/no active	kg/m²	−0.25 (−0.36 to −0,14)	Larouche, Saunders, Faulkner, Colley, and Tremblay (2014)
Physical activity	Cognitive functions (Math, English, mood, academic performance, etc.)	6–10 years	Active/no active	Multiple	Benefit	Biddle and Asare (2011)
Physical activity	Depression	11–18 years	Vigorous PA/no active	Multiple	Benefit	Biddle and Asare (2011)
Physical activity	Anxiety	3–18 years	Vigorous PA/no active	Multiple	Benefit	Biddle and Asare (2011)
PM10	Asthma	5–19 years	mg/m³	Cases	1028 (10006–1051)	HRAPIE (2013)
PM10	Bronchitis	6–12 years	mg/m³	Cases	108 (1–119)	HRAPIE (2013)

DRF: dose-response function; PM10: particulate matter less than 10μm of diameter; PA: physical activity.

measurements of health determinants related to transport (e.g., measurement of physical activity, air pollution, and traffic incidents).

An example is the measurement of walking or cycling using questionnaires asking the number of trips, the trip duration or distance. Physical activity can also be measured using pedometers, accelerometers and geographical positioning systems (GPS). This more direct measurement can result in a more precise exposure assessment than questionnaires. Another example is the inhalation of air pollution during walking or cycling. Exposure assessment could be done measuring the concentration of air pollution (individual measurement) during walking or cycling combined with physical activity measurements using an accelerometer combined with heart rate or breath rate monitoring. Finally, the last step of a comparative risk assessment is risk characterization. When all previous steps are combined in an analysis that results in a relative risk of the specific exposure levels (of health determinants) in the population studied (using the dose-response functions) and the estimation of the attributable fraction, to estimate the proportion of disease that can be attributed to a particular level of exposure.

Quantitative risk assessment can also be translated into monetary terms, adding an economic assessment (Mueller et al., 2015). The economic assessment translates the health outcomes into health costs associated with each case of disease prevented or increased (morbidity) with the travel policy, through the estimation of a health care cost related with diagnosis or treatment (direct health cost) and the cost related with work absences due to disease incapacity (indirect health costs). The societal costs related to mortality can also be included in this economic assessment, estimating the economic cost related to a premature death based on the value of a statistical life or the value of each year of life lost. Many stakeholders especially policy-makers are interested to know the economic cost of their policies and include an economic assessment could facilitate benefit-cost analysis. So, this economic assessment is a valuable step to increase the applicability and usefulness of quantitative HIA results.

It is important to highlight that not all health determinants related to transport policies (in travelers and the general population) can be quantified in an HIA. For this reason, quantitative HIA should be considered as a partial part of the assessment. The main reasons that do not allow quantification of health determinants in a quantitative risk assessment are usually the lack of robust and quantitative epidemiological evidence and the lack of data in the study population. Many of the health determinants related to transport such as social capital or ultraviolet radiation and their health outcomes have not been described in quantitative dose-response functions in children, so this makes it difficult to include them in a quantitative risk assessment. As well, many of the epidemiological studies have been performed only in high-income countries, where cities have a more homogeneous pattern of exposures. This can make it difficult to use these studies in other countries with different urban contexts.

An example of a recent quantitative HIA of transport interventions in children performed in Barcelona, Spain, estimated the health impacts of increasing walking to school in those children who lived less than 1 km from their school. This study focused on the car-trip substitution by walking-trips, taking into account three health determinants, namely: physical activity, air pollution exposure during the trip, and traffic incidents (see Fig. 5). The study found many health benefits related to increased walking, few risks due to the increased exposure to air pollution during walking to school and a reduction of minor transport injuries due to the substitution of motorizing trips to walking trips in those children (see Table 4).

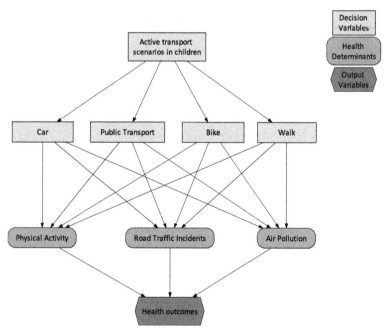

Fig. 5 Quantitative HIA conceptual framework of walking to school promotion in Barcelona.

Table 4 Estimated results of car substitution by walk to school in 37,000 children in Barcelona

Risk factor	Health outcome	Population	Cases/year
Physical activity	Pediatric hypertension	6–10 years	−500
	Hypertriglyceridemia	6–10 years	−378
	Overweight	6–10 years	−605
	Obesity	6–10 years	−363
PM10	Asthma	6–10 years	0.006
	Bronchitis	6–10 years	0.03
Traffic injuries	Minor injury	6–10 years	−100
	Major injury	6–10 years	0.71
	Traffic fatality	6–10 years	0.23

PM10: particulate matter less than 10 μm of diameter.

6 Monitoring and evaluation for HIA in transport related to children

One main product of any HIA (qualitative or quantitative) is providing a list of indicators for monitoring and evaluation. Monitoring and evaluation are the sixth step of HIA and focus on providing indicators to follow the health determinants and health outcomes included in the HIA (Harris et al., 2007). This step is important for stakeholders and policy-makers, as these indicators will help them to identify if the HIA estimations were correct and if there is any deviation of the health determinants or/and outcomes from the main estimation. If any deviation occurs, the monitoring process will help to prevent future unexpected changes. There are two different types of indicators: indicators of health determinants, and indicators of health outcomes. Health determinant indicators are those factors that summarize the level of exposure. For example, a health determinant is physical activity, and its indicator could be the amount of walking that can be expressed at the population (number of children walking to school) or individual level (minutes walked per day). Another example for health determinants is air pollution, and its indicator could be the concentration of a specific air pollutant in the city/neighborhood/street, expressed as the annual average concentration of particulate matter (or any other pollutant) in the city/neighborhood/street for example.

Health indicators are measurement units of the levels of health outcomes related to health indicators. For example, considering physical activity (health determinant), the incidence (new cases) or prevalence (current cases) of obesity in the studied population at a certain time could be considered.

Another example is for air pollution (health determinant), specifically for particulate matter less than $10 \mu m$ in diameter, a health indicator could be the incidence or prevalence of asthma in the study population. As can be noted, health determinant indicators (number of pedestrians or the level of air pollution) sometimes could be an easier and more effective indicator to follow because the change of health determinants (physical activity or air pollution) will happen before the health outcomes (obesity or asthma). This mainly applies to those health outcomes where the natural history of the disease is long (years). In other words, this mainly applies to those diseases, such as obesity, where it takes many years to see any development of the disease. For other diseases or symptoms with a shorter time development, such as asthmatic crises, the change in the health indicators (emergency room visits for asthma) could appear in only a few hours after the change in the health determinant (hourly concentrations of air pollutants). Health indicators could be a mix of a short, medium and long-term impacts, and the choose of those indicators will be determined by the type health determinants involved and policy context.

In summary, health determinant and health outcome indicators for transport policies should be provided for any HIA. These indicators will help stakeholders and policy-makers to prevent any unexpected changes and detect the benefits of their policy. The indicators should also be presented with a list of possible information sources in the study population where stakeholders could identify these indicators. This will reduce the effort to collect (and invest valuable resources) some indicators that possibly already exist in other data sources. An example of those data sources where health determinants and outcome indicators can be identified include travel surveys (e.g., the number of children walking to school or trip duration); air quality surveillance systems (e.g. hourly/daily/annual concentration of particulate matter or gases); health surveys (e.g., incidence or prevalence of multiple diseases or levels of physical activity); emergency room visit reports (e.g., specific health conditions visits per day/month); traffic safety reports (e.g., number of traffic injuries or fatalities in pedestrians or cyclists), among others.

7 Participatory process for HIA in transport related to children

Participatory approaches in HIA can increase the utility, applicability, and acceptance for stakeholders (Nieuwenhuijsen et al., 2017). The HIA (qualitative and quantitative) should always include a participatory approach,

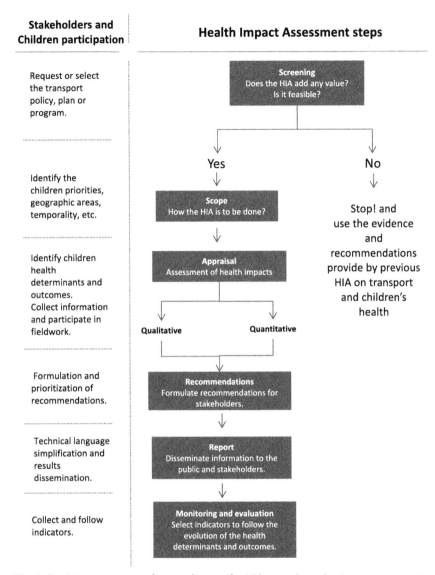

| Stakeholders and Children participation | Health Impact Assessment steps |

Request or select the transport policy, plan or program.

Screening
Does the HIA add any value?
Is it feasible?

Yes   No

Identify the children priorities, geographic areas, temporality, etc.

Scope
How the HIA is to be done?

Stop! and use the evidence and recommendations provide by previous HIA on transport and children's health

Identify children health determinants and outcomes. Collect information and participate in fieldwork.

Appraisal
Assessment of health impacts

Qualitative   Quantitative

Formulation and prioritization of recommendations.

Recommendations
Formulate recommendations for stakeholders.

Technical language simplification and results dissemination.

Report
Disseminate information to the public and stakeholders.

Collect and follow indicators.

Monitoring and evaluation
Select indicators to follow the evolution of the health determinants and outcomes.

Fig. 6 Participatory approach according to the HIA steps in active transport context.

especially (but not exclusively) in the screening step (see Fig. 6). As mentioned above, the screening step provides the justification (relevance and utility) of an HIA for a specific transport policy or intervention. Not all transport policies or interventions will require an HIA. Only those that could affect the majority of the population, or a vulnerable population, or have particular societal relevance should be considered for an HIA. The local stakeholders or policy-makers should then perform this screening process. Examples of this participatory approach in the screening process could be depth interviews with relevant stakeholders or stakeholder workshops. These participatory approaches will provide invaluable information regarding the appropriateness of an HIA for a specific policy or intervention. This participatory approach will also provide information on the different scenarios to be included in the HIA, and the necessity to perform a quantitative or economic assessment in the HIA. The participatory approach in the screening step will define whether a HIA is necessary and if so, what type should be performed.

The participatory approach can also be implemented in the rest of the HIA as described in Fig. 6. In the scoping step of an HIA, the participatory approach could help to identify the main population of interest, if there is a vulnerable group of children to consider, the temporality and geographical boundaries of the HIA. In the appraisal step, stakeholder involvement through participatory approaches will help to identify possible health determinants and health outcomes that could have been missed in the first assessment. It is important to highlight that the local stakeholders, citizens (including children), and policy-makers are the experts in the local context. In the scoping step, citizens and stakeholders can also help in the collection of data, for example, they can contribute to recruiting other citizens to answer travel or health surveys, they can also be part of data collection performing measurements (air quality, traffic counts, etc.). In the recommendation step, participatory approaches could help to identify priorities for the local population (including children), and context that could help to develop more effective recommendations and identify the stakeholders or authorities that should receive the recommendations. In the reporting step, a participatory approach can also improve the language and content of the report; this is especially useful for increasing the efficacy and utility of the HIA resulting in increased understanding between stakeholders, citizens and children on the issues related to transport policies and empowering the population. Finally, participatory approaches could be used in the sixth step of an HIA, monitoring, and evaluation. In this last step, participatory approaches can help to design the most valuable and practical indicators.

8 Conclusions and future for HIA in transport related to children

The HIA in transport related to children is a valuable tool to include children in the context of transport policies, to promote a healthy environment for children and health in all policies. Under the current situation, qualitative HIA should be considered as a complete tool to help policy-makers, stakeholders and researchers to introduce and translate health evidence and perspective in to transport policies and interventions. Introducing a participatory perspective in the HIA process will increase the acceptability and usefulness of the HIA results and transport policies. In the future, the epidemiological studies will produce more and better quantitative evidence to produce quantitative HIA for transport and childhood.

References

Biddle, S. J., & Asare, M. (2011). Physical activity and mental health in children and adolescents: A review of reviews. *British Journal of Sports Medicine, 45*(11), 886–895. https://doi.org/10.1136/bjsports-2011-090185.

Cesa, C. C., Sbruzzi, G., Ribeiro, R. A., Barbiero, S. M., de Oliveira Petkowicz, R., Eibel, B., et al. (2014). Physical activity and cardiovascular risk factors in children: meta-analysis of randomized clinical trials. *Preventive Medicine, 69*, 54–62. https://doi.org/10.1016/j.ypmed.2014.08.014.

de Nazelle, A., Nieuwenhuijsen, M. J., Antó, J. M., Brauer, M., Briggs, D., Braun-Fahrlander, C., et al. (2011). Improving health through policies that promote active travel: a review of evidence to support integrated health impact assessment. *Environment International (Internet), 37*(4), 766–777. Available from: http://www.ncbi.nlm.nih.gov/pubmed/21419493 [cited 22 August 2014].

Ezzati, M., Lopez, A. D., Rodgers, A., & Murray, C. J. (2004). *Comparative quantification of health risks global and regional burden of disease. Comparative quantification of health risks global and regional burden of disease.*

Harris, P., Harris-Roxas, B., Harris, E., & Kemp, L. (2007). *Health impact assessment: A practical guide. Liverpool.*

Health Risks of Air Pollution in Europe—HRAPIE Project. (2013). WHO Regional Office for Europe UN City, Marmorvej 51 DK-2100 Copenhagen Ø, Denmark. World Health Organization. http://www.euro.who.int/__data/assets/pdf_file/0006/238956/Health_risks_air_pollution_HRAPIE_project.pdf.

Larouche, R., Saunders, T. J., Faulkner, G., Colley, R., & Tremblay, M. (2014). Associations between active school transport and physical activity, body composition, and cardiovascular fitness: A systematic review of 68 studies. *Journal of Physical Activity & Health, 11*(1), 206–227. https://doi.org/10.1123/jpah.2011-0345.

Mindell, J., Biddulph, J., Taylor, L., Lock, K., Boaz, A., Joffe, M., et al. (2010). Improving the use of evidence in health impact assessment. *Bulletin of the World Health Organization, 88*(7), 543–550. https://doi.org/10.2471/BLT.09.068510.

Mueller, N., Rojas-Rueda, D., Cole-Hunter, T., de Nazelle, A., Dons, E., Gerike, R., et al. (2015). Health impact assessment of active transportation: A systematic review. *Preventive Medicine (Baltim) (Internet), 76*, 103–114. https://doi.org/10.1016/j.ypmed.2015.04.010.

Nieuwenhuijsen, M. J., Khreis, H., & Verlinghieri, E. (2017). Participatory quantitative health impact assessment of urban and transport planning in cities: A review and research needs. *Environment International (Internet), 103*, 61–72. https://doi.org/10.1016/j.envint.2017.03.022.

Rojas-Rueda, D., de Nazelle, A., Andersen, Z. J., & Braun, C. (2016). Health impacts of active transportation in Europe. *PLoS ONE, 423*, 1–14.

Rojas-Rueda, D., de Nazelle, A., Tainio, M., & Nieuwenhuijsen, M. J. (2011). The health risks and benefits of cycling in urban environments compared with car use: Health impact assessment study. *BMJ, 343*, d4521.

Rojas-Rueda, D., De Nazelle, A., Teixidó, O., & Nieuwenhuijsen, M. J. (2012). Replacing car trips by increasing bike and public transport in the greater Barcelona metropolitan area: A health impact assessment study. *Environment International, 49*, 100–109. https://doi.org/10.1016/j.envint.2012.08.009.

Rojas-Rueda, D., de Nazelle, A., Teixidó, O., & Nieuwenhuijsen, M. J. (2013). Health impact assessment of increasing public transport and cycling use in Barcelona: a morbidity and burden of disease approach. *Preventive Medicine (Baltim) (Internet), 57*(5), 573–579. Available from: http://www.ncbi.nlm.nih.gov/pubmed/23938465 [cited 17 December 2014].

Further reading

Gascon, M., Rojas-Rueda, D., Torrico, S., Torrico, F., Manaca, M., Plasencia, A., & Nieuwenhuijsen, M. J. (2016). Urban policies and health in developing countries: The case of Maputo (Mozambique) and Cochabamba (Bolivia). *The Open Public Health Journal, 1*(2), 24–31.

Rutter, H., Cavill, N., Racioppi, F., Dinsdale, H., Oja, P., & Kahlmeier, S. (2013). Economic impact of reduced mortality due to increased cycling. *American Journal of Preventive Medicine (Internet), 44*(1), 89–92. Available from: http://www.ncbi.nlm.nih.gov/pubmed/23253656 [cited 17 December 2014].

PART THREE

Solutions for transport and children's wellbeing

CHAPTER NINE

Policy and culture

Ben Shaw

Department of Sociology, University of Surrey, Guildford, United Kingdom

Contents

1 Introduction

This chapter is about how policy and policymakers can respond to the challenges current transport patterns and infrastructures pose to children and their health and wellbeing. Policymaking is about making interventions in systems to drive and deliver desirable change. Policymakers need to be clear about the problems they wish to address, the outcomes that are desired and the means by which these will be delivered. Earlier chapters have articulated some of the problems transport brings generally, and for children in particular, and the pathways and mechanisms by which these impacts occur. However, transport policy often tends to overlook the needs of children or forget about the need and desire of children to be able do more than just get to and from school safely. Asking the question, 'what would a child-centred transport policy look like?' results in a very different set of policy responses to the ones we typically see.

With these points in mind, different framings of children's needs, built environment and transport that are particularly relevant for development of transport policy are presented below. A range of policy interventions that have been made are then given. These range from enabling children to survive in current transport systems, to more forward-looking approaches intended to enable children to flourish in the built environment. A chapter of this length can't be comprehensive or prescriptive in the policies it covers. Policy must always be developed and implemented with careful consideration of its context. However, the aim is to illustrate both some general principles that are needed to address the needs of children and their well-being in policy and give specific examples of where this has been done.

2 Significant change happens over time: Policy can shape the future we want

While many of the problems associated with development of modern transport systems can seem like they have always been with us, over longer timescales, very significant changes can be seen. My mother, born in the late 1930s, tells a story about how in her village one of her 7 year-old school classmates would leave school to go home by herself and on the way singlehandedly collect a herd of cows from the fields and take them along the public road back to the farm for milking. My father brought up in post-war London, and still living there, can point to residential streets which didn't have a single car parked in them when he was a child growing up in the late 1940s, but now have cars parked nose-to-tail. As a child I remember in the early 1980s making a day trip from London to Boulogne with two other 12 year-old friends unaccompanied by adults. The trip involved a pre-dawn cycle ride across London, catching a train to Dover, a ferry to Boulogne, where we were surprised to find that in France they drive on the other side of the road to the UK, before fairly rapidly retracing our steps.

Not too much should be read into these personal anecdotes, although similar more formal accounts of the changes in childhood mobility and freedoms are recorded in the literature (e.g., Gaster (1991) for the period from 1915 to 1976). Pooley, Turnbull, and Adams (2005) also acknowledge the changes in car use and independence on the journey to school, but also highlight there are also continuities over time.

These examples, from research and anecdote are intended to illustrate the scale of change we have seen in transport and children's lives, freedoms and mobility over only a few generations. Ask any adult and they will be able to give a story of their first or early experiences of traveling independently. Ask most children today and they will say that they would like more freedom to be able to get about, or play outside, by themselves and with their friends. Policymakers need to respond to this.

Car ownership and use has grown enormously. Total annual vehicle mileage in the UK grew tenfold between 1949 and 2017 to a total of 327 billion vehicle kilometers (Department for Transport, 2018). This increase has been accompanied by changes in lifestyles, behaviors and infrastructures, both positive and negative. However, for children, as discussed in Chapters 6–8 on physical health impacts (speed, emissions, and health impact assessment) these changes have largely been negative.

The issues associated with traffic have long preoccupied the public and policymakers. 'Too many motor vehicles, using too few suitable roads give Britain the highest traffic density in the world, and an acute economic and social problem', is the opening line of the 1959 Fabian pamphlet, *What shall we do about the Roads?* (Rodgers, 1959). Shortly after, the landmark *Buchanan Report* was published in the UK (Ministry of Transport, 1963). This is perhaps prehistory for the purposes of current policy debates, now that we have the Internet, smart phones, are developing autonomous vehicles, and smart cities and other related infrastructures. However, the report's foreword is perceptive and vivid, and especially so given its formal status as a government publication, in its statement of the coming challenges posed by traffic:

> *It is impossible to spend any time on the study of the future of traffic in towns … without being at once appalled at the magnitude of the emergency coming upon us …*
> *We are nourishing at immense cost a monster of great potential destructiveness. And yet we love him dearly. Regarded in its collective aspect as 'the traffic problem' the motor car is clearly a menace which can spoil our civilisation. But translated into terms of the particular vehicle that stands in our garage… we regard it as one of most treasured possessions or dearest ambitions, an immense convenience, an expander of the dimensions of life, an instrument of emancipation, a symbol of the modern age. Paragraph 55, Report of the Steering Group (Ministry of Transport, 1963).*

Over 50 years later the tensions inherent in this statement are still far from resolved. In spite of the ever growing evidence of negative impacts, we have continued to nourish the monster. The practical benefits of cars, whether real or perceived, and cultural significance and aspirational importance of car ownership holds sway over much of our society, culture, government and policy. This extends to children, with toy cars being an important part of play for many children. It is not just a matter of introducing policies to drive change to respond to these problems. The cultural and political factors at play need to be explored and worked within.

In the UK at the national level there have been periodic attempts to deal with the problems of traffic and transport more widely. These have oscillated between 'predict and provide', i.e., predicting demand for traffic and providing the infrastructure needed to accommodate it, and more integrated approaches based on the realization that building our way out of the problem isn't going to work. *Roads for Prosperity* (Department of Transport, 1989) and *A new deal for transport – better for everyone* (Department of the Environment Transport and the Regions, 1998) illustrating these differing approaches well. It is the latter government white paper that led to the enabling powers for congestion charging being introduced in London, one of the most significant policy interventions seen in transport in the UK.

At the time of writing, we seem to moving in the UK into another phase of building roads to meet demand with investment in road building being announced, aimed at 'delivering the largest ever strategic roads investment package' (Treasury, 2018). This is in spite of the long-standing realization that:

We consider it should be a basic objective of a sustainable transport policy: To improve the quality of life, particularly in towns and cities, by reducing the dominance of cars and lorries and providing alternative means of access. (paragraph 4.32 (Royal Commission on Environmental Pollution, 1995).

Of course children don't drive so how are their transport needs met through a car-dominated transport system. It can be argued that children have benefitted from the automobile society. Fotel and Thomsen (2003) have gone as far as to argue, not without some apparent qualms and nuances, that far from seeing themselves as powerless victims of the hegemony of the car and of unequally distributed access to mobility, children can see themselves as both suffering and benefiting from automobility (e.g., traveling by car). Therefore, rather than being 'othered', they should be treated as partaking members of the automobile society. This may be the case, but the shift from children being active and autonomous in their transport habits has implications. These go beyond just the ability to be independently mobile or not and concerns the well-being, health and physical, mental and social development of children.

3 The decline of children's independent mobility

A frustration at government claims that roads were safer than they had ever been lead Hillman, Adams, and Whitelegg (1990) to publish *One False*

Move… A study of Children's Independent Mobility. On one hand, on the basis of casualty rates the then government claimed the roads were safer than ever. On the other, it highlighted that roads were extremely dangerous in public information campaigns such as 'One False Move and You're Dead'. These two positions seemed incompatible and Hillman et al. sought to explain and challenge this.

Comparing data from 1971 and 1990 Hillman et al. noted that while child road traffic fatalities had halved, the volume of traffic had nearly doubled. The study, conducted in England, then measured children's independent mobility (CIM), that is, the ability of children to get about their local neighborhood unaccompanied by adults. The data gathered revealed a huge drop in children's independent mobility between 1971 and 1990. The headline finding was that in 1971, 80% of seven and eight year-old children surveyed were able to go to school without adult supervision. By 1990 this had fallen to 9%. The explanation for the drop in road casualties was not that roads had become safer, but that children had been removed from the danger posed by the increasing volume and speed of traffic on the roads. As such, casualty statistics alone are not a very good measure of the safety of roads. Essentially, children had lost their freedom for the advantage of vehicle users.

The approach of Hillman et al. was revisited in Shaw et al. (2013, 2015) with the surveys being repeated in England and Germany and then extended to 14 other countries. This work revealed widespread restrictions on children's independent mobility in many of the countries studied and, where longitudinal data exists, drops over time in the level of independent mobility, as shown in Tables 1 and 2 (Björklid & Gummesson, 2013).

Does the drop in children's ability to get around and play independently in their local neighborhood matter? Are there issues policymakers need to respond to? Or is the drop in independent mobility just a reflection that we now live in different times with pros and cons associated both with past and current behaviors?

Hillman et al. (1990) and subsequent authors, including in other chapters of this book, note that a reduction in independent mobility has consequences for children's health and their social, physical and mental development. Stone, Faulkner, Mitra, and Buliung (2014) summarize the range of impacts identified by other workers succinctly, highlighting that children's independent mobility is critical to healthy development, cognitive development, building relationships which impact, social capital and allowing children to engage and form bonds with one another and the natural environment. Children on foot are children who are not in cars so there

Table 1 Percentage of primary school children (7- to 11-year-olds) granted independent mobility, England and Germany, 1971–2010

	England 1971	England 1990	England 2010	Germany 1990	Germany 2010
Cross main roads alone (children's response)	72	51	55	75	61
Cross main roads alone (parents' response)	–	22	36	70	66
Travel to places other than school alone	63–94	37	7–33[a]	70	27–85[a]
Travel home from school alone	86	35	25	91	76
Go out alone after dark	–	2	2	5	7
Cycle to go places (children's response)[b] as % of bicycle owners	–	–	60	–	76
Use buses alone (children's response)	48	15	12	31	31
Use buses alone (parents' response)	–	7	5	29	25

[a]A range is given due to the way the question was asked in 2010, with some parents reporting that their children 'traveled alone' and others reporting that it 'varies'.
[b]A meaningful comparison for the changes between 1990 and 2010 in the license to cycle in England and Germany is not possible due to changes to the way the question was asked between surveys
Source: Hillman, M., Adams, J. A., & Whitelegg, J. (1990). *One false move… A study of children's independent mobility.* London: PSI Publishing; Shaw, B., Watson, B., Frauendienst, B., Redecker, A., Jones, T., & Hillman, M., 2013. *Children's independent mobility: A comparative study in England and Germany (1971–2010).* London: Policy Studies Institute.

Table 2 Percentage of parents granting 7- to 9-year-old children license to go to different activities, Sweden

Is the child allowed to walk unaccompanied by an adult to...	1981 N = 1485	2009 N = 558	2012 N = 577
School	94	46	46
Friends	98	63	67
Play areas	98	63	61
Green spaces	96	58	67
Sports grounds	72	21	24
Shops	82	23	24
Library	60	15	13
Indoor swimming, pool/bathing place	36	7	7
Cinema	34	2	3

Source: Table 27, Björklid, P., & Gummesson, M. (2013). *Children's independent mobility in Sweden.* Borlänge: Swedish Transport Administration.

are environmental benefits as well. Waygood, Friman, Olsson, and Taniguchi (2017) expand on these points.

Additionally, being independently mobile is something children desire and value and have a right to, as highlighted by Freeman and Tranter (2011), Shaw et al. (2015), and Waygood et al., 2017. On the basis of children's rights, independent mobility is something of intrinsic value to children which they should be able to enjoy. A safe outside environment is a prerequisite for this which should be provided. This right is expressed in the United Nations' *Convention on the Rights of the Child* (United Nations, 1989). The Convention enshrines the right of children to rest and leisure and to engage in play and recreational activities appropriate to the age of the child, and requires that states should promote this right and encourage provision to satisfy it (Article 31), and also that every child has the right to a standard of living that is good enough to meet their physical, social and mental needs (Article 27).

With these benefits in mind, children's independent mobility is not just a measure of the age that children are able to get about by themselves, but also a measure of road safety and a proxy for many other desirable attributes of the built environment, transport and well-being.

So if children have a right to a safe environment and both desire and benefit from being independently mobile, what policy interventions are needed to deliver this? We first need to ask what is accounting for the drop in children being able to get about by themselves. The age at which a particular child is allowed to get about independently results from of the interaction of factors related to the child, their parents, the external environment they live in and the cultural attitudes that affect attitudes and behavior (Shaw et al., 2015) (see also Chapter 5 on the Socio-Ecological Model). However, danger from traffic is consistently cited by parents as a barrier to the granting of independent mobility (Shaw et al., 2015, citing Hillman et al., 1990; Johansson, 2006; Karsten, 2002; Lynch, 1977; Shaw et al., 2013; Zwerts, Allaert, Janssens, Wets, & Witlox, 2010). Other factors include (see also Chapters 11 and 12):

- living in urban areas, with higher population density and connectivity/ accessibility of destinations having a positive effect,
- gender, with boys often, but not always, being more independently mobile than girls,
- proximity of desired destinations,
- parental behavior and attitudes,
- socio-economic status and household car ownership,

- 'stranger danger' (more usefully framed in some sources as 'social fear'), and, the strength of community relations,
- social pressures and conventions of 'good' parenting,
- changed parental lifestyles and preferences for car use which has resulted in greater distances to access local services.

Given the growth in traffic it is not surprising that it is cited as the major concern of parents in relation to letting their children out. As well as the threat from the increase in speed and volume in traffic (see Chapter 6), the growth in car use and dependency has also had knock-on effects on the availability and accessibility of local amenities, the urban form and wider spatial development. The places children may want to go are now often more widely distributed and hard or even impossible to access independently. This is a reality that has developed over the last century of development that has accommodated the needs of drivers and vehicles. We can't turn back the clock and remove motor traffic from our lives or rebuild and reconfigure our cities overnight. However, we can develop and implement policies that place a higher priority on the needs of children in transport and related areas and address the impacts other chapters in this book have already so clearly articulated. With the right policies and the cultural and political support to implement them change can occur, and surprisingly quickly.

4 Developing a transport policy that takes children into account

The title of this chapter is Policy and Culture. Addressing the impact of transport on children requires major policy interventions but also significant cultural change in societal attitudes to mobility and the value of children's lives. Traditional road safety campaigns, in countries such as the UK, intended to mitigate the effects of dangerous road environments by educating children how to navigate them safely are not enough. The *source* of the danger needs to be addressed. Below some examples of approaches that do this are described before conclusions about the steps needed to reduce the impact of current impacts on children and their wellbeing.

4.1 Policy must address unsafe environments for children

There is an apparent high-level societal acceptance of the dangerous environments in which most children are expected to live and develop and a tolerance of the danger and harms posed by the speed, volume, emissions and noise of traffic (as detailed in Chapters 6–8). It is surprising that there is not a more widespread call to resolve this issue, especially so, given the high levels of concern parents have reported about the risks of injury to their children from traffic. To a great extent, children's rights to a safe environment seem to be considered less justified than allowing drivers to travel at speeds which are clearly not safe for others who are entitled to use the road. Hüttenmoser (1995) captures it well, 'the disadvantages to these children over many years cannot be justified by the insatiable drive of adults to use their living surroundings for their own mobility and to disrespect the vital needs of children'.

4.2 Vision zero and the safe system approach

Johnston (2010) attributes the apparent social or cultural acceptance of death and injury on the roads to the historical focus on driver error as the predominant cause of crashes, combined with a normalizing drip-feed of daily crashes, deaths and injuries, the relatively low risk of being a casualty on any particular trip and the perception of personal control over safety when driving. He sums this up as, 'While personal safety is valued, community safety is not'. This needs to be changed if transport's impact on children's lives and wellbeing is to be reduced.

The Vision Zero concept, first adopted in Sweden in 1997,[a] is one approach that seeks to achieve this change. The Vision Zero Network contrasts the difference in approach with traditional road safety (Fig. 1). Vision Zero rejects the traditional view that death and serious injury on the road are an inevitable, albeit tragic, result of traffic and modern mobility. Instead, the long-term aim is to have zero fatalities or serious injuries resulting from road traffic crashes. Vision Zero provides a conceptual approach to road safety; a toolkit for road design and enforcement approaches; and redefines road safety as a public health issue, that is road crashes are a preventable health threat (Kim, Muennig, & Rosen, 2017).

Conceptually, Vision Zero adopts a systems approach. Drivers, and more widely all road users, are part of a system created by many actors—traffic engineers, planners, vehicle designers and manufacturers, public health professionals and others. Everyone in this system has responsibility for eliminating crashes, and where they are unavoidable, ensuring they are survivable

---

[a]See (Belin, Tillgren, & Vedung, 2012) for details of the development and implementation of the Vision Zero approach in Sweden.

Fig. 1 A new vision for safety—traditional road safety vs. vision zero. *Reproduced with permission from https://visionzeronetwork.org/about/what-is-vision-zero/.*

without life-changing injuries. The ideal road system is one in which the human tolerance for mechanical forces is not exceeded (an idea proposed by William Haddon Jr., as noted in (Kim et al., 2017). This results in the setting of maximum speeds for vehicles and road users in different situations above which these tolerable forces are exceeded. As an example, 70 km/h for frontal impact in a car, or less than 30 km/h for an unprotected pedestrian. Road design is used to limit speed and where speed cannot be limited road users should be separated (Kim et al., 2017).

Vison Zero has been built on and implemented in countries and states apart from Sweden under different names. The World Resources Institute and Global Road Safety Facility have reviewed these schemes that share 'a common set of principles that focus on creating a mobility system that is forgiving of human error' under the general term of the Safe System approach (Welle et al., 2018), with Fig. 2 summarizing the key components of the approaches. Countries that have adopted a Safe Systems approach have 'both the lowest rate of fatalities per 100,000 inhabitants and the fastest change in fatality levels' (Welle et al., 2018).

This chapter is not the place to review the details of the approaches adopted in each setting. Different authors highlight that the approach is principles-driven rather than a design manual and that strategies should be specific to local context and informed by local knowledge (Welle et al., 2018). However, it can be seen that eliminating crashes and serious injury requires considerably broader action than road safety campaigns just focused on changing children's behaviors. It extends to integrated actions across different areas of policymaking and sectors of the economy.

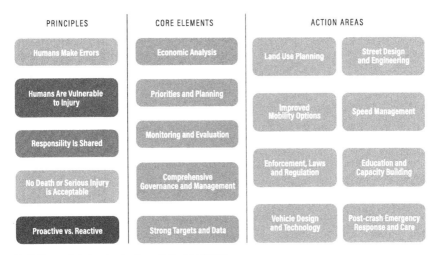

PRINCIPLES   CORE ELEMENTS   ACTION AREAS

Humans Make Errors   Economic Analysis   Land Use Planning   Street Design and Engineering

Humans Are Vulnerable to Injury   Priorities and Planning   Improved Mobility Options   Speed Management

Responsibility Is Shared   Monitoring and Evaluation

No Death or Serious Injury is Acceptable   Comprehensive Governance and Management   Enforcement, Laws and Regulation   Education and Capacity Building

Proactive vs. Reactive   Strong Targets and Data   Vehicle Design and Technology   Post-crash Emergency Response and Care

Note: Principles are multicolored, core elements are in grey, and action areas are in orange.

Fig. 2 Principles, core elements, and action areas of the safe systems approach. *Reproduced with permission from Welle, B., Sharpin, A. B., Adriazola-Steil, C., Bhatt, A., Alveano, S., Obelheiro, M., et al. (2018). Sustainable & safe: A vision and guidance for zero road deaths. Washington: World Resources Institute.*

In relation to children it is clear that Vision Zero and Safe Systems design principles have significant implications. If followed they would, and apparently do, result in a very different road systems especially at the local and neighborhood level. Children behave unpredictably, their judgment can be poor, and their size means they are easily hidden from drivers by vehicles, trees, and street furniture. The road system needs to be built around these innate characteristics of children so that entirely predictable behaviors do not result in their death or serious injury.

4.3 Building a child friendly city

It is striking that children, their needs and vulnerabilities don't feature more prominently in transport or wider policy and planning. As found in a previous review of policy interventions conducted in relation to children's independent mobility (Shaw et al., 2015) there are some good examples of cities and neighborhoods that have tried to address the negative impacts of motor transport on children with both Rotterdam and Vancouver being regularly cited. Beyond this the wider picture is less positive. For example, the National Planning Policy Framework (Ministry of Housing, Communities, & Local Government, 2019), which sets out the Government's planning policies for England and how they should be applied, refers to children only once in the context of providing sufficient homes for different groups including 'families with children'. The section on 'Promoting healthy and safe communities', an obvious place to highlight the specific needs of children in the planning and development process doesn't differentiate the needs of children from wider community needs. Given children (0–17 year-olds) form over a fifth of England's population[b] the lack of any national planning guidance on meeting their needs is a startling omission.

While there are worthwhile initiatives being undertaken where they exist they tend to be smaller in scale, hard to find and be site-specific rather than trying to address the problems across a wider urban area. They also tend to be focused on action to mitigate the impact of traffic, rather than transforming the environments children live and play in to be safe (Shaw et al., 2015).

Against this Rotterdam has an international reputation for its work to become a child friendly city. However, this has only been acquired relatively recently. The catalyst to the change was Rotterdam being found in 2006 to be the least child-friendly of 500 Dutch municipalities (Steketee, Mak, Tierolf, & Flikwert, 2006). The exodus of families posed a threat to the city, both socially and economically. The 'Child Friendly Rotterdam' program (City of Rotterdam, 2010) set to turn this around and aimed to: enhance the city as a residential location, keep families in the city, strengthen the economy, and improve the quality of life for children from birth to 18 years-old.

Working in partnership across city services, district councils, housing corporations and developers the approach was based on four 'Building blocks for a Child Friendly Rotterdam':

1. Child-friendly housing: conditions for family-friendly homes and apartments were formulated covering internal space requirements, access to outside space, internal storage and a room for each child.

2. Public space: with space requirements for outdoor play areas, and play space immediately outside a home's front door—including a 3–5 m wide pavement on at least one side (and ideally the sunny side) of the street.

3. Local facilities: such as shops, sport clubs and extended schools: i.e. a primary or a secondary school offering additional activity programs.

[b]Children (0–17 year-olds) form 21.3% of England population based on the Office for National Statistics interactive population pyramids tool available at: https://www.ons.gov.uk/peoplepopulationand community/populationandmigration/populationestimates/bulletins/annualmidyearpopulationestimates/ mid2017#main-points.

4. Safe traffic routes: a network of child-friendly traffic routes to encourage children to explore the city and engage in city life; strategic location of public amenities; speed reduction and no-through traffic measures.

Putting these building blocks into practice has resulted in real change. Rotterdam's own monitoring against indicators of the percentage of private housing, traffic and playground safety, youth facilities, environmental factors, housing, social cohesion and image, found that 8 out of the 11 areas where the child friendly approach was piloted were performing better. Child friendly neighborhoods are now 'an intrinsic part of city policy' and 'on everyone's agenda' (Wapperom, 2016). In 2014, the Academy of Urbanism considered Rotterdam's progress against its child friendly city objectives and concluded that the 'realisation of these objectives is already evident in projects completed and underway throughout the city centre' (Academy of Urbanism, 2014). It also awarded Rotterdam its 2015 Best City Award intended to recognize the best, most enduring or most improved urban environments (Academy of Urbanism (Producer), 2014).

Tim Gill, one of the leading advocates and independent researchers on childhood, has reviewed Rotterdam's progress in 2018 as part of his recent Churchill Fellowship. He found the Rotterdam's focus on being family-friendly has had a measurable impact and helped turn the city around economically, environmentally and culturally. Some criticisms have been raised about the approach 'gentrifying' Rotterdam and attracting affluent families at the expense of poorer ones. This aside, the aim of making Rotterdam more child friendly has been a success. Gill notes factors of success including the scale of the City's investment, its clarity of focus, the development of new planning norms (highlighted above), the support of other relevant policy areas such as transport and mobility, a shift away from a focus on playgrounds to better public space for children everywhere, the important role of non-profit organizations and the involvement of children in developing proposals (Gill, 2018).

4.4 Understanding children's needs

All these factors of success in Rotterdam are important, but the last two points (local facilities and safe traffic routes) are worth expanding upon. Debates and policy on transport and planning for children often seems to only be about playgrounds and the journey to school. However, children play everywhere, not just in formally allocated play areas. Going to school is an important part of a child's life and the journey to school should be one that is safe for the child. However, it is not the only journey a child makes and people are often surprised by the high proportion of time children are not at school once weekends and holidays are taken into account. In the UK only just over half the days in the year are spent at school. Children's needs, desires and actual use of space should not be assumed by adults involved in planning public space or the adults who care for them.

These issues were explored in a recent study with two classes of 9–10 year old children from an inner-city London school (Bornat & Shaw, 2019). The work experimented with a range of methods for engaging children in discussion about their lives and local neighborhood including surveys, whole class discussions, small focus groups, walking tours, photography, and map-making over a whole school term. It explored the nature of their lived experience in the local community but also sought to link these experiences to specific spatial features of the neighborhood and the attributes that enable children's play and mobility. The full detail of the work cannot be reported here but a few points are worth highlighting. The participating children reported playing everywhere but the proximity and range of spaces to play was hugely important to them. The children's ability to play and get about was significantly affected by adult behaviors, with the children being at the bottom of the hierarchy on claims to use of public space. The children also provided important insights into the use of space in their local neighborhood which would not have been obvious to the professionals involved in designing and refurbishing public space. Children's voices therefore need to be brought into public debate about these issues more effectively (see Chapter 13).

4.4.1 Small changes can catalyze bigger changes

Rotterdam is a compelling example of the change that can be made by a major program of investment and policy development. It was catalyzed by a real problem the city faced. The lack of political will or scale of challenge can often be a major barrier to progress. But small, and importantly in times of austerity in many countries, cheap initiatives can make or catalyze much bigger differences. Examples include The Playing Out approach developed in Bristol, UK; the London Borough of Hackney's School Streets; and programs of 'filtered permeability' and 'mini-Hollands' which restrict motorized through traffic and encourage active travel modes currently being implemented in various areas of London.

'Playing Out' is an initiative that was started by two neighbors in Bristol, UK in 2009. It is a simple model in which residents close their street to traffic for a few hours thereby creating a safe place for children to play. Playing Out give four steps to organizing a session: 1. Talk to your neighbors and set a date, 2. Get permission and support, 3. Tell everybody and get ready, 4. Play Out! (Playing Out, 2018). From starting in one street in 2009, five other local streets trialed it the following year. Media coverage created enquires from other communities on how to set up Playing Out sessions and a Community Interest Company was set up to provide this advice. Local Authorities, led by the example of Bristol City Council, created policies that enabled easier temporary road closures and national government funded the network to create a national Playing Out movement which, by 2018, had over 660 streets in 67 local authority areas running Playing Out sessions.[c]

In 2012 Hackney became the first borough in London to introduce play streets and there are now over 40 in the borough. An early evaluation by Hackney Play in 2014, found that it had 'enabled over 8,100 child-hours of physical activity, on par with 14 additional classes of weekly term-time PE lessons' and 'revealed a strong consensus amongst organisers about the perceived benefits of the scheme.... especially in terms of social interaction, but also as a way to expand children's freedom and choice in their play.' (Gill, 2015). An evaluation of the Street Play Project of Play England found Playing Out initiatives increased the time children spent outdoors and their activity levels and have significant community building benefits (Play England, 2016).

As such Playing Out is an important initiative. However, the challenge is how play streets and spaces can be reclaimed more permanently rather than as a temporary respite from the dominance of cars and other adult uses. Playing Out is an easy, low cost and low risk approach that demonstrates the possibilities of making spaces child friendly and is a stepping stone in building more ambitious responses to the problem of communities and children's lives dominated by traffic (see also Chapter 10).

Hackney School Streets is another initiative that challenges existing conventions around traffic and children. Again it is a simple and easy to implement concept—roads outside schools are temporarily closed to traffic at the beginning and end of the school day with only pedestrians and cyclists being allowed to use them. The aim is to tackle congestion, improve air quality and make it easier and safer to walk and cycle to school. Exemptions can be

[c]This synopsis of the development of Playing Out is based on material from the Playing Out website https://playingout.net (accessed 1/2/2019).

granted for local residents but vehicles entering the school street without permission during its operation receive a fine. Five pilots have been run with one street being made permanent on basis of the beneficial impact and the other four being evaluated[d] and more are being planned.

The filtered permeability approach being implemented in various London Boroughs including Camden, Hackney and Waltham Forest and across London to create a network of cycling 'Quietways' is based on the Dutch 'street hierarchy' approach. The street hierarchy is based on the principles of 'homogeneity' of traffic in terms of speed, direction and mass and 'functionality of roads into access, distributor or through roads all with associated and appropriate speed limits (Schepers, Twisk, Fishman, Fyhri, & Jensen, 2017) The London approach varies in scale of implementation but seeks to cut 'rat-running' through residential or other destination areas by introducing single or larger numbers of strategically-placed road closures, restricted turns and/or one way streets and road treatments. The more ambitious 'mini-Hollands' are a program of schemes in outer-London Borough intended to create pedestrian and cycle friendly environments through multiple interventions. Though more expensive then single road closures and while politically controversial in implementation, even initial evaluations suggest a 'measureable and early impact on active travel behavior and perceptions of the local cycling environment', (Aldred, Croft, & Goodman, 2018).

5 Concluding comments: Children's needs must be given much greater prominence in transport and planning policy

The initiatives and approaches discussed above are intended to be illustrative of the range of options that have been used to tame the impact of transport on children's health and well-being. They have been chosen to illustrate the importance of viewing the issue from a systems perspective (Vision Zero); the impact of political leadership, strategic and cross-cutting, city-wide policy combined with practical action (Rotterdam); and the ability of small actions at the local level to drive change (Playing Out, School Streets, filtered permeability). The idea that children should be involved in shaping their local environments is a further critical observation.

[d]Based on information from Hackney Council's website available at https://hackney.gov.uk/article/4379/School-streets (accessed 1/2/2019).

It is neither a comprehensive nor systematic review of policies and is biased to the experience of northern Europe. With further space available other initiatives could have been included. For example, the work of the City of Toronto to develop its planning guidelines: 'Growing Up: Planning for Children in New Vertical Communities'. This directs how new development can better function for larger households at three scales: the unit, the building and the neighborhood and is supported by case studies at each of these levels.[e] Vancouver's living first policies and planning guidelines from the late 1980s and 1990s have similar objectives (see Shaw et al., 2015 for summary details).

An alternative approach is the Play Sufficiency Duty and Assessment process in Wales, UK which places a duty on local authorities to assess the sufficiency of play opportunities for children and develop action plans to ensure this. Play is an intrinsic and fundamental part of childhood. A focus on assessing whether children have sufficient opportunities for play frames policy action on delivering a key need of children. Wrexham Borough Council has lead the way with its approach to implementing this Duty.[f] Its response seeks to embed play in policies and programs across the council to help create environments where children can freely play and which encourages communities to be more play friendly.

There are also organizations, networks and foundations promoting the concept and practice of the child friendly city, all of which could have been drawn upon for this chapter. The interested reader is urged to explore them further. These include the Child Friendly City initiative of UNICEF,[g] the European Child in the City network[h] and the Urban95 initiative of the Bernard van Leer Foundation, which asks the question 'If you could experience a city from 95 cm – the height of a 3-year-old – what would you change?'[i]

There is no one-size-fits-all template for developing and implementing policies that will address the impact of transport on children's health and well-being. However, there are solutions and approaches that can make a fundamental difference to children and wider society and these need to be implemented more widely. Children's lives and daily activity tends to be focused on their local neighborhoods, especially for younger children,

---

[e]See   https://www.toronto.ca/city-government/planning-development/planning-studies-initiatives/ growing-up-planning-for-children-in-new-vertical-communities/.

[f]See http://www.wrexham.gov.uk/english/leisure_tourism/play/play_sufficiency.htm.

[g]See https://childfriendlycities.org/.

[h]See https://www.childinthecity.org/.

[i]See https://bernardvanleer.org/solutions/urban95/.

and this is where change must occur. Local authorities and communities have shown that change is possible. The spread of Playing Out in the UK is also suggestive of a latent demand for action. However, support is required from higher levels of policymaking, whether regional, national or international levels to support and scale local initiatives to address the current impacts of transport on children. These approaches are not about being anti-car or seeking to halt economic and social progress to return to some imaginary pre-motorized idyll. It is about a not unreasonable desire to rebalance the focus of our streets, cities, towns and villages so they accommodate the need and desire of children to grow and develop in healthy, safe environments. These are as much about cultural and conceptual framings as technical policy. The changes they require will in cases be considered controversial and often opposed very vocally by some vested, and often minority, interests but policymakers and politicians must remember to give due weight to the little heard voice and interests of children in the debate.

References

Academy of Urbanism. (2014). *Assessments, urbanism awards, Rotterdam.* Retrieved from: https://www.academyofurbanism.org.uk/rotterdam/.

Academy of Urbanism (Producer). (2014). Urbanism awards: Rotterdam takes top prize. Retrieved from: http://www.academyofurbanism.org.uk/urbanism-awards-rotterdam-takes-top-prize/.

Aldred, R., Croft, J., & Goodman, A. (2018). Impacts of an active travel intervention with a cycling focus in a suburban context: One-year findings from an evaluation of London's in-progress mini-Hollands programme. *Transportation Research Part A: Policy and Practice.* https://doi.org/10.1016/j.tra.2018.05.018. (Corrected proof, in press).

Belin, M. -Å., Tillgren, P., & Vedung, E. (2012). Vision zero—A road safety policy innovation. *International Journal of Injury Control and Safety Promotion, 19*(2), 171–179. https://doi.org/10.1080/17457300.2011.635213.

Björklid, P., & Gummesson, M. (2013). *Children's independent mobility in Sweden.* Borlänge: Swedish Transport Administration.

Bornat, D., & Shaw, B. (2019). *Neighbourhood design: Working with children towards a child friendly city.* London: ZCD Architects. Retrieved from: https://www.zcdarchitects.co.uk/estate-regeneration-and-childrens-needs.

City of Rotterdam. (2010). *Rotterdam, city with a future: How to build a Child Friendly City.* Rotterdam: Youth, Education and Society Department, City of Rotterdam.

Department for Transport. (2018). *Road traffic (vehicle miles) by vehicle type in Great Britain, annual from 1949, table TRA0101.* Retrieved from: https://www.gov.uk/government/statistical-data-sets/road-traffic-statistics-tra#traffic-volume-in-miles-tra01.

Department of the Environment Transport and the Regions. (1998). *A new deal for transport—Better for everyone: The Government's white paper on the future of transport.* London: The Stationery Office Ltd.

Department of Transport. (1989). *Roads for prosperity.* London: HMSO.

Fotel, T., & Thomsen, T. U. (2003). The surveillance of children's mobility. *Surveillance & Society, 1*(4), 535–554.

Freeman, C., & Tranter, P. (2011). *Children and their urban environment.* London: Routledge. https://doi.org/10.4324/9781849775359.

Gaster, S. (1991). Urban children's access to their neighborhood: Changes over three generations. *Environment and Behavior*, *23*(1), 70–85. https://doi.org/10.1177/0013916591231004.

Gill, T. (2015). *Hackney play street evaluation report*. London: Hackney Play Association and Hackney Council.

Gill, T. (2018). *How a focus on child-friendliness revived one city's fortunes.* Retrieved from: https://rethinkingchildhood.com/2018/04/26/rotterdam-child-friendly-city-urban-planning-gentrification/#more-6722.

Hillman, M., Adams, J. A., & Whitelegg, J. (1990). *One false move… A study of children's independent mobility*. London: PSI Publishing.

Hüttenmoser, M. (1995). Children and their living surroundings: Empirical investigations into the significance of living surroundings for the everyday life and development of children. *Children's Environments*, *12*(4), 403–413.

Johansson, M. (2006). Environment and parental factors as determinants of mode for children's leisure travel. *Journal of Environmental Psychology*, *26*(2), 156–169.

Johnston, I. (2010). Beyond "best practice" road safety thinking and systems management—A case for culture change research. *Safety Science*, *48*(9), 1175–1181. https://doi.org/10.1016/j.ssci.2009.12.003.

Karsten, L. (2002). Mapping Childhood in Amsterdam: The spatial and social construction of children's domains in the city. *Tijdschrift voor Economische en Sociale Geografie/Journal of Economic & Social Geography*, *93*(3), 231–241.

Kim, E., Muennig, P., & Rosen, Z. (2017). Vision zero: A toolkit for road safety in the modern era. *Injury Epidemiology*, *4*(1), 1. https://doi.org/10.1186/s40621-016-0098-z.

Lynch, K. (1977). *Growing up in cities*. Cambridge, MA: The MIT Press.

Ministry of Housing, Communities & Local Government. (2019). *National Planning Policy Framework*. London: HMSO.

Ministry of Transport. (1963). *Traffic in towns: A study of the long term problems of traffic in urban areas*. London: HMSO.

Play England. (2016). *Why temporary street closures for play make sense for public health*. London: Play England.

Playing Out. (2018). *How to organise playing out session on your street—A step by step manual.* Retrieved from: https://playingout.net/wp-content/uploads/2018/04/Playing-Out-manual-2018-smaller.pdf.

Pooley, C. G., Turnbull, J., & Adams, M. (2005). The journey to school in Britain since the 1940s: Continuity and change. *Area*, *37*(1), 43–53. https://doi.org/10.1111/j.1475-4762.2005.00605.x.

Rodgers, W. T. (1959). *What shall we do about the roads?* London: Fabian Society.

Royal Commission on Environmental Pollution. (1995). *Transport and the environment: Eighteenth report*. Oxford; New York: Oxford University Press.

Schepers, P., Twisk, D., Fishman, E., Fyhri, A., & Jensen, A. (2017). The Dutch road to a high level of cycling safety. *Safety Science*, *92*, 264–273. https://doi.org/10.1016/j.ssci.2015.06.005.

Shaw, B., Bicket, M., Elliott, B., Fagan-Watson, B., Mocca, E., & Hillman, M. (2015). *Children's independent mobility: An international comparison and recommendations for action*. London: Policy Studies Institute.

Shaw, B., Watson, B., Frauendienst, B., Redecker, A., Jones, T., & Hillman, M. (2013). *Children's independent mobility: A comparative study in England and Germany* (pp. 1971–2010). London: Policy Studies Institute.

Steketee, M., Mak, J., Tierolf, B. A., & Flikwert, M. (2006). *Kinderrechten als basis voor lokaal jeugdbeleid. Kinderen in Tel Databoek 2006 [Children's rights as the basis for local youth policy. Dutch kids Count 2006]*. Retrieved from: http://www.kinderenintel.nl/docs/Excerpt_KinderenInTel2006.pdf.

Stone, M. R., Faulkner, G. E. J., Mitra, R., & Buliung, R. N. (2014). The freedom to explore: Examining the influence of independent mobility on weekday, weekend and after-school physical activity behaviour in children living in urban and inner-suburban neighbourhoods of varying socioeconomic status. *International Journal of Behavioral Nutrition and Physical Activity, 11*(1), 5. https://doi.org/10.1186/1479-5868-11-5.

Treasury, H. M. (2018). *Budget 2018.* London: HMSO.

United Nations. (1989). *Convention on the rights of the child. General assembly resolution 44/25 of 20 November 1989.* Geneva: United Nations.

Wapperom, R. (2016). *Rotterdam: City with a future. Presentation to a vision for 2026—Hackney the child friendly city. 15th November 2016, Hackney London.* .

Waygood, E. O. D., Friman, M., Olsson, L. E., & Taniguchi, A. (2017). *Transport and child well-being: An integrative review.* Travel Behaviour and Society. https://doi.org/10.1016/j.tbs.2017.04.005.

Welle, B., Sharpin, A. B., Adriazola-Steil, C., Bhatt, A., Alveano, S., Obelheiro, M., et al. (2018). *Sustainable & safe: A vision and guidance for zero road deaths.* Washington: World Resources Institute.

Zwerts, E., Allaert, G., Janssens, D., Wets, G., & Witlox, F. (2010). How children view their travel behaviour: A case study from Flanders (Belgium). *Journal of Transport Geography, 18*(6), 702–710.

CHAPTER TEN

Making the economic case for active school travel

Noreen C. McDonald[a], W. Mathew Palmer[b] and Ruth L. Steiner[c]

[a]Department of City & Regional Planning, University of North Carolina at Chapel Hill, Chapel Hill, NC, United States
[b]Durham Public Schools, Durham, NC, United States
[c]Department of Urban and Regional Planning, University of Florida, Gainesville, FL, United States

Contents

1 Introduction

Discussions of active school travel emphasize health benefits accruing from increased physical activity as well as social benefits from children's increased knowledge of their communities. Less attention has been paid to economic benefits of designing communities where children can safely access school by foot and bicycle. We make an argument for considering the economic case for the promotion of active school travel. The economic costs and benefits we consider are wide-ranging. For example, we provide information on health benefits from physical activity and injury reduction but also consider how investments in active school travel can reduce out of pocket and time costs to school districts and families from transporting children to school. We also highlight the complexity of the system where decisions on school siting, school enrollment, and bus policies impact potential benefits of investments in active travel infrastructure.

The key finding is that investing in non-motorized infrastructure has significant economic benefits accruing from reductions in child pedestrian injury and school transportation costs, but that these links have not been well-researched and deserve more attention (Gordon, 2018). This chapter provides brief background on active school travel (AST) and then summarizes health, injury prevention, school transportation, and school siting impacts of encouraging youth to walk and bike to school.

2 Background: Prevalence of active school travel and health linkages

School travel patterns vary greatly across countries. Active travel is least common in the United States (12.7%) but higher in Australia (22.5% in urban areas), Canada (~25%), the United Kingdom (53% for 5–10 year olds), and especially the Netherlands (58% for children under 11) (Department for Transport, 2017; Gray et al., 2014; McDonald, Brown, Marchetti, & Pedroso, 2011; Merom, Tudor-Locke, Bauman, & Rissel, 2006; Wegman & Aarts, 2006). Outside northern Europe, walking is substantially more common than biking. Rates of walking and bicycling to school have decreased over time in North American countries and regions (Buliung, Mitra, & Faulkner, 2009; McDonald et al., 2011). For example, 48% of US elementary and middle school students walked to school in 1969, but the share dropped to 13% in 2009 (McDonald, 2007; McDonald et al., 2011).

Efforts to increase walking and biking to school in the 21st century have been based in a desire to increase physical activity levels among youth. School travel represents an everyday opportunity to increase activity if active modes substitute for motorized modes (Tudor-Locke, Ainsworth, & Popkin, 2001). The desire to increase physical activity links to sharp increases in overweight and obesity among American youth (Centers for Disease Control and Prevention, National Center for Health Statistics, 2017). Obese children and adolescents face a range of health impacts, including sleep-associated breathing disorders, including increased resistance to airflow, heavy snoring, reduction in airflow (hypopnea) and cessation of breathing (apnea), and asthma (Lobstein, Baur, & Uauy, 2004). Childhood obesity is associated with type 2, the so-called "adult onset" diabetes, menstrual problems and early menarche in girls and delayed maturation in boys and obese children are at also at higher risk for hypertension and high cholesterol (Cooper et al., 2006; Lobstein et al., 2004). Children and adolescents who are obese are at greater risk for being stigmatized, bullied and other adverse impacts to self-esteem that result in higher rates of depression (Erickson, Robinson, Haydel, & Killen, 2000; Lobstein et al., 2004). Children who are obese are also more likely be obese as adults and the childhood health concerns are likely to continue into adulthood where they can reduce quality of life and life span and increase health care costs (Lobstein et al., 2004; Must et al., 1999).

Reducing the rate of childhood obesity is a function of changing the energy balance of children by decreasing food intake and increasing the level of physical activity, including active school travel. Active school travel interventions have the potential to increase the daily physical activity levels of children. They can be classified to include health promotion (e.g., walk to school days), community enforcement/safety initiatives (e.g., walking school bus and bicycle trains), and modifications of infrastructure (e.g., building of sidewalk or bicycle paths). As originally passed in 2005, the Safe Routes to School (SRTS) program in the United States required expenditures for both infrastructure and non-infrastructure programs, such as education, enforcement and encouragement. Research on active school travel has found that programs such as SRTS are associated with increased walking and biking (Larouche, Mammen, Rowe, & Faulkner, 2018; Villa-González, Barranco-Ruiz, Evenson, & Chillón, 2018).

3 Economic impacts related to injury prevention and physical activity

3.1 Injury and fatality reduction

Strong evidence exists that programs to increase walking and biking have been effective at reducing injury and fatality risk. Looking at 18 US states from 1995 to 2010, researchers found that the Safe Routes to School program was associated with a 23% decline in school-age pedestrian and bicyclist injury risk and a 20% decline in school-age pedestrian and bicyclist fatality risk compared to risks for adults aged 30–64 (DiMaggio, Frangos, & Li, 2016). Similar results were found in an analysis of New York City's SRTS program (DiMaggio, Chen, Muennig, & Li, 2014; DiMaggio & Li, 2013).

While the authors do not quantify the economic benefits of these safety improvements, it seems likely they are substantial. The US Department of Transportation (DOT) places the value of a statistical life at $9.6 million (2015 dollars) with a range of $5.4 to $13.4 million (Moran & Monje, 2016). The economic costs of injuries are substantial as well. DOT finds that minor injuries are valued at $29,000 (0.3% of VSL) and severe injuries at $1.01 million (10.5% of VSL) (Moran & Monje, 2016).

3.2 Physical activity

Outside of injury prevention, the health impacts of AST are less clear (Larouche, Saunders, Faulkner, Colley, & Tremblay, 2014). Generally, children who use active travel modes show higher levels of physical activity than children who are taken to school in a vehicle (Larouche et al., 2014). Children who bicycle are significantly more fit than children who walk or travel by motorized travel (Cooper et al., 2006) and have higher aerobic power and muscle endurance than walkers and travelers in vehicles (Andersen, Lawlor, Cooper, Froberg, & Anderssen, 2009; Voss & Sandercock, 2010). Users of active modes of travel also had enhanced academic performance (Dwyer, Sallis, Blizzard, Lazarus, & Dean, 2001; Lucken et al., 2018). Rosenberg, Sallis, Conway, Cain, and McKenzie (2006) showed reductions in the level of obesity for boys after 2 years of active school travel but not for girls, while Abbott, Macdonald, Nambiar, and Davies (2009) found that "walking to school was associated with higher school-day steps in older children" and Hinckson, Garrett, and Duncan (2011) found that "students of high socio-economic status background improved … compared to those from mid … and low."

Economic benefits from increased physical activity in children related to increased active school travel have not been well-studied. Many possible pathways for long-term economic benefits exist including reductions in conditions associated with overweight and obesity and establishing patterns of life-long physical activity. However, due to the inconsistent findings on the impacts of active school travel on obesity and other conditions, little research exists on this topic and firm conclusions about economic benefits resulting from active school travel cannot currently be drawn.

4 Economic impacts on school transportation costs

Motorized transport is required when children do not walk or bike to school. In the United States, about 54% of students aged 5–17 use private vehicles and 33% use school buses (McDonald et al., 2011). In Canada, 24% of schoolchildren rely on private vehicles (Gray et al., 2014). While school buses are largely a North American phenomena, families—using autos—provide substantial shares of school transportation even in countries with high rates of walking and biking. For example, 41% of 5–10 year olds in England access school by private vehicle and 40% of Dutch primary schoolchildren use autos (Department for Transport, 2017; Wegman & Aarts, 2006).

Of course, motorized transport is often required for longer trips which would untenable to conduct on foot or bike due to time and effort. However, survey data from the US shows that many children are driven or take the bus for short trips of less than one mile. For example, elementary and middle school students living within a quarter-mile of school are 14 times more likely to walk to school than those living 1–2 miles from school (McDonald et al., 2011).

Programs aimed at increasing active school travel target students living near school where distance is not a barrier. Even for children living close to school, the out-of-pocket and opportunity cost to families and school systems of providing transport for these short trips is substantial. Using data for the US, my colleagues and I estimated that families drive an extra 1.5 billion miles and spent an extra 50 million hours driving elementary and middle school students to school when the distance is less than one mile (McDonald et al., 2016). Using the American Automobile Association's estimate of driving costs and standard values of time, this equates to an economic cost of $720 million ($300 million for vehicle costs and $420 million for time) (McDonald et al., 2016). Little research has been done on how parents perceive these costs. For some, school may be a convenient stop on the way to work or they may value spending time with their children. However, for short trips to school, the positive utility of spending time with children can be replicated by accompanying children to school by foot or bike.

In North America, schools also spend substantial amounts on school transportation. School bus service originated to provide children from rural areas with the opportunity to attend school. However, as school travel patterns have evolved school buses increasingly provide service to children living close to school. In some cases, this is because the walking conditions are considered hazardous. In Florida, 1% of all students receive hazard busing. However, in some counties the rate is much higher. For example Escambia county which includes Pensacola has a hazard busing rate of 12% (McDonald et al., 2016). The cost to school districts of transporting students living within 1 mile of school is between $100 and $500 million in the US or about $200 per student (McDonald et al., 2016).

An obvious question is whether communities might be safer and healthier if, instead of providing hazard busing, hazardous walking conditions were eliminated. The answer is yes. Our research team looked across the US to identify examples of communities implementing this strategy. Austin, Texas constructed a pedestrian bridge to provide an off-road connection between apartments and the local elementary school. The bridge cost $750,000, but the school system planned to eliminate three bus routes with an estimated annual savings of $130,000 (McDonald et al., 2016). Other researchers have identified similar examples. Auburn, Washington implemented several SRTS projects including new sidewalks and bike lanes. Funding for these efforts came from a 2 SRTS grants totaling $307,000 (Crowe, Rivas, & Watts, 2009). The school system was ultimately able to save $240,000 per year in hazard busing costs (Safe Routes to School National Partnership, 2010).

5 Economic implications of school siting, student enrollment policies and bus operations

School transportation systems are complex multimodal networks. Several components influence the costs of school travel through their impact on the distance from home to school. Of relevance for walking and bicycling to school, active school travel research indicates that the distance from home to school is the most commonly cited barrier to parents permitting their child to walk or bicycle to school (National Center for Safe Routes to School, 2016). Yet, the distance from home to school is a byproduct of land use and built environment decisions made by land use planning and zoning, residential development design choices, and school facility site location decisions. Further adding to the distance from home factor, student assignment geographies are determined by educational leaders through consideration of district educational policies (Hanley, 2007; Wilson, Wilson, & Krizek, 2007).

5.1 Land use planning

Municipal and county land use planners regulate residential developments through planning and zoning, tools which influence where, when and what types of homes are built. School facility planners are influential in the location of school facilities through district decisions to open, close or renovate a school. During periods of development growth and decline, coordination between city planners and school planners can increase the efficiency and safety of school transportation networks by locating school facilities within corridors that afford multimodal options (Murtagh, Dempster, & Murphy, 2016; Steiner et al., 2011). Conversely, lack of coordination between city and school planners can increase the travel distance from home to school (McDonald, 2010).

5.2 Student enrollment geographies

In addition to the physical distance from a family's home to the nearest public school, emerging school choice and student assignment policy trends in the United States complicate the home-to-school distance dynamic. Moreover, student enrollment in public education is not limited to geographic base school assignment; rather, students have increasing options to enroll in special curriculum and magnet options through public school districts seeking to attract and retain student families during a time in which charter school enrollment is increasing. According to research by Wilson et al. (2007), city-wide school choice in public school districts decrease rates of children walking, increase vehicle miles traveled, and are 4.5 times as costly.

5.3 School bus policies and operations

The provision of bus service is a key variable in school travel mode choices. A driving force of school bus service provision is school transportation funding; several states cover the bulk of the cost of school bus service (capital, operations, and maintenance), whereas others contribute very little and delegate local school bus service to the community level. Concurrently, for those states that do reimburse, there is wide variability in the definition of process for identifying hazard routes to school. The study by McDonald et al. (2015) outlined the importance of defining the distance as both Euclidean-spatial and network. Further, research suggests that the definition and responsibility for identifying a hazardous route varies by state—in some states the school district transportation director marks the route as unsafe and receives state reimbursement; in others a professional engineer must assess the safety of the route and qualify it as hazardous in order for the school district to receive state reimbursement for bus service.

6 Access for all

The research presented in this chapter focused on the benefits to children and adolescents of programs to increase active school travel. This ignores the co-benefits of SRTS on all travelers. For example, road safety improvements that reduce mortality and injury for children likely do so for all road users. Similarly, new sidewalks and bike lanes create networks that make it easier for all to travel by foot and bike. Assessment of the co-benefits of SRTS as well as provision of pedestrian and bicycle facilities has identified some evidence of positive social and environmental sustainability co-benefits (Sallis et al., 2015).

7 Conclusions

Supporting active school travel provides economic benefits to communities, families, and school districts through reductions in the costs of motorized transport and decreases in injuries and fatalities. Long-term assessments of the economic benefits of increased physical activity from school travel do not yet exist. These economic benefits can inform debates about infrastructure investments, school siting, and school transportation operations and funding.

Yet few studies quantify economic benefits of increased walking and biking for children thereby requiring more work on this topic. At present, this gap in research exists along two areas of inquiry: the cost of injury and loss of life and the operational, regulatory and financial systems of school districts. We see an acute need to quantify the economic benefits of mortality and morbidity reductions due to road safety improvements. SRTS programs have made demonstrable safety improvements but the economic benefits have not been systematically quantified.

Research into the system of school travel, which includes school bus operations and maintenance, passenger vehicle ownership, and walking and bicycling, is nested in a large system of school district operations, regulation and finance. Yet, little research has been done focusing on the complex set of decisions facing school districts and how these decisions interact with school travel decisions and costs. To illustrate the need for this systems-level analysis, consider: If a urban-growth school district builds a centrally located school to accommodate increased demand for urbanizing families, do they receive any land acquisition or facilities construction financial assistance from the county or state for their predicted decrease in school bus costs, which are state-reimbursed? Similarly, if a school district needs to renovate a school that produces public health, social and economic benefits to the community, are there coordinated systems of public finance and regulation to support smart school priorities? Research into school operations, and their coordinated planning in the context of a rapidly changing urban landscape, is necessary to fully grasp the economic complexity of systems-level school travel costs. Concurrent with this effort, we recommend case study research to quantify how public sector investments in encouraging walking and biking have reduced operations expenditures around school transportation and potentially school construction capital costs.

References

Abbott, R. A., Macdonald, D., Nambiar, S., & Davies, P. S. W. (2009). The association between walking to school, daily step counts and meeting step targets in 5- to 17-year-old Australian children. *Pediatric Exercise Science, 21*(4), 520–532. https://doi.org/10.1123/pes.21.4.520.

Andersen, L. B., Lawlor, D. A., Cooper, A. R., Froberg, K., & Anderssen, S. A. (2009). Physical fitness in relation to transport to school in adolescents: The Danish youth and sports study. *Scandinavian Journal of Medicine & Science in Sports, 19*(3), 406–411. https://doi.org/10.1111/j.1600-0838.2008.00803.x.

Buliung, R. N., Mitra, R., & Faulkner, G. (2009). Active school transportation in the greater Toronto area, Canada: An exploration of trends in space and time (1986–2006). *Preventive Medicine, 48*(6), 507–512. https://doi.org/10.1016/j.ypmed.2009.03.001.

Centers for Disease Control and Prevention, National Center for Health Statistics. (2017). *Prevalence of obesity among adults and youth: 2015–2016*. Retrieved from: https://www.cdc.gov/nchs/products/databriefs/db288.htm.

Cooper, A. R., Wedderkopp, N., Wang, H., Andersen, L. B., Froberg, K., & Page, A. S. (2006). Active travel to school and cardiovascular fitness in Danish children and adolescents. *Medicine & Science in Sports & Exercise, 38*(10), 1724–1731.

Crowe, R., Rivas, R. G., & Watts, K. N. (2009). Safe routes to school—Making a big different via small steps. *Public Roads, 73*(1). Retrieved from: https://www.fhwa.dot.gov/publications/publicroads/09julaug/01.cfm.

Department for Transport. (2017). *Transport statistics Great Britain 2017*. Statistics, *(November)* (pp. 1–288). ISBN: 9780115530951.

DiMaggio, C., Chen, Q., Muennig, P. A., & Li, G. (2014). Timing and effect of a safe routes to school program on child pedestrian injury risk during school travel hours: Bayesian changepoint and difference-in-differences analysis. *Injury Epidemiology, 1*(1), 17. https://doi.org/10.1186/s40621-014-0017-0.

DiMaggio, C., Frangos, S., & Li, G. (2016). National Safe Routes to school program and risk of school-age pedestrian and bicyclist injury. *Annals of Epidemiology, 26*(6), 412–417. https://doi.org/10.1016/j.annepidem.2016.04.002.

DiMaggio, C., & Li, G. (2013). Effectiveness of a safe routes to school program in preventing school-aged pedestrian injury. *Pediatrics, 131*(2), 290–296. https://doi.org/10.1542/peds.2012-2182.

Dwyer, T., Sallis, J. F., Blizzard, L., Lazarus, R., & Dean, K. (2001). Relation of academic performance to physical activity and fitness in children. *Pediatric Exercise Science, 13*(3), 225–237. https://doi.org/10.1123/pes.13.3.225.

Erickson, S. J., Robinson, T. N., Haydel, K. F., & Killen, J. D. (2000). Are overweight children unhappy?: Body mass index, depressive symptoms, and overweight concerns in elementary school children. *Archives of Pediatrics & Adolescent Medicine, 154*(9), 931–935. https://doi.org/10.1001/archpedi.154.9.931.

Gordon, C. (2018). Economic benefits of active transportation. In R. Larouche (Ed.), *Children's active transportation* (pp. 39–52). Elsevier.

Gray, C. E., Larouche, R., Barnes, J. D., Colley, R. C., Bonne, J. C., Arthur, M., et al. (2014). Are we driving our kids to unhealthy habits? Results of the active healthy kids

Canada 2013 report card on physical activity for children and youth. *International Journal of Environmental Research and Public Health, 11*(6), 6009–6020. https://doi.org/10.3390/ijerph110606009.

Hanley, P. F. (2007). Transportation cost changes with statewide school district consolidation. *Socio-Economic Planning Sciences, 41*(2), 163–179. https://doi.org/10.1016/j.seps.2005.10.004.

Hinckson, E. A., Garrett, N., & Duncan, S. (2011). Active commuting to school in New Zealand children (2004–2008): A quantitative analysis. *Preventive Medicine, 52*(5), 332–336. https://doi.org/10.1016/j.ypmed.2011.02.010.

Larouche, R., Mammen, G., Rowe, D. A., & Faulkner, G. (2018). Effectiveness of active school transport interventions: A systematic review and update. *BMC Public Health, 18*(1), 206. https://doi.org/10.1186/s12889-017-5005-1.

Larouche, R., Saunders, T. J., Faulkner, G. E. J., Colley, R. C., & Tremblay, M. S. (2014). Associations between active school transport and physical activity, body composition and cardiovascular fitness: A systematic review of 68 studies. *Journal of Physical Activity and Health, 11*(1), 206–227.

Lobstein, T., Baur, L., & Uauy, R. (2004). Obesity in children and young people: A crisis in public health. *Obesity Reviews, 5*(s1), 4–85. https://doi.org/10.1111/j.1467-789X.2004.00133.x.

Lucken, E., Soria, J., Niktas, M. -A., Wang, T., Stewart, M., & Nikoui, R. (2018). Impact of information about health and academic benefits on parent perception of the feasibility of active transportation to school. *Journal of Transport & Health, 10*, 28–36. https://doi.org/10.1016/j.jth.2018.07.005.

McDonald, N. C. (2007). Active transportation to school. Trends among U.S. schoolchildren, 1969–2001. *American Journal of Preventive Medicine, 32*(6), 509–516. https://doi.org/10.1016/j.amepre.2007.02.022.

McDonald, N. C. (2010). School siting: Contested visions of the community school. *Journal of the American Planning Association, 76*(2), 184–198.

McDonald, N. C., Brown, A. L., Marchetti, L. M., & Pedroso, M. S. (2011). U.S. school travel, 2009: An assessment of trends. *American Journal of Preventive Medicine, 41*(2), 146–151. https://doi.org/10.1016/j.amepre.2011.04.006.

McDonald, N. C., Steiner, R. L., Palmer, W. M., Bullock, A. N., Sisiopiku, V. P., & Lytle, B. F. (2016). Costs of school transportation: Quantifying the fiscal impacts of encouraging walking and bicycling for school travel. *Transportation, 43*(1), 159–175. https://doi.org/10.1007/s11116-014-9569-7.

McDonald, N. C., Steiner, R. L., Sisiopiku, V. P., Palmer, W. M., Lytle, B. F., Tsai, J., et al. (2015). Quantifying the costs of school transportation *(no. 2012-022S)*. Retrieved from: https://stride.ce.ufl.edu/wp-content/uploads/2017/03/STRIDE_QSTC_Final Report.pdf.

Merom, D., Tudor-Locke, C., Bauman, A., & Rissel, C. (2006). Active commuting to school among NSW primary school children: Implications for public health. *Health and Place, 12*(4), 678–687. https://doi.org/10.1016/j.healthplace.2005.09.003.

Moran, M., & Monje, C. (2016). *Guidance on treatment of the economic value of a statistical life (VSL). In US Department of Transportation Analyses—2016 Adjustment*. Retrieved from US Department of Transportation website: https://www.transportation.gov/sites/dot.gov/files/docs/2016%20Revised%20Value%20of%20a%20Statistical%20Life%20Guidance.pdf.

Murtagh, E. M., Dempster, M., & Murphy, M. H. (2016). Determinants of uptake and maintenance of active commuting to school. *Health & Place, 40*, 9–14. https://doi.org/10.1016/j.healthplace.2016.04.009.

Must, A., Spadano, J., Coakley, E. H., Field, A. E., Colditz, G., & Dietz, W. H. (1999). The disease burden associated with overweight and obesity. *JAMA, 282*(16), 1523–1529. https://doi.org/10.1001/jama.282.16.1523.

National Center for Safe Routes to School. (2016). *Trends in walking and bicycling to school from 2007 to 2014*. Retrieved from Federal Highway Administration website http://www. pedbikeinfo.org/pdf/Community_SRTSfederal_Trends.pdf.

Rosenberg, D. E., Sallis, J. F., Conway, T. L., Cain, K. L., & McKenzie, T. L. (2006). Active transportation to school over 2 years in relation to weight status and physical activity. *Obesity (Silver Spring, Md.)*, *14*(10), 1771–1776.

Safe Routes to School National Partnership. (2010). *Local success stories: Reducing bus transportation costs*. Vol. 2014.

Sallis, J. F., Spoon, C., Cavill, N., Engelberg, J. K., Gebel, K., Parker, M., et al. (2015). Co-benefits of designing communities for active living: An exploration of literature. *International Journal of Behavioral Nutrition and Physical Activity*, *12*(1), 30. https://doi.org/10.1186/s12966-015-0188-2.

Steiner, R. L., Bejleri, I., Wheelock, J. H., Perez, B. O., Provost, R. E., Fischman, A., ... Cahill, M. (2011). *How policy drives mode choice in children's transportation to school: An analysis of four Florida school districts* (R. Miles, M. Wyckoff, & A. Adelaja, eds.). East Lansing: Michigan State University Press.

Tudor-Locke, C., Ainsworth, B. E., & Popkin, B. M. (2001). Active commuting to school: An overlooked source of children's physical activity. *Sports Medicine*, *31*(5), 309–313.

Villa-González, E., Barranco-Ruiz, Y., Evenson, K. R., & Chillón, P. (2018). Systematic review of interventions for promoting active school transport. *Preventive Medicine*, *111*, 115–134. https://doi.org/10.1016/j.ypmed.2018.02.010.

Voss, C., & Sandercock, G. (2010). Aerobic fitness and mode of travel to school in English schoolchildren. *Medicine and Science in Sports and Exercise*, *42*(2), 281–287. https://doi.org/10.1249/MSS.0b013e3181b11bdc.

Wegman, F., & Aarts, L. (2006). *Advancing sustainable safety*. SWOV Institute for Road Safety Research. https://doi.org/10.1016/j.ssci.2007.06.013.

Wilson, E. J., Wilson, R., & Krizek, K. J. (2007). The implications of school choice on travel behavior and environmental emissions. *Transportation Research D*, *12*(7), 506–518.

CHAPTER ELEVEN

Engaging children in neighborhood planning for active travel infrastructure

Karen Witten[a] and Adrian Field[b]
[a]SHORE & Whariki Research Centre, Massey University, Auckland, New Zealand
[b]Director of Dovetail Consulting Ltd., Auckland, New Zealand

Contents

1 Introduction

Walking, scootering, skating or biking to school enables children and young people to accumulate the regular levels of physical activity needed for good health. Compared to children who travel to school by car, those who use active modes are more likely to reach recommended levels of physical activity (Faulkner, Buliung, Flora, & Fusco, 2009; Larouche et al., 2014). Children also play and socialize with friends as they make their way to school, especially when unaccompanied by an adult. As they traverse their local environment, they learn to negotiate space, and as they encounter others, they learn to assess risk and make decisions (Carroll, Witten, Kearns, & Donovan, 2015; Mackett, Brown, Gong, Kitazawa, & Paskins, 2007; Pooley et al., 2010). However, despite the many benefits of active travel to school, rates have declined drastically in New Zealand over recent decades and a third of children and young people are now insufficiently active for good health (Maddison et al., 2016).

Declining rates of active travel and independent mobility have been attributed to a number of factors. In New Zealand these include parents' and children's fears of traffic speeds and volumes, strangers and bullying by older youth, a rise in out-of-zone schooling, the allure of screen time, increasing participation in after school activities, parent trip-chaining, and fewer mothers at home to nurture neighborhood relationships (Carroll et al., 2015; Witten, Kearns, Carroll, Asiasiga, & Tava'e, 2013). Recent systematic reviews of international research suggest a combination of social and built environment features are necessary to encourage active travel. Ikeda et al. (2018), for example, identified perceptions of traffic safety and social relationships with neighbors, friends and families to be positively associated with active school travel. Reviewing twenty-eight empirical studies (natural experiments and prospective, retrospective, experimental, and longitudinal research), Smith et al. (2017) revealed that physical activity and/or travel behaviors in adults and children is enabled by the provision of active travel infrastructure and high quality parks and playgrounds. These reviews support the contention that child-friendly neighborhoods not only feel safe and welcoming to children but they also offer children the freedom to move about independently without fear of exposure to traffic or other dangers (Freeman & Tranter, 2011; Nordstrom, 2010). Research evidence also suggests wider community benefits where children can interact safely and openly with local people in neighborhood settings (Malone, 2006; Weller & Bruegel, 2009).

New Zealand suburban street environments are generally not child-friendly. They are car-friendly which encourages high motor vehicle ownership and mode share. In the 2013 Census 82.6% of Auckland commuters reported traveling to work by car, 8.4% by bus or train and 6.5% by active travel modes (StatsNZ, 2014). In Auckland, NZ's largest city, transport planning over recent decades has focused on building road capacity to meet the demands of increasing motor vehicle traffic. Efficiency and travel-time savings have been the underpinning rationale for investment. Substantial changes are needed to this approach if adult commuting patterns are to change in favor of active modes and children's rates of active travel to school are to rebound.

In this chapter, we present Te Ara Mua—Future Streets—a case study of an alternative approach to designing and delivering transport infrastructure, discuss why children's engagement in transport planning is desirable, and highlight the involvement of children and young people in the Future Streets participatory design process.

2 Te Ara Mua-future streets

Te Ara Mua—Future Streets, is a neighborhood scale streetscape retrofit located in Mangere, Auckland, New Zealand. A streetscape retrofit entails redesigning on- and-off street public space in an existing neighborhood. At the heart of the project is the hypothesis that suburban streets can be modified to improve safety on the roads and support healthier mobility options, particularly walking and cycling.

The Mangere area was developed in the 1950s and 60s and has a curvilinear street network with many cul-de-sacs (short dead-end streets) branching off collector roads. Alleyways are common, linking the cul-de-sacs to greenway routes and other residential streets. The Future Streets intervention has involved redesigning local streets by applying self-explaining roads theory, an approach that posits both positive and negative road user behaviour can be reinforced by the design of streets and mobility networks (Charlton et al., 2010; Mackie, Charlton, Baas, & Villasenor, 2013). Traffic calming and prioritizing walking and cycling infrastructure have been central to the design rationale.

Te Ara Mua—Future Streets has been a partnership project between a team of transport and health researchers, Mangere residents, supported by the Mangere-Otahuhu Local Board, and the city's transport agency, Auckland Transport. The research team has had primary responsibility for generating concept designs for the street intervention, and Auckland Transport has had responsibility for developing designs and for funding and constructing the new streetscapes. The research team engaged local residents in a participatory design process. This was an iterative, co-design process that took place over eighteen-months. It began by establishing how local people moved about the neighborhoods, the modes and routes they used to common destinations and their aspirations for neighborhood change to support alternative mobility options. Stalls held in the local shopping mall during Saturday morning markets days provided an opportunity to talk with local people, gather information and share emerging design concepts. Local children frequented the stalls in the mall and engaged with the research team (Fig. 1), however, the main strategy for consulting children on their use,

Fig. 1 Engaging the public on street redesign proposals. *(Courtesy of the Future Streets team.)*

experiences and aspirations for the re-design of local streetscapes was through focus groups held at three local schools.

3 Why should children be included in the planning process?

As citizens, children have a right to be consulted—to have their views sought out and considered on matters that affect them (Simpson, 1997; United Nations, 1989). Transport affects children's daily life, not only in terms of whether they get to and from school safely but also whether their journeys between home and school and other routine destinations enable them to engage with friends, gain independence and participate in community life. The United Nations Convention on the Rights of the Child (UNCROC) challenges the commonplace exclusion of children from public life and policymaking and sets out parameters for children's rights as citizens to express their views on matters affecting them. Ratified by many countries, including New Zealand, the convention has increased calls for children's participation in public realm planning. However, despite being in place for nearly three decades, examples of meaningful—as opposed to tokenistic—participation are still rare (Cele & van der Burgt, 2015; Freeman & Tranter, 2011; Wilks & Rudner, 2013). On an individual level, participation fosters competence in communication and decision making, builds confidence and self-esteem, and strengths children's sense of community (Chawla & Heft, 2002; Derr & Kovacs, 2017; Derr & Rigolon, 2017).

4 Why are children's voices seldom heard in planning processes?

Freeman, Nairn, and Sligo (2003) attribute the absence of children's voices in public realm planning to established, unchallenged ways of working, lack of training on how to work with children and young people, tight planning timeframes, limited budgets and hierarchical power structures in the planning sector. Individuals who hold power in agencies largely determine who has a voice in decision-making and the limits of any influence they may have (Freeman et al., 2003; Shier, 2010). The absence of children's voices in transport planning suggests children are seldom front of mind as valued consumers of transport infrastructure. Reporting on occasions in which children are involved in urban planning processes, Freeman et al. (2003) observe that the 'mere fact of an initiative being undertaken' (p. 55) is heralded as a success, irrespective of the form it takes and without reflection on how it worked for the young people or the planning practitioners involved.

Alternative explanations for the absence of children's voices lie in notions of children as 'adults in the making' rather than young people with agency and rights in the here and now (Uprichard, 2008). We argue that cities miss out if children are side-lined in planning processes, as children are not only 'experts' on childhood and what works for children (Christensen & Prout, 2002; Tisdall & Bell, 2006) but they also bring fresh ideas and ways of imagining public spaces (Carroll, Witten, & Stewart, 2017; Graham & Fitzgerald, 2010; Malone, 2017).

5 What does meaningful participation with children look like?

Several models depicting levels of participation with children have been developed, informed by Arnstein's (1969) 'Ladder of Citizen Participation'. Widely used examples include Hart's (1992) 'Ladder of Participation' and Shier's (2001) 'Pathways to Participation'. The latter model includes five levels of participation: (1) children are listened to; (2) children are supported in expressing their views; (3) children's views are taken into account; (4) children are involved in decision-making processes; (5) children share power and responsibility for decision-making. The third step on Shier's pathway 'children's views are taken into account' is the minimum level of participation required to comply with UNCROC requirements.

To participate meaningfully and contribute to decision-making, children need to have access to information presented in an age-appropriate way and the relevance of the task to their lives explained to them (Freeman & Tranter, 2011; Shier, 2010). Friendly adults play an important role facilitating children's participation by selecting interactive methods that engage children's interest; establishing a trusting atmosphere that encourages children to share their ideas; conducting participatory processes in familiar settings; and ensuring children find the experience enjoyable (Carroll et al., 2018; Carroll, Witten, Asiasiga, & Lin, 2019; Wilks & Rudner, 2013). The formality of an institutional setting can be overwhelming and constrain participation.

The literature on children's engagement in planning is primarily case study based and the outcomes observed commonly pertain to the effectiveness or otherwise of the strategies used to engage children, the benefits for children's agency, activity, learning and self-esteem or planners views on the process of participatory design with children (Carroll & Witten, 2017; Derr, Chawla, & van Vliet, 2017; Derr & Kovacs, 2017; Malone, 2017). Children often seek meeting places and natural features—trees, water elements, habitats for wildlife—the benefits of which go unchallenged (Carroll et al., 2017; Derr & Rigolon, 2017; Malone, 2013). While there are accounts of city plans being modified to take account of children's advice (Carroll & Witten, 2017; Nordstrom, 2017), we are not aware of studies that have compared the design solutions of infrastructure projects that have and have not involved, or compared the success of design outcomes from the perspectives of different population groups. Longitudinal studies have been advocated to build evidence of the impacts of children's participation in planning on design outcomes (Derr & Kovacs, 2017).

The scarcity of published accounts of children's engagement in transport planning suggests it does not occur often, and the articles that are available mainly focus on school travel (Babb & Curtis, 2013; Pooley et al., 2010; Rõivas, Antov, Oja, Abel, & Sepp, 2011) and young people's perceptions of local environmental factors that influence their mode use (Davis, 2001; Marzoughi, 2011). Surveys, sometimes integrating maps, have been the most commonly used method in these studies with the occasional addition of focus groups (Davis, 2001) and photovoice techniques (e.g. Pooley et al., 2010). Planning for real and other 3D modeling techniques have also been used to consult children on school travel planning (Kelly et al., 2004, p. 244). A more novel approach was reported by Magnussen and Elming (2015). They engaged young people in a neighborhood scale planning exercise in Copenhagen that using Minecraft and LEGO. In this study young people's local knowledge was drawn upon as they applied science gaming processes to construct models of redesigned neighborhoods.

6 Method

The engagement of children and young people in the Te Ara Mua— Future Streets project was part of a multi-layered participative approach. Perspectives were elicited from leaders in the community, social, health, housing and education sectors; mana whenua (Māori, the indigenous people with tribal affiliations in the area); local business people; police; disabled people; and the elected Local Board, as well as from children and young people. These targeted consultation processes were in addition to informal consultations held in the local town centre with residents on Saturday market days during the pre-design (issues identification) and design testing phases.

Children and young people were invited to take part in school-based focus groups, pre and post intervention. Four focus groups were held at three local schools (two primary and one secondary). Primary school participants were Year 5 and 6 students (aged 9–11 years), and secondary school focus groups were held with Year 9 and 10 students (13–15 years). Separate male and female groups were held at one primary school, while at the other primary and the secondary school, mixed gender focus groups were held. Each focus group had around seven or eight participants.

The pre-intervention phase occurred in late 2013, and enabled children and young people to discuss how they traveled through their community, and to identify strengths and challenges of the local street and greenways networks for moving about the neighborhood. Findings from this phase informed the re-design of neighborhood streets and open space interventions, alongside other parallel engagement and design processes. The post-intervention phase occurred in late 2017.

During the pre-intervention focus groups, participants were shown photographs from around the intervention area and asked to locate them on a large aerial photograph of Māngere. This helped orient them to the local streetscapes. Following this the children/young people used different colored dots to mark up the places they most liked/disliked visiting, and the places they felt most safe/unsafe; and the reasons for these were discussed. Conversations then traversed how they traveled around Māngere and the reasons for this, the modes of travel and extent of active transport, and what would make it safer to undertake active (and independent) travel in the area.

The post-intervention process followed the same approach. Children and young people's knowledge of, and responses to, the street change interventions were explored using before and after photographs. Topics covered in the pre intervention focus groups relating to how they commonly moved around the neighborhoods and barriers to active and independent travel were revisited.

Discussions from each focus group were transcribed and analyzed thematically, drawing on approaches developed by Braun and Clarke (2006), to explore and map out emerging themes.

7 Key findings: Pre-intervention

School, shops, parks, sports facilities, churches and the homes of friends and relatives were the local destinations the children and young people visited most often. Getting to and from these destinations was generally by car or on foot with walking trips almost always in the company of friends, siblings or other family members. The children said they did not want to walk alone, and many indicated they were not allowed to by their parents, primarily because of fears about violence and bullying from older youth and concerns about crossing roads safely (Witten, Kearns, Carroll, & Asiasiga, 2017).

A number of participants had bikes or scooters but they were seldom used to get to and from neighborhood destinations. Biking or scootering to school was rare, other than on school sponsored 'wheels day' events, and biking within the neighborhood was largely restricted to playing in the street near the children's homes. If children ventured further afield on bikes they were generally accompanied by parents or other adult family members.

Many of the children talked about being scared of encountering youth gangs who they said drank in local parks, alleyways and dead-end streets and several described specific incidents during which they had felt threatened or frightened.

> ...my park sometimes it is dangerous cause there is a group of boys in a gang they always drink there and sometime when another group ... looking for a fight and then they throw bottles...

Alleyways were singled out as being particularly worrying, described by one child as 'really long, slim and scary'.

> …they have gangs around here, they're mostly in alleyways. Yeah. That's why I don't like going places.

Consistent with concerns raised by Mangere adults, the prospect of coming across roaming and/or barking dogs also put children off being out and about.

> …there is two rottweiler dogs, me and my brothers were going for a walk and we were just walking …we tried to speed past and they were running after us.

Broken glass contributed to children sensing places as unsafe and, along with stories of children's bikes being stolen, was a reason given for not biking.

> …sometimes because the glass is kind of big and you can get punctures and my wheels pop'.

Turning to safety on the roads, of particular note were children's comments on how hard it could be to cross busier local roads especially when cars were traveling quickly. At times their concerns were illuminated with vivid accounts of local children who had been injured by cars while crossing roads. A few children also said they worried about adults not looking and seeing them as they backed out of driveways. As illustrated by the following excerpt, similar concerns were raised with respect to biking.

> Um, crossing the roads, in case someone's quickly speeding past. And I'm about to pedal off, I might not be fast enough to get there.

In light of the experiences children reported while out and about in neighborhood spaces, it is not surprising that the changes they wanted centred on making the area safer from people in cars and people in streets, parks and walkways. The children wanted playgrounds to be alcohol-free, dogs to be chained up, and drivers to watch out for them.

> To make my street more safer like a park like a playground so alcohol free… yeah alcohol free zone…'.

Better lighting on streets and in alleyways, more pedestrian crossings, speed bumps and signs to slow cars, and traffic lights, were all suggested as way to make Mangere safer for kids. They also suggested basketball hoops in the park to make it more fun.

8 Intervention design and construction

The children's observations and experiences were analyzed, along with data gathered through other community engagement and participatory design processes to generate the following list of key community concerns:

- Personal Safety—especially on off-road pathways, poor lighting, youth drinking and crime
- Speeding traffic impacting on perceptions of walking and cycling safety
- Lack of crossings—especially on busier arterial roads
- Confusion about road user priorities, especially around the shopping mall
- Dogs in the area posing a threat to pedestrians and cyclists

In turn, these community concerns, as well as community aspirations for mobility and accessibility in the area, informed the development of the following design principles for the intervention:

- Street/route hierarchy giving greater priority to pedestrians and cyclists
- People feel safe on routes
- Reduce traffic speed and make it more consistent
- Improve people's ability to cross the road safely
- Schools and the mall are priority destinations for the walking and cycling network
- A separated bike network on main roads is important
- Improvements reflect the identity of Māngere people

A design committee, including representatives from the research team, Auckland Transport and other consultants, debated and developed the design concepts in conjunction with a community reference group. A 'human centred design' approach was adopted, the key characteristics of which are inclusion of multidisciplinary perspectives; understanding the users experience and involving users throughout iterative design and development phases, and user-centred evaluation (Giacomin, 2014).

Building on the 'human-centred design' approach, a hypothetical scenario of a 12-year old traveling to school independently was used to help with decisions about the level of safety and amenity required from the proposed infrastructure changes. This was particularly useful for choosing cycling infrastructure and pedestrian crossing facilities. During a second round of market-day stalls in the local mall, residents viewed and provided feedback on the preliminary designs. Alternative design options were considered for particular locations. Children were among the local people who made their preferences known to the project team.

In the construction phase, the main intervention devices were traffic calming measures such as raised tables and buildouts; increased pavement widths; bike lanes; and cultural landscaping that reflected mana whenua identity and the historic flora of the area. The interventions encompassed the street network to improve safety for all forms of transport, as well as improvements to the local greenway network to make it more attractive to active travel modes (examples are illustrated in Fig. 2). The designs took into account Crime Prevention Through Environmental Design (CPTED) principles, to improve visual surveillance and use of the area.

Fig. 2 Before and after images of selected street and open space changes. *(Courtesy of the Future Streets team.)*

9 Key findings: Post-intervention

Feedback from the participating children indicated that some key areas of community concerns were being addressed through the street changes. Noted improvements were in addressing perceptions and experience of speeding traffic, making it clearer where to walk and cycle, and improving the availability of crossings in the areas. Raised tables (described by children as "speed bumps") were generally approved of and were thought to slow traffic down and made crossing roads safer for all users:

> ...cars slow down and before there was just a crossing and no speed bumps so they could just keep going and hit someone.

Older students recognized the safety value for pedestrians and the signal that raised tables sent to drivers to slow down:

> I think the whole point of changing it was for safety, most of it was changing the road and actually adding the crossing addition, so that makes it easier for cars to know when to stop, for people to cross safely.

Bike lanes, intended to help reduce confusion of road user priorities, were also seen as positive safety improvements, although many younger children did not use them, apart from at organized events led by a local bike activator. Even then, broken glass left on the lanes was an issue. Some also raised the loss of parking from the bike lanes and the way people would still occasional park in the lanes:

> My opinion is half and half because... normally they park on the side of the road and when they made the bike lanes the parents had nowhere to park... Half of me is yes because there has to be some space for bikers and speed bumps because there are lot of people who speed.

Some also noted that few people bike in Māngere:

> I think the bike lanes are good but they could have at least made it smaller because bikes [number riding] are not like humungous.

Where there was mixed feedback was the buildouts on a local street that reduced traffic to one lane in some areas. One boy was a resident and appreciated that it slowed the traffic down in his street—"people are going slow and they wait". He also noted there were fewer large trucks using the street. However, those who traveled through the street with parents were less approving:

> I had to go to my first cousin's birthday and we had to wait because there was like five cars and we just had to wait.

Some children also reported frustration from parents at slower speed, loss of parking and different routes being taken due to the bike lanes.

Changes to the local Windrush Reserve were thought to be a substantial improvement for shade, walkways, plantings and playground, with one child saying they were "more stylish and cool".

Although some road safety issues were recognized as being addressed by the changes, personal safety and roaming dogs in the area remained concerns. Most primary school children still traveled by car to school. This appeared to be due to normative expectations regarding school travel, a sense of 'stranger danger' and established patterns of family travel. Many primary school students however would walk home from school, and this seemed to be a time that was thought to be safer for many.

> because I am the youngest in my family and my parents are over protective so I can't walk to school in the mornings but I can walk after school because everybody is around.

Some older children, whilst approving the changes, noted that other aspects of the area were less conducive to the safety aspirations of the project.

> What they're doing with the road is good because, it puts us all in safety, but it doesn't change how Mangere is like… You can't change people.

Children and young people continued to raise safety issues with regards to neighbors and other residents who took part in antisocial and frightening behaviors, and alleyways that were thought to be unsafe. Younger children raised concerns about students at other schools who were often seen as rivals, or bullies and troublemakers. Older children were more likely to point to particular gang-related areas, where "you just don't want to be around them."

Home was a place that many highlighted as refuges of safety and family members they trusted, but many were fearful of their streets:

> I don't like my street too much because people have a fight and they crack their glasses and that, and then our babies go out barefoot and glass gets in their feet.
> Most of them have fights down at the park and there is this one dog, every time I go for a normal walk the dog always chases me down the road.

10 Discussion

To engage children in transport planning is to acknowledge that they are competent social actors who have valuable knowledge and experiences to share, and a right to be consulted on matters of relevance to their lives. The effective engagement of children requires thoughtful planning to ensure methods used are child-friendly and age appropriate and that participants have the necessary contextual and information resources to contribute meaningfully. Non-tokenistic engagement is also more likely if children are consulted in familiar settings where they are comfortable and confident to express their points of view.

The Te Ara Mua—Future Streets consultation took place in schools, a familiar setting, and involved a representative group of children. Regarding methods, the children were highly engaged exploring the aerial photograph of the area, commonly looking for their homes and schools, before identifying wider landmarks. Our initial focus on the routes taken, and mode used, on the trip to school was useful as it had relevance to all participants and also provided a conduit into conversations about trips to other destinations and reasons for and against using alternative routes and transport modes. The children enthusiastically shared their knowledge and experiences of local routes, how these influenced their mobility habits and preferences and what would need to change to encourage greater active travel.

The post-intervention feedback from children was taken at a relatively early stage, before many behaviour changes could be expected to be bedded in. Noticeably however, many children recognized the changes had happened and generally felt that the changes could improve safety in the area. Whilst at the time of interview, it doesn't appear that behaviors had changed substantially (that participants were aware of), there were widely perceived safety improvements through street and open space changes. The research highlights the importance of access to shops, schools, activities, churches, markets and other community resources in the intervention area. The recognition given by children and young people to the potential of the improvements to active travel across the area gives some indication that the changes have laid foundations for more active travel by children.

The changes, whilst generally welcomed, could not impact on all aspects of safety and perceptions of safety. Key perceptual or actual barriers to active travel in the area that remained were the presence of threatening dogs, and antisocial behaviour, often linked to alcohol and other drugs.

The research also revealed some issues specific to the ethnicity mix of the area. Walking was more common among the older age groups interviewed, particularly boys. However, there was a driving ethos that appeared to be culturally based for the older girls, in which female children in Pacific families are more likely to be driven to destinations. There are also commonalities with the findings reported by O'Sullivan, O'Connell, and Byrne (2017) in a social housing development in Cork City, Ireland, where anti-social behaviour, public drinking and personal safety were key stressors for children, all of which impacted their access to amenities in the local environment.

The involvement of children in the Future Streets intervention design was both purposeful and limited. Reflecting on Shier's (2001) Pathway to Participation there is no doubt that children were purposefully consulted and their views were taken into account in the development of the project's design principles and design solutions. This level of engagement equates to step three on Shier's (2001) pathway, falling short of children being involved in design development and decision-making. Children are significant stakeholders if the Te Ara Mua—Future Streets goal of curbing the decline in the active travel trajectory is to be met, but children's wellbeing did not set the agenda for the project. Streets that are safer and easier for walking, better air quality, and lower road traffic injury rates are goals set for all residents, and the engagement for the project was intended to obtain a population-wide process of input and reflection, including, but not limited to, children.

11 Conclusions

Transport planning has an immense influence on children's lives—on their play, their mobility, where and how they socialize with peers, and whether or not they are afforded independent mobility. The Te Ara Mua—Future Streets experience highlights opportunities for children's perspectives and experiences to be actively considered within transport planning, and moreover, for the safe interaction of children with the build environment to be an overarching goal of intervention design. Streets designed with children in mind, and informed by children's knowledge, will facilitate safe travel and provide opportunities for play and exploration. If children's mobility needs are not taken seriously, transport planning will undermine children's wellbeing and cast gloom over the urban futures of us all.

References

Arnstein, S. (1969). A ladder of citizen participation. *Journal of the American Planning Association, 35*(4), 216–224.

Babb, C., & Curtis, C. (2013). Evaluating the built environment for children's active travel to school. In Australasian Transport Research Forum, ATRF 2013—Proceedings. *Brisbane, Australia.*

Braun, V., & Clarke, V. (2006). Using thematic analysis in psychology. *Qualitative Research in Psychology, 3*(2), 77–101.

Carroll, P., & Witten, K. (2017). Children as urban design consultants: A children's audit of a central city square in Auckland, Aotearoa/New Zealand. In K. Bishop & L. Corkery (Eds.), *Designing cities with children and young people: Beyond playgrounds and skate parks* (pp. 105–119). Abingdon, Oxon: Routledge.

Carroll, P., Witten, K., Asiasiga, L., & Lin, E. -Y. (2019). Kids in the City: Reflecting on children's engagement as urban researchers and consultants in Aotearoa/New Zealand. *Children & Society.* https://doi.org/10.1111/chso.12315.

Carroll, P., Witten, K., Calder-Dawe, O., Smith, M., Kearns, R., Asiasiga, L., et al. (2018). Enabling participation for disabled young people: Study protocol. *BMC Public Health, 18* (712) https://doi.org/10.1186/s12889-12018-15652-x.

Carroll, P., Witten, K., Kearns, R., & Donovan, P. (2015). Kids in the City: Children's use and experiences of urban neighbourhoods in Auckland, New Zealand. *Journal of Urban Design, 20*(4), 417–436. https://doi.org/10.1080/13574809.2015.1044504.

Carroll, P., Witten, K., & Stewart, C. (2017). Children are citizens too: Consulting with children on the redevelopment of a central city square in Auckland, Aotearoa/New Zealand. *Built Environment, 43*(2), 272–289.

Cele, S., & van der Burgt, D. (2015). Participation, consultation, confusion: professionals' understandings of children's participation in physical planning. *Children's Geographies, 13*(1), 14–29.

Charlton, S., Mackie, H., Baas, P., Hay, K., Menezes, M., & Dixon, C. (2010). Using endemic road features to create self-explaining roads and reduce vehicle speeds. *Accident Analysis and Prevention, 42*(6), 1989–1998. https://doi.org/10.1016/j.aap.2010.06.006.

Chawla, L., & Heft, H. (2002). Children's competence and the ecology of communities: A functional approach to the evaluation of participation. *Journal of Environmental Psychology, 22*, 201–216.

Christensen, P., & Prout, A. (2002). Working with ethical symmetry in social research with children. *Childhood, 9*(4), 477–497.

Davis, A. (2001). Getting around: Listening to children's views. *Proceedings of the Institution of Civil Engineers: Municipal Engineer, 145*(2), 191–194.

Derr, V., Chawla, L., & van Vliet, W. (2017). Children as natural change agents: Child friendly cities as resilient cities. In K. Bishop & L. Corkery (Eds.), *Designing cities with children and young people: Beyond playgrounds and skate parks* (pp. 24–35). New York: Routledge.

Derr, V., & Kovacs, I. (2017). How participatory processes impact children and contribute to planning: A case study of neighbourhood design from Boulder, Colorado, USA. *Journal of Urbanism: International Research on Placemaking and Urban Sustainability, 10*(1), 29–48.

Derr, V., & Rigolon, A. (2017). Participatory schoolyard design for health and wellbeing; policies that support play in urban green spaces. In C. Freeman & P. Tranter (Eds.), *Risk, protection, provision and policy (volume 12 of geographies of children and young people)* (pp. 125–148). Springer.

Faulkner, G., Buliung, R., Flora, P., & Fusco, C. (2009). Active school transport, physical activity levels and body weight of children and youth: A systematic review. *Preventive Medicine, 48*(1), 3–8.

Freeman, C., Nairn, K., & Sligo, J. (2003). 'Professionalising' participation: From rhetoric to practice. *Children's Geographies, 1*(1), 53–70.

Freeman, C., & Tranter, P. (2011). *Children and their urban environment: Changing worlds.* London: Earthscan.

Giacomin, J. (2014). What is human Centred design? *The Design Journal, 17*(4), 606–623. https://doi.org/10.2752/175630614X14056185480186.

Graham, A., & Fitzgerald, R. (2010). Children's participation in research: Some possibilities and constraints in the current Australian research environment. *Journal of Sociology, 46*, 133–147.

Hart, R. (1992). *Children's participation: From tokenism to citizenship.* Florence, Italy: UNICEF International Child Development Centre.

Ikeda, E., Stewart, T., Garrett, N., Egli, V., Mandic, S., Hosking, J., et al. (2018). Built environment associates of active school travel in New Zealand children and youth: A systematic meta-analysis using individual participant data. *Journal of Transport & Health, 9*, 117–131.

Kelly, J., Jones, P., Barta, F., Hossinger, R., Witte, A., & Wolf, A. (2004). *Successful transport decision-making: A project management and stakeholder engagement handbook.* European Commission. *http://civitas.eu/sites/default/files/guidemapshandbook_web.pdf.*

Larouche, R., Oyeyemi, A., Prista, A., Onywera, V., Akinroye, K., & Tremblay, M. (2014). Associations between active school transport and physical activity, body composition, and cardiovascular fitness: A systematic review of 68 studies. [journal article]. *Journal of Physical Activity & Health, 11*, 206–227.

Mackett, R., Brown, B., Gong, Y., Kitazawa, K., & Paskins, J. (2007). Children's independent movement in the local environment. *Built Environment, 33*(4), 454–468.

Mackie, H., Charlton, S., Baas, P., & Villasenor, P. (2013). Road user behaviour changes following a self-explaining roads intervention. *Accident Analysis & Prevention, 50*, 742–750. https://doi.org/10.1016/j.aap.2012.06.026.

Maddison, R., Marsh, S., Hinckson, E., Duncan, S., Mandic, S., Taylor, R., et al. (2016). Results from New Zealand's 2016 report card on physical activity for children and youth. *Journal of Physical Activity and Health, 13*(Suppl. 2), S225–S230. https://doi.org/10.1123/jpah.2016-0323.

Magnussen, R., & Elming, A. (2015). Cities at play: Children's redesign of deprived neighbourhoods in Minecraft. In *Proceedings of the European conference on games-based learning* (pp. 331–337). Sonning Common, England: Academic Conferences and Publishing International Limited.

Malone, K. (2006). United Nations: A key player in a global movement for child friendly cities. In B. Gleeson & N. Sipe (Eds.), *Creating child friendly cities* (pp. 13–32). New York: Routledge.

Malone, K. (2013). "The future lies in our hands": Children as researchers and environmental change agents in designing a child-friendly neighbourhood. *International Journal of Justice and Sustainability, 18*(3), 372–395.

Malone, K. (2017). In K. Bishop & L. Corkery (Eds.), Child friendly cities: A model of planning for sustainable development. *Designing cities with children and young people: Beyond playgrounds and skate parks* (pp. 11–23). New York: Routledge.

Marzoughi, R. (2011). Barriers to teenage mobility in the greater Toronto area, Ontario, Canada: Attitudes, concerns, and policy implications. *Transportation Research Record, 2231*(1), 61–67.

Nordstrom, M. (2010). Children's views on child-friendly environments in different geographical, cultural and social Neighbourhoods. *Urban Studies, 47*(3), 514–528.

Nordstrom, M. (2017). In K. Bishop & L. Corkery (Eds.), *Designing Cities with Children and Young People. How are child impact assessments used in planning and child friendly environments? The Swedish experience* (pp. 150–160). New York: Routledge.

O'Sullivan, S., O'Connell, C., & Byrne, L. (2017). Hearing the voices of children and youth in housing estate regeneration. *Children, Youth and Environments, 27*(3), 1–15.

Pooley, C., Whyatt, D., Walker, M., Davies, G., Coulton, P., & Bamford, W. (2010). Understanding the school journey: Integrating data on travel and environment. *Environment and Planning A: Economy and Space, 42*(4), 948–965.

Rõivas, T., Antov, D., Oja, T., Abel, K., & Sepp, E. (2011). Children's risks on their way to school: The example of Tallinn. In *WIT transactions on ecology and the environment* (pp. 529–538). Southampton: Ashurst.

Shier, H. (2001). Pathways to participation: Openings, opportunities and obligations. *Children & Society, 15*(2), 107–117.

Shier, H. (2010). Pathways to participation revisited: Learning from Nicaragua's child coffee workers. In B. Percy-Smith & N. Thomas (Eds.), *A handbook of children and young people's participation* (pp. 215–229). London: Routledge.

Simpson, B. (1997). Towards the participation of children and young people in urban planning and design. *Urban Studies, 34*(5/6), 907–925.

Smith, M., Hosking, J., Woodward, A., Witten, K., MacMillan, A., Field, A., et al. (2017). Systematic literature review of built environment effects on physical activity and active transport—An update and new findings on health equity. *International Journal of Behavioral Nutrition and Physical Activity. 14*(158). https://doi.org/10.1186/s12966-12017-10613-12969.

StatsNZ (2014). *Commuting patterns in Auckland: Trends from the Census of Population and Dwellings 2006–13.* http://m.stats.govt.nz/Census/2013-census/profile-and-summary-reports/commuting-patterns-auckland/commuting-modes (aspx> Accessed 28 September 2017).

Tisdall, E., & Bell, R. (2006). In E. Tisdall, J. Davis, & M. Hillet al.*Included in governance? Children's participation in 'public' decision making. Children, Young People and Social Inclusion: Participation for What? (pp. 103–119). Bristol: Policy Press.

United Nations (1989). *Convention on the Rights of the Child.* http://www.unicef.org.uk/Documents/Publication-pdfs/UNCRC_PRESS200910web.pdf. Accessed 25 July 2018.

Uprichard, E. (2008). Children as 'being and becomings': Children, childhood and temporality. *Children & Society, 22,* 303–313.

Weller, S., & Bruegel, I. (2009). Children's 'Place' in the development of Neighbourhood social capital. *Urban Studies, 46*(3), 629–643.

Wilks, J., & Rudner, J. (2013). A voice for children and young people in the city. *Australian Journal of Environmental Education, 29*(1), 1–17.

Witten, K., Kearns, R., Carroll, P., & Asiasiga, L. (2017). Children's everyday encounters and affective relations with place: Experiences of hyperdiversity in Auckland neighbourhoods. *Social & Cultural Geography.* https://doi.org/10.1080/14649365.14642017.11347700. 10.1080/14649365.2017.1347700 published online 3 July.

Witten, K., Kearns, R., Carroll, P., Asiasiga, L., & Tava'e, N. (2013). New Zealand parents' understandings of the intergenerational decline in children's independent outdoor play and active travel. *Children's Geographies, 11*(2), 215–229. https://doi.org/10.1080/14733285.2013.779839.

CHAPTER TWELVE

Urban space for children on the move

Maria Johansson[a], Fredrika Mårtensson[b], Märit Jansson[c] and Catharina Sternudd[d]

[a]Environmental Psychology, Dept of Architecture and Built Environment, Lund University, Lund, Sweden
[b]Dept of Work Science, Business Economics and Environmental Psychology, Swedish University of Agricultural Sciences, Alnarp, Sweden
[c]Dept of Landscape Architecture, Planning and Management, Swedish University of Agricultural Sciences, Alnarp, Sweden
[d]Dept of Architecture and Built Environment, Lund University, Lund, Sweden

Contents

1 Introduction

There is a worldwide call to increase children's physical activity (WHO, 2011), where transport by foot and bicycle, even at modest distances, makes a substantial contribution (Chillón et al., 2010; Tudor-Locke, Ainsworth, & Popkin, 2001; van Sluijs et al., 2009). Children's physical activity is related to their overall opportunities for independent action, exploration and socializing with friends in local environments (Cook, Whitzman, & Tranter, 2015; Evans, 2007; Mårtensson & Nordström, 2017; Prezza & Pacilli, 2007). Today, such independent active mobility is largely withheld from children, and most children under 11 years cannot move freely about in their local area, as found in an international study of 16 countries (Shaw et al., 2015). This highlights the need to deepen the understanding of children's independent active mobility. This chapter suggests an integrated approach to children's outdoor environment. We use the terms *urban open spaces* that encompasses a variety of hard-paved 'open' spaces such as streetscapes, pedestrian paths and squares as well as vegetation-dominated green spaces such as parks, gardens, woodlands, street trees, and playgrounds accessible for a child moving around in their neighborhood (Randrup & Persson, 2009) and *independent active mobility*, which encompasses physically active transport and play without adult supervision in the urban environment.

Pedestrians and cyclists are affected by the immediate contact they have with their surroundings while moving (Kärrholm, Johansson, Lindelöw, & Ferreira, 2014; Wunderlich, 2008). Children who are allowed to move independently are in an ongoing transaction with the urban environment, as they move at low speed and are curious and attentive to the things and places that appear around them (Cele, 2005). Pathways and streets are interchangeably used for travel, play and exploration (Björklid & Gummesson, 2013), but also woodlands, parks, and playgrounds, become important paths, nodes and destinations for children. When choosing their own routes, children tend to alternate between visiting places experienced as familiar and safe, and approaching sites that are fascinating and more challenging (Agans, Säfvenbom, Davis, Bowers, & Lerner, 2013). The properties and design of the urban environment as perceived by the child thereby constitute a key to increased physical activity in general and independent active mobility in particular. The contexts of children's positive experiences of movement in the urban environment during transport and play may, as among adults, strengthen their motivation to walk and cycle independently (Johansson, Sternudd, & Kärrholm, 2016).

Opportunities for independent active mobility have broad implications for children's well-being, by impacting physical, psychological, cognitive, social, and economic parameters (Waygood, Friman, Olsson, & Taniguchi, 2017). There are also good arguments for believing that children's bonds to a place are established through opportunities for independent play and transport (Chawla, 2015; Chawla, Keena, Pevec, & Stanley, 2014). Traffic safety has long been on the agenda, but there is also a need to look beyond the volume and speed of cars and into the more complex interdependencies between qualities of urban environments and children's independent active mobility (Villanueva et al., 2016).

The UN Convention on the Rights of the Child includes rights to provision of spaces for play and leisure, but also the right of children to have a voice in community development (Skelton, 2007). In some neighborhoods across the world, children have been involved in work to create spaces for play and socializing (Chawla & Driskell, 2006). The UN 2030 Agenda for Sustainable Development Goal 11, stating that the urban environment should be inclusive, safe, resilient and sustainable for everyone, challenges societies to scale up the work and make the urban environment at large child-friendly (Mårtensson & Nordström, 2017). Children's needs and aspirations can be placed at the heart of development with no risk of jeopardizing the overall challenge of sustainability, since environments for children tend to work also for others (Shaw et al., 2015).

Planning, architecture and landscape architecture practices are largely responsible for the qualities of our everyday outdoor environments. These practices are commonly engaged in three main domains, which can also be considered as the phases of planning, design and management (Rodiek, 2006). Planning shapes urban environments and their structures on the larger scale, and design on the more detailed level, while management maintains and develops existing structures (Jansson & Lindgren, 2012). All three domains of practice need to be engaged in the shaping of urban environments supporting children's independent active mobility. In this chapter a selection of theories from people-environment studies, and environmental psychology in particular, are presented and elaborated to provide concepts that highlight the role of urban environments in children's mobility.

2 Opportunities for mobility embedded in neighborhood

Children's mobility is embedded in and inseparable from its wider psychological, social, environmental and policy context, at all levels (Bringlof-Isler et al., 2008; Ferreira et al., 2006; Fyhri, Hjorthal, Mackett, Fotel, & Kyttä, 2011; Napier, Brown, Werner, & Gallimore, 2011). Research on walkability indicates the importance of the 'D variables' when planning for walking and cycling – Density and Diversity of land use, Design of the street network, Destination accessibility and Distance to transit bus stops – and also pedestrian-oriented Designs at a more detailed level (Cervero & Kockelman, 1997; Ewing & Cervero, 2010). Research reviews suggest that these results largely, but not entirely, can also be applied to children and adolescents: Their access to a neighborhood and independent active mobility being associated with residential density, land-use mix and proximity to school, parks and recreational facilities (van Loon & Frank, 2011). Davison and Lawson (2006) also report positive associations between children's and adolescents' physical activity and pedestrian safety and the availability of public transport, but negative associations with crime. Ding, Sallis, Kerr, Lee, and Rosenberg (2011) differentiates between studies on children and adolescents, and report the strongest evidence for associations between adolescents' mobility and residential density and land-use mix, whereas for children access to recreation facilities, walking/biking facilities, traffic speed/volume pedestrian safety structures, incivilities/disorders and vegetation seem to have a stronger impact. It has been argued that children's independent active mobility perhaps is associated more with factors related to proximity and safety, and when they enter adolescence their territory grows as they gain experience and become more mature (Johansson, 2006; Mitra, 2013). The proximate environments of home, school and the neighborhood are critical for children's independent active mobility, both in terms of physical features and social aspects such as socio-economic status and social capital (Merom, Tudor-Locke, Bauman, & Rissel, 2006). The neighborhood thereby constitutes the focal point of research on children's mobility (Carver, Timperio, Hesketh, & Crawford, 2010) and in the development of child-friendly cities (Horelli, 2007).

The relationship between the outcome in terms of walking and objective planning parameters, such as residential density and street connectivity, is likely to depend on how users perceive the environmental qualities (Alfonzo, 2005; Nasar, 2008). In the planning, design and management of urban open spaces, user perspectives must be integrated, and children's own perceptions and experiences are vital in enabling a child-friendly, inclusive, safe and resilient neighborhood (Horelli, 1998). Children's local knowledge and understanding of particular places should be utilized (Bonaiuto, Fornara, & Bonnes, 2006; Fornara, Bonaiuto, & Bonnes, 2010; Uzzell, Pol, & Badenas, 2002). A child-oriented approach allows planners and designers to obtain a thorough understanding of how children experience and use their local environments and what features may support or hinder their mobility. An illustrative example is that neighborhoods with cul-de-sacs and low street connectivity provide locations for children's safe outdoor play, whereas adults seem to regard such neighborhoods features as hindering active modes of transport (Ding et al., 2011).

Making use of children's perspectives, de Vries, Bakker, van Mechelen, and Hopman-Rock (2007) found the perceived quality of neighborhood in terms of safety, state of repair and suitability to the wishes of children to be more important determinants of their physical activity than the frequency and availability of facilities for sports and play. Jamme, Bahl, and Banerjee (2018) found that children felt comfortable walking in neighborhoods that they experienced had "eyes on the street" from residents, shopkeepers, and patrons, but expressed discomfort in the presence of "broken windows" as cues of social disorder. Children's perspectives may differ depending on their access to the neighborhood. Children in a high walkability neighborhood depicted, for example, more active transport in their mental maps of the surroundings than children in low walkability neighborhoods (Holt, Spence, Sehn, & Cutumisu, 2008). Alton, Adab, Roberts, and Barrett (2007) identified how children categorized as high walkers perceived heavy traffic around their homes and on the roads as dangerous, while those categorized as low walkers worried more about strangers and reported a lack of parks and sportsgrounds for play near their homes.

Westford (2010) argues that current professional design ideals of mixed traffic and high density are unsupportive of children's independent active mobility, and calls for new priorities in urban planning and design as part of a transportation policy. Planning for walking and cycling largely focuses on the presence and quality of infrastructure, such as pedestrian paths, pavements and zebra crossings. However, children are interacting with their lived environment as a whole, which also incorporates other types of areas than those planned specifically for their use (Jansson, Sundevall, & Wales, 2016).

In this chapter we draw attention to urban open spaces accessible to the public, which may contain many values for people and society. An overview of the particular benefits of green open spaces for children's mental resilience highlights their implications for children's capability to live in good health by adding sensory experiences and stimulating their imagination, and generally facilitating their ability to be in control and capable of planning and leading their lives (Chawla, 2015). Looking beyond the transport infrastructure and focusing on urban open spaces allows an examination of the physical features of entire neighborhoods, including overall landscape characteristics and elements from nature in relation to children's independent active mobility.

3 Integrating the playfulness of mobility in the equation

Play is a salient track in children's ways of approaching the world. When developing urban environments and strengthening a neighborhood's capacity to promote independent active mobility, children's goal-oriented transports need to be understood as merged with activity of a playful character when the child interacts with landscape characteristics and elements. Playgrounds, woodlands and other settings attractive for children (Noschis, 1992) contribute to an "outward pull" from home (Chatterjee, 2005). Video-tracking of how children's play evolves has highlighted landscape characteristics that trigger them to move, and how particular elements can help them coordinate and negotiate their interplay (Mårtensson, 2004; Wells, Jimenez, & Mårtensson, 2018). Attributes that serve as cues to play and destinations with an outward pull need to be part of an overall landscape structure that can house all the activity that the natural elements might spur. Patches of trees, shrubs and hilly terrain need to be well-distributed across the open spaces and well-integrated with any built elements or equipment (Mårtensson, 2013; Wells et al., 2018).

Four theoretical concepts from environmental psychology can be used to analyze a neighborhood with regard to its potential for children's active independent mobility: place attachment, affordance, wayfinding and prospect-refuge. These concepts have in common that they acknowledge children's perceptions and experiences of open spaces at neighborhood level and allow for an integrated view on children's mobility as both play and transport.

4 Conceptualizing neighborhoods in relation to children's independent active mobility

4.1 Attachment, the foundation of independent mobility

Place attachment can be understood as emotional ties that people develop with a place, and both physical features and social aspects of the place contribute (Bonaiuto, Aiello, Perugini, Bonnes, & Ercolani, 1999). Attachment is usually investigated at neighborhood level (Lewicka, 2010) and can be seen as the foundation for children to independently enter their neighborhood and make it their place. People may feel attached to a place due to the social factors of having close ties with people, but physical features such as beautiful nature, options for recreation and other stimulating environmental characteristics also contribute to place attachment (Hidalgo & Hernández, 2001; Lewicka, 2011; Scannell & Gifford, 2010).

The relative importance children assign to physical features and social aspects in their place of residence seems to vary across regions, with children in Sweden reporting more about physical attributes, while children in France report more the social aspects (Nordström, 2010). Ferreira, Johansson,

Sternudd, and Fornara (2016) showed a positive association between place attachment and walking behavior in adults. Children's independent active mobility is also explained by the neighborhood relationships of adults and the informal supervision such networks might add (Prezza et al., 2001). The literature on children's more active place-making tends to focus on 'favorite places' (Korpela, 1992), while we know much less about how children form their own networks with peers in a neighborhood and how these add to their and other's bonds with place (Morrow, 1999).

The planning of neighborhoods, including the open spaces, should also consider physical features (e.g. building density, aesthetics and greenery) and social aspects (e.g. security, discretion and sociability) that contribute to a positive atmosphere and place attachment (Bonaiuto et al., 2006; Bonaiuto, Fornara, & Bonnes, 2003). Literature on what particular attributes children tend to favor can provide information for planning, design and strategic management, but to truly uncover and document people's bonds to particular places their user experiences must be included. This should therefore be one of the fundamental tasks when preparing any environmental change. Children's own documentation of their perception and use of their neighborhood, for example in terms of favorite places, can be helpful in this task. These places can be documented through child-led walks in which children show their places (Cele, 2005), place mapping (Gifford, 2016) or by means of participatory GIS (Kyttä, Broberg, & Kahila, 2012).

4.2 Affordances supporting movement

Children's mobility in their neighborhoods has been connected to Gibson's (1979) affordance theory, which proposes that objects hold instantly detectable functions and are perceived by the observer in terms of what they offer. The concept of affordances, described by Heft (1988, p. 32) implies that: "the functionally significant properties of the environment are perceived qualities that emerge from person-environment relations". This means that one and the same object may provide many different affordances depending on the observer's needs and aspirations (Fig. 1). Kyttä (2004) has described child-friendly environments at neighborhood level as areas where high independent active mobility among children is combined with a richness in affordances that invite and allow children to different activities. Independent active mobility is supported when there are many affordances encouraging children to be outdoors (Chatterjee, 2005; Jansson et al., 2016; Kyttä, 2004; Lerstrup & Konijnendijk van den Bosch, 2017).

Fig. 1 Vegetation offers many affordances for children and play, especially if varied and containing for example multistemmed trees.

The actual affordances at a site are partly situational and context-bound (Broberg, Kyttä, & Fagerholm, 2013), but attempts have been made to define the physical feature attributes of particular affordances to particular user groups. Overall, a large variation in types of environments and elements provided for children is positive (Kyttä, 2004). This can include highly designed and managed open spaces such as playgrounds and parks, but also woodland areas, overgrown gardens and other less maintained spaces that tend to be attractive to children (Jansson et al., 2016). While younger children opt for traffic-free environments with variation and complexity of more dense vegetation areas (Mårtensson, 2004, 2013; Wells et al., 2018), older children also seem to look out for more managed places facilitating their pursuit of social interaction and organized games (Clark & Uzzell, 2002; Mårtensson et al., 2014). Babb, Olaru, Curtis, and Robertson (2017) found that green open spaces afforded the highest number of functions supporting children's independent active mobility. Gray open spaces, such as street environments, afforded walking and being with friends while appreciating street trees and gardens, but were also deemed negative due to the traffic and these spaces forming barriers in the neighborhood.

The concept of affordances can guide land use policy into claiming and providing land rich in affordances. The inter-connected sequences of places and spaces suitable for children's mobility across a neighborhood are quintessential, along with attention to details in architecture and design. In the planning phase, this could mean allowing nodes of nature to remain, or designing green infills in the development of the urban fabric; smaller ones in the streetscape and larger ones as recreation facilities and in proximity to child-care facilities, schools and after-school clubs.

The design process may benefit from affordance-based design, described by Refshauge, Stigsdotter, Lamm, and Thorleifsdottir (2013) as a way to provide play spaces for children. This involves starting with a large number of affordances for children's play and adding both experiences and aspects of the requests that support children's playful movement in open spaces linking between play and transport. The management approach to urban open space can also radically improve the availability of affordances to form more unique places that are more attractive to children. From a child perspective, the general increase of biodiversity associated with low-intensity management suggested by some contemporary approaches to urban forestry and garden design can often be preferred over more traditional park management.

4.3 Wayfinding via mind and body

Children need to develop familiarity with their neighborhood in order to practice independent active mobility. They are explorers by nature and their wayfinding skills develop with age (Segal, 2015). The term wayfinding was introduced by Kevin Lynch (1960), who suggested that recalled images of environmental features form mental maps that guide our movements in cities. Lynch identified five kinds of elements that seemed to support orientation in urban environments: *landmarks* referring to easily recognized points of orientation such as towers, buildings or mountains, *districts* referring to identifiable areas of park or housing for example, *edges* which are linear elements in the environment that cut through and separate, such as walls, railroads or shores, *paths* that are the 'channels' along which people move, such as streets, pavements or walkways, and finally *nodes*, representing focus points in the urban environment, such as crossings or squares (Fig. 2).

Later research confirms that children, and especially the younger ones, rely heavily on visual reference points and landmarks when they find their way around (Lingwood, Blades, Farran, Courbois, & Matthews, 2015). Brightly colored objects, such as large green waste bins and yellow lines on the road, were recalled. Similar-looking buildings were hard for the younger ones to distinguish, while older children were able to recall less eye-catching environmental features, such as particular buildings and hedges (Fenner, Heathcote, & Jerrams-Smith, 2000). Pedestrian paths can support wayfinding, and may also include barriers that may form obstacles for an adult walker but that can be useful for children by helping them stick to the path (Lueder & Rice, 2008).

Fig. 2 The trampled grass between the stones shows that they afford interesting possibilities for children's use.

Places of particular interest to children support them in their wayfinding. When asked to draw maps of a route, children included playgrounds, benches for gathering in groups, parks and other green areas, but signage, posters and unfamiliar buildings were also portrayed (Segal, 2015).

Children, and adults, depend on similar visual cues in their wayfinding. Lynch's five environmental elements can guide the analysis of this dimension of child-friendly urban environments. To act as landmarks, buildings and other environmental characteristics need to catch the interest of the child, which suggests that complexity and variation should be in focus when planning and designing neighborhoods that support children's active independent mobility. Children's multimodal way of approaching their surroundings seems to make them better at handling complexity, and inclined to make use of more subtle cues to orientation provided by detailed environmental objects of their particular interest. Complexity in child-oriented planning and design can be provided through the rich use of colors and bold expression in buildings, signs, urban furniture and strategically located playgrounds. Close attention should also be paid to green areas, where complexity in terms of hills and slopes, different kinds of vegetation, and ground cover can be used to support wayfinding and mobility.

4.4 Asking for prospect and refuge

Perceptions of open spaces as unsafe may threaten the development of place attachment in ways that limit children's opportunities to explore the neighborhood for affordances and find their own ways around. Prospect-refuge theory, originally developed by Appleton (1975), sheds light on two important dimensions in environmental perception. Prospect refers to a preference of having a clear unobstructed view of the landscape, and refuge refers to a preference for a place to hide that provides shelter. Dosen and Ostwald (2016) confirmed the importance of prospect to environmental preference, and Nasar and Fisher (1992) applied the theory to understand aspects of the social environment in urban areas, focusing on fear of crime. These authors slightly adapted the theory, and argued that people would perceive places as less safe if the environment provided potential hiding places, in this case for offenders (refuge), while limiting the pedestrian's overview of the nearby surroundings (prospect).

Perceived personal safety tends to have large effects on the use of urban environments, including in green open spaces (Jansson, Fors, Lindgren, & Wiström, 2013; Keane, 1998). Rahm and Johansson (submitted) found that perceived prospect encouraged pedestrian use of open spaces after dark, because of adequate lighting and well-kept greenery. Adults' trust in the environment being safe and secure is also associated with children's independent active mobility (Johansson, 2003, 2006). Children from the age of around eleven start to perceive the neighborhood more like adults, making references to how personal safety is associated with maintained greenery (Jansson et al., 2016). Younger children tend to appreciate more complex green settings, which awaken their curiosity (Mårtensson, 2004). For play and socializing, children tend to prefer sites containing both prospect and refuge. They like to hang out by an open space that gives them an overview, but that also provides shelter and the opportunity for themselves to hide (Mårtensson et al., 2014) (Fig. 3).

Urban open spaces should be planned, designed and managed to provide for children's perceived personal safety. Importantly, the presence of built structures and green elements should provide places where children who are short can get an overview or prospect of the spaces and also partly be overviewed and seen from nearby buildings. Refuge works in both ways in relation to children's independent active mobility. This means that there is need for a sound balance in providing interesting environments with, for example, shrubbery and bushes where children on the move can play and hide, but these places should not be so secluded that they offer refuge for potential offenders. To counteract perceptions of open spaces being unsafe, planning, design and management also need to consider the change between daylight and dark hours. At high latitudes, mornings and afternoons when

Fig. 3 The park provides overview and prospect over the lawns and the winding path as well refuge in terms of places for children to hide behind the bushes.

children travel to and from school and leisure activities are dark during the winter season, so at least feasible alternative routes should be available when it is dark outside.

5 Planning, designing and managing open spaces to support independent active mobility

Local initiatives to strengthen children's opportunities for independent active mobility are reported from all over the world. However, the design and content of interventions are diverse, systematic evaluations of their impact are scattered, and the long-term effects largely unknown (Shaw et al., 2015). This is confirmed by the increasing number of studies analyzing the effectiveness of interventions aiming to promote active travel modes to school. Interventions targeting physical features of open spaces have primarily aimed to improve basic pedestrian designs by improving traffic safety for children, such as pavement and crossing improvements on the one hand, and traffic control and speed reduction on the other (Chillón, Evenson, Vaughn, & Ward, 2011; Larouche, Mammen, Rowe, & Faulkner, 2018). The effect of improved pedestrian design on children's actual independent active mobility is mixed, and the effect seems to be dependent on the local context (e.g. Boarnet, Anderson, Day, McMillan, & Alfonzo, 2005; Boarnet, Day, Anderson, McMillan, & Alfonzo, 2005; Buliung, Faulkner, Beesley, & Kennedy, 2011; Crawford & Garrard, 2013). This is an argument supporting the conclusion by Shaw et al.

(2015) that the best interventions are those focusing on transforming urban environments to enable children's overall independence and development, as part of a wider program for social, environmental and economic development.

The Child Friendly Cities Initiative, launched by UNICEF, and the UN-Habitat initiative to help local governments implement the UN Convention on the Rights of the Child, are presented as positive examples contributing to the street design concepts of Woonerf in the Netherlands, Home Zones in the UK, the participation tool Kid's Tracks in Norway, and the urban design strategy of Vauban, Germany. In the Woonerf concept, streets in a residential area are designed in a way that gives people who walk or cycle priority over motorized vehicles, with cars traveling at walking speed being welcome (Gill, 2006). The concept was adapted in the UK (Home Zones or Shared Streets), Sweden and many other countries (Ben-Joseph, 1995; Biddulph, 2010). Besides promoting physical activity and non-motorized travel, the Woonerf concept seems to support social interaction among residents in the neighborhoods (Karsten & van Vliet, 2006).

6 Implications for practice

We argue that, to achieve optimal urban open spaces, children's independent active mobility should be regarded as a constant transaction with the surroundings, because of its continuous interchange between transport and play. Planning, design and management should involve the expertise of children and other locals, including parents (Timperio, Crawford, Telford, & Salford, 2004; McDonald, Deakin, & Aalborg, 2010), and consider research findings on attributes of open spaces that are compatible with children's independent active mobility. Early in the planning process, an empathic stance must be taken towards children on the move and their particular ways of approaching urban open spaces, such as to retain, enhance, and develop existing qualities.

Without doubt, there are fundamentals of planning that must be met regarding a land use mix, residential density, proximity to school, parks and recreational facilities, a safe traffic environment, freedom from crime, and pedestrian facilities. In addition, we propose four conceptualizations to further improve the interface between children and their environment, to make open spaces more child-friendly and safeguard children's independent active mobility.

Urban planning, design and management need to: (i) consider and provide physical features and social aspects that enable children to develop and maintain emotional bonds, such as attachment to their neighborhood; (ii) seek to understand what various places and physical features might offer, or afford, to children, what patterns of behavior these objects may trigger, and how these affordances can build and support children's independent active mobility; (iii) understand how the urban environment facilitates children's orientation and wayfinding and thereby provide control in the urban environment; and (iv) address how the environment supports the perception of personal safety during light and dark hours by attending to prospect and refuge.

It is fundamental to physical active transportation that urban open spaces are developed to ensure interlinkage through neighborhoods and cityscapes, and that are inclusive for everyone. Taking the perspective of children's independent active mobility as a point of departure would be a way to ensure that not only the UN Convention on the Rights of the Child, but also the sustainability target for urban environments in UN Agenda 2030 are met.

References

Agans, J. P., Säfvenbom, R., Davis, J. L., Bowers, E. P., & Lerner, R. M. (2013). Positive movement experiences: Approaching the study of athletic participation, exercise, and leisure activity through relational developmental systems theory and the concept of embodiment. *Advances in Child Development and Behavior, 45*, 261–286.

Alfonzo, M. A. (2005). To walk or not to walk? The hierarchy of walking needs. *Environment and Behavior, 37*, 808–836.

Alton, D., Adab, P., Roberts, L., & Barrett, T. (2007). Relationship between walking levels and perceptions of the local neighbourhood environment. *Archives of Disease in Childhood, 92*, 29–33.

Appleton, J. (1975). *The experience of landscape.* London: Wiley.

Babb, C., Olaru, D., Curtis, C., & Robertson, D. (2017). Children's active travel, local activity spaces and wellbeing: A case study in Perth, WA. *Travel Behaviour and Society, 9*, 81–94. https://doi.org/10.1016/j.tbs.2017.06.002.

Ben-Joseph, E. (1995). Changing the residential street scene—Adapting the shared street (Woonerf) concept to the suburban environment. *Journal of the American Planning Association, 61*(4), 504–515. https://doi.org/10.1080/01944369508975661.

Biddulph, M. (2010). Evaluating the English home zone initiatives. *Journal of the American Planning Association, 76*(2), 199–218.

Björklid, P., & Gummesson, M. (2013). *Children's independent mobility in Sweden (No. 2013:113).* Borlänge: The Swedish Transport Administration.

Boarnet, M. G., Anderson, C. L., Day, K., McMillan, T., & Alfonzo, M. (2005). Evaluation of the California safe routes to school legislation: Urban form changes and children's active transportation to school. *American Journal of Preventive Medicine, 28*(2 Suppl. 2), 134–140.

Boarnet, M. G., Day, K., Anderson, C., McMillan, T., & Alfonzo, M. (2005). California's safe routes to school program: Impacts on walking, bicycling, and pedestrian safety. *Journal of the American Planning Association, 71*(3), 301–317.

Bonaiuto, M., Aiello, A., Perugini, M., Bonnes, M., & Ercolani, A. P. (1999). Multi-dimensional perception of residential environment quality and neighbourhood attachment in the urban environment. *Journal of Environmental Psychology, 19*, 331–352.

Bonaiuto, M., Fornara, F., & Bonnes, M. (2003). Indexes of perceived residential environment quality and neighbourhood attachment in urban environments: A confirmation study on the city of Rome. *Landscape and Urban Planning, 65*, 41–52.

Bonaiuto, M., Fornara, F., & Bonnes, M. (2006). Perceived residential environment quality in middle- and low-extension Italian cities. *Revue Européenne de Psychologie Appliquée, 56*, 23–34.

Bringlof-Isler, B., Grize, L., Mäder, U., Ruch, N., Sennhauser, F. H., Braun-Fahrländer, C., et al. (2008). Personal and environmental factors associated with active commuting to school in Switzerland. *Preventive Medicine, 46*, 67–73.

Broberg, A., Kyttä, M., & Fagerholm, N. (2013). Child-friendly urban structures: Bullerby revisited. *Journal of Environmental Psychology, 35*, 110–120.

Buliung, R., Faulkner, G., Beesley, T., & Kennedy, J. (2011). School travel planning: Mobilizing school and community resources to encourage active school transportation. *Journal of School Health, 81*(11), 704–712. https://doi.org/10.1111/j.1746-1561.2011.00647.x.

Carver, A., Timperio, A., Hesketh, K., & Crawford, D. (2010). Are children and adolescents less active if parents restrict their physical activity and active transport due to perceived risk? *Social Science & Medicine, 70*, 1799–1805.

Cele, S. (2005). On foot in the city of children. *Nordic Journal of Architectural Research, 1*, 85–98.

Cervero, R., & Kockelman, K. (1997). Travel demand and the 3Ds: Density, diversity, and design. *Transportation Research D, 2*, 199–219.

Chatterjee, S. (2005). Children's friendship with place: A conceptual inquiry. *Children Youth and Environments, 15*, 1–26.

Chawla, L. (2015). Benefits of nature contact for children. *Journal of Planning Literature. 30*, https://doi.org/10.1177/0885412215595441.

Chawla, L., & Driskell, D. (2006). The growing up in cities project. *Journal of Community Practice, 14*, 183–200.

Chawla, L., Keena, K., Pevec, I., & Stanley, E. (2014). Green schoolyards as havens from stress and resources for resilience in childhood and adolescence. *Health & Place, 28*, 1–13.

Chillón, P., Evenson, K. R., Vaughn, A., & Ward, D. S. (2011). A systematic review of interventions for promoting active transportation to school. *International Journal of Behavioral Nutrition and Physical Activity. 8*, https://doi.org/10.1186/1479-5868-8-10.

Chillón, P., Ortega, F. B., Ruiz, J. R., Veidebaum, T., Oja, L., Mäestu, J., & Sjöström, M. (2010). Active commuting to school in children and adolescents: An opportunity to increase physical activity and fitness. *Scandinavian Journal of Public Health, 38*, 873–879.

Clark, C., & Uzzell, D. L. (2002). The affordances of the home, neighbourhood, school and town centre for adolescents. *Journal of Environmental Psychology, 22*, 95–108.

Cook, A., Whitzman, C., & Tranter, P. (2015). Is citizen kid an independent kid? The relationship between children's independent mobility and active citizenship. *Journal of Urban Design, 20*, 526–544.

Crawford, S., & Garrard, J. (2013). A combined impact-process evaluation of a program promoting active transport to school: Understanding the factors that shaped program effectiveness. *Journal of Environmental and Public Health, 2013.* https://doi.org/10.1155/2013/816961.

Davison, K. K., & Lawson, C. T. (2006). Do attributes in the physical environment influence children's physical activity? A review of the literature. *International Journal of Behavioral Nutrition and Physical Activity, 3*, 19.

de Vries, S. I., Bakker, I., van Mechelen, W., & Hopman-Rock, M. (2007). Determinants of activity-friendly neighborhoods for children: Results from the space study. *American Journal of Health Promotion, 21*, 312–316.

Ding, D., Sallis, J., Kerr, J., Lee, S., & Rosenberg, D. E. (2011). Neighborhood environment and physical activity among youth. A review. *American Journal of Preventive Medicine, 41,* 442–455.

Dosen, A. S., & Ostwald, M. J. (2016). Evidence for prospect-refuge theory: A meta-analysis of the findings of environmental preference research. *City, Territory and Architecture, 3,* 4. https://doi.org/10.1186/s40410-016-0033-1.

Evans, S. D. (2007). Youth sense of community: Voice and power in community contexts. *Journal of Community Psychology, 35,* 693–709.

Ewing, R., & Cervero, R. (2010). Travel and the built environment. *Journal of the American Planning Association, 76,* 265–294.

Fenner, J., Heathcote, D., & Jerrams-Smith, J. (2000). The development of wayfinding competency: Asymmetrical effects of visuo-spatial and verbal ability. *Journal of Environmental Psychology, 20,* 165–175.

Ferreira, I. A., Johansson, M., Sternudd, C., & Fornara, F. (2016). Transport walking in urban neighbourhoods—Impact of perceived neighbourhood qualities and emotional relationship. *Landscape and Urban Planning, 150,* 60–69.

Ferreira, I., van der Horst, K., Wendel-Vos, W., Kremers, S., van Lenthe, F. J., & Brug, J. (2006). Environmental correlates of physical activity in youth—A review and update. *Obesity Reviews, 8,* 129–154.

Fornara, F., Bonaiuto, M., & Bonnes, M. (2010). Cross-validation of abbreviated perceived residential environment quality (PREQ) and neighborhood attachment (NA) indicators. *Environment and Behavior, 20,* 1–26.

Fyhri, A., Hjorthal, R., Mackett, R., Fotel, T., & Kyttä, M. (2011). Children's active travel and independent mobility in four countries: Development, social contributing trends and measures. *Transport Policy, 18,* 703–710.

Gibson, R. (1979). *An ecological approach to visual perception.* Boston: Houghton Mifflin.

Gifford, R. (2016). *Research methods for environmental psychology.* Wiley and Blackwell.

Gill, T. (2006). Home zones in the UK: History, policy and impact on children and youth. *Children, Youth & Environments, 16,* 90.

Heft, H. (1988). Affordances of children's environments: A functional approach to environmental description. *Children's Environments Quarterly, 5,* 29–37.

Hidalgo, M. C., & Hernández, B. (2001). Place attachment: Conceptual and empirical questions. *Journal of Environmental Psychology, 21,* 273–281.

Holt, N. L., Spence, J. C., Sehn, Z. L., & Cutumisu, N. (2008). Neighborhood and developmental differences in children's perceptions of opportunities for play and physical activity. *Health & Place, 14,* 2–14.

Horelli, L. (1998). Creating child-friendly environments: Case studies on children's participation in three European countries. *Childhood, 5,* 225–239.

Horelli, L. (2007). Constructing a theoretical framework for environmental child-friendliness. *Children, Youth and Environments, 17,* 267–292.

Jamme, H., Bahl, D., & Banerjee, T. (2018). Between "broken windows" and the "eyes on the street:" walking to school in inner city San Diego. *Journal of Environmental Psychology, 55,* 121–138.

Jansson, M., Fors, H., Lindgren, T., & Wiström, B. (2013). Perceived safety in relation to urban woodland vegetation—A review. *Urban Forestry & Urban Greening, 12,* 127–133.

Jansson, M., & Lindgren, T. (2012). A review of the concept 'management' in relation to urban landscapes and green spaces: Toward a holistic understanding. *Urban Forestry & Urban Greening, 2,* 139–145.

Jansson, M., Sundevall, E., & Wales, M. (2016). The role of green spaces and their management in a child-friendly urban village. *Urban Forestry & Urban Greening, 18,* 228–236.

Johansson, M. (2003). Social dangers as constraints for pro-environmental travel modes— The perception of parents in England and Sweden. *Medio Ambiente y Comportamiento Humano, 4,* 49–69.

Johansson, M. (2006). Environment and parental factors as determinants of mode for children's leisure travel. *Journal of Environmental Psychology, 26,* 156–169.

Johansson, M., Sternudd, C., & Kärrholm, M. (2016). Perceived urban design qualities and affective experience of walking. *Journal of Urban Design, 21,* 256–275.

Kärrholm, M., Johansson, M., Lindelöw, D., & Ferreira, I. A. (2014). Interseriality and different sorts of walking: Suggestions for a relational approach to urban walking. *Mobilities.* https://doi.org/10.1080/17450101.2014.969596.

Karsten, L., & van Vliet, W. (2006). Children in the city: Reclaiming the street. *Children, Youth & Environments, 16,* 151–167.

Keane, C. (1998). Evaluating the influence of fear of crime as an environmental mobility restrictor on women's routine activities. *Environment and Behavior, 30,* 60–74.

Korpela, K. (1992). Adolescents' favourite places and environmental self-regulation. *Journal of Environmental Psychology, 12,* 249–258.

Kyttä, M. (2004). The extent of children's independent mobility and the number of actualized affordances as criteria for child-friendly environments. *Journal of Environmental Psychology, 24,* 179–198.

Kyttä, A. M., Broberg, A. K., & Kahila, M. H. (2012). Urban environment and children's active lifestyle: Softgis revealing children's behavioral patterns and meaningful places. *American Journal of Health Promotion, 26,* 137–148.

Larouche, R., Mammen, G., Rowe, D. A., & Faulkner, G. (2018). Effectiveness of active school transport interventions: A systematic review and update. *BMC Public Health. 18,* https://doi.org/10.1186/s12889-017-5005-1.

Lerstrup, I., & Konijnendijk van den Bosch, C. (2017). Affordances of outdoor settings for children in preschool: Revisiting heft's functional taxonomy. *Landscape Research, 42,* 47–62.

Lewicka, M. (2010). What makes neighborhood different from home and city? Effects of place scale on place attachment. *Journal of Environmental Psychology, 30,* 35–51.

Lewicka, M. (2011). Place attachment: How far have we come in the last 40 years? *Journal of Environmental Psychology, 31,* 207–230.

Lingwood, J., Blades, M., Farran, E. K., Courbois, Y., & Matthews, D. (2015). The development of wayfinding abilities in children: Learning routes with and without landmarks. *Journal of Environmental Psychology, 41,* 74–80.

Lueder, R., & Rice, V. B. (2008). *Ergonomics for children: Designing products and places for toddlers to teens.* New York/London: Taylor & Francis, Cop.

Lynch, K. (1960). *The image of the City.* Cambridge, Mass.: M.I.T. Press.

Mårtensson, F. (2004). *The landscape in children's play. A study of outdoor play in preschools:* (p. 464). (Dissertation)Alnarp, Agraria: Swedish University of Agricultural Sciences, Acta Universitatis (in Swedish).

Mårtensson, F. (2013). Guiding environmental dimensions for outdoor play. *Journal of Social Medicine, 90,* 658–665.

Mårtensson, F., Jansson, M., Johansson, M., Raustorp, A., Kylin, M., & Boldemann, C. (2014). The role of greenery for physical activity play at school grounds. *Urban Forestry & Urban Greening, 13,* 103–113.

Mårtensson, F., & Nordström, M. (2017). Nordic child-friendly planning reconsidered. In K. Bishop & L. Corkery (Eds.), *Designing cities with children and young people; beyond playgrounds and skate parks.* Routledge.

McDonald, N. C., Deakin, E., & Aalborg, A. E. (2010). Influence of the social environment on children's school travel. *Preventive Medicine, 50*(Suppl), S65–S68.

Merom, D., Tudor-Locke, C., Bauman, A., & Rissel, C. (2006). Active commuting to school among NSW primary school children: Implications for public health. *Health & Place*, *12*, 678–687.

Mitra, R. (2013). Independent mobility and mode choice for school transportation: A review and framework for future research. *Transport Reviews*, *33*, 21–43.

Morrow, V. (1999). Conceptualising social capital in relation to the well-being of children and young people: A critical review. *The Sociological Review*, *47*, 744–765.

Napier, M. A., Brown, B. B., Werner, C. M., & Gallimore, J. (2011). Walking to school: Community design and child and parent barriers. *Journal of Environmental Psychology*, *31*, 45–51.

Nasar, J. L. (2008). Assessing perceptions of environments for active living. *American Journal of Preventive Medicine*, *34*, 357–363.

Nasar, J. L., & Fisher, B. (1992). Design for vulnerability. Cues and reactions to fear of crime. *Sociology and Social Research*, *76*, 48–58.

Nordström, M. (2010). Children's views on child-friendly environments in different geographical, cultural and social neighbourhoods. *Urban Studies*, *47*, 514–528.

Noschis, K. (1992). Child development theory and planning for neighbourhood play. *Children's Environments*, *9*, 3–9.

Prezza, M., & Pacilli, M. G. (2007). Current fear of crime, sense of community and loneliness in Italian adolescents: The role of autonomous mobility and play during childhood. *Journal of Community Psychology*, *35*, 151–170.

Prezza, M., Pilloni, S., Morabito, C., Sersante, C., Alparone, F. M., & Giuliani, M. V. (2001). The influence of psychological and environmental factors on children's independent mobility and relationship to peer frequentation. *Journal of Community and Applied Psychology*, *11*, 435–450.

Rahm, J., & Johansson, M. (submitted). "In the evening, I don't walk in the park": Urban greenery, outdoor lighting and the perception of safety. Urban Design International.

Randrup, T. B., & Persson, B. (2009). Public green spaces in the Nordic countries: Development of a new strategic management regime. *Urban Forestry & Urban Greening*, *1*, 31–40.

Refshauge, A. D., Stigsdotter, U. K., Lamm, B., & Thorleifsdottir, K. (2013). Evidence-based playground design: Lessons learned from theory to practice. *Landscape Research*, *40*, 226–246.

Rodiek, J. E. (2006). Landscape planning: Its contribution to the evolution of the profession of landscape architecture. *Landscape and Urban Planning*, *1*, 291–297.

Scannell, L., & Gifford, R. (2010). Defining place attachment: A tripartite organizing framework. *Journal of Environmental Psychology*, *30*, 1–10.

Segal, R. (2015). *Playfinding: Child-friendly wayfinding as a tool for children's independent mobility in the Exchange District of Winnipeg, Manitoba.*

Shaw, B., Bicket, M., Elliott, B., Fagan-Watson, B., Mocca, E., & Hillman, M. (2015). *Children's independent mobility: An international comparison and recommendations for action.* London: Policy Studies Institute.

Skelton, T. (2007). Children, young people, UNICEF and participation. *Children's Geographies*, *5*, 165–181.

Timperio, A., Crawford, D., Telford, A., & Salford, J. (2004). Perceptions about the local neighborhood and walking and cycling among children. *Preventive Medicine*, *38*, 39–47.

Tudor-Locke, C., Ainsworth, B. E., & Popkin, B. M. (2001). Active commuting to school and overlooked source of children's physical activity. *Sports Medicine*, *31*, 309–313.

Uzzell, D., Pol, E., & Badenas, D. (2002). Place identification, social cohesion, and environmental sustainability. *Environment and Behavior*, *34*, 26–53.

van Loon, J., & Frank, L. (2011). Urban form relationships with youth physical activity: Implications for research and practice. *Journal of Planning Literature*, *26*, 280–308.

van Sluijs, E. M., Fearne, V. A., Mattocks, C., Riddoch, C., Griffin, S. J., & Ness, A. (2009). The contribution of active travel to children's physical activity levels: Cross-sectional results from the ALSPAC study. *Preventive Medicine, 48*, 519–524.

Villanueva, K., et al. (2016). Can the neighbourhood built environment make a difference in children's development? Building the research agenda to create evidence for place-based children's policy. *Academic Pediatrics, 16*, 10–19.

Waygood, E. O. D., Friman, M., Olsson, L. E., & Taniguchi, A. (2017). Transport and child well-being: An integrative review. *Travel Behaviour and Society, 8*, 32–49.

Wells, N., Jimenez, F. E., & Mårtensson, F. (2018). Chapter 6.1: Children and nature. In M. van den Bosch & W. Bird (Eds.), *The role of nature in improving the health of a population* (pp. 167–176). Oxford Textbooks in Public Health.

Westford, P. (2010). *Neighborhood design and travel a study of residential quality, child leisure activity and trips to school.* (Doctoral dissertation) Stockholm: Royal Institute of Technology.

WHO, World Health Organization (2011). http://www.who.int/dietphysicalactivity/publications/recommendations5_17years/en/.

Wunderlich, F. M. (2008). Walking and rhythmicity: Sensing urban space. *Journal of Urban Design, 13*, 125–239.

Further reading

Carver, A., Timperio, A., & Crawford, D. (2008). Playing it safe: The influence of neighbourhood safety on children's physical activity—A review. *Health & Place, 14*, 217–227.

Foster, S., Villanueva, K., Wood, L., Christian, H., & Giles-Corti, B. (2014). The impact of parents' fear of strangers and perceptions of informal social control on children's independent mobility. *Health & Place, 26*, 60–68.

van den Brink, A., Bruns, D., Tobi, H., & Bell, S. (Eds.), (2016). *Research in landscape architecture: Methods and methodology.* New York, NY: Routledge.

CHAPTER THIRTEEN

Bringing back play to urban streets

Raktim Mitra and Zainab Abbasi
School of Urban and Regional Planning, Ryerson University, Toronto, ON, Canada

Contents

1 Introduction

Most children today are deprived of the opportunity to explore their neighborhoods by themselves or with friends and to engage in outdoor play of any kind outside of their backyards or front lawns. Streets have historically played an important role as locations for social encounters, and places for pleasure and civic engagement (Fyfe, 1998; Malone, 2002). Neighborhood streets have been common places for children to meet friends and play outdoors. But with the evolution and popularity of automobiles over the past century, transportation infrastructure are often conceptualized, designed and built as "roads", primarily to facilitate the movement of motorized vehicles, undermining the role of streets as a critical component of the public realm. As vehicles have taken over street right-of-ways, adults have discouraged children's presence on their neighborhood streets. In addition, a shift in culture around children's mobility, where adults are expected to constantly supervise a child's every movement outside of their home, as well as increased parental concerns over safety from traffic, have severely limited children's presence on outdoor public spaces including streets (Carver, Timperio, & Crawford, 2008; Faulkner, Mitra, Buliung, Fusco, & Stone, 2015; Jarvis, Newman, & Swiniarski, 2014). Some of these concerns are supported by evidence of how transportation affects a child's health and safety. Chapters 6 and 7 in this book elaborately discuss detrimental effects of traffic speed and emissions on children.

In addition to providing an opportunity to be independent, spontaneous and creative, outdoor play offers immense physical- and social health-related benefits for children (Cheng & Johnson, 2010; Faulkner et al., 2015; Gleave & Cole-Hamilton, 2012; Valentine & McKendrick, 1997). Play also provides benefits to parents and community members. While children play independently without direct parental supervision, adults can use this time to meet and interact with one another, develop a sense of community and build social capital (Murray & Devecchi, 2016; Weller & Bruegel, 2009; Wilson, 1996).

Despite many potential benefits, lack of availability and accessibility to open spaces have largely limited children to the confines of their homes (Carver et al., 2008; Faulkner et al., 2015; Karsten, 2005; Read, 2011; Tandy, 1999). Eroding parental support toward children's presence on neighborhood streets, coupled with regulatory mechanisms that separate land uses and define the desired users of each use, have also engineered children out of the streets over the past century, and consequently had a further detrimental affect on children's health and wellbeing.

Re-introducing urban and suburban neighborhood streets for children's outdoor play, and at the same time limiting automobile access and speed, can be a way of providing easy access to outdoor play space and enable independent mobility by providing safer environments for a vast majority of our children. This chapter discusses one such programming approach, popularly known as "play streets". Examples of successful play streets are discussed, with a particular focus on the StreetPLAY pilot conducted in Toronto, Canada, in 2017. We have analyzed the benefits to such programming for children and the community and identified key conditions for successful implementation of play streets.

2 Bringing back play to urban streets

Since the mid-1900s, playgrounds have been used as a means to steer children away from playing on the streets and into controlled spaces where behavior could be monitored closely and where 'appropriate' play would occur (Hart, 2002). Children were being kept out of our streets through mechanisms such as play bans. More importantly, children are often made to feel marginalized around vehicles on streets. A study of 11- and 12-year-old Danish children (Fotel, 2009) found that children did not feel respected by car drivers even when they had the right of way.

The City of Toronto, Canada, for example, banned street hockey and ball play on streets under the City of Toronto Act in 2006. A key purpose of this ban was to maintain streets for the safe passage of vehicular and pedestrian traffic (City of Toronto, 2011a, 2016). The ban was also placed to ensure the safety of children who may be less aware of their surroundings when parents or supervisors are not watching them. Leaving hockey nets or basketballs on the street would result in a $90 fine under the ban (City of Toronto, 2011a). The ban prevented the opportunity for children to take advantage of local streets as play spaces in close proximity of their homes, where parents or caregivers are within earshot distance. Similar regulations became a common practice in many other municipalities across Canada and the US. Recently in 2016, the City of Toronto followed many other North American municipalities by passing a motion to lift the ban and welcomed the use of local streets for outdoor play (City of Toronto By-law 775-2016). This new policy environment offers an exciting opportunity to welcome children out onto the street for play once again.

However, bringing outdoor free play back to neighborhood streets has become almost impossible without some form of community-led programmed intervention. These interventions, known broadly as "tactical urbanism" in the field of Urban Planning, are citizen-organized, quick and inexpensive tactics to improve the local environment as a response to the lengthy bureaucratic process of implementing changes in the local environment (Lydon & Garcia, 2015). Where broader policies and urban norms do not support such opportunities for play, citizens may mobilize in reimagining, reclaiming and reprogramming public spaces and demonstrating the effects of short term actions on long term changes in improving livability and building social capital (Lydon & Garcia, 2015). Typically, the aim of these tactics and short-term interventions is to bring attention to the benefits and garner wider popular and municipal policy support. Inspired by this broader tactical urbanism movement, play street programs have become increasingly common across the western countries.

3 The emergence of play street programs

The basic idea behind play streets is simple—to open up neighborhood streets for children's play by limiting or eliminating access by automobile, during specific times of the day. Volunteers from the community ensure 'eyes on street', eliminating the need for constant parental supervision when children play on their local street, meet with friends or simply explore the street. These programs are motivated by the need for play and independence in a child's life and the historical role that urban streets have played in enabling children's outdoor play and mobility (Ferguson & Page, 2015; Hart, 2002). While the nature and scope of play street programs vary widely depending on context, needs and supports from communities, programs from North America, Europe and Australia have emphasized the importance of community advocacy, neighborhood-level support and supportive policy as some of the key facets of successful implementation of play streets.

3.1 Playing out program, Bristol, England

The Playing Out model in Bristol, England was initiated by local parents frustrated with the lack of opportunities for children to play freely on the street (Ferguson & Page, 2015). The low-cost intervention was developed to provide safe spaces for children's free play. It consists of a partial road closure after school hours on designated days for a given period of time, organized and supervised by neighbors. Since its inception in 2009, the program has grown tremendously and the Playing Out team now provides hands-on support to other streets in Bristol in organizing street plays in their neighborhoods. The positive impact of the program is felt across the country with 40 towns and cities in UK having organized over 250 Playing Out sessions by 2015 (Ferguson & Page, 2015).

3.2 Play streets, London, England

The non-profit organization London Play, in London, England began implementing play streets across the city in 2008 as part of their commitment to and advocacy around outdoor play. The first play streets were also influenced by supportive policy, such as "The Children's Plan" by the Ministry of Children, Schools and Families, that emphasized the development of play strategies nationally and across municipalities in England (Ministry of Children, Schools and Families, UK, 2007). Significant financial commitment was made by the government to develop and implement these strategies. In 2012, the Mayor of London published new supplementary planning guidance for play in London. Also in 2013, the Government of England formally recognized the benefits of play streets, leading to a re-emergence of play streets in recent years (London Play, n.d.-a).

Currently, the majority of the boroughs in London have play street programs in some of their streets. As part of a recent multi-sectoral collaboration that includes the Playing Out program in Bristol, and that is funded by the Department of Health, London Play is working toward building community capacity in developing and sustaining play streets programs in London and across the country (London Play, n.d.-b). With specific focus on 12 of London's 32 boroughs, London Play is also working with councils to enable municipality-supported and community-led play streets across London.

3.3 Street renaissance program, New York City, USA

With a population density that has the city bursting at the seams, children in New York City do not have adequate access to safe outdoor play (Hart, 2002). Local community leaders in many neighborhoods have recognized the potential of streets for safe outdoor play. Building on this momentum, in 2005 and 2006 community organizations, non-profit organizations and the City governance collaborated in developing various street play programs which improved community members' access to streets for play all over the city.

The Streets Renaissance Program in New York City runs through a partnership between urban planning, transportation and several non-profit organizations, namely—Project for Public Spaces, Transportation Alternatives and the Open Planning Project. Together, they have developed a campaign model to spur positive change in transportation policy in New York City (Project for Public Spaces, 2006). The program resulted in various block parties and street play programs through partnerships with local community organizations in each neighborhood.

In New York City, residents can apply for a block party permit for $15 to temporarily close off the street for all community members to enjoy. Transportation Alternatives provided thirty $300 grants to low-income neighborhoods to encourage them and to help cover costs of hosting the block parties, such as the permit expenses, food, drinks and supplies. Grants were primarily awarded to neighborhoods hosting community events for the first time. Transportation Alternatives also provided hands-on support during the events. As a result, nearly 3300 block parties took place between 2007 and 2008.

For example, in the Jackson Heights neighborhood, community members advocated to close the street next to their park (78th Street) in order to extend the play space of the often crowded park. The Streets Renaissance

Program helped the community navigate liability and insurance issues by working with the City to develop an agreement. The program ensured that the City's transportation department maintains liability for safety and the maintenance of the street. Local residents were responsible for maintaining the street closure. The neighborhood successfully closed the street every Sunday from June to November. The pilot project gained a lot of popularity with the community. The community collaborated with the Jackson Heights Green Alliance (JH Green) to establish a long-term program for 78th Street (Project for Public Spaces, 2015). Through the collaborative efforts, JH Green successfully turned 78th Street into a car-free zone from June through November. As a result, today it is a popular site for community events and gathering, and the Department of Transportation is redesigning the site into a pedestrianized plaza to reflect the community's needs (Project for Public Spaces, 2015).

3.4 Play streets, San Francisco, USA

San Francisco was one of ten cities selected as part of the national Play Streets program run by the Partnership for a Healthier America and Blue Cross and Blue Shield Association. The Play Streets program in San Francisco was implemented through a partnership between local non-profit Livable City, and was financially sponsored by the San Francisco Municipal Transportation Agency (SFMTA). Between June and August of 2013, the program activated smaller scale one to two car-free city blocks for children's outdoor play in four underserved neighborhoods.

The program was flexible for neighborhoods to tailor to their own preferences and use. As a result, the program significantly contributed to the amount of usable open space for recreation, in proximity to the residents' homes. There was strong agreement throughout the neighborhood that the program strengthened the community (Zeif, Chaudhuri, & Musselman, 2016).

Recently in 2017 the SFMTA, the San Francisco Planning Department and the Department of Public Health launched a new Play Streets program two-year pilot with the aim of implementing the program city-wide. Subsequently, two play street programs were run in 2017 and 2018.

3.5 Play street program, Seattle, USA

In 2014, the Seattle Department of Transportation (SDOT) piloted the Play Streets Program in Seattle. SDOT developed a pilot program which consisted of a free and simple permit to which interested neighborhoods applied.

The permit system was free to encourage all neighborhoods to participate. Play Streets events were held in all seven districts of the city. During the pilot, the SDOT issued over 185 permits for play streets. Following the success of the initial pilots, the SDOT formalized the program in 2016. They have since developed a Play Streets Handbook, a checklist and video tutorials to equip interested communities with all the information they need to successfully host Play Streets events (Seattle Department of Transportation, 2016).

4 The StreetPLAY program in Toronto, Canada

Earth Day Canada, a non-profit organization based in Toronto, collaborated with the City of Toronto in 2017 to introduce StreetPLAY programming onto residential streets in the city (Earth Day Canada, 2019). The pilot project took place in one neighborhood (Seaton Village), where there was existing political support from local city councilors, as well as interested community members. Seaton Village is an inner-urban neighborhood located to the west of downtown Toronto with a median household income in the neighborhood that is higher than the city of Toronto average (City of Toronto, 2011b). It is also a rapidly gentrifying neighborhood; the detached, semi-detached and row houses have appreciated by 62% in terms of property values, in a short span of 2 years (Metro News, 2017).

Several community meetings were held to identify residential streets for the pilot project. In the end, 7 residential street sections were selected: 4 sections of Clinton Street between Bloor St and Dupont St; Palmerston Gardens; Markham St & Follis Ave; and Pendrith Street (Fig. 1). Each day of the week, one or two different streets were closed to vehicles and activated for children's street play. On weekdays the street closure was from 4 to 8 pm and on Sundays from 2 to 5 pm. A total of 155 StreetPLAY events took place in June, September and October of 2017 (Earth Day Canada, 2019).

As a result of further collaboration with the City of Toronto, the Transportation Services Department waived the street closure permit fee and did not require a third-partly liability insurance, making the event free for all residents. Parents and community members were recruited to supervise the street closures. Earth Day Canada's Street Team and local volunteers (often parents or high school students) supervised the events and managed the street closure during the StreetPLAY events. Locally available materials such as recycling bins and hockey nets with a StreetPLAY sign attached were

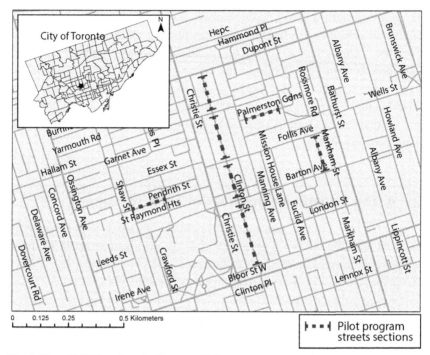

Fig. 1 StreetPLAY locations in Toronto, 2017.

used as a physical barrier to close off the street to vehicular traffic, except for residents living on the street.

5 Benefits to children and community

A limited literature has provided evidence of the benefits of play street programs, particularly in the European context. For example, Ferguson and Page (2015) studied the Playing Out project in Bristol, England and identified increased independence and confidence among children. The project also provided an opportunity for active after-school time for children. Murray and Devecchi's (2016) investigation of a play street program in a large British town also identified several benefits. Children were more likely to spend time outdoor after the programming. Parents also reported improved perceptions of street safety, reducing the need for direct parental supervision in the presence of community volunteers.

The StreetPLAY pilot in Toronto also offered an opportunity to provide novel insights into the benefits of such programming. The pilot ran for

4 months and a total of 155 events (i.e., street closures) were held; the communities got prolonged exposure reducing the potential biases in response. We conducted field observations as well as parent surveys at each participating StreetPLAY street on three randomly selected event days, in July, September and October of 2017 (two weekdays and a Sunday at each street). A total of 104 responses from parents and caregivers were collected, representing 157 children who participated in these events. In addition, neighborhood surveys were conducted after the completion of the StreetPLAY pilot, to collect data from community members, regardless of whether they or their children (if any) had participated in the StreetPLAY event or not. These surveys were collected in November 2017 on two randomly selected weekday evenings. Each address on both sides of the streets where the StreetPLAY event took place ($n = 545$) was tried at least twice, on different days. One adult household member was asked to fill out a short survey. In the end, a total of 105 completed neighborhood surveys were collected (19% response rate).

Our results show that as the StreetPLAY pilot brought play back to the streets in the Seaton Village neighborhood, children aged 4–11 years were particularly benefited. Three-quarters (74%) of children participating were between 4 and 11 years of age, and only 1 in 10 children were 12 years or older (Table 1). Overall, more girls attended the events than the boys

Table 1 Characteristics of participating children: participant survey results

Variable	Frequency	Percent (%)
Age of children ($n = 154$)		
0–3 years old	24	15.6
4–7 years old	62	40.3
8–11 years old	53	34.4
12 years and up	15	9.7
Gender of children ($n = 157$)		
Girl	87	55.4
Boy	69	44.2
Other	1	0.01
Time children spent at StreetPLAY ($n = 156$)		
Less than 30 min	22	14.1
30–60 min	38	24.4
1–2 h	53	33.9
More than 2 h	43	27.6
Frequency of visit to StreetPLAY ($n = 154$)		
This was my first time	8	5.2
More than once since the program started	102	66.2
I have come to all of the events on my street	44	28.6

(58% vs 42%). The majority of the children spent at least 1 hour outside as they participated. Also encouraging is the finding that at the time of the survey, 29% of them would have come to every StreetPLAY event on their street, and nearly a two-thirds (66%) reported coming to the event more than once (Table 1).

Our neighborhood surveys provided a better picture of the participation rate among children who live in the Seaton Village community. Results from the neighborhood survey indicated that the majority of children aged <4 years (57%) and 4–7 years (55%), and 44% of 8–11 year old children attended more than one StreetPLAY events (parent reports after completion of pilot) (Fig. 2). At least one fifth of children in each age group (29%, 20% and 34% respectively) attended at least one event each week.

As the streets became community play spaces, many participating children were able to engage in a diverse range of activities alone or with friends with minimum adult supervision. Popular activities according to parents were running (81%), cycling/skateboarding (70%), ball games (63%), drawing/coloring (45%), bubbles (32%), skipping (31%), water play (17%), hula hooping (15%), hopscotch (13%) and scooter (6%) (Fig. 3). Many parents brought their children out to the streets and helped the younger ones with their outdoor play. Parents also spent time socializing with other community members. With more eyes on the street and safe environmental conditions without the cars, there were less concerns about children's traffic or personal safety.

In order to assess broader implications of the StreetPLAY pilot programming on the local community, our neighborhood survey asked a set of questions that aimed to capture the community's perceptions on benefits, safety and (in)convenience. The community members responded to a group

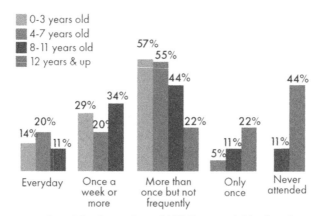

Fig. 2 Frequency of participation at StreetPLAY Event: neighborhood survey results.

(A)

(B)

Fig. 3 Children of different ages playing at StreetPLAY events. *(Photo courtesy: Earth Day Canada (2019). The Toronto StreetPLAY pilot project (TSPP). https://bit.ly/2AYkvXn.)*

of statements on a 5-point scale ranging from 'strongly agree' to 'strongly disagree'. For easier interpretation, the proportion of positive responses (i.e., strongly agree or agree) were compared with the proportion of more negative responses. In this chapter, we have highlighted perceived benefits to a child, and perceived inconveniences, as reported by community members (Table 2).

Table 2 Perceptions of StreetPLAY: neighborhood survey results

Variable	Frequency	Percent (%)
Benefits		
StreetPLAY has offered a safe outdoor play environment for children		
Agree	96	91.4
Neutral or disagree	9	8.6
StreetPLAY requires less adult supervision when children play outside		
Agree	71	67.6
Neutral or disagree	34	32.4
StreetPLAY provides an opportunity for a child to make new friends		
Agree	88	83.8
Neutral or disagree	17	16.2
Inconveniences		
StreetPLAY makes me uncomfortable when running daily errands		
Agree	9	8.6
Neutral or disagree	96	91.4
StreeyPLAY creates congestion on nearby street		
Agree	6	5.7
Neutral or disagree	99	94.3
StreetPLAY creates problems with parking		
Agree	14	13.3
Neutral or disagree	91	86.7

Almost all of the community members (91.4%) felt that the StreetPLAY events offered a safe play environment for children, and that such events were better for children's social wellbeing as they provided opportunities to make new friends (83.8%). There appears to be not much disagreement about the benefits of these events to children in the community. However, a smaller proportion of community members felt that StreetPLAY enabled an environment where, according to them, children needed less supervision (67.7%). In other words, despite a recognition of improved personal and traffic safety, a third of the residents in the neighborhood were still hesitant to consider more independent mobility for their children or other children living in the neighborhood.

Interestingly, very few residents outlined their concerns about the mobility inconveniences that may occur (e.g., discomfort due to limited access to cars, congestion in nearby streets and parking) as a result of the StreetPLAY events, when streets are closed off for automobiles, allowing only limited and controlled access to local residents (Table 2). Problems with finding parking came out as the biggest concern, with 13% residents identifying this as a problem. The finding may not be surprising when the urban context of this neighborhood is considered. Seaton Village is an inner urban neighborhood with excellent connection to downtown Toronto (i.e., the major employment center) via multiple public transportation options and the bicycle network. The majority of residents either use transit or bicycle to get to work in summer and fall, and as a result, afternoon street closures would not create much problem for commuting adults. The smaller proportion of residents who would drive to/from work and other activities/places could still use alternative routes and park (perhaps temporarily) on other streets without creating major congestion issues.

6 Conclusion and way forward

Children's access to neighborhood and the opportunity for unsupervised exploration and free play have been overlooked across the western world in recent decades (Mitra, Faulkner, Buliung, & Stone, 2014; Wood, 2017). Historically, neighborhood streets were common places for children to meet, play and socialize. A shift in mobility culture and automobile-centric urban planning approaches has slowly moved children away from streets and into the backyards, playgrounds and recreational facilities. In recent decades, tactical urbanism-inspired interventions, broadly known as play streets, which is a community-led play intervention that opens up neighborhood streets for children's play by limiting or restricting access by automobiles, have gained popularity. We have discussed international examples of successful play street interventions, with a particular emphasis on findings from a pilot project in Toronto, Canada.

The case studies discussed in this chapter are almost always led by the community-advocacy groups, or by neighborhood groups that evolved into advocacy organizations over time. However, support from the communities and local parents, and supportive policy environment, are the keys to successful implementation of play street programs. The programs that have sustained and grown over time were directly supported by the municipalities or other upper-levels of the government.

In Toronto, political leadership from the city councilors helped bring the StreetPLAY program to the Seaton Village neighborhood. Earth Day Canada engaged with the interested communities on multiple events, which led to a greater awareness of the pilot project. Later, coordination between Earth Day Canada and City of Toronto's Transportation Services Division facilitated the planning and delivery of the StreetPLAY pilot project. The City did not require residents to pay a fee for the street closure permit, and as a result, the events were free and open for everyone to enjoy. The City also did not require third party liability insurance, which significantly facilitated program implementation. In addition, local city councilors were consistently kept informed of the progress of the pilot project; strong, open communication made it easier to solve any issues with the implementation along the way.

Our research based in Toronto confirmed previous literature in showing that play street events can create new and exciting opportunities for outdoor play for children, and may contribute to improved physical, mental and social health and wellbeing. It should be noted that the StreetPLAY pilot was implemented in a neighborhood that is inhabited by relatively more educated and high-income people, and the community already has strong social capital. In fact, these characteristics probably helped with bringing the pilot to this community in the first place. However, some have argued that children living in low-income and deprived communities may benefit even more from such programming interventions, as many children in those communities are deprived of the opportunities to safely engage in outdoor play (Humbert et al., 2006; Jarvis et al., 2014). Implementing community-led programming in these communities is often harder because of poor infrastructure and lower social capital or community organizational capacity (Reitsma-Street, Maczewski, & Neysmith, 2000). The impact of play street programming on children and adults living in low-income and disadvantaged communities, particularly in the context of Toronto or other North American communities, remains a topic for future research.

In addition, when it comes to the broader concerns around children's independent mobility, our findings are less conclusive. Previously, Murray and Devecchi (2016) argued that play streets may not necessarily enable "play", which by definition should be freely chosen, spontaneous, generally self-directed, and fun (Faulkner et al., 2015; Gleave & Cole-Hamilton, 2012; Gray, 2011). In comparison, the StreetPLAY events were somewhat programmed, and our surveys indicated that one-third of the residents in the community did not feel that the events reduced the need for adult supervision when children played outdoors. While it is difficult to change the culture of mobility that has taken almost a century to develop, we argue that interventions such as play streets that open up opportunities for children to use public space, even when under limited supervision, is a step toward greater independence of children.

To conclude, we found that re-introducing streets for all users of the space has its benefits, but it requires support from politicians, municipal governments and more importantly, the community. There is an opportunity for the Urban Planning policy and practice to learn from these experiences across the western world, and we hope that these short-term actions can ultimately result in broader changes in community planning practice where children's independence and safe outdoor presence will be more clearly recognized.

References

Carver, A., Timperio, A., & Crawford, D. (2008). Playing it safe: The influence of neighbourhood safety on children's physical activity—A review. *Health and Place*, *14*(2), 217–227.

Cheng, M., & Johnson, J. (2010). Research on children's play: Analysis of developmental and early education journals from 2005 to 2007. *Early Childhood Education Journal*, *37*, 249–259.

City of Toronto. (2011a). *Playing of ball sports on residential streets in Toronto. City of Toronto staff report to public works and infrastructure committee.* https://www.toronto.ca/legdocs/mmis/2011/pw/bgrd/backgroundle-37328.pdf.

City of Toronto. (2011b). *Neighbourhood profile—Annex.* City of Toronto Social Policy Analysis and Research. https://www.toronto.ca/ext/sdfa/Neighbourhood%20Profiles/pdf/2016/pdf1/cpa95.pdf.

City of Toronto. (2016). *By-law no. 775-2016. Public works and infrastructure committee item PW14.11.* City of Toronto.

Earth Day Canada. (2019). *The Toronto StreetPLAY pilot project (TSPP).* https://bit.ly/2AYkvXn.

Faulkner, G., Mitra, R., Buliung, R., Fusco, C., & Stone, M. (2015). Children's outdoor play time, physical activity and parental perceptions of neighbourhood environment. *International Journal of Play*, *4*(1), 84–97.

Ferguson, A., & Page, A. (2015). Austerity as opportunity supporting healthy street play on a budget: A winner from every perspective. *International Journal of Play*, *4*(3), 266–269.

Fotel, T. (2009). Marginalized or empowered? Street reclaiming strategies and the situated politics of children's mobilities. *Geography Compass*, *3*(3), 1267–1280.

Fyfe, N. R. (1998). *Images of the streets: Planning, identity and control in public space.* New York: Routledge.

Gleave, J., & Cole-Hamilton, I. (2012). *A world without play: A literature review.* London: Play England. http://www.playengland.org.uk/media/371031/a-world-without-play-literature-review-2012.pdf.

Gray, P. (2011). The decline of play and the rise of psychopathology in children and adolescents. *American Journal of Play*, *3*, 443–463.

Hart, R. (2002). Containing children: Some lesson on planning for play from New York City. *Environment & Urbanization*, *14*(2), 135–148.

Humbert, M., Chad, K., Spink, K., Muhajarine, N., Anderson, K. D., Bruner, M. W., et al. (2006). Factors that influence physical activity participation among high- and low-SES youth. *Quality Health Research*, *16*(4), 467–483.

Jarvis, P., Newman, S., & Swiniarski, I. (2014). On "becoming social": The importance of collaborative free play in childhood. *International Journal of Play*, *3*(1), 53–68.

Karsten, L. (2005). It all used to be better? Different generations on continuity and change in urban children's daily use of space. *Children's Geographies*, *3*(3), 275–290.

London Play (n.d.-a) London play—Our history. https://www.londonplay.org.uk/content/29919/about_us/our_history/our_history.

London Play (n.d.-b) Street play project. https://www.londonplay.org.uk/content/30773/our_work/recent_work/play_streets/street_play_project.

Lydon, M., & Garcia, A. (2015). *Tactical urbanism: Short-term action for long-term change.* Washington, DC: Island Press.

Malone, K. (2002). Street life: Youth, culture and competing uses of public space. *Environment & Urbanization, 14*(2), 157–168.

Metro News. (2017). *Home in Toronto's Seaton village neighbourhood appreciates 62% in two years.* Torstar News Service.

Ministry of Children, Schools and Families, UK. (2007). *The children's plan—Building brighter futures.* https://webarchive.nationalarchives.gov.uk/20130323053208/https://www.education.gov.uk/publications/eOrderingDownload/The_Childrens_Plan.pdf.

Mitra, R., Faulkner, G. E. J., Buliung, R. N., & Stone, M. R. (2014). Do parental perceptions of the neighbourhood environment influence children's independent mobility? Evidence from Toronto, Canada. *Urban Studies, 51*(16), 3401–3419.

Murray, J., & Devecchi, C. (2016). The Hantown street play project. *International Journal of Play, 5*(2), 196–211.

Project for Public Spaces. (2006). *New York City streets renaissance.* https://www.pps.org/projects/new-york-city-streets-renaissance.

Project for Public Spaces. (2015). *78th street play street.* https://www.pps.org/places/78th-street-play-street.

Read, J. (2011). Gutter to garden: Historical discourses of risk in interventions in working class children's street play. *Children & Society, 25*(1), 421–434.

Reitsma-Street, M., Maczewski, M., & Neysmith, S. (2000). Promoting engagement: An organizational study of volunteers in community resource centres for children. *Children and Youth Services Review, 22*(8), 651–678.

Seattle Department of Transportation. (2016). *Play streets program briefing report.* www.seattle.gov/transportation/playstreets.htm

Tandy, C. (1999). Children's diminishing play space: A study of inter-generational change in children's use of their neighbourhoods. *Australian Geographical Studies, 37*(2), 154–164.

Valentine, G., & McKendrick, J. (1997). Children's outdoor play: Exploring parental concerns about children's safety and the changing nature of childhood. *Geoforum, 28*(2), 219–235.

Weller, S., & Bruegel, I. (2009). Children's 'Place' in the development of neighbourhood social capital. *Urban Studies, 46*(3), 629–643.

Wilson, W. J. (1996). *When work disappears: The world of the new urban poor.* New York: Knopf.

Wood, J. (2017). Planning for children's play: Exploring the 'forgotten' right in Welsh and Scottish policy. *The Town Planning Review, 88*(5), 579–602.

Zeif, S., Chaudhuri, A., & Musselman, E. (2016). Creating neighbourhood recreational space for youth and children in the urban environment: Play (ing in the) streets in San Francisco. *Children and Youth Services Review, 70*, 95–101.

CHAPTER FOURTEEN

Individual and household influences

E. Owen D. Waygood[a] and Kevin Manaugh[b]
[a]Department of Civil, Geological, and Mining Engineering, Polytechnique Montréal, Montreal, QC, Canada
[b]Department of Geography, McGill School of Environment, McGill University, Montreal, QC, Canada

Contents

1 Introduction

Children's active and independent travel are positively related to many measures of wellbeing (Waygood, Friman, Olsson, & Taniguchi, 2017a, 2017b; also see Chapters 1–5). Such travel increases social capital, which is itself then associated with greater independent travel, as it reduces the stress and anxiety that individuals feel about social dangers (e.g. Bonner, 1997; Pacilli, Giovannelli, Prezza, & Augimeri, 2013). Unfortunately, research in English-speaking countries has documented that with each successive generation such travel begins later in children's lives, and their levels of independence at each age are smaller (e.g. Gaster, 1991; Pooley, Turnbull, & Adams, 2005). Though to a lesser extent, this trend is also evident in other countries, accompanied with increases in travel by car (Shaw et al., 2013; Susilo & Waygood, 2012; Xu, Taniguchi, Ishigami, & Hirata, 2015).

Transport and Children's Wellbeing
https://doi.org/10.1016/B978-0-12-814694-1.00010-5

Fyhri, Hjorthol, Mackett, Fotel, and Kyttä (2011) propose a contextual framework of social trends that leads to these decreases in independence. Many of the aspects proposed in this framework relate to the decisions by parents within these general social changes. These changes include: choosing homes that are larger and more dispersed, choosing non-local schools, giving priority to structured-play over free-play, and even letting children use cellphones to call for a ride no matter the child's location. All of these decisions are associated with greater car use.

With respect to the child, their physical and cognitive development will influence their transport options, but also their developing attitudes and beliefs. These are cached within the parental attitudes and beliefs that will affect the choices listed previously. Today's children are not evolutionary different from the children of previous generations who enjoyed more freedom when traveling. However, motor vehicle traffic keeps increasing, residential development has changed, and beliefs related to children's travel and personal safety, along with parenting styles, are in constant flux. This chapter aims to discuss these points and what might better support children's active and independent travel.

2 Individual level

2.1 Age

Children generally show an increase in independence at the population level as their age increases (e.g. Curtis, Babb, & Olaru, 2015; Shaw, Bicket, & Elliott, 2015). However, the age at which this independence begins differs between cultures (e.g. Joshi & Maclean, 1997), and between generations (e.g. Gaster, 1991). Joshi and Maclean (1997) found that middle-class parents in Japan expected their children to have some independent travel at around age 6, in India at around age 8, and in England at a bit past 10 years old. This cultural expectation can be seen in the literature on children's independent and active travel in Japan which illustrates that the majority of children walk to school at age six (Waygood, Taniguchi, Craig-St-Louis, & Xu, 2015) and that active travel levels, though diminishing, are still quite high (Xu et al., 2015). In English-speaking cultures (e.g. the U.K., Canada, U.S.A., Australia, and New Zealand), the majority of children do not walk without being accompanied by an adult until around 10 years old (e.g. Hillman, Adams, & Whitelegg, 1990; Carver, Watson, Shaw, & Hillman, 2013). Traveling independently in such contexts may not even occur during primary/elementary school (children under 12 years old) (e.g. Janssen, Ferrao, &

King, 2016; Shaw et al., 2013). An international comparison found that Northern European countries (including Germany) and Japan had the highest levels of CIM. Among these countries, Finland had the highest level of CIM, though at age 7 children from Japan were nearly always more likely to engage in independent travel (apart from going out alone at night). Shaw et al. (2015) find that along with the countries mentioned above, many southern European countries as well as less wealthy countries such as Sri Lanka, Brazil, and South Africa had very low levels of CIM. The suggestion here is that it is not necessarily true that children are less capable in this modern age, and that it is not a dichotomy between wealthy and developing countries, but that there are perhaps expectations, beliefs, and practices that differ between these places that explain these differences.

Countries with currently low levels of CIM have not always had low levels. A study examining childhood travel from 1915 until the mid-1970s in the USA found that with each successive generation, the barriers to independent travel increased (Gaster, 1991). Part of this change was due to increasing traffic, as streets changed from places used by children and society in general as an extension of their private living space (Appleyard, 1980), to corridors of danger traversed by vehicles at lethal speeds. The participants in Gaster's (1991) study were grouped into three categories: those whose childhoods started before 1935, between 1935 and 1945, and after 1945 and before 1960. The participants recounted at what age they were allowed to roam freely. This was found to be generally at ages under 8 years old, but with each successive group, the age increased by over 1 year. For the earliest group, the average age was five and a half. The author noted that as the years progressed, the type of play changed from being unstructured, to organized and structured. This change occurred as children began losing independence and traffic danger lead to children being escorted. The result for traffic can be seen in a more recent study in Switzerland where the majority of children aged five (with no older siblings) were allowed to independently play outside in public areas (Hüttenmoser, 1995). The author also found that it was parents who live on streets with unfavorable traffic conditions who thought that it was irresponsible to let children play outside independently. These parents thus organized play for their children. The author argued that as a result of the traffic conditions, parents naturally grew to believe that children could not freely move about.

Another reason for limiting children's independent travel is the concern that children may not be competent enough to travel independently. There are two main points here. One point is that if independent mobility is not demonstrated and children are not given the opportunity to practice these skills, much like other skills in life, they will not be developed. If parents are not walking or cycling with their children and helping them to develop the necessary skills to navigate their contexts, then it is perhaps not surprising that the children do not develop the competency to get around by themselves. The second point is that the perception of competence seems to relate to traffic conditions. As traffic conditions get worse and danger (real or perceived) increases, parents are going to feel that greater maturity and mastery is needed to navigate these complex and dangerous environments.

Some authors argue that children cannot walk long distances due to their limited physical capacity to do so (Davis & Jones, 1996). However, evidence is scant in this regard. Recent research has shed light on what most parents know to be true from personal experience. For example, anecdotally, the lead author's children walk with him everywhere. At the ages of 5 and 6, the author's two children played in playgrounds while the author sat for breaks, despite having walked nearly 30,000 steps with him that day. Moreover, the children's legs were shorter, so they were taking more steps than their father. Parents take their children to the park, and those children are likely running around for longer than the parents would be able to. In fact, a recent study showed that prepubertal children have as much energy as well-trained adult endurance athletes (Birat et al., 2018). If anything, it is more likely that parents lack the energy, while children need the physical activity.

Main points: Independence generally increases with age, though it is evident at quite young ages (for nearby trips). The main problem seems to be limiting the negative impacts of traffic. Much of that can be done through better street and neighborhood design (see Chapters 6 and 12). The activity space (i.e. how far they roam) of children will increase with age, so developing the skills to use mobility tools such as scooters and bicycles will allow them to access locations outside their immediate neighborhoods (likely sufficient for primary school aged children). Next, knowing how to use public transport would give the children access to the larger range of destinations that is likely necessary for them to meet most of their daily travel needs into adolescence. Such experiences are evident in countries with high CIM such as Japan (see Chapter 16).

2.2 Gender

Differences in CIM have been observed between genders, though these differences depend on the country and the type of travel being studied. Various research has found that girls are less independent than boys during the week

(Kyttä, 1997; Mitra, Faulkner, Buliung, & Stone, 2014). Others find no statistical difference between the two genders during the week, or find that girls are slightly more independent on weekends (Cervesato & Waygood, 2019; Waygood & Kitamura, 2009). In an international study of CIM (Shaw et al., 2015), not many differences were found for the "licenses[a]" of CIM, with only Italy consistently giving boys more licenses than girls. One interesting and conflicting result from that study was found in France. French parents reported that they were more likely to allow their sons to cross main roads alone compared to their daughters, but when the children themselves responded to the same question the inverse result was found; that is, girls were more likely to self-report that they were allowed this behavior. That may suggest that parents may feel (for whatever reason) that they should restrict girls, but that the girls themselves felt highly confident with the behavior.

In studies of routes and travel patterns, it is variously observed that boys may explore more and have larger ranges of travel, often using modes such as bicycles and scooters more frequently (Alparone & Pacilli, 2012; Brown, Mackett, Gong, Kitazawa, & Paskins, 2008; Mikkelsen & Christensen, 2009; Pacilli et al., 2013). Whether this is related to their own personal desire, a lower perception of danger, or parental/social practice is not always clear. However, there does seem to be evidence that the higher use of bicycles by boys may be linked to preference. Evidence from Denmark found that boys (aged 10–13) have a higher preference for bicycles than girls (Mikkelsen & Christensen, 2009). In Japan, boys (aged 10–12) ranked bicycles as more fun, faster, and cooler than girls (Waygood, 2009a). And finally, in Australia, boys were more likely to be active commuters than girls and their preference was cycling (alone) as their commute mode (Curtis et al., 2015; Mikkelsen & Christensen, 2009).

Some research finds that boys are more likely to travel alone and more likely to desire traveling alone (Curtis et al., 2015; Mikkelsen & Christensen, 2009). On the other hand, girls will often seek a companion (Brown et al., 2008; Mikkelsen & Christensen, 2009), whether it be for social reasons, personal safety perceptions, or to assuage parental concerns (Mikkelsen & Christensen, 2009). It is perhaps important to note here once again that CIM is taken as travel without an adult, rather than travel alone. In cases when children travel with other children, they will typically do

---

[a] A "license" here is the right (the license) given to the child by the parents to do certain travel-related behaviors such as cross a main road, ride a bicycle on the street, walk to school alone, go out at night alone, etc.

more; they play more and for longer duration (Loptson, Muhajarine, & Ridalls, 2012). Although boys may mention traveling to school alone on a bicycle as their preferred mode, evidence also exists that boys want a companion to make things more interesting (Morrow, 2000).

Main points: Gender differences may exist in terms of what parents allow and what types of travel are preferred, but both genders are capable of independent travel. International comparisons find that in most cases, both genders have equal license to be independent.

2.3 Perceptions and attitudes

When children are asked what their preference is for travel, the majority mention walking and cycling (Barker, 2006; Curtis et al., 2015; Mitchell, Kearns, & Collins, 2007; O'Brien, 2008; Shaw et al., 2015). However, children that are driven around are more likely to prefer travel by car (Curtis et al., 2015), suggesting that they may be conditioned to like this mode (Baslington, 2008; Hjorthol & Fyhri, 2009). This can be seen in children's attitudes towards cars and their anticipated future use (Baslington, 2009). Some research finds that children also perceive walking as easier than driving. Children who discuss different travel modes with an open mind expressed greater social and personal norms to use alternative modes (Haustein, Klöckner, & Blöbaum, 2009). *Social norms* reflect the expectations of members of a particular peer group and guide behavior (Bamberg, Hunecke, & Blöbaum, 2007; Doran & Larsen, 2016). *Personal norms* guide an individual through internal concepts of right and wrong and may vary from external social norms. Both can impact travel behavior through the avoidance of internal guilt (in the case of personal norms) or social ostracizing (in the case of social norms). For example, if a person believes that they should walk, then using another mode when walking is an option could cause feelings of guilt. If the social norm prefers cycling, then traveling by a mode that is a deterrent to cycling could cause ostracizing.

Social norms can be broken down into a number of different types, but here, two types will be briefly introduced. Descriptive norms are those that are perceived to be the common behavior in a certain situation (Lapinski & Rimal, 2005). It does not need to be the actual case, but just the perceived one. As an example, perhaps most children walk to school, but a large number of parents drive their children to school. The large space that is occupied and the attention given to the cars may make it seem like they are the majority. Thus, if a parent sees this, they will often be subtly influenced towards this behavior. An injunctive norm is one that society feels is the "correct" behavior in a situation, or that it is what is ought to be done (Lapinski & Rimal, 2005). This can be seen in systems such as the national walking bus in Japan (Waygood et al., 2015), where the societal belief is that walking to school is the correct behavior. This injunctive norm leads to solutions that protect walking and limits the dangers (such as parents dropping children off by car; Rothman, Buliung, Howard, Macarthur, & Macpherson, 2017).

With respect to traffic, most studies focus on the parental concerns about traffic safety, as it is generally thought that parents are the ones who make the decisions. However, a number of studies have examined children's perceptions. One study found that the vast majority of children identified roads as "scary and dangerous" (Matthews, 1995), while another more recent paper found that parents mention traffic danger, but not children (Crawford et al., 2017). Whether this is due to traffic danger being normal for children now as opposed to over 20 years ago, is not clear. In a review, Carver, Timperio, and Crawford (2008) give evidence that perceptions of traffic danger by children was found to diminish the rate of girls walking, while in another study, no relationship was found. In the U.K., girls' perceptions of traffic safety reduced their likelihood of playing outside every day (Page, Cooper, Griew, & Jago, 2010). Although gender was not analyzed, children who were classified as frequent walkers were more likely to worry about traffic safety where they lived, but less likely to worry about dangers posed by others (i.e. "stranger danger" or fear of being abducted, attacked or harassed by unknown persons) than children who did not walk frequently. In Canada, all children expressed concerns about being hit by a car, though these fears were magnified in the children who did not use active modes to get to school (Fusco, Moola, Faulkner, Buliung, & Richichi, 2012). They found that the mode that children used directly influenced their perspective and the visual representations (the children took photos of their trip to school) they used to express their trips to school. All children also expressed "disdain" for traffic and took photos of busy intersections and vehicles, which made their travel environments hostile. In New Zealand, the most frequent complaint by children of their living environment was the danger imposed by traffic (Mitchell et al., 2007).

In terms of perceptions of danger when traveling, girls were found to speak of "stranger danger" (Foster, Villanueva, Wood, Christian, &

Giles-Corti, 2014; Mikkelsen & Christensen, 2009), while boys spoke of threats from older boys (Mikkelsen & Christensen, 2009). Although no gender differences were given, children reported concerns about bullying, getting lost, and strangers (Crawford et al., 2017).

Main points: Children, no matter their actual travel patterns, generally prefer active modes such as walking and cycling as their means of travel. However, children who predominantly use cars show a tendency to like car travel, suggesting a socialization to cars with use. In terms of their perceptions of danger, children are acutely aware of traffic danger (again, a negative influence on their mental well-being). However, the fear of traffic is lower for children who actually experience it through active modes. As well, children who travel by active modes have a lower perception of "stranger danger", which again may relate to simply knowing the actual conditions through first-hand experience rather than imagining them.

2.4 Actions

Children as young as five (Hüttenmoser, 1995) who go out and practice their independent movement build and maintain social connections with other children and adults. In the example of Zurich, Switzerland, over 50% of five year-olds (with no older sibling) consistently played outside alone, with only 10% being consistently supervised. Children in countries around the world are more likely to make incidental social interactions with their neighbors if they are walking and independent (Waygood et al., 2017a; Waygood & Friman, 2015). Children who knew more neighboring adults were found to have more confidence in their ability to get around by themselves (Crawford et al., 2017). The social connections that are developed in this way support CIM. Social support (Pacilli et al., 2013) and social control (McDonald, Deakin, & Aalborg, 2010) are both positively correlated with increased active travel to school, thus supporting a reinforcing relationship.

The use of modes influences attitudes, which is a practice of socializing the children to different? modes (Baslington, 2008). Although (almost) all children naturally walk, travel by other modes is a learned behavior that requires different skills (Baslington, 2008). As with any other skill, practice is required. In order to practice their skills, the child must make progressively longer or more difficult trips as their experience and confidence increases. It is sometimes forgotten that children are capable, problem solving agents. They are also capable of negotiating with their parents for freedoms (Davis & Jones, 1996).

One child who is traveling independently can help stimulate more children to also travel independently. One way this could happen is that other children would see the independent traveler as an example for how they could do the same. Another effect would be on parents, who have the very human tendency to be aware (consciously or not) of and affected by social norms. If the child or parent sees no other children doing a particular action, they may question whether there might be a reason to not to do that action. If a child is independent, they can seek out others to travel with them and potentially help to break down barriers that may exist for that child.

Although this decision is not entirely in their hands, children should look to participate in the planning process. Unfortunately, even for planning that directly affects them, children are typically not given the opportunity to participate (Davis & Jones, 1996). This is a loss to the planners as children often intimately know their local regions better than adults. They know where there are such things as shortcuts, shops, vacant spaces, as they walk and explore their life space. How the environment is mediated for children is likely one of the most important influences on CIM (Hüttenmoser, 1995). No matter how they travel, they are well aware of the impacts that building for cars have imposed on them and their freedom (Fusco et al., 2012). As highlighted by numerous authors, children are a marginalized group who suffer the consequences of poorly designed neighborhoods and cities (Davis & Jones, 1996; Freeman & Tranter, 2011; Gleeson & Sipe, 2006; Hillman et al., 1990; Lennard & Lennard, 2000; Lynch & Banerjee, 1976; Matthews & Limb, 1999; Taniguchi, Hara, Takano, Kagaya, & Fujii, 2003). Children have valuable inputs that help create more livable cities. Further reading on the topic of involving children in the planning process can be found in Chapters 16 (Waygood and Taniguchi) and 17 (van de Craats et al.) in this book.

3 Household level

Parents both restrict and facilitate children's independent travel (Mikkelsen & Christensen, 2009; Pacilli et al., 2013). Parents can facilitate CIM by teaching children the required skills for getting around, but also through knowing their neighbors (Prezza et al., 2001). Walking with children helps to build their experience and also to develop connections with neighbors (Grannis, 2011). If a child is always driven places, then it is perhaps not surprising that parents might not have confidence in the child's capacity for CIM (Curtis et al., 2015).

Authors have written variously of the "domestification of childhood" (Mikkelsen & Christensen, 2009) or "bubble wrapped" children (Malone, 2007). In both cases, this relates to children who are more and more restricted in their freedoms and typically remain indoors more than outside. Parents may want to "park" their children in safe locations (Davis & Jones, 1996), but this often limits the amount and variety of play (e.g. Hüttenmoser, 1995). Children who are independent (Cooper, Page, Foster, & Qahwaji, 2003) and who conduct more active travel are overall more physically active (Schoeppe, Duncan, Badland, Oliver, & Curtis, 2013). Unfortunately, CIM and active travel seem to be decreasing with each passing generation. This decrease is related to the increasing amount of traffic, among other changes. Some parents may see the car as an essential tool for getting their children around, but it ultimately is connected to the loss of freedom, and the reduced physical and social development of their children (see Chapters 2 and 4).

Many factors influence parents' choices with respect to their child's travel. The influencers that are often mentioned are traffic safety and personal safety (social danger or "stranger danger") (Hillman et al., 1990; McDonald & Aalborg, 2009; Salmon, Salmon, Crawford, Hume, & Timperio, 2007) and convenience (Fyhri & Hjorthol, 2009; McDonald & Aalborg, 2009; Wen et al., 2008). Generally, traffic danger is found to be more important than social danger in explaining CIM (Carver et al., 2008; Crawford et al., 2017; Faulkner, Richichi, Buliung, Fusco, & Moola, 2010). However, distance is nearly always the primary explanatory factor (Curtis et al., 2015). Distance also relates to how strongly those perceptions of danger are (Pacilli et al., 2013). In a study that examined 48 different perceptions of a neighborhood, and 11 reasons for having chosen a home, across different city sizes and built environments, the strongest explanatory factor for a child walking to school or not was the distance threshold (in this case 0.78 km; Waygood & Susilo, 2015). In other studies, social danger was not an explanatory factor for CIM, once the built or social environments were considered (Foster et al., 2014). Parents were found to have a higher sense of social danger if they were less connected to their neighbors (Alparone & Pacilli, 2012), and walking with children is connected to increased neighborhood networks (Grannis, 2011). Thus, it would seem that walking with one's children provides positive feedback for the community and works towards building supportive social environments.

The perception that children need to be protected and escorted could be a result of traffic. In a study of children's independence in Switzerland, those parents who lived on streets with traffic conditions that were unfavorable for children were more likely to state that it was irresponsible to let children out alone (Hüttenmoser, 1995). That author writes, "the disadvantages to these children over many years cannot be justified by the insatiable drive of adults to use their living surroundings for their own mobility and to disrespect the vital needs of children." This is also reflected by another author who wrote about children's use of streets for social and physical play versus the desire of adults to use those streets for a throughway (Abu-Ghazzeh, 1998). Thus, the suggestion is that there is a disconnect between what may actually be best for the child and demanding easy access by car.

Many parents believe that the car is the safest means of travel and use this as a justification for driving their children around (Johansson, 2006; Pacilli et al., 2013). However, this is in conflict with the fact that cars and traffic are the primary cause of death of children worldwide (Toroyan & Peden, 2007). For wealthy countries, it is children in cars themselves who represent the majority of fatalities. The danger around schools is frequently caused by parents dropping their own children off (Rothman et al., 2017). Thus, it is a classic example of a "tragedy of the commons": when the limited social good is safety, each individual creates a worse overall situation by taking what is *perceived* to be the best for themselves, leading to continued deterioration.

Parents may choose to use whatever mode is "quickest and easiest" (Faulkner et al., 2010). In a situation where the child gets to school by themselves, this should be seen as the quickest and easiest option from the parents' point of view (they use no time of their own) (Hillman et al., 1990). However, if a certain threshold (distance or other) is surpassed, and options such as school buses are not available, the decision that seems quickest and easiest may be the parents' default travel mode. In many cases this is believed to be the car. In some situations where car travel is facilitated, this may indeed be "quickest and easiest" for that individual. However, other studies find that driving was not in fact easy due to parking and congestion which lead to increased levels of stress (Barker, 2006). Some authors argue that speed is actually stealing time and money from parents (Freeman & Tranter, 2011; Tranter & May, 2006). The argument for this is that when the amount of time necessary to work to pay for the high mobility of a car is taken into account, it is not quicker. Unfortunately, even if a parent may not want to drive, they may still drive their child as this is sometimes perceived as "good parenting" (Valentine, 1997).

In many instances, parents prefer living in low-density neighborhoods. These low-density developments impact the majority of trips because of longer distances and because alternatives such as public transport are less common. This effectively maroons the child. Children seek stimulation from other children and they are more active when other children are present (Loptson et al., 2012), yet the low-density neighborhood limits this. In rural areas, children are more likely to feel isolated, travel alone, and put more importance on their pets than friends (Mikkelsen & Christensen, 2009). Having places to go and play nearby that are perceived as safe leads to more active children (Johansson, 2003). Although some societies may consider small, low-density developments as better places to raise children (Bonner, 1997), research finds that these developments can isolate children, limit their interactions and reduce physical activity.

In most studies examining the gender of caretakers, mothers are found to escort their children more often than fathers (Waygood, 2009b). They sacrifice their own leisure time to escort their children, and this is more common in more rural locations (Mattsson, 2002). As the one who is more likely to escort the child, it is also found that the mother's perception of social danger is more important than the father's (Alparone & Pacilli, 2012; Carver et al., 2008; Crawford et al., 2017). It is not necessarily true that mothers want to escort their children everywhere. Many appreciate the numerous advantages of active travel (Ramanathan, O'Brien, Faulkner, & Stone, 2014). Mothers may want children to walk, but feel that they are powerless to change the situation (Barker, 2006). One should not blame a mother or parent for doing what they feel is right, but it must be acknowledged that the system needs to change in a way that favors/better facilitates travel that is more advantageous to children.

Main points: Many negative impacts on children's independent mobility can be linked to the choice of neighborhood. A neighborhood that may seem attractive due to its cheap living spaces comes at the cost of children being completely dependent on adults for their travel. Travel is more likely to be in cars, which reduces local social connections and increases traffic for others, further diminishing the conditions for children. This constant travel by car socializes children to believe that it is the only means of travel and reduces their knowledge of simply how to get around.

3.1 Actions

In situations where they feel they have no choice, parents chauffeur their children around and make great efforts to meet their children's needs. However, the result of this behavior is that typically, children do not get as much physical activity (Schoeppe et al., 2013) or social interaction as children who are independent (Hüttenmoser, 1995; Waygood et al., 2017a). Parents must fit the child's needs and activities into their own spare time, which is generally less than the child's spare time (Davis & Jones, 1996). As such, parents must find additional time, which was found to usually result in the mother sacrificing her own leisure time to do so (Mattsson, 2002). As some authors argue, purchasing more vehicles in order to have more than one adult chauffeur children does not in fact save time; the additional income needed to purchase the extra car must be obtained through working more, thus further reducing available time (Tranter, 2006). So, how might parents help make their children more independent, so that everyone gains time for more leisure and development.

A first step is to realize that along with great mobility, car use poses many negative impacts on children, and there are many advantages to children's independent mobility (see Chapter 1). Parents and society teach children to fear traffic, as it is the leading cause of childhood fatalities. However, in many cases parents seem reticent to suggest that car traffic should be reduced, even though it is the source of danger (Davis & Jones, 1996; De Groof, 2008). Often, the burden of safety is placed on children (Davis & Jones, 1996; Hillman et al., 1990), and when a child dies from a traffic collision the blame is often placed on their (child-like) behavior (Roberts & Coggan, 1994). As one author wrote, "In place of victim blaming, public health approaches would emphasize environmental and social influences on children's quality of life" (Davis & Jones, 1996). This can be seen in Sweden, where it was recognized that if children are not fully capable of dealing with traffic, traffic must adjust to this vulnerable, highly valued, but marginalized group (Björklid & Gummesson, 2013). Thus, one way to protect children would be for parents to support traffic taming measures as proposed by approaches such as Sweden's Vision Zero (see Chapters 6 and 9; visionzeronetwork.org).

We (as researchers/members of society/adults) talk about adjusting children to fit into the adult world through educating children about the dangers of traffic, but we do not educate the more capable adults (Davis & Jones, 1996). This may be because children are considered to be easier to reach (and perhaps are less likely to phone and complain to politicians). However, the source of the danger is adult activity. We must understand the difference between suffering danger and causing danger. The victim blaming of children should not be accepted, and there should be stronger support to limit the dangers of cars.

Social danger such as "stranger danger" is mentioned by some parents. In a study of previous generations, women did not speak of "stranger danger" when they recounted their childhood travel experiences (Gaster, 1991), suggesting it is a more recent fear. Typically, this type of fear is more associated with parents who drive more, and it often restricts girls more than boys (Brown et al., 2008; De Groof, 2008). Parents who mention such concerns often restrain their children more, which results in lower activity participation (Carver, Timperio, Hesketh, & Crawford, 2010). Even the adolescents (i.e. older children) of "supervising parents" fear crime more (De Groof, 2008), and a greater sense of danger is associated with negative mental health outcomes for children and adolescents (Leventhal & Brooks-Gunn, 2000). Research from social psychology finds that parents who are overprotective were 40% more likely to have children with social phobias (Lieb et al., 2000). As Gatersleben and colleagues showed in a simulation experiment, how one gets around can impact their perceptions of others. In the experiment, people viewed the same scene of youth in a park, but from the perspective of different modes of transport. Car drivers were more likely to feel "threatened" or "annoyed" by the youths compared to cyclists or pedestrians, who had higher degrees of "positive attitudes" towards the same youths (Gatersleben, Murtagh, & White, 2013). Thus, walking and experiencing life at the speed that we evolved with not only reduces the danger for others in one's community, but it can better inform people about their community and lead to positive interactions.

Walking with children can further help improve children's independent mobility by improving connections with neighbors. Sociological studies find that 80% of neighbor networks relate to local travel with children (Grannis, 2011). Building a local network is associated with better health outcomes for children (Helliwell & Putnam, 2004) along with increased CIM (Prezza et al., 2001). Parents who are more active tend to have children who are more active (Loptson et al., 2012; Sidharthan, Bhat, Pendyala, & Goulias, 2011). Part of this is due to these parents encouraging the child to be more active (Loptson et al., 2012), but part of it is also related to social learning (Bandura, 1977; Baslington, 2008). Simply walking and cycling with children shows them that these are feasible means of travel and gives them the experience that will help them when they become independent (and like it or not, they will!). There does not seem to be much of a link between how parents traveled when they were children and how their children travel, though parents who cycled more were found to have children who were more likely to be classified as "free range" (Curtis et al., 2015).

Thus, the way the parents traveled during their childhoods do not matter as much as what they choose to do now.

Of course, parents are also subjected to social norms. These social norms can relate to "peer pressure", where parents sense that others disapprove of their behavior. Parents in the United Kingdom spoke of feeling that other parents disapproved of them letting their child walk, or even walking with their child (Valentine, 1997). Valentine (ibid) described this as a cultural idea of the "ideal mother": one who is ever present to provide for and protect her child. It seems that this idea is more present in parents who escort their children (Hüttenmoser, 1995), and is linked with children who are classified as "bubble wrapped" (Curtis et al., 2015). Parents of "bubble wrapped" children are more likely to think that it is irresponsible to let children roam free, but also they are more likely to believe that others would judge them for allowing their child to be independently mobile (Curtis et al., 2015). Furthermore, these parents are more likely to believe that their children are not competent, which may be related to continuously escorting them.

Parents whose children are not active commuters are less likely to believe that there is any benefit to such behavior (Curtis et al., 2015; Ramanathan et al., 2014). This is common in behavior-change frameworks where people downplay the positive health impacts that would result from an action they *are not* taking, and think nothing of the negative health impacts that result from an action they *are* taking (e.g. Prochaska et al., 1994). As was documented in previous research reviews (Schoeppe et al., 2013; Waygood et al., 2017b), CIM is positively associated to all domains of child-wellbeing, while car travel is typically negatively associated. Again, part of the action that parents can take is to understand and speak about these negative consequences of unrestrained car use with other parents, their community, and decision makers such as politicians and school boards.

Children's independent mobility is decreasing with each passing generation due to the restrictions from the increasing levels of traffic that adults and authorities cause (police officers and custodians) (Gaster, 1991). Rather than seeking to escape traffic by driving greater distances to live in low-density areas (a touch ironic) and then demanding greater infrastructure to reduce car commute times (which is linked with increased traffic), parents could recognize the impact that traffic is having on the lives of their children and support initiatives to reduce traffic on their streets and those of other residents. Much of this relates to limiting speeds, but if access to cars can be limited as well, children's use of common spaces becomes more common (Biddulph, 2012).

4 Conclusions

Children of both sexes are capable of independent travel from a young age, and parents can help facilitate this. Currently, part of the difficulty is that the free movement of cars is prioritized over the free movement of children (and society in general), to their detriment. A street that is difficult or limiting for cars is one that facilitates children (and their parents) to play and interact with their neighbors. Simply walking with children can help them build the skills to get around by themselves, and can help build the local social networks which increase social support. A key point is that long distances and traffic have significant negative impacts on children, but this is not the foregone conclusion of a modern society as is shown through examples such as those highlighted in the international comparison of children's independent mobility.

References

Abu-Ghazzeh, T. M. (1998). Children's use of the street as a playground in Abu-Nuseir, Jordan. *Environment and Behavior, 30*(6), 799–831.

Alparone, F. R., & Pacilli, M. G. (2012). On children's independent mobility: The interplay of demographic, environmental, and psychosocial factors. *Children's Geographies, 10*(1), 109–122.

Appleyard, D. (1980). Livable streets: Protected neighborhoods? *The Annals of the American Academy of Political and Social Science, 451*(1), 106–117.

Bamberg, S., Hunecke, M., & Blöbaum, A. (2007). Social context, personal norms and the use of public transportation: Two field studies. *Journal of Environmental Psychology, 27*(3), 190–203.

Bandura, A. (1977). *Social learning theory*. NJ: Prentice-Hall: Englewood Cliffs.

Barker, J. (2006). "Are we there yet?": Exploring aspects of automobility in children's lives. In *Faculty of geography and earth sciences*. Brunel University.

Baslington, H. (2008). Travel socialisation: A social theory of travel mode behaviour. *International Journal of Sustainable Transportation, 2*(2), 91–114.

Baslington, H. (2009). Children's perceptions of and attitudes towards, transport modes: Why a vehicle for change is long overdue. *Childrens Geographies, 7*(3), 305–322.

Biddulph, M. (2012). Street design and street use: Comparing traffic calmed and home zone streets. *Journal of Urban Design, 17*(2), 213–232.

Birat, A., Bourdier, P., Piponnier, E., Blazevich, A. J., Maciejewski, H., Duché, P., et al. (2018). Metabolic and fatigue profiles are comparable between prepubertal children and well-trained adult endurance athletes. *Frontiers in Physiology, 9*(387).

Björklid, P., & Gummesson, M. (2013). *Children's independent mobility in Sweden. Trafikverket.* Stockholm: The Swedish Transport Administration.

Bonner, K. (1997). *A great place to raise kids: Interpretation, science, and the urban-rural debate.* Quebec: McGill-Queen's University Press.

Brown, B., Mackett, R., Gong, Y., Kitazawa, K., & Paskins, J. (2008). Gender differences in children's pathways to independent mobility. *Children's Geographies, 6*(4), 385–401.

Carver, A., Timperio, A., & Crawford, D. (2008). Playing it safe: The influence of neighbourhood safety on children's physical activity—A review. *Health & Place, 14* (2), 217–227.

Carver, A., Timperio, A., Hesketh, K., & Crawford, D. (2010). Are children and adolescents less active if parents restrict their physical activity and active transport due to perceived risk? *Social Science & Medicine, 70*(11), 1799–1805.

Carver, A., Watson, B., Shaw, B., & Hillman, M. (2013). A comparison study of children's independent mobility in England and Australia. *Children's Geographies, 11*(4), 461–475.

Cervesato, A., & Waygood, E. O. D. (2019). Children's independent trips on weekdays and weekends: Case study of Quebec City. *Transportation Research Record, 2673*(4), 907–916. https://doi.org/10.1177/0361198119837225.

Cooper, A. R., Page, A. S., Foster, L. J., & Qahwaji, D. (2003). Commuting to school: Are children who walk more physically active? *American Journal of Preventive Medicine, 25*(4), 273–276.

Crawford, S., Bennetts, S., Hackworth, N., Green, J., Graesser, H., Cooklin, A., et al. (2017). Worries, 'weirdos', neighborhoods and knowing people: A qualitative study with children and parents regarding children's independent mobility. *Health & Place, 45*, 131–139.

Curtis, C., Babb, C., & Olaru, D. (2015). Built environment and children's travel to school. *Transport Policy, 42*, 21–33.

Davis, A., & Jones, L. J. (1996). Children in the urban environment: An issue for the new public health agenda. *Health & Place, 2*(2), 107–113.

De Groof, S. (2008). And my mama said: The (relative) parental influence on fear of crime among adolescent girls and boys. *Youth & Society, 39*(3), 267–293.

Doran, R., & Larsen, S. (2016). The relative importance of social and personal norms in explaining intentions to choose eco-friendly travel options. *International Journal of Tourism Research, 18*(2), 159–166.

Faulkner, G. E., Richichi, V., Buliung, R. N., Fusco, C., & Moola, F. (2010). What's "quickest and easiest?": Parental decision making about school trip mode. *International Journal of Behavioral Nutrition and Physical Activity, 7*(1), 62.

Foster, S., Villanueva, K., Wood, L., Christian, H., & Giles-Corti, B. (2014). The impact of parents' fear of strangers and perceptions of informal social control on children's independent mobility. *Health & Place, 26*, 60–68.

Freeman, C., & Tranter, P. J. (2011). *Children and their urban environment: Changing worlds.* Routledge.

Fusco, C., Moola, F., Faulkner, G., Buliung, R., & Richichi, V. (2012). Toward an understanding of children's perceptions of their transport geographies: (Non)active school travel and visual representations of the built environment. *Journal of Transport Geography, 20*(1), 62–70.

Fyhri, A., & Hjorthol, R. (2009). Children's independent mobility to school, friends and leisure activities. *Journal of Transport Geography, 17*(5), 377–384.

Fyhri, A., Hjorthol, R., Mackett, R. L., Fotel, T. N., & Kyttä, M. (2011). Children's active travel and independent mobility in four countries: Development, social contributing trends and measures. *Transport Policy, 18*(5), 703–710.

Gaster, S. (1991). Urban children's access to their neighborhood: Changes over three generations. *Environment and Behavior, 23*(1), 70–85.

Gatersleben, B., Murtagh, N., & White, E. (2013). Hoody, goody or buddy? How travel mode affects social perceptions in urban neighbourhoods. *Transportation Research Part F: Traffic Psychology and Behaviour, 21*, 219–230.

Gleeson, B., & Sipe, N. (2006). *Creating child friendly cities: Reinstating kids in the city.* Routledge.

Grannis, R. (2011). *From the ground up: Translating geography into community through neighbor networks*. Princeton University Press.

Haustein, S., Klöckner, C. A., & Blöbaum, A. (2009). Car use of young adults: The role of travel socialization. *Transportation Research Part F: Traffic Psychology and Behaviour, 12*(2), 168–178.

Helliwell, J. F., & Putnam, R. D. (2004). The social context of well-being. *Philosophical Transactions-Royal Society of London Series B Biological Sciences*, 1435–1446.

Hillman, M., Adams, J., & Whitelegg, J. (1990). *One false move... a study of children's independent mobility*. London: Policy Studies Institute.

Hjorthol, R. J., & Fyhri, A. (2009). Are we socializing our children to Car use? *Tidsskrift for Samfunnsforskning, 50*(2), 161–182.

Hüttenmoser, M. (1995). Children and their living surroundings: Empirical investigations into the significance of living surroundings for the everyday life and development of children. *Children's Environments, 12*(4), 403–413.

Janssen, I., Ferrao, T., & King, N. (2016). Individual, family, and neighborhood correlates of independent mobility among 7 to 11-year-olds. *Preventive Medicine Reports, 3*, 98–102.

Johansson, M. (2003). Social dangers as constraints for pro-environmental travel modes— The perception of parents in England and Sweden. *Medio Ambiente y Comportamiento Humano, 4*(1), 49–69.

Johansson, M. (2006). Environment and parental factors as determinants of mode for children's leisure travel. *Journal of Environmental Psychology, 26*(2), 156–169.

Joshi, M. S., & MacLean, M. (1997). Maternal expectations of child development in India, Japan and England. *Journal of Cross-Cultural Psychology, 28*, 219–234.

Kyttä, M. (1997). Children's independent mobility in urban, small town, and rural environments. In R. Cammstra (Ed.), *Growing up in a changing urban landscape* (pp. 41–52). Assen: Van Gorcum.

Lapinski, M. K., & Rimal, R. N. (2005). An explication of social norms. *Communication Theory, 15*(2), 127–147.

Lennard, H. L., & Lennard, S. H. C. (2000). *The forgotten child: Cities for the well-being of children*. Gondolier Press.

Leventhal, T., & Brooks-Gunn, J. (2000). The neighborhoods they live in: The effects of neighborhood residence on child and adolescent outcomes. *Psychological Bulletin, 126*(2), 309.

Lieb, R., Wittchen, H. -U., Höfler, M., Fuetsch, M., Stein, M. B., & Merikangas, K. R. (2000). Parental psychopathology, parenting styles, and the risk of social phobia in offspring: A prospective-longitudinal community study. *Archives of General Psychiatry, 57*(9), 859–866.

Loptson, K., Muhajarine, N., & Ridalls, T. (2012). Walkable for whom? Examining the role of the built environment on the neighbourhood-based physical activity of children. *Canadian Journal of Public Health = Revue canadienne de sante publique, 103*(9 Suppl. 3), eS29–eS34.

Lynch, K., & Banerjee, T. (1976). Growing up in cities. *New Society, 37*(722), 281–284.

Malone, K. (2007). The bubble-wrap generation: Children growing up in walled gardens. *Environmental Education Research, 13*(4), 513–527.

Matthews, H. (1995). Living on the edge: Children as 'outsiders'. *Tijdschrift voor Economische en Sociale Geografie, 86*(5), 456–466.

Matthews, H., & Limb, M. (1999). Defining an agenda for the geography of children: Review and prospect. *Progress in Human Geography, 23*(1), 61–90.

Mattsson, K. T. (2002). Children's (in)dependent mobility and parents' chauffeuring in the town and the countryside. *Tijdschrift voor Economische en Sociale Geografie, 93*(4), 443–453.

McDonald, N. C., & Aalborg, A. E. (2009). Why parents drive children to school: Implications for safe routes to school programs. *Journal of the American Planning Association, 75*(3), 331–342.

McDonald, N. C., Deakin, E., & Aalborg, A. E. (2010). Influence of the social environment on children's school travel. *Preventive Medicine, 50*(Supplement), S65–S68.

Mikkelsen, M. R., & Christensen, P. (2009). Is children's independent mobility really independent? A study of children's mobility combining ethnography and GPS/mobile phone technologies. *Mobilities, 4*(1), 37–58.

Mitchell, H., Kearns, R. A., & Collins, D. C. A. (2007). Nuances of neighbourhood: Children's perceptions of the space between home and school in Auckland, New Zealand. *Geoforum, 38*(4), 614–627.

Mitra, R., Faulkner, G. E. J., Buliung, R. N., & Stone, M. R. (2014). Do parental perceptions of the neighbourhood environment influence children's independent mobility? Evidence from Toronto, Canada. *Urban Studies, 51*(16), 3401–3419.

Morrow, V. M. (2000). 'Dirty looks' and 'trampy places' in young people's accounts of community and neighbourhood: Implications for health inequalities. *Critical Public Health, 10*(2), 141–152.

O'Brien, C. (2008). Sustainable happiness and the trip to school. *World Transport Policy & Practice, 14*(1), 15–26.

Pacilli, M. G., Giovannelli, I., Prezza, M., & Augimeri, M. L. (2013). Children and the public realm: Antecedents and consequences of independent mobility in a group of 11–13-year-old Italian children. *Children's Geographies, 11*(4), 377–393.

Page, A. S., Cooper, A. R., Griew, P., & Jago, R. (2010). Independent mobility, perceptions of the built environment and children's participation in play, active travel and structured exercise and sport: The PEACH project. *International Journal of Behavioral Nutrition and Physical Activity, 7*, 17.

Pooley, C. G., Turnbull, J., & Adams, M. (2005). The journey to school in Britain since the 1940s: Continuity and change. *Area, 37*(1), 43–53.

Prezza, M., Pilloni, S., Morabito, C., Sersante, C., Alparone, F. R., & Giuliani, M. V. (2001). The influence of psychosocial and environmental factors on children's independent mobility and relationship to peer frequentation. *Journal of Community & Applied Social Psychology, 11*(6), 435–450.

Prochaska, J. O., Velicer, W. F., Rossi, J. S., Goldstein, M. G., Marcus, B. H., Rakowski, W., et al. (1994). Stages of change and decisional balance for 12 problem behaviors. *Health Psychology, 13*(1), 39–46.

Ramanathan, S., O'Brien, C., Faulkner, G., & Stone, M. (2014). Happiness in motion: Emotions, well-being, and active school travel. *Journal of School Health, 84*(8), 516–523.

Roberts, I., & Coggan, C. (1994). Blaming children for child pedestrian injuries. *Social Science & Medicine (1982), 38*(5), 749–753.

Rothman, L., Buliung, R., Howard, A., Macarthur, C., & Macpherson, A. (2017). The school environment and student car drop-off at elementary schools. *Travel Behaviour and Society, 9*, 50–57.

Salmon, J., Salmon, L., Crawford, D. A., Hume, C., & Timperio, A. (2007). Associations among individual, social, and environmental barriers and children's walking or cycling to school. *American Journal of Health Promotion, 22*(2), 107–113.

Schoeppe, S., Duncan, M. J., Badland, H., Oliver, M., & Curtis, C. (2013). Associations of children's independent mobility and active travel with physical activity, sedentary behaviour and weight status: A systematic review. *Journal of Science and Medicine in Sport, 16*(4), 312–319.

Shaw, B., Watson, B., Frauendienst, B., Redecker, A., Jones, T., & Hillman, M. (2013). *Children's independent mobility: A comparative study in England and Germany*: (pp. 1971–2010). London, UK: Policy Studies Institute.

Shaw, B., Bicket, M., & Elliott, B. (2015). *Children's independent mobility: An international comparison and recommendations for action*. London: Policy Studies Institute.

Sidharthan, R., Bhat, C. R., Pendyala, R. M., & Goulias, K. G. (2011). Model for children's school travel mode choice accounting for effects of spatial and social interaction. *Transportation Research Record*, (2213), 78–86.

Susilo, Y. O., & Waygood, E. O. D. (2012). A long term analysis of the mechanisms underlying children's activity-travel engagements in the Osaka metropolitan area. *Journal of Transport Geography*, *20*(1), 41–50.

Taniguchi, A., Hara, F., Takano, S. e., Kagaya, S. i., & Fujii, S. (2003). Psychological and behavioral effects of travel feedback program for travel behavior modification. *Transportation Research Record: Journal of the Transportation Research Board*, *1839*, 182–190.

Toroyan, T., & Peden, M. (2007). *Youth and road safety*. Geneva: World Health Organization.

Tranter, P. (2006). Overcoming social traps. In B. Gleeson & N. Sipe (Eds.), *Creating child friendly cities: New perspectives and prospects* (pp. 121–135). Routledge.

Tranter, P., & May, M. (2006). The hidden benefits of walking: Is speed stealing our time and money. In *Conference on walking and liveable communities*: Citeseer.

Valentine, G. (1997). Gender, children, and cultures of parenting. *Gender, Place and Culture*, *4*(1), 37–62.

Waygood, E. O. D. (2009a). Keeping it close: Why compact development helps children travel. In *Urban management engineering*. Kyoto University.

Waygood, E. O. D. (2009b). What is the role of mothers in transit-oriented development? The case of Osaka–Kyoto–Kobe, Japan. In *Women's issues in transportation 4th international conference* (pp. 163–178). Irvine, CA: Transportation Research Board.

Waygood, E. O. D., & Friman, M. (2015). Children's travel and incidental community connections. *Travel Behaviour and Society*, *2*(3), 174–181.

Waygood, E. O. D., Friman, M., Olsson, L. E., & Taniguchi, A. (2017a). Children's incidental social interaction during travel international case studies from Canada, Japan, and Sweden. *Journal of Transport Geography*, *63*, 22–29.

Waygood, E. O. D., Friman, M., Olsson, L. E., & Taniguchi, A. (2017b). Transport and child well-being: An integrative review. *Travel Behaviour and Society*, *9*, 32–49. Supplement C.

Waygood, E. O. D., & Kitamura, R. (2009). Children in a rail-based developed area of Japan travel patterns, independence, and exercise. *Transportation Research Record*, (2125), 36–43.

Waygood, E. O. D., & Susilo, Y. O. (2015). Walking to school in Scotland: Do perceptions of neighbourhood quality matter? *IATSS Research*, *38*(2), 125–129.

Waygood, E. O. D., Taniguchi, A., Craig-St-Louis, C., & Xu, X. (2015). International origins of walking school buses and child fatalities in Japan and Canada. *Traffic Science Japan*, *46*(2), 30–42.

Xu, X., Taniguchi, A., Ishigami, T., & Hirata, S. (2015). The current status and transition of Japanese children's travel behavior. In *Annual Meeting of the Japanese Society of Civil Engineering*. Okayama, Japan: Japanese Society of Civil Engineering.

Wen, L. M., Fry, D., Rissel, C., Dirkis, H., Balafas, A., & Merom, D. (2008). Factors associated with children being driven to school: Implications for walk to school programs. *Health Education Research*, *23*(2), 325–334.

Further reading

Mitra, R. (2013). Independent mobility and mode choice for school transportation: A review and framework for future research. *Transport Reviews*, *33*(1), 21–43.

CHAPTER FIFTEEN

Inclusive research design: Accounting for childhood disability in school transportation research

Timothy Ross
Department of Geography and Planning, University of Toronto, Toronto, ON, Canada

Contents

Over the past decade, transportation research has shown more concern for children. This concern has been prompted by children undergoing more parent-chauffeured automobile trips between their 'island geographies' (i.e., their home, school, and organized activities), which has contributed to their increased isolation from public life (Milne, 2009; Mitchell, Kearns, & Collins, 2007). Correspondingly, they are making fewer trips using active modes that offer opportunities for physical activity and engagement with local environments and public life (Fusco, Moola, Faulkner, Buliung, & Richichi, 2012). Further, children's independent mobility has decreased (Barker, Kraftl, Horton, & Tucker, 2009; Hillman, Adams, & Whitelegg, 1990) and they are exhibiting troubling overweight and obesity rates (Tremblay et al., 2010). These disconcerting children's health and transportation trends have brought the school transportation research subfield into focus. Advancing children's use of active modes for school travel

Transport and Children's Wellbeing
https://doi.org/10.1016/B978-0-12-814694-1.00015-4

has come to be regarded as an opportunity to increase children's physical activity and independent mobility levels, and to gain the related health and well-being benefits (Larsen, Gilliland, & Hess, 2012).

Much of the school transportation literature has come from studies concerned about understanding how environmental and social factors affect children's travel behaviour and mode choice (Rothman, Macpherson, Ross, & Buliung, 2018; Rothman, To, Buliung, Macarthur, & Howard, 2014; Mitra & Buliung, 2014; Larsen et al., 2012[a]), and recognizing trends in their travel behaviors over space and time (Buliung, Mitra, & Faulkner, 2009; Faulkner, Richichi, Buliung, Fusco, & Moola, 2010; Ham, Martin, & Kohl III, 2008). While this work has been valuable, much of it has essentialized childhood as a developmental life stage and scoped out children's bodily and physiological diversity in favor of considering children whose bodies fit into a simplified, normalized able body type. This has arguably left much of the research with a limited, homogenized understanding of childhood that does little in terms of recognizing its intersects with other forms of social difference, such as disability. Inattention to childhood disability in school transportation research is disconcerting in a North American context. In the United States, 2.8 million (5.2%) of the 53.9 million school-aged (i.e., 5–17 years old) children were reported as having a disability in 2010 (U.S. Census Bureau, 2010). In Canada, there were 174,810 children (aged 5–14 years) reported as living with disability in 2006, almost 43% of them were reported to be living with severe to very severe disability (Statistics Canada, 2008c), and almost three quarters of them were reported to have multiple disabilities (Statistics Canada, 2008b). Of Canada's children aged 5 to 9 and 10 to 14, 4.2% and 4.9% were reported as having disabilities, respectively (Statistics Canada, 2008a). Given the prevalence of childhood disability, the ways in which it is experienced in relation to transportation and, especially, school transportation warrant greater attention.

This chapter considers how disabled children's experiences and perspectives have gone largely unconsidered in school transportation research. This is followed by a discussion about using the new sociology of childhood (James, Jenks, & Prout, 1998; James & Prout, 1997; Prout, 2005) and participatory methods from childhood studies (Stafford, 2017) to work towards including them in research. I propose three considerations to help (school) transportation researchers with crafting and carrying out participatory research designs that adequately include disabled children. They are: (1) enabling disabled children's participation via inclusive technologies;

---

[a] See also McDonald, 2007; McMillan, 2007.

(2) supporting their engagement by providing them with opportunities to have positive participation experiences; and (3) emphasizing researcher reflexivity to help ensure the children's experiences and perspectives are adequately represented. In discussing these considerations, I reference inclusive measures used in a recent ethnographic study of how families of disabled children experience school travel in the Greater Toronto and Hamilton Area (GTHA) in Ontario, Canada.

1 Childhood disability, school transportation, and mobility

School transportation research has been criticized for largely disregarding children's critical perspectives and experiences of disability. For example, Ross and Buliung (2018) found that the active school travel (AST) and children's independent mobility (CIM) fields have given disability remarkably less consideration than other forms of social difference (i.e., gender, age, class, and race/ethnicity). They also found that of the AST/CIM studies involving disabled children's participation, most ask them to describe experiences, but not to provide critical input (i.e., they are not asked what should be changed or how they would change things to improve their experiences) (Ross & Buliung, 2018). Not engaging disabled children's critical thinking seems illogical since their unique positionality can afford them the ability to deliver invaluable insights that others (e.g., able-bodied children, parents, student transportation service providers) may very well not be able to provide. It also seems illogical because engaging disabled children's critical perspectives has been useful in studies about how they view the accessibility of school sites and buildings (see Pivik, 2010; Stephens et al., 2015). Inattention to disabled children has some carry-over into related policy. For example, Metrolinx (2018) – Ontario, Canada's crown agency for managing transport in the GTHA – is working to have 60% of children in the GTHA actively traveling to school by 2041 and notes the importance of advancing accessibility. However, disability has been largely scoped out of its published school travel reports (e.g., Metrolinx, 2013, 2014; Metrolinx and Green Communities Canada, 2013).

Ross and Buliung (2018) also found that most school transportation studies considering childhood disability have used theoretical approaches that ignore the normalcy of disabled children's exclusionary experiences and the ableism that allows the experiences to occur. 'Ableism' can be regarded as a set of beliefs, processes, and practices that produce favoritism for certain abilities (e.g., cognition, competitiveness or consumerism) and frequently negative sentiments towards the lack of such abilities (Wolbring, 2007; in Goodley, 2014: 22). It presumes able-bodiedness, which in turn socially constructs disabled people's marginalization (Chouinard, 1997: 380). By leaving ableist thinking, values, and actions inherent in school transportation unquestioned and unchallenged, scholars may be contributing to the quiet continuation of disabled children's exclusionary experiences during school travel.

While the disability/mobility relationship has received more attention over the past 30 years, our understanding of it remains in its early stages (Goggin, 2016). Disability has been folded into 'geographies of mobility' research to explore, among other things, how hegemonic, normatively ordered conceptions of mobility prioritize and privilege the presence and modes of movement and mobility of certain bodies over others (Imrie, 2000, 2003); how disabled people's identities shift across socio-spatial locations and positions (Imrie & Edwards, 2007); and how they negotiate access and inclusion using mobile technologies (Goggin, 2016; Saltes, 2018). Our understanding of the relationship between childhood disability, in particular, and mobility remains underdeveloped. For example, we are only beginning to understand how dominant social values affect mobility choices and behaviors of families of children with mobility impairments (Gibson et al., 2012; Palisano, Hanna, Rosenbaum, & Tieman, 2010). Also, inattention to childhood disability has only recently come into focus in CIM research, which has maintained a long-time ableist bias by having "remarkably little explicit regard for 'non-normative' bodies/mobilities or, more broadly, experiences of dis/ability in general" (Buliung, Larsen, Faulkner, & Ross, 2017: 9).

An ableist homogenization of childhood has underpinned school trans-portation and mobility research and contributed to disabled children being overlooked as active research participants, having their voices go unheard, and having their experiences not well understood, if not devalued (Stafford, 2017). Disregarding them in research can help to allow school transportation planners, student transportation service providers, and other parties not to recognize or question the provision of limited status quo transportation options that discount childhood disability. For example, limited status quo options typically exclude disabled children from AST initiatives and fre-quently require them to be transported outside their neighborhoods to a subset of schools equipped with resources to serve them. Requiring a dis-abled child to attend a school in this subset can separate them from siblings and neighborhood peers, prevent informal peer interaction during school trips, and the added distance/travel time to school may require them to wake up and leave home earlier than if they attended school locally. Waking up and leaving home earlier can be a major challenge for some families who must undertake remarkably time-consuming and work-intensive morning routines. For example, some disabled children may require support from parents, other family, personal support workers, and/or nurses to wake-up, get dressed and fed; undergo muscle mobilization/stretching routines, lift-and-carry transitions, and tube-feeding; and to leave to go to school. Requiring a disabled child to travel farther to school also creates demand for specialized student transportation services and, consequently, more administrative and logistical work for families.

Crafting inclusive research designs that value disabled children's experiences and perspectives is a practical way to work towards understanding and accounting for the presence and diversity of childhood disability, as well as eliminating ableism from the material conditions involved in school travel. The new sociology of childhood can help with recognizing disabled children's agency and including them in research.

2 Recognizing and including disabled children's perspectives

The new sociology of childhood perspective emerged from a dissatisfaction with a prevailing conception of childhood as a developmental life stage, which often scoped out childhood's historical and social contexts, and the variability in how it is experienced (Prout, 2005). New sociology of childhood scholars aimed to move beyond "psychologists' deterministic, positivistic, and medicalized models and ideals of childhood development" (Barker et al., 2009: 2). They acknowledge a multitude of diverse, socially constructed childhoods that are experienced in countless ways within and across societies, and recognize these differences have ties to the same social categories that differentiate adulthood (e.g., age, gender, race, ethnicity, class, disability, sexuality) (James et al., 1998; Prout, 2005). The new sociology of childhood lens also rejects that children are passive beings of socialization (Prout, 2005). Instead, it regards children as active, sense-making social actors capable of thinking critically and providing valuable input about their experiences and how they would like their worlds to be (Holloway & Valentine, 2000). The lens encourages direct engagement with children in research and broader social processes to recognize their agentic capacities, and to stop perpetuating a reliance on (and privileging of) adults' second-hand knowledge of children's experiences, needs, and desires (Holloway & Valentine, 2000; James et al., 1998; Prout & James, 1990). This has contributed to childhood studies emphasizing participatory methods that support children's inclusion.

Numerous participatory research methods have been advanced over recent decades to support conducting research 'with' (rather than 'for' or 'on') children so that scholars can directly access their experiences, viewpoints, and ideas. Some of these methods include photovoice and photo elicitation (Moola, Johnson, Lay, Krygsman, & Faulkner, 2015; Briggs, Stedman, & Krasny, 2014; Fusco et al., 2012[b]); participatory photo-mapping (Dennis Jr., Gaulocher, Carpiano, & Brown, 2009; Teixeira & Gardner, 2017); story-telling (LeBron et al., 2014); drawing activities (Elden, 2012); and activity-based interviews (Stafford, 2017). While conducting research with children has become more common, the methods for doing so have been criticized for not adequately accounting for the diversity of children and childhoods and, in turn, discounting some children (Beazley, Bessel, Ennew, & Waterson, 2009; Stafford, 2017; Tisdall, 2012). Disabled children represent a group whose experiences and views have been discounted. Their frequent exclusion from research participation has been attributed to assumptions about their capacity, not being considered legitimate research participants, and the use of restrictive methods that do not account for their participation (Lewis, 2001; Priestley, 1998; Stafford, 2017).

Although participatory research about how disabled children experience their environments has produced invaluable insights (see Stafford, 2017; Stephens et al., 2015; Pivik, 2010[c]), little has been done to include them in school transportation-related participatory research. For example, while Fusco et al. (2012, 2013) conducted useful participatory photovoice research about children's school journeys, disabled children's experiences were not considered. If we are to provide student transportation that is inclusive to disabled children, it is undeniably logical to include their voices. We must understand their unique school transportation experiences, challenges, and desires to inform efforts to realize inclusive school transportation. In the following section, I outline an inclusive research design used to study how families of disabled children experience school travel. Certain aspects of the study are then referenced to discuss some suggested inclusive research design considerations.

---

[b] See also Dyches, Cichella, Olsen, & Mandleco, 2004; Aitken & Wingate, 1993.
[c] See also Dyches et al., 2004; Aitken & Wingate, 1993.

3 Inclusive research design

To engage school transportation's childhood disability gap, I conducted an ethnographic study involving a photovoice (Wang & Burris, 1997) component. Photovoice involves having a certain group photograph their lived experiences concerning a certain topic, reflect on their photos, and then use them as aids to communicate their views to a researcher (Wang & Redwood-Jones, 2001). I also used conceptual tools of institutional ethnography (Smith, 1987, 2005) to support inquiry into inequitable, work-intensive aspects of the families' school travel. Using photovoice and institutional ethnographic conceptual tools helped to facilitate understanding of how families of disabled children experience the material conditions of their school travel, including inequitable aspects.

I chose photovoice over other participatory approaches because taking photos can be an engaging exercise for children (Fusco et al., 2012) and it offers them multiple means of communication (Lewis, 2001; Stafford, 2017). Photovoice would also engage all participants' critical thinking by requiring them to consider and photograph what aspects of their school travel experiences they wish to share with researchers. This enabled participants to think about their school travel experiences before interviews, and to have their photographs for reference during the interviews. This may have helped them to feel more confident and to provide richer input during interviews. Carrying out photovoice would also be less intrusive than using video-recordings or having a researcher observe families' routines. Lastly, participants' photos would help with clearly understanding the families' material conditions of school travel, as well as how they are experienced and regarded. I briefly note these reasons for selecting photovoice to emphasize that methodological choices must of course be made with great care and with attention to a study's aims, participants, and sensitivities. In this chapter, I am suggesting that a similar level of care and attention is warranted with respect to decisions about inclusive research design. Since I reference the school travel study in discussing researcher considerations for inclusive research design, I offer an overview of the study's research design for context.

4 Research design overview

Working with two GTHA-based hospital clinics, 13 families (i.e., child–parent dyads) living with childhood disability were recruited for a total of 30 participants (15 disabled children and 15 parents[d]). Each child had one of three conditions: osteogenesis imperfecta (OI), Duchenne muscular dystrophy (DMD), and spinal muscular atrophy (SMA) type two. OI is a chronic disease characterized by bone fragility and deformity, as well as periods of severe disability caused by regular bone fractures (Harrington, Sochett, & Howard, 2014). DMD and SMA are neuro-muscular disorders characterized by progressive muscle weakness, as well as declines in respiratory systems and motor functions (Birnkrant et al., 2018; Farrar et al., 2017). These conditions restricted the children's mobility such that they usually needed mobility support from an adult and/or mobility aids to achieve school trips.

Each family received an adaptive photo kit that supported the child's independent photo-taking. The child was asked to photograph things or experiences they like or dislike, find easy or difficult, or anything they wanted researchers to know about how they get ready and travel to school. The parent was asked to do the same on a different day. After the photography exercises, the child and parent participated in separate semi-structured, in-depth interviews inside their home. They were asked about their biographic and demographic backgrounds, their school trip experiences, school travel decisions, body and identity, and their photographs. I broke down school trip experience questions into four groups that reflected a disaggregation of the typical morning school trip routine and its micro-environments. This was done to help ensure rich, focused descriptions of how they experience the material conditions of their everyday school trips. I also incorporated numerous measures to help ensure that the disabled children (and parents) were enabled to participate as fully as possible, provide meaningful input, and feel included as they do so. Measures were also incorporated to help ensure that I could adequately represent and communicate (and therefore include) the families' experiences and perspectives in my work. I reference some of this study's measures below in proposing three considerations to help researchers craft studies that adequately include disabled children.

---

[d] Child and parent participant totals were each 15 because two families had two children participate, and two families had two parents participate.

5 Enablement via inclusive technologies

Using child-friendly participatory methods with disabled children may not ensure their inclusive participation. This is because some disabled children may require enabling technologies. Researchers could benefit from questioning if a study involving disabled children needs to incorporate inclusive technologies (i.e., in relation to study aims, methods, and children's conditions and capacities) and incorporating them as required. For example, such questioning occurred while designing the school travel study. It led to the realization that technologies would be crucial to enabling some children with OI, DMD, and SMA to independently photograph their school trips. Therefore, I developed adaptive photo kits and then piloted them with two families of children with different medical conditions (i.e., OI and SMA). I arrived at a photo kit with the components shown in Fig. 1.

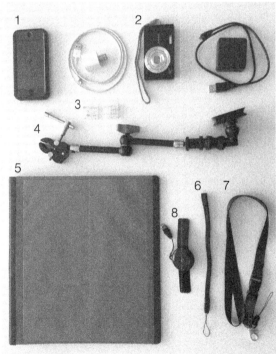

1. 6th generation iPod Touch in protective Otterbox case, power cord, and A/C adapter

2. Sony Cyber-Shot W800 digital camera (back-up), power cord, and A/C adapter

3. Two spare 3M Dual Lock Fasteners for attaching iPod Touch to Tecla mount

4. Customized Tecla mount for attaching iPod Touch to wheelchair

5. Photo kit binder with a list of photo kit contents, a study summary sheet, photography exercise instructions, and researcher business cards

6. Wrist lanyard for holding iPod Touch in hand, if preferred

7. Neck lanyard for holding iPod Touch around neck, if preferred

8. Bluetooth remote control to take photos with reduced movement, if preferred

Fig. 1 Adaptive photo kit components. *(Source: author.)*

Choosing an easy-to-use, intuitive camera was viewed as crucial to successful data collection. I chose a sixth-generation iPod Touch. Its touchscreen camera application was simpler to use than many standalone cameras and it was correctly assumed that many families (children included) would be familiar with the camera application and its operation. The iPod Touch camera application could be operated with light touches, which enabled some children with strength and/or dexterity conditions. I removed extraneous applications (e.g., games) from the iPod Touch and configured its home-screen to display on a few applications to help make photo-taking as straightforward as possible.

Finding a mount to connect an iPod Touch to the front of participants' wheelchairs such that it could be used for photo-taking proved difficult. This led to the collaborative[e] development of a customized mount. After testing multiple mounts with a pilot study child participant with SMA who uses a wheelchair, we arrived at the design shown above in Fig. 1 (see item 4). The mount has a clamp for wheelchair tubing on one end and a 3D-printed iPod Touch connector on the other. Between the clamp and 3D-printed iPod Touch connector are two metal bars and three joints that can be loosened and tightened at one juncture to facilitate easy positioning. The two metal bars offered the rigidity needed to keep the iPod Touch in place while traveling over bumps. Two pieces of gooseneck tubing next to the iPod Touch connector allowed micro-adjustments of the device to make photo-taking easier. If a child opted not to use the mount and to instead hold the iPod Touch, they were asked to use the photo kit's wrist or neck lanyard to help secure the device. I asked this to help minimize opportunities for dropping, losing, and breaking the iPod Touch, and to avoid situations where children might feel the need to pick up a dropped device and endanger themselves if they opt to do so.

I explain the camera selection rationale and the customized mount's development to offer insight into the time and effort that may be needed to enable disabled children's participation. Identifying, developing, and providing inclusive technologies can be a work-intensive and time-consuming aspect of research design. However, providing an adaptive photo kit allowed children to take photos independently and participate as fully as possible. Without the kit, it is likely that some children would have been unable to take photos or may have become frustrated in trying to do so. The adaptive photo kit's absence may have also led to photo-taking by proxy,

---

[e] I collaborated with Komodo OpenLab and Tecla (gettecla.com).

meaning that parents may have taken child participants' photos and, in turn, selected and inflected the photos with their own adult/parent perspectives. This could have led to the misrepresentation (and therefore exclusion) of children's experiences and viewpoints.

6 Engagement via positive participation experiences

If a child participant is disinterested in or feels burdened by participating, it may quickly diminish their engagement and prevent meaningful input. This can of course make it difficult to account for, include, and communicate their experiences and viewpoints in research. Disabled children's inclusion in research could be helped by questioning if their participation process (e.g., recruitment incentives; activities; meeting times, locations, and durations) offers them (and their families) an opportunity to have positive participation experiences. Is their participation convenient? Is it work-intensive and/or time-consuming? Are they offered a benefit that recognizes the value of their time and effort? Asking such questions while designing the school travel study led to greater emphasis on researcher flexibility and the use of atypical gift card recruitment incentives.

Researcher flexibility measures were incorporated into the school travel study to make the families' participation convenient. I offered to conduct all meetings at the families' homes across the GTHA to prevent them from having to travel. I also offered to meet on weekends if it was more convenient (almost half of the meetings were on weekends). Other flexibility measures were borne out of an understanding of these families' difficult schedules and the potential for children's health issues to occur. It was communicated that meetings would be (and indeed, were) re-scheduled, if requested, without question or pushback. I also duplicated the adaptive photo kit because having two would allow each participating family to have a kit for one week. While the photography exercise required two days, giving each family a kit for one week allowed them to have flexibility with photo-taking and to avoid feeling undue stress if they could not take photos on a day.

Gift card recruitment incentives were used to support the recruitment of families of disabled children as 'expert knowers' who were the best people to speak about their embodied experiences (Smith, 2006: 224). A nurse and doctor, each with pre-existing relationships with the to-be-recruited families, led recruitment efforts. They informed parents that for full participation, they could choose one $250 gift card or two valued at $125. Gift card options were for a movie theater, drug store, and well-known stores that sold toys, online music, computers/technology, and discount clothing. I offered multiple card options, and to divide their values across two options, so that families could enhance the benefit of their full participation by choosing the option(s) that best suited their needs and desires. Only companies with online gift card options were used to ensure cards' timely delivery and to avoid lost gift cards.

The hospital involved in the study initially challenged the study's gift card amount, noting that it was higher than usual and perhaps excessive. I contended that the amount may be atypical, but it accurately reflected the value of the time and effort requested of the families. Each family was anticipated to spend 270 min on the project, and 30 min of buffer time was added to this to account for time overruns, bringing the total to 300 min (5 h). The gift card amounts were based on $50 per hour (i.e., $50 × 5 h = $250) of participation time. This rate nearly doubles the average hourly rate of $27.70 paid to full-time payroll employees in Canada in 2016 (Statistics Canada, 2017). The $250 amount was regarded as necessary to incentivize families who experience childhood disability-related time and financial constraints (e.g., dealing with accessible home/vehicle costs; spending more time helping children with daily tasks such as eating and getting dressed) and who may be hesitant to participate since school mornings can already be stressful. Moreover, these families might be hesitant to participate since they regularly receive requests to participate in studies concerning their children's medical conditions. As intended, the $250 gift cards seemed to help the families have positive participation experiences, as evidenced by numerous conversations with children and parents, and the below parent email excerpts:

> *Thank you so very much for the gift cards!! Just wanted to let you know they were received and greatly appreciated!! (Parent, Family 2, personal communication, February 26, 2017)*
> *Thank you so much we will enjoy the movies! (Parent, Family 6, personal communication, March 14, 2017)*
> *It was wonderful sharing our experience with you. … [My partner] and I are glad that you and your colleagues are taking the initiative to bring out our experiences to a larger audience especially who could make a difference to the future of our kids… Also, I did receive gift card emails, appreciate it. (Parent, Family 8, personal communication, March 30, 2017)*
> *I am glad that you got some valuable input with this interview, thank you [for] doing this research to improve school travel for families with disability. GREAT JOB! … I received the gift card, thank you. (Parent, Family 9, personal communication, April 4, 2017)*

If the families were not offered a benefit that recognized the value of their time and effort, and if I had not emphasized researcher flexibility to make their participation convenient, it is likely that fewer families would have been willing to participate and those willing to participate may have been less engaged. These research design measures clearly required notable funding and more data collection work (e.g., traveling to all families' homes; working on weekends); however, they reduced families' participation workloads, offered them a tangible benefit for their efforts, and allowed them the opportunity to have a positive participation experience. This seems to have supported the families' engagement, which in turn helped with better understanding and including their experiences and viewpoints in the research.

7 Adequate representation via researcher reflexivity

Incorporating researcher reflexivity into a research design can be invaluable to including disabled children. This is because even if disabled children are enabled to fully participate via inclusive technologies, and their engagement is supported by the opportunity to have a positive participation experience, a lack of researcher reflexivity may lead to researchers unwittingly dismissing or misrepresenting the children's experiences, viewpoints, and ideas. This can occur via unrecognized and thus unchecked researcher bias (e.g., an ableist bias), the privileging of a researcher's voice over the children's, and using methods that discount children's desire or need to communicate via different (i.e., not verbal and written) means, such as drawing, video, role-playing, and photography (Stafford, 2017; Tisdall, 2012). Reflexivity helps to ensure respect for and acceptance of disabled children's sense-making as their reality, and aids the prioritization of faithfully representing their understandings, experiences, and ideas (Stafford, 2017: 604).

Researcher reflexivity was integral to including disabled children and their parents in the school travel study. To understand and communicate their experiences and viewpoints, I embraced 'uncomfortable reflexivity' (Pillow, 2003) as I collected and analyzed data. This meant recognizing that while there is of course a need to represent and find meaning in the collected data, the representations of the families' experiences produced in the research should be continuously challenged (Pillow, 2003). I used uncomfortable reflexivity as a tool to continuously question if and how I could adequately describe and explain the families' experiences, and to challenge my efforts through a process involving deep reflexivity, heightened self-awareness, and discomfort. This involved spending time after meetings with families, as well as during data analysis and writing, to question assumptions and the collected data in relation to any ableist bias I might hold, as well as my privileged positionality as a white, able-bodied, adult male researcher. I also questioned if described experiences were in fact a major issue for the families, or if I merely viewed them as such due to my own positionality.

Practicing reflexivity helped me to more fully realize that my personal history provided me with no tacit knowledge of how families living with childhood disability experience everyday school travel, nor the remarkable (but often unnoticed) workloads and time/financial constraints they some-times face. It also helped with better understanding the ways (and the extent to which) my positionality offers me advantages regarding movement and mobility, independence, transportation access, physical/mental health, and notably, experiencing fewer constraints in everyday life (e.g., temporal, socio-spatial, and institutional). For example, I came to better understand that my able-bodied childhood afforded me school transportation privileges by allowing me to walk to school without difficulty (or thought, even), ride buses with other children aboard and without any safety concerns, and by not needing to wake up early for time-consuming routine tasks (e.g., tube-feeding and requiring support with toileting and in-house transfers). These realizations were integral to carrying out a thoughtful research project that valued and emphasized faithfully representing the families' experiences. Without purposeful reflexivity in participatory research involving disabled children, a researcher runs the risk of unwittingly misrepresenting (and therefore excluding) the children's voices due to unchecked biases and/or privileging the researcher's voice. In other words, a lack of reflexivity can undo the inclusivity of an otherwise inclusively designed research project by producing findings that misrepresent and exclude children's experiences and perspectives.

8 Participant inclusion, researcher insight

By carefully selecting a child-friendly, participatory approach and emphasizing the three researcher considerations discussed above, I was able to craft an inclusive research design that enabled disabled children and parents to openly and effectively communicate their experiences and view-points. In turn, the research design facilitated a detailed, insightful under-standing of how the families experience school travel in inequitable, work-intensive ways. For example, it allowed me to clearly understand how the routine act of getting a child with OI, DMD, or SMA out of bed each day to get ready for school can, in and of itself, present challenges that demand planning and work. The act can involve difficult physical lifts (or, the use of an in-home sling-lift) that can be dangerous to child and parent. Further, it may extend into the night, as some parents described periodically or routinely sleeping in the same room as their child to monitor them. The families' school day wake-ups are also typically early. Many parents described starting their days during the 5:00 AM and 6:00 AM hours to accommodate night nurses leaving and/or personal support workers arriving, and to undertake daily health-related wake-up procedures (e.g., rolling a child onto their side for 30–60 min before their wake-up, applying cough assist machines, removing night-time bilevel positive airway pressure ventilator masks).

Beyond wake-up routines, the families indicated that they must regularly perform inequitable work to achieve school trips and gain education access. Such work is required to overcome challenges involved in, among other things, obtaining funding for accessible private vehicles and home renovations, communicating with student transportation service providers, gaining access to school sites' accessible parking, entering school buildings via inaccessible entrances, and managing support worker schedules and staff changes. Constantly taking on these (and various other) challenges involves emotional work. By helping participants to feel included, the research design helped participants to be open about the emotional aspects of their experiences. Children generally described feeling sad and angry when they encountered disabling barriers, nervous in certain scenarios (e.g., when hitting speed bumps in vehicles, using bus steps and lifts, moving through crowds), and feeling lonely during accessible bus trips because they often had no peers with whom they could interact. Many parents indicated feeling isolated from family, friends, and other parents; worried about their child's well-being; as well as feeling exhausted from and frustrated with the work they must do to overcome inaccessible design and gain education access for their child(ren).

In briefly discussing how the families experienced and felt about their school travel, my intent is not to present study findings (that is not this chapter's purpose); rather, my aim is to stir thought about the participant engagement and detailed, insightful understanding that an inclusive research design can offer. Without emphasizing participant inclusion, it is unlikely that the school travel study's participants would have been as engaged as they were;

moreover, it is doubtful that the study would have yielded the detailed, insightful understandings of the families' experiences and emotions that it did. Whether families' engagement was spurred on by the children's ability to fully participate via inclusive technologies, receiving a benefit that adequately acknowledged their effort, or because they knew that voicing their experiences and viewpoints in findings was a priority, the time and effort that went into crafting an inclusive research design was worthwhile. It allowed me to gain a comprehensive and insightful understanding of the families' school travel experiences, including their laborious and emotional aspects.

9 Conclusion

School transportation, a transportation research subfield that should clearly have regard for childhood disability, has largely disregarded it. While the subfield has come into focus for researchers as an opportunity to advance children's physical activity levels, independent mobility, and well-being, its inherent ableism has contributed to disabled children being frequently overlooked as active research participants and, in turn, their experiences and viewpoints being mostly ignored. Given childhood disability's prevalence in North America, conducting school travel research involving disabled children's participation could help to improve many children's school travel experiences and well-being.

This chapter has suggested that the new sociology of childhood perspective can be useful for including disabled children in school transportation research. The perspective offers a lens through which the children are regarded as active, sense-making social actors capable of thinking critically and participating in research. Moreover, it supports recognizing children's agency in research through participatory methods that allow them to directly present their experiences and perspectives. However, merely incorporating participatory methods into a study involving disabled child participants may not be enough to ensure their inclusion. This is because participatory methods have been found to frequently overlook some children, such as those living with disability (Stafford, 2017; Tisdall, 2012). To conduct participatory research that involves and adequately includes disabled children in school transportation, three useful researcher considerations have been suggested: (1) enabling participation via inclusive technologies; (2) supporting engagement by providing them with opportunities to have positive participation experiences; and (3) using researcher reflexivity to help ensure experiences and perspectives are faithfully represented in research.

Questioning if inclusive technologies are needed to enable disabled children's participation, and incorporating them as required, is encouraged because such technologies may be essential to their participation. Identifying, developing, and incorporating inclusive technologies may be work-intensive and time-consuming, but having them on hand during data collection may mean the difference between a child being able to participate and being frustrated with participating, or entirely unable to do so.

Questioning if a research design provides disabled children the opportunity to have positive participation experiences is suggested as a useful inclusive research design practice. This is because the children's engagement and input may be diminished if they are disinterested in or feeling burdened by their participation. This can make it difficult to account for and include their experiences and viewpoints in research. Greater researcher flexibility (i.e., to make participation more convenient), understanding and respecting the families' potential time and financial constraints, and offering a benefit commensurate with the value of the time and effort requested (e.g., gift card recruitment incentives) can help to create the opportunity for positive participation experiences. Creating such opportunities may require notable work (e.g., meeting on weekends; traveling to families to reduce their travel) and funding to recognize the value of their time and effort. However, making participation more convenient and offering families a benefit commensurate to their time and effort can help to support their engagement, produce meaningful input, and, in turn, support the inclusion of their experiences in research.

Without researcher reflexivity, a researcher risks misrepresenting and excluding disabled child participants' voices from what could be an otherwise inclusively designed study. For this reason, researchers could benefit from incorporating reflexivity practices into research designs involving disabled children. Practicing reflexivity can help with checking researcher bias, questioning whose voices are being prioritized or privileged, and challenging if children's and parents' voices are being faithfully represented in the research. Researcher reflexivity can be uncomfortable, as it may involve questioning one's own understandings and assumptions, positionality and privilege, and relations to participants and the research. However, embracing these uncomfortable tasks and incorporating them into studies can be invaluable, if not essential, to faithfully reporting and including participant's experiences and perspectives in research.

Crafting an inclusive research design involving disabled children can require substantial time and effort, as evidenced by the work involved in crafting the school travel study referenced in this chapter. However, embracing this work in school transportation research and transportation research in general can help us better recognize and understand the diversity of childhoods; children's bodies, physiologies, and cognitive capacities; and the multitude of ways in which children experience everyday life. Engaging the proposed inclusive research design considerations and embracing the work involved in doing so may lead to important lessons learned from disabled children, which may in turn help with questioning and unsettling the normalized ableism inherent in school transportation research.

References

Aitken, S., & Wingate, J. (1993). A preliminary study of the self-directed photography of middle-class, homeless, and mobility-impaired children. *The Professional Geographer*, 45(1), 65–72.

Barker, J., Kraftl, P., Horton, J., & Tucker, F. (2009). The road less travelled—New directions in children's and young people's mobility. *Mobilities*, 4(1), 1–10.

Beazley, H., Bessel, S., Ennew, J., & Waterson, R. (2009). The right to be properly researched: Research with children in a messy, real world. *Children's Geographies*, 7(4), 365–378.

Birnkrant, D. J., Bushby, K., Bann, C. M., Apkon, S. D., Blackwell, A., Brumbaugh, D., et al. (2018). Diagnosis and management of Duchenne muscular dystrophy, part 1: Diagnosis, and neuromuscular, rehabilitation, endocrine, and gastrointestinal and nutritional management. *Lancet Neurology*, 17(3), 251–267.

Briggs, L. P., Stedman, R. C., & Krasny, M. E. (2014). Photo-elicitation methods in studies of children's sense of place. *Early Childhood Education*, 24(3), 153–172.

Buliung, R., Larsen, K., Faulkner, G., & Ross, T. (2017). Children's independent mobility in the City of Toronto, Canada. *Travel Behaviour and Society*, 9, 58–69.

Buliung, R., Mitra, R., & Faulkner, G. (2009). Active school transportation in the greater Toronto area, Canada: An exploration of trends in space and time (1986–2006). *Preventive Medicine*, 48(6), 507–512.

Chouinard, V. (1997). Making space for disabling differences: Challenging ableist geographies. *Environment and Planning D: Society and Space*, 15, 379–387.

Dennis, S. F., Jr., Gaulocher, S., Carpiano, R. M., & Brown, D. (2009). Participatory photo mapping (PPM): Exploring an integrated method for health and place research with young people. *Health & Place*, 15, 466–473.

Dyches, T. T., Cichella, E., Olsen, S. F., & Mandleco, B. (2004). Snapshots of life: Perspectives of school-aged individuals with developmental disabilities. *Research and Practice for Persons with Severe Disabilities*, 29(3), 172–182.

Elden, S. (2012). Inviting the messy: Drawing methods and 'children's voices'. *Childhood*, 20 (1), 66–81.

Farrar, M. A., Park, S. B., Vucic, S., Carey, K. A., Turner, B. J., Gillingwater, T. H., et al. (2017). Emerging therapies and challenges in spinal muscular atrophy. *Annals of Neurology*, 81(3), 355–368.

Faulkner, G. E. J., Richichi, V., Buliung, R. N., Fusco, C., & Moola, F. (2010). What's quickest and easiest?': Parent decision making about school trip mode. *International Journal of Behavioral Nutrition and Physical Activity*, 7(1), 1.

Fusco, C., Moola, F., Faulkner, G., Buliung, R., & Richichi, V. (2012). Toward an understanding of children's perceptions of their transport geography: (non)active school travel and visual representations of the built environment. *Journal of Transport Geography*, *20*, 62–70.

Gibson, B. E., Teachman, G., Wright, V., Fehlings, D., Young, N. L., & McKeever, P. (2012). Children's and parents' beliefs regarding the value of walking: Rehabilitation implications with cerebral palsy. *Child: Care, Health and Development*, *38*(1), 61–69.

Goggin, G. (2016). Disability and mobilities: Evening of social futures. *Mobilities*, *11*(4), 533–541.

Goodley, D. (2014). *Dis/ability studies: Theorising disablism and ableism*. London: Routledge.

Ham, S. A., Martin, S., & Kohl, H. W., III (2008). Changes in the percentage of students who walk or bike to school–United States, 1969 and 2001. *Journal of Physical Activity and Health*, *5*(2), 205–215.

Harrington, J., Sochett, E., & Howard, A. (2014). Update on the evaluation and treatment of Osteogenesis Imperfecta. *Pediatric Clinics of North America*, *61*(6), 1243–1257.

Hillman, M., Adams, J., & Whitelegg, J. (1990). *One false move: A study of children's independent mobility*. London: Policy Studies Institute.

Holloway, S., & Valentine, G. (2000). Children's geographies and the new social studies of childhood. In S. Holloway & G. Valentine (Eds.), *Children's Geographies: Playing, Living, Learning* (pp. 1–22). New York: Routledge.

Imrie, R. (2000). Disability and discourses of mobility and movement. *Environment and Planning A*, *32*(9), 1641–1656.

Imrie, R. (2003). Architects conceptions of the human body. *Environment and Planning D: Society and Space*, *21*(1), 47–65.

Imrie, R., & Edwards, C. (2007). The geographies of disability: Reflections on the development of a sub-discipline. *Geography Compass*, *1*(3), 623–640.

James, A., Jenks, C., & Prout, A. (1998). *Theorizing childhood*. Cambridge: Wiley.

James, A., & Prout, A. (Eds.), (1997). *Constructing and reconstructing childhood: Contemporary issues in the sociological study of childhood*. London: RoutledgeFalmer.

Larsen, K., Gilliland, J., & Hess, P. M. (2012). Route-based analysis to capture the environmental influences on a child's mode of travel between home and school. *Annals of the Association of American Geographers*, *102*(6), 1348–1365.

LeBron, A. M. W., Schulz, A. J., Bernal, C., Gamboa, C., Wright, C., Sand, S., et al. (2014). Storytelling in community intervention research: Lessons learned from the walk your heart to health intervention. *Prog Community Health Partnership*, *8*(4), 477–485.

Lewis, M. (2001). *Learning to listen: Consulting children and young people with disabilities*. London: Save the Children.

McDonald, N. C. (2007). Active transportation to school: Trends among U.S. schoolchildren, 1969–2001. *American Journal of Preventive Medicine*, *32*, 509–516.

McMillan, T. E. (2007). The relative influence of urban form on a child's travel mode to school. *Transportation Research Part A*, *41*(1), 69–79.

Metrolinx (2013). *Active and sustainable school transportation in Ontario: Barriers and enablers*. Ontario: Metrolinx.

Metrolinx (2014). *The Costs and Benefits of School Travel Planning Projects in Ontario, Canada, January 2014*. Ontario: Metrolinx.

Metrolinx (2018). *2041 Regional transportation plan: For the Greater Toronto and Hamilton Area*. Ontario: Metrolinx.

Metrolinx and Green Communities Canada (2013). *School Travel Planning in Action in Ontario: Successes and Lessons in Active and Sustainable School Transportation*. Ontario: Metrolinx.

Milne, S. (2009). Moving into and through the public world: Children's perspectives on their encounters with adults. *Mobilities*, *4*(1), 103–118.

Mitchell, H., Kearns, R. A., & Collins, D. C. A. (2007). Nuances of neighbourhood: Children's perceptions of space between home and School in Auckland, New Zealand. *Geoforum*, *38*(4), 614–627.

Mitra, R., & Buliung, R. N. (2014). The influence of neighbourhood environment and household travel interactions on school travel behavior: An exploration using geographically weighted models. *Journal of Transport Geography*, *36*, 69–78.

Moola, F., Johnson, J., Lay, J., Krygsman, S., & Faulkner, G. (2015). The heartbeat of Hamilton': Researcher's reflections on Hamilton children's engagement with visual research methodologies to study the environment. *International Journal of Qualitative Methods*, *14* (4), 1–14.

Palisano, R. J., Hanna, S. E., Rosenbaum, P., & Tieman, B. (2010). Probability of walking, wheeled mobility, and assisted mobility in children and adolescents with cerebral palsy. *Developmental Medicine and Child Neurology*, *52*, 66–71.

Pillow, W. S. (2003). Confession, catharsis, or cure? Rethinking the uses of reflexivity as methodological power in qualitative research. *Qualitative Studies in Education*, *16*(2), 175–196.

Pivik, J. R. (2010). The perspective of children and youth: How different stakeholders identify architectural barriers for inclusion in schools. *Journal of Environmental Psychology*, *30*, 510–517.

Priestley, M. (1998). Childhood disability and disabled childhoods: Agendas for research. *Childhood*, *5*(2), 207–223.

Prout, A. (2005). *The future of childhood*. New York: Routledge.

Prout, A., & James, A. (1990). A new paradigm for the sociology of childhood? In A. James & A. Prout (Eds.), *Constructing and reconstructing childhood: Contemporary issues in the sociological study of childhood* (pp. 7–33). London: RoutledgeFalmer.

Ross, T., & Buliung, R. (2018). A systematic review of disability's treatment in the active school travel and children's independent mobility literatures. *Transport Reviews*, *38*(3), 349–371.

Rothman, L., Macpherson, A. K., Ross, T., & Buliung, R. N. (2018). The decline in active school transportation (AST): A systematic review of the factors related to AST and changes in school transport over time in North America. *Preventive Medicine*, *111*, 314–322.

Rothman, L., To, T., Buliung, R., Macarthur, C., & Howard, A. (2014). Influence of social and built environment features on children walking to school. *Preventive Medicine*, *60*, 10–15.

Saltes, N. (2018). Navigating disabling spaces: Challenging ontological norms and the Spatialization of difference through 'embodied practices of mobility. *Mobilities*, *13*(1), 81–95.

Smith, D. (1987). *The everyday world as problematic: A feminist sociology*. Toronto, ON: University of Toronto Press.

Smith, D. (2005). *Institutional ethnography: A sociology for people*. California: AltaMira Press.

Smith, D. (2006). Introduction. In D. E. Smith (Ed.), *Institutional Ethnography as Practice* (pp. 1–11). Lanham, MD: Rowman & Littlefield.

Stafford, L. (2017). 'What about my voice': Emancipating the voices of children with disabilities through participant-Centred methods. *Children's Geographies*, *15*(5), 600–613.

Statistics Canada (2008a). *Table 1—Disability Rates for Children under the Age of 15, by Sex and Age Groups, Canada, 2006*. Retrieved from: https://www150.statcan.gc.ca/n1/pub/89-628-x/2008009/tables/5201059-eng.htm.

Statistics Canada, 2008b. Table 6—Number of Disabilities Reported for Children Aged 5 to 14 Years with Disabilities, Canada, 2006. Retrieved from: https://www150.statcan.gc.ca/n1/pub/89-628-x/2007002/t/4125015-eng.htm.

Statistics Canada, 2008c. Table 8—Severity of disability among children aged 5 to 14 years with disabilities, Canada, 2001 and 2006. Retrieved from: https://www150.statcan.gc.ca/n1/pub/89-628-x/2007002/t/4183076-eng.htm.

Statistics Canada (2017). Wages by occupation, 2016. June 15, 2017. http://www.statcan.gc.ca/daily-quotidien/170615/dq170615a-eng.htm?HPA=1.

Stephens, L., Scott, H., Aslam, H., Yantzi, N., Young, N. L., Ruddick, S., et al. (2015). The accessibility of elementary schools in Ontario, Canada: Not making the grade. *Children, Youth and Environments*, *25*(2), 153–175.

Teixeira, S., & Gardner, R. (2017). Youth-led participatory photo mapping to understand urban environments. *Children and Youth Services Review*, *82*, 246–253.

Tisdall, E. K. M. (2012). The challenge and challenging of childhood studies? Learning from disability studies and research with disabled children. *Children & Society*, *26*, 181–191.

Tremblay, M., Shields, M., Laviolette, M., Craig, C. L., Janssen, I., & Connor Gorber, S. (2010). Fitness of Canadian children and youth: Results from the 2007–2009 Canadian health measures survey. *Health Reports*, *21*, 1–7.

U.S. Census Bureau, 2010. School-aged children with disabilities in U.S. metropolitan statistical areas: 2010. Retrieved from: https://www.census.gov/prod/2011pubs/acsbr10-12.pdf.

Wang, C., & Burris, M. A. (1997). Photovoice: Concept, methodology, and use for participatory needs assessment. *Health Education & Behavior*, *24*(3), 369–387.

Wang, C., & Redwood-Jones, Y. (2001). Photovoice ethics: Perspectives from Flint photovoice. *Health Education & Behavior*, *29*(5), 560–572.

Wolbring, G. (2007). New and emerging sciences and technologies, Ableism, transhumanism and region, faith, theology and churches. *International Journal of Contextual Theology in East Asia*, *7*, 79–112.

Further reading

Fusco, C., Faulkner, G., Moola, F., Buliung, R., & Richichi, V. (2013). Urban school travel: Exploring children's qualitative narratives about their trip to school. *Children, Youth and Environments*, *23*(3), 1–23.

Gleeson, B. (2006). *Geographies of disability*. London: Routledge.

PART FOUR

Examples from different cultures

CHAPTER SIXTEEN

Japan: Maintaining high levels of walking

E. Owen D. Waygood[a] and Ayako Taniguchi[b]

[a]Department of Civil, Geological, and Mining Engineering, Polytechnique Montréal, Montreal, QC, Canada
[b]Risk Engineering, University of Tsukuba, Tsukuba, Japan

Contents

1 Current state of children's travel in Japan
1.1 Walking is still dominant

Japan has had considerable success in maintaining high levels of children walking to school in comparison to other wealthy nations (Drianda & Kinoshita, 2011; Shaw, Bicket, & Elliott, 2015; Susilo & Waygood, 2012; Waygood, 2009; Waygood & Kitamura, 2009; Xu, Taniguchi, Ishigami, & Hirata, 2015). As well, unlike many other countries, the differences between "licenses" (i.e., permission from parents) for children to travel independently have not noticeably changed between the current generation and the previous one (Shaw et al., 2015). Nationally, walking is still the dominant mode for children for weekday travel (Taniguchi & Xin,

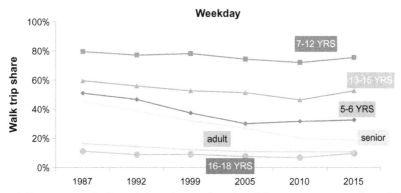

Fig. 1 Percentage of all weekday trips on foot by different age groups from 1987 to 2015.

2018). Over a twenty-year period (Fig. 1), although decreases in walking can be seen, the majority of trips are still on foot for seven to 17 year olds (Xu et al., 2015) (Table 1). For high school students, travel on foot has historically been low (as most trips are by public transport and cycling), but is now under 10%. However, these high school students may actually be walking further than children going to elementary schools in order to use public transport (Waygood, Sun, & Letarte, 2015). The overall modal shares can be seen in Table 1. The largest growth has been in private vehicle travel, though the percentage remains below 20%. As such, Japan offers a contrast from other wealthy countries such as the USA where private vehicle travel is dominant.

1.2 High levels of independence

When considering children's independent mobility (CIM), children in Japan are highly independent during the week, though less so on the weekend (Waygood & Kitamura, 2009). For weekend travel, considerable growth in car travel can be seen, increasing from 38% in 1992 to 63% in

Table 1 Change in weekday modal share for children aged 5–17

Year	Rail	Bus	Car	Bicycle	On foot
1992	8%	4%	11%	23%	54%
1999	7%	3%	14%	23%	53%
2005	8%	3%	17%	21%	51%
2010	9%	2%	19%	21%	49%
2015	10%	2%	18%	18%	51%

(*Source:* Japanese nationwide PT data.)

2015 (Xu et al., 2015). Licenses for CIM (i.e., what the children and their parents say they are allowed to do with respect to travel alone) for children aged seven are among the highest in the world (Shaw et al., 2015). These results reflect the findings published elsewhere on CIM licenses in Japan (Drianda & Kinoshita, 2011). Independent travel in Japan is most associated with more urbanized areas (Drianda & Kinoshita, 2011; Waygood & Kitamura, 2009). On average, children (in grade five, aged 10 and 11) in the most urbanized areas did 91% of their trips without an adult during the week, and this remained above 85% for the other urban areas (Waygood & Kitamura, 2009). The percentage measured in the less dense towns and rural areas falls to below 60% (children typically walked to school, but then some were picked up by car). In some suburban areas where children are not granted as much freedom, parents expressed that they wished their children could be independent, but were more worried about the traffic than those in urban areas (Drianda & Kinoshita, 2011). Finally, parents in the least urbanized areas were the most unlikely to give licenses to their children. Also, the children in these areas expressed more concerns over both traffic and stranger danger (Drianda & Kinoshita, 2011), perhaps reflecting a similar finding to other countries where this type of development is more common. Perhaps contrary to expectations is that children in rural areas are given more license to travel by public transport (Drianda & Kinoshita, 2011) which is likely related to the fact that distances are much greater and therefore such modes are necessary to facilitate independent travel.

1.3 Interactions with their world while walking: Impacts on social and psychological wellbeing

As children walk around, they consciously observe other people (Waygood & Friman, 2015; Waygood & Kitamura, 2009) and interact with people that they know (Waygood, Friman, Olsson, & Taniguchi, 2017). The rates of incidental interaction are much higher in Japan than those that were found for Canada or Sweden (Waygood et al., 2017), but in all cases it was walking and independent travel that was most associated with these interactions. According to Shiina (2009), conversations with friends and locals on the school road broadens children's living experience, writing that "the school trip was one of the most important for a child's growth environment". These connections with neighbors likely lowers parental concerns about letting children out alone, as there are other adults there to assist and keep an eye out for them if needed.

The things that children do while walking is different from other modes. Kinoshita (Kinoshita, 2009) describes the importance of taking their time (e.g., dilly dallying, wandering) while children commute to or from school. Kinoshita wrote that activities such as "looking at the roadside flowers, walking [a] slow speed, sometimes stopping, playing, thinking, competing with friends, and greeting or chatting with neighbors along the road" is very important for the growth of children. One can see that as with incidental interactions being associated with active modes, social interactions are much higher than travel by car (Fig. 2; Taniguchi, 2018). These incidental interactions and greetings, often called "*aisatsu*" in Japanese, were found to be positively associated with children's life satisfaction and their quality of life (Taniguchi, 2018). Such findings relate to work that shows that children's subjective wellbeing is positively associated to their social capital (Helliwell & Putnam, 2004). Thus, we can see that there are intrinsic aspects to walking that better connect children to their social and physical environments.

1.4 Physical wellbeing and transport

For the majority of schools in Japan, children walk to school in a walking school bus, a system that has been in existence since at least the early 1960s (Waygood, Taniguchi, Craig-St-Louis, & Xu, 2015), with evidence

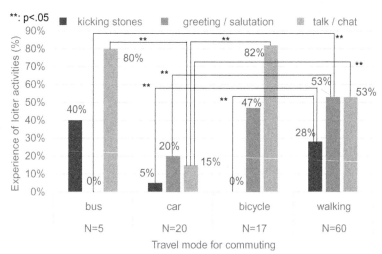

Fig. 2 The percentages of different activities that children do while commuting by different modes. The stars indicate that there are statistically significant differences between the findings, linked by the lines.

dating back to the 19th century (Senda & Kamioka, 2009). Although mandatory, it is preferred by most children, though the greatest latent demand is for cycling (Drianda & Kinoshita, 2011). Children typically obtain roughly 20 min of daily exercise through these walking school buses, though in this case the children in less urban areas generally get more exercise as they walk further to get to school (Waygood & Kitamura, 2009). Participating in these walking school buses contributes to the overall goal of children having 60 min a day of physical activity.

Although the children are walking at very high rates, the population-based death rates by traffic for children aged 10 are the lowest in the world. In places where children walk less frequently such as Canada, the rates for pedestrian deaths are the same as in Japan. However, due to the number of children who die in cars in Canada, the overall death rate is about three times higher than in Japan (Waygood, Taniguchi, et al., 2015). This raises a serious question about how car travel can be considered a safe means of travel for children (Johansson, 2006; Pacilli, Giovannelli, Prezza, & Augimeri, 2013). On a positive note, children's (aged 5–17) fatality rates by traffic have been going down rapidly since 1992 (Taniguchi & Xin, 2018), though over this period car use has been increasing for all trips. The number of traffic fatalities was 2079 in 1992 and 270 in 2015. In 1992 (Table 1), the modal share for cars was only 11% nationally, while in 2015 it represented 18% on weekdays. Thus, this small percentage change can't explain the major reduction in traffic fatalities. A study (Waygood, Taniguchi, et al., 2015) that looked at child fatalities by mode in Japan observed a reduction in child (<15 years old) pedestrian deaths by half between 2002 and 2007 (0.6–0.3 per 100,000 children under 15 years old), while deaths in motor-vehicles and on bicycles decreased by one-third (0.3–0.2 per 100,000 people of that age range) (Waygood, Taniguchi, et al., 2015). A general decrease was observed for all modes. This might suggest that the overall transport system is getting safer, though an increase in the amount driven results in an increase in the number of injuries per capita (Waygood, Taniguchi, et al., 2015). It could also be that medical technology or other factors are reducing deaths while the actual transport system is not improving.

2 What might explain the high levels of active and independent travel seen in Japan?

This section will focus on what might explain these high levels of active and independent travel. The influences will be grouped according to the socio-ecological model (see Chapter 5 for details) starting from the level of culture down to the individual level (Bronfenbrenner, 1979). The socio-ecological model is a framework proposed to understand behavior. It suggests that behavior is influenced by numerous different levels from cultural, policy, and the social and built environment, to the household and the individual.

2.1 Culture

One of the explanations for high levels of CIM is simply that children's independent travel is expected and valued by the society (Joshi & MacLean, 1997). One can imagine that if something is valued, it will work its way (consciously or subconsciously) into the policies and practices that support that behavior. Those outcomes are discussed below.

Children are typically taught to be aware of their impact on others around them, which is an important cultural value. This can relate to children being aware of other users of transport infrastructure. Of course, this perspective may create stress for some parents of young children on public transport, as they are acutely aware of the negative impacts of a noisy child in a public space (Ohmori, Taniguchi, Manabe, Terauchi, & Aono, 2014). However, this cultural attitude may also help explain the reason cars are expected to watch out for the more vulnerable road users (rather than the other way around).

Rural areas are less idealized as "great places to raise kids", as is the case often in Anglo-Saxon cultures (Bonner, 1997). In Japan, rural areas are more associated to lacking access to the resources for children. This does not mean that Japanese people do not appreciate nature. On the contrary, connectedness with nature is often more evident in Japan, through children tending to gardens at the majority of schools, and through their adoration of celebrating nature's seasonal changes through food and outings to see natures changes.

As mentioned, "aisatsu" (which simply translates to "a greeting") is encouraged (Fig. 3). This is partly because it is recognized to help protect children. As was discussed in Chapter 4, children who are better connected to their neighborhoods feel more secure, and their parents also feel more secure. In Canada, this type of community connection is mentally associated to small centers (Bonner, 1997), but as was shown, aisatsu more commonly occurs in more urbanized areas of Japan (Waygood & Friman, 2015). A key difference may simply be that urban areas in Japan are typically built for and support walking for daily activities and for accessing public transport

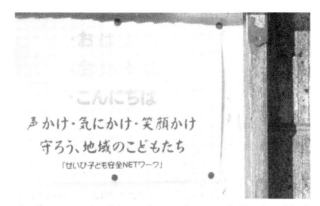

Fig. 3 Example of encouraging "aisatsu" posted on a neighborhood bulletin board in Nara, Japan, which translates as: good morning, welcome back, hello; Greet. Care. Smile. Let's protect our areas' children. *(Photo credit: E.O.D. Waygood.)*

(Kitamura, Sakamoto, & Waygood, 2008; Sun, Waygood, Fukui, & Kitamura, 2009; Waygood, Sun, & Letarte, 2015).

2.2 National policies and programs

Commuting to school plays a large role in a child's health (Kimura & Itoi, 2008). As mentioned above, the majority of children in elementary schools participate in a walking school bus program called "*shuudantōgekō*" (Waygood, Taniguchi, et al., 2015). Evidence of this idea dates back to 1894 (Senda & Kamioka, 2009). At that time, it was not nationally organized, but numerous communities developed a walking school bus as a solution to the new problem of traffic. While walking to school, the children walk in a line with the oldest children at the front and back. The younger children, and often also the older ones, wear yellow hats on their commute. This feature increases the safety of the children by making them more visible. Driving and cycling to school are generally not permitted due to safety concerns. Driving is associated with creating danger for children, whereas cycling may increase the risk of danger for the child. This is generally the case in urban areas, though in some less developed areas these modes may be permitted due to the extreme distances involved.

Part of facilitating walking to school relates to where the school is located. Elementary schools are typically built in the center of neighborhoods, while middle and high schools are typically located within walking distance of (high quality) public transport. Having an elementary school in the center of a neighborhood decreases the average commuting distance for the community, whereas building a school retrospectively (i.e., after developing an area) on the edge of a neighborhood will increase overall distances. Public elementary schools are not built with consideration to public transport, as typically children will walk to attend their local school.

Traffic safety is a concern of parents around the world. The number of vehicles entering an intersection is the main determinant of collisions with children, not the number of pedestrians (Miranda-Moreno, Morency, & El-Geneidy, 2011). Acknowledging the danger that traffic imposes, Japan has a national law restricting traffic within 500 m of schools between 7:00 am and 9:30 am (交通安全対策基本法第24条 = Basic traffic safety law Article 24) (Inada et al., 2017), though in practice it is often applied between 7:30 and 8:30. With the combined efforts of the walking school bus system, very few deaths occur during this time (Waygood, Taniguchi, et al., 2015). It is also sometimes implemented after school (after 3:30 pm), and one might consider that its implementation everywhere as this is often the time of day when the most deaths occur (Inada et al., 2017; Waygood, Taniguchi, et al., 2015).

2.2.1 Residential roads and speed

Speed is a crucial determinant of danger. The amount of energy in a collision increases exponentially, which likely explains why death is highly unlikely with collisions at 30 km/h but highly likely at 60 km/h (Huguenin-Richard, 2010). In Japan, streets are often narrow, especially in the older neighborhoods. As a result, drivers naturally drive slower and therefore death and injury rates are lower (Inada et al., 2017). Further, the speeds on residential streets are generally limited to 30 (such as on "seikatsu" (life) streets) or 40 km/h. Moreover, these residential streets typically do not have separate sidewalks, so the streets are shared by a mixture of pedestrians and other forms of traffic. Although the thought in North America is often that sidewalks are necessary for safety, they can actually promote higher traffic speeds due to the segregation of different modes. The problem is that anyone using that street to play or simply to cross to the other side is thus exposed to higher danger. Mixed streets (known also as "shared space") reduce speeds (e. g., Fitzpatrick, Carlson, Brewer, & Wooldridge, 2001) and thus reduces traffic danger (e.g., review by Ewing & Dumbaugh, 2009), which apply to both pedestrians (Stoker et al., 2015) and cyclists (e.g., Schramm & Rakotonirainy, 2010). Local streets in Japan can often only accommodate vehicle traffic in only one direction, or require vehicles to negotiate with each other when navigating the narrow streets. Single lane roads are found to reduce the number of fatalities (e.g., Aziz, Ukkusuri, & Hasan, 2013;

Ukkusuri, Miranda-Moreno, Ramadurai, & Isa-Tavarez, 2012) and pedestrian-vehicle collisions are less likely with more narrow streets (Ukkusuri et al., 2012). The shared streets cause the mixing of traffic, but it also causes drivers to be more alert when the space is used by elderly and children (Kaparias, Bell, Miri, Chan, & Mount, 2012). In Japan, the rates for children killed and seriously injured were higher on streets with curb-stones than on those that were shared (side strip or none; Fig. 4; Inada et al., 2017).

In addition to narrow roads, there is very little build setback in much of Japan's urban development which means that the visual perception of roads is narrower. Drivers judge their speeds by the rate of movement in their peripheral vision, so the further the set-back, the lower the driver's perceived speed. For example, in a study comparing a two lane arterial with no buildings to the sides, and a single lane road with empty parking bays on a commercial street with no set-back (i.e., the road was the same width), the mean speed was roughly 10% lower for the latter (Edquist, Rudin-Brown, & Lenné, 2012).

2.3 City level

City planning, known as "*machi-zukuri*" (which translates to "town making") requires the collaboration between various planning organizations

Fig. 4 Local street in Kyoto with a speed limit of 20 km/h, a sign (foreground sign with two children walking) indicating that this is a school access corridor, the elementary school on the left, and the "side strip" indicating where pedestrians should walk on the right. *(Photo credit: E.O.D. Waygood.)*

so that the living contexts supports a good quality of life. This requires that there is support for local medical, welfare, and commercial services through the public transport network. As such, it is recognized that modes must be available to the whole population, including children, so they do not need a parent to access these locations.

Parking is another factor to consider. Parking on streets is generally forbidden in Japan's urban areas. Despite narrower street sizes not generally permitting on-street parking, it could be argued this is not provided due to the fact that on-street parking is a personal gain that is paid for by the public. Parking also affects child safety. Some individuals argue that parked cars create a physical barrier between the moving vehicles and pedestrians, and as such, improves the safety of these vulnerable users. However, evidence of this proposed advantage cannot be found. One study that might support this found that in a context of a commercial arterial (i.e., a street with shops) with parking bays on the road, slower speeds were observed when the bays were filled with cars (Edquist et al., 2012). The opposing argument is that parked cars create a dangerous visual barrier between the driver and children. Children are often shorter than vehicles (especially the increasingly popular box-type SUVs, or other such trucks), meaning that they are not visible to the driver and vice versa (e.g., Fig. 1 of Mitchell, Kearns, & Collins, 2007). If there are parked cars, the child must go out to the edge of the parked vehicle in order to check for passing cars, bringing them into potential conflict with a driver who might not see them until the instant they are upon them. Even when it is an adult pedestrian, the reaction times of passing drivers are longer when there are parked cars (Edquist et al., 2012). In that study, even though the drivers were going slower with the presence of the parked cars, they were much more likely to crash into the pedestrian. Thus, the potential gain of narrowing the street through parked cars is outweighed by the loss from the visual barrier created. Further, allowing parked cars on a street may result in the street being two lanes wider than it would otherwise be, which can add roughly 6 m to the distance needed to cross the street, increasing the child's exposure time to traffic.

2.4 Neighborhood level

In an international study on CIM (Shaw et al., 2015), parents from numerous countries were asked whether they agree or disagree with this statement: "Most adults who live in the neighbourhood look out for other people's children in the area". Japan was the top ranked nation with over 75%

agreeing or strongly agreeing, and with less than 10% disagreeing (with no strong disagreement) for that question. In another study on Japan, it was found that this trust is higher in more urban areas than suburban ones (Drianda & Kinoshita, 2011), again reflecting that the biases against city living that are evident in Anglo-Saxon cultures (Bonner, 1997) may not hold up to empirical study. This section describes some features of neighborhoods that likely explain this high level of social trust.

Japan has a strong tradition of festivals and many of these are at the neighborhood level. Policies such as the *furusato-zukuri* (1984; Robertson, 1987) aim to increase the feelings of attachment and commitment to neighborhoods through various means, including local festivals. The children's festival (*kodomo matsuri*) is an example of a common festival that can be found in most neighborhoods. Festivals involving *mikoshi* (portable shrines) often involve the cooperation of numerous local men as they carry the heavy wooden shrine through the streets while being cheered on by both the participants and the watching crowd. These events foster the chance for neighbors to get together, interact, develop and maintain social bonds. These social bonds are important for reducing the anxiety about "stranger danger" and creating larger networks of "allo-parents" (adults who support the child, but who are not their parents). The festivals often mix traditional practices, food, alcohol, and games for children, thus allowing for a variety of people with varied interests to be there and mingle. Western countries are beginning to bring back such local events through projects such as play streets (see Chapter 10).

Walking school buses in Japan are generally organized through the collaboration between the local school and the parent-teacher association (PTA) (Waygood, Taniguchi, et al., 2015). The local parents are involved at various times to help ensure that the walking school bus is functioning correctly. The parental contribution is not a daily occurrence, but parents are expected to contribute at some point during the year. As well, the PTA generally has a safety committee that deals with local problems. Local individuals such as retired workers may also contribute as crossing guards. Thus, the community works together to protect the children's safety and independence.

As children walk around, they are also encouraged to participate in "*aisatsu*" (i.e., greeting people). In contrast to the cultural approaches seen in Anglo-Saxon countries, teachers in Japan encourage children to actively say "hi" to adults, especially unknown ones, as they walk around their neighborhoods. Children are thus actively engaged in developing their local social capital which has numerous benefits related to both CIM and wellbeing (see Chapter 4).

Police officers and, in some cases, members of the PTA actively patrol neighborhoods. This gives individuals further confidence that someone is there to help children if needed, but it also reaffirms that there are "eyes on the street". The officers and PTA members walk and cycle the neighborhood while saying hello to people. These actions likely add an extra sense of personal security for parents. Through continually experiencing walking and cycling first hand, the police officers themselves remain aware of the problems related to traveling by these modes. Further, the fact that a pedestrian or cyclist might in fact be a police officer likely deters dangerous driver behavior. In literature from the UK, when children and parents were asked about improving their neighborhoods, they said that "police on the street" would help (Morrow, 2000). In addition to patrolling the neighborhoods, police also visit preschools and kindergartens to instruct children on how to navigate traffic safely.

Japan's land-use laws allow for various uses in nearly all zone types such as public institutions (such as day-cares, Fig. 5), non-toxic industry, clinics, and commercial establishments, thus facilitating local trips (Koohsari et al., 2018), even in the most restrictive residential zoning areas (Sorenson, 2002). As a result, parents often send their children on local errands. The first time a child goes out to run an errand is commonly known as "*hajimete no otsukai*". The children walk independently to a local destination, often in order to buy food for the family (there is even a book about this aimed at children 3 and 4 years old; Tsutsui, 1977). Without mixed land-use and policies that protect small local shops, the possibility to carry on this practice will

Fig. 5 The morning drop-off at a local day-care. *(Photo credit: E.O.D. Waygood.)*

diminish. This "cultural practice" allows the child (and the parent) to test their independence in a familiar environment. Going to small "mom and pop" type stores means the individual at the store likely knows the child. This is perhaps a demonstration of the "popsicle test" which states that a child of eight should be able to go buy a popsicle independently (e.g., Bartlett, 2003). This requires that there is a shop that would sell such a child-oriented product and that conditions support independent travel. Children in areas that are more built up are more independent (Drianda & Kinoshita, 2011; Waygood & Kitamura, 2009), whereas the notion of stranger danger is more prevalent in rural and less urban areas, partly because there are fewer people around walking to various destinations (Drianda & Kinoshita, 2011). Urban areas showed little concern over stranger danger or traffic danger, as people commonly walk around and traffic movement is restricted by the narrow roads and congestion (Drianda & Kinoshita, 2011).

Along with increased social capital, access to local shops, and general walkability, walking is also associated with the upkeep of a neighborhood (Renalds, Smith, & Hale, 2010). In Japan, local upkeep is connected to the local neighborhood association (*chounaikai*) which has existed for many generations (Sorenson, 2002). In one study, over 90% of participants belonged to a *chounaikai* and over 70% participated in its activities (Otani, 1999). The *chounaikai* organizes neighborhood cleaning, helps keep households informed of changes such as new recycling practices, and partakes in other locally relevant topics. Acting as a group likely builds a sense of community, and activities such as cleaning the neighborhood can also create environments that demonstrate a certain amount of local pride and personal responsibility. A clean local area can also make public areas more inviting. Enhanced community engagement is associated with measures such as local upkeep, access to facilities, security and safety, and walkability (Hassen & Kaufman, 2016). This may help explain why community participation is still high in Japan, though there is likely a two-way positive relationship.

The social interactions mentioned above perhaps explain the tendency for people in Japan to list their neighbors and co-workers as among their close relationships, more than those in western cultures (Otani, 1999). Another explanation might be that Japanese are less likely to move than Americans, and reside in their neighborhoods for longer (32 years for Japan compared to 20 years for the USA) (Otani, 1999). As described by Schoppa (2013), the housing approach in the USA is often to buy into a better neighborhood when you can, or buy a home in another area if there are problems. However, the approach in Japan is often to buy into a neighborhood then work with the community to fix problems, if any should arise.

2.5 Household

Walking and cycling with children is still common in Japan, though families are increasingly using cars, particularly on weekends (Xu et al., 2015). Parents who walk and cycle with their children (Fig. 6) allow their children to learn about negotiating traffic and demonstrates to them that active and independent modes are an option (Baslington, 2008; Haustein, Klöckner, & Blöbaum, 2009; Hjorthol & Fyhri, 2009). In Japan, children are expected to be able to get around by themselves at around age six (Joshi & MacLean, 1997). This may relate to the walking school bus system, where from their first year at school (around age six or seven), children start walking to school in groups but may return by themselves or with friends. These children are taught how to navigate traffic, for example by raising their arm while crossing roads. This makes them visually taller, increasing the likelihood that drivers in elevated vehicles (trucks and such) would see them, and signals to drivers the child's intent to cross (and that they're not just standing and staring at vehicles). Children are often taught which streets are dangerous, and how to interact with other road users.

In major centers, shopping is still mostly done with active modes (Kitamura et al., 2008). For children in urban settings (Ohmori et al., 2014), accompanied trips are often for shopping (Waygood, 2009), but the majority of trips to shops were found to be independent of adults

Fig. 6 A parent traveling with children by bicycle is a common sight in Japan. *(Photo credit: E.O.D. Waygood.)*

(Waygood, 2009), suggesting that they may also be doing such trips *for* the household. The ability of these children to travel independently could thus change the parental perspective that children are a burden when it comes to travel. The independent child could possibly be a bonus to the parent. The child does not need to be chauffeured to school or activities, and they can run errands for the parent (thus reducing travel burden).

Recently, the general number of children is decreasing and so catchment areas are increasing. As a result, the distances that children must travel are increasing. Although in many cases the walking school bus system is able to overcome this barrier, in extreme cases (e.g., over 3 km or over a 30-min walk) school buses are beginning to be used. A school bus can also be set up for safety reasons related to traffic (MECSST, 2008). Although school buses can be found in 62% of municipalities, they represented just 1.7% of school trips by elementary and middle school children (MECSST, 2008). In 55% of those municipalities, local public bus routes are part of the school bus program. The exact system varies significantly depending on the context of each location, but integrating school commutes with the existing public transport system is recommended. Due to the costs of school buses, this has recently become a big issue for local government.

Middle and high school students typically use public transport to travel to their schools (Fig. 7). This means that children contribute to the use of public transport, allowing greater overall service levels to exist. Through this practice, the children learn and become familiar with using public transport. This eliminates the psychological barriers related to using public transport when they are older and start making their own choices on travel modes (Muromachi, 2017).

When children are infants or toddlers, parents may travel around with them in strollers or on bicycles (seeing bicycles with two child seats is not uncommon, Fig. 8). However, it is not always easy to travel this way due to the numerous challenges, including having sufficient space in public transport for strollers (Ohmori, 2015) or even worrying about whether the child will disturb others. These barriers vary according to the built environment. There are more problems related to public transport access in very urban areas, walking and cycling barriers in suburbs, and car access problems in less built-up areas (Ohmori et al., 2014). The Japanese Association for an Inclusive Society puts out information on going out with strollers using various modes, and barrier-free design is promoted in many locations (Ohmori, 2015).

Fig. 7 High school children arriving by foot after taking the train. *(Photo credit: E.O.D. Waygood.)*

(A)   (B)

Fig. 8 A bicycle with seats for two small children is still a common site in Japan. *(Photo credit: E.O.D. Waygood.)*

3 Conclusion

Japan is a wealthy country that has maintained high levels of active travel, but is also struggling against the siren call of car travel. Car use for children's travel is increasing, especially on weekends for the youngest age groups. Fatality rates have decreased significantly, with no major shift in mode share observed on weekdays. Social interaction rates are much higher for children who walk, and lowest for children who are driven. Finally, life satisfaction and quality of life are positively associated with incidental social interactions. Thus, there is much evidence that suggests that walking for children needs to be protected for their overall well-being.

This chapter outlined the numerous ways that Japan supports children walking at different levels of the socio-ecological model. The expectation that children should be able to travel independently may explain why Japanese children have some of the highest levels of independent travel in the world. Parents and the community support children's independent travel both directly (e.g., teaching road crossing skills at young ages) and indirectly (e.g., developing social connections at local levels). In many cases, the influences in Japan that are described in the chapter can be transferred to other cultures, as various supporting literature shows that the same relationships exist elsewhere. Influences such as having local shops to facilitate walking is not unique to Japan, nor are the traffic calming effects of narrow streets and shared streets. These characteristics can be applied outside of Japan, as well as planning to build elementary schools in the heart of neighborhoods. It is also feasible to develop a network of public transport that supports independent travel to middle and high schools. Building social capital by organizing local activities such as festivals may require greater effort in cultures where this is not the norm, but incorporating these activities would be beneficial across different cultures, as most people enjoy spending time with their friends and neighbors. Such examples can be seen in recent road closures for play streets.

References

Aziz, H. A., Ukkusuri, S. V., & Hasan, S. (2013). Exploring the determinants of pedestrian–vehicle crash severity in New York City. *Accident Analysis & Prevention, 50,* 1298–1309.

Bartlett, R. (2003). Testing the 'Popsicle Test': Realities of retail shopping in new 'Traditional Neighbourhood Developments'. *Urban Studies, 40*(8), 1471–1485.

Baslington, H. (2008). Travel socialisation: A social theory of travel mode behaviour. *International Journal of Sustainable Transportation, 2*(2), 91–114.

Bonner, K. (1997). *A great place to raise kids: Interpretation, science, and the urban-rural debate.* Quebec: McGill-Queen's University Press.

Bronfenbrenner, U. (1979). *The ecology of human development.* Harvard University Press.

Drianda, R. P., & Kinoshita, I. (2011). Danger from traffic to fear of monkeys: Children's independent mobility in four diverse sites in Japan. *Global Studies of Childhood, 1*(3), 226–242.

Edquist, J., Rudin-Brown, C. M., & Lenné, M. G. (2012). The effects of on-street parking and road environment visual complexity on travel speed and reaction time. *Accident Analysis & Prevention, 45,* 759–765.

Ewing, R., & Dumbaugh, E. (2009). The built environment and traffic safety: A review of empirical evidence. *Journal of Planning Literature, 23*(4), 347–367.

Fitzpatrick, K., Carlson, P., Brewer, M., & Wooldridge, M. (2001). Design factors that affect driver speed on suburban streets. *Transportation Research Record: Journal of the Transportation Research Board, 1751,* 18–25.

Hassen, N., & Kaufman, P. (2016). Examining the role of urban street design in enhancing community engagement: A literature review. *Health & Place, 41,* 119–132.

Haustein, S., Klöckner, C. A., & Blöbaum, A. (2009). Car use of young adults: The role of travel socialization. *Transportation Research Part F: Traffic Psychology and Behaviour, 12*(2), 168–178.

Helliwell, J. F., & Putnam, R. D. (2004). The social context of well-being. *Philosophical Transactions-Royal Society of London Series B Biological Sciences,* 1435–1446.

Hjorthol, R. J., & Fyhri, A. (2009). Are we socializing our children to Car use? *Tidsskrift for Samfunnsforskning, 50*(2), 161–182.

Huguenin-Richard, F. (2010). La mobilité des enfants à l'épreuve de la rue: Impacts de l'aménagement de zones 30 sur leurs comportements. *Enfances, Familles, Générations,* (12), 66–87.

Inada, H., Tomio, J., Nakahara, S., Xu, X., Taniguchi, A., & Ichikawa, M. (2017). National 10-year trend in road injuries involving school children on the way to and from school in Japan, 2003–2012. *Injury Prevention, 23*(5), 297–302.

Johansson, M. (2006). Environment and parental factors as determinants of mode for children's leisure travel. *Journal of Environmental Psychology, 26*(2), 156–169.

Joshi, M. S., & MacLean, M. (1997). Maternal expectations of child development in India, Japan and England. *Journal of Cross-Cultural Psychology, 28,* 219–234.

Kaparias, I., Bell, M. G. H., Miri, A., Chan, C., & Mount, B. (2012). Analysing the perceptions of pedestrians and drivers to shared space. *Transportation Research Part F: Traffic Psychology and Behaviour, 15*(3), 297–310.

Kimura, M., & Itoi, A. (2008). Children's physical activities and commuting time by walking (in Japanese). *Growth and Development study (Supplement),* 93.

Kinoshita, I. (2009). Chapter 5: Qualitative change of children's play in Japan (in Japanese). In *Town development in which children can wander on their way: Consider traffic problems on school roads, Gakugei publishing Co., Ltd.* (pp. 82–91).

Kitamura, R., Sakamoto, K., & Waygood, O. (2008). Declining sustainability: The case of shopping trip energy consumption. *International Journal of Sustainable Transportation, 2*(3), 158.

Koohsari, M. J., Sugiyama, T., Shibata, A., Ishii, K., Hanibuchi, T., Liao, Y., et al. (2018). Walk Score® and Japanese adults' physically-active and sedentary behaviors. *Cities, 74,* 151–155.

MECSST. 国内におけるスクールバス活用状況等調査報告概要 *(Report overview on the use of school buses within Japan),* 2008.

Miranda-Moreno, L. F., Morency, P., & El-Geneidy, A. M. (2011). The link between built environment, pedestrian activity and pedestrian–vehicle collision occurrence at signalized intersections. *Accident Analysis & Prevention, 43*(5), 1624–1634.

Mitchell, H., Kearns, R. A., & Collins, D. C. A. (2007). Nuances of neighbourhood: Children's perceptions of the space between home and school in Auckland, New Zealand. *Geoforum, 38*(4), 614–627.

Morrow, V. M. (2000). 'Dirty looks' and 'trampy places' in young people's accounts of community and neighbourhood: Implications for health inequalities. *Critical Public Health, 10* (2), 141–152.

Muromachi, Y. (2017). Experiences of past school travel modes by university students and their intention of future car purchase. *Transportation Research Part A: Policy and Practice, 104*, 209–220.

Ohmori, N. (2015). Mitigating barriers against accessible cities and transportation, for child-rearing households. *IATSS Research, 38*(2), 116–124.

Ohmori, N., Taniguchi, A., Manabe, R., Terauchi, Y., & Aono, S. (2014). How different are barriers against out-of-home activity participation for women raising children? In: *5th International conference on women's issues in transportation federation Internationale De L'Automobile (FIA) Institut Francais des Sciences et Technologies des Transports, de l'Aménagement et des Réseaux (IFSTTAR) Bureau of Transportation Statistics Transportation Research Board.*

Otani, S. (1999). Personal community networks in contemporary Japan. In *Networks in the global village: Life in contemporary communities* (pp. 279–298).

Pacilli, M. G., Giovannelli, I., Prezza, M., & Augimeri, M. L. (2013). Children and the public realm: Antecedents and consequences of independent mobility in a group of 11–13-year-old Italian children. *Children's Geographies, 11*(4), 377–393.

Renalds, A., Smith, T. H., & Hale, P. J. (2010). A systematic review of built environment and health. *Family & Community Health, 33*(1), 68–78.

Robertson, J. (1987). A dialectic of native and newcomer: The Kodaira Citizens' festival in suburban Tokyo. *Anthropological Quarterly, 60*(3), 124–136.

Schoppa, L. (2013). Residential mobility and local civic engagement in Japan and the United States: Divergent paths to school. *Comparative Political Studies, 46*(9), 1058–1081.

Schramm, A., & Rakotonirainy, A. (2010). The effect of traffic lane widths on the safety of cyclists in urban areas. *Journal of the Australasian College of Road Safety, 21*(2), 43.

Senda, M., & Kamioka, N. (2009). *Town development in which children can wander on their way: Consider traffic problems on school roads (in Japanese)*. Gakugei publishing Co., Ltd.

Shaw, B., Bicket, M., & Elliott, B. (2015). *Children's independent mobility: An international comparison and recommendations for action*. London: Policy Studies Institute.

Shiina, F. (2009). Chapter 7: Policy of commuting to/from school in Japan (in Japanese). In *Town development in which children can wander on their way: Consider traffic problems on school roads, Gakugei publishing Co., Ltd.* (pp. 114–124).

Sorenson, A. (2002). *Making of urban Japan: Cities and planning from Edo to the twenty-first century*. New York: Routledge.

Stoker, P., Garfinkel-Castro, A., Khayesi, M., Odero, W., Mwangi, M. N., Peden, M., et al. (2015). Pedestrian safety and the built environment: A review of the risk factors. *Journal of Planning Literature, 30*(4), 377–392.

Sun, Y., Waygood, E., Fukui, K., & Kitamura, R. (2009). Built environment or household life-cycle stages: Which explains sustainable travel more? *Transportation Research Record: Journal of the Transportation Research Board, 2135*(1), 123–129.

Susilo, Y. O., & Waygood, E. O. D. (2012). A long term analysis of the mechanisms underlying children's activity-travel engagements in the Osaka metropolitan area. *Journal of Transport Geography, 20*(1), 41–50.

Taniguchi (2018). A. In 通学状況が子どもの心身の健康に与える影響 *(How school travel affects children's mental and physical health)*.

Taniguchi, A., & Xin, X. (2018). The relationship between transitions in children's travel behaviour and mental and physical health in Japan. In: *Presented at international conference on transport & health, Mackinac Island, USA.*

Tsutsui, Y. (1977). *Hajimete no otsukai (English title: Miki's first errand)*.

Ukkusuri, S., Miranda-Moreno, L. F., Ramadurai, G., & Isa-Tavarez, J. (2012). The role of built environment on pedestrian crash frequency. *Safety Science, 50*(4), 1141–1151.

Waygood, E. O. D. (2009). What is the role of mothers in transit-oriented development? The case of Osaka–Kyoto–Kobe, Japan. In *Women's issues in transportation 4th international conference, No. 2, transportation research board, Irvine California* (pp. 163–178).

Waygood, E. O. D., & Friman, M. (2015). Children's travel and incidental community connections. *Travel Behaviour and Society, 2*(3), 174–181.

Waygood, E. O. D., Friman, M., Olsson, L. E., & Taniguchi, A. (2017). Children's incidental social interaction during travel international case studies from Canada, Japan, and Sweden. *Journal of Transport Geography, 63*, 22–29.

Waygood, E. O. D., & Kitamura, R. (2009). Children in a rail-based developed area of Japan travel patterns, independence, and exercise. *Transportation Research Record, 2125*, 36–43.

Waygood, E. O. D., Sun, Y., & Letarte, L. (2015). Active travel by built environment and lifecycle stage: Case study of Osaka metropolitan area. *International Journal of Environmental Research and Public Health, 12*(12), 15900–15924.

Waygood, E. O. D., Taniguchi, A., Craig-St-Louis, C., & Xu, X. (2015). International origins of walking school buses and child fatalities in Japan and Canada. *Traffic Science Japan, 46*(2), 30–42.

Xu, X., Taniguchi, A., Ishigami, T., & Hirata, S. (2015). The current status and transition of Japanese children's travel behavior. In: *Annual meeting of the Japanese society of civil engineering, No. 51, Japanese Society of Civil Engineering, Okayama, Japan*.

Further reading

Hüttenmoser, M. (1995). Children and their living surroundings: Empirical investigations into the significance of living surroundings for the everyday life and development of children. *Children's Environments, 12*(4), 403–413.

CHAPTER SEVENTEEN

Children's school travel and wellbeing in the Netherlands

Iris van de Craats[a], Pauline van den Berg[a], Astrid Kemperman[a]
and E. Owen D. Waygood[b]
[a]Built Environment, Eindhoven University of Technology, Eindhoven, Netherlands
[b]Department of Civil, Geological, and Mining Engineering, Polytechnique Montréal, Montreal, QC, Canada

Contents

1 Introduction

Active travel (i.e., travel using human powered mobility options such as cycling and walking) among children of the current 'backseat generation' is decreasing worldwide (e.g., Buliung, Mitra, & Faulkner, 2009), including in the Netherlands. This is an unfavorable development because children that miss out on active travel also miss out on related valuable health and cognitive development benefits. For example, active travel to school can make a valuable contribution to everyday physical activity and to developing an active lifestyle in general, which is likely to track into adulthood (Telama, 2009). Moreover, children's active travel has been found to be associated with positive emotions such as feeling happy or relaxed (Ramanathan,

O'Brien, Faulkner, & Stone, 2014). Active travel has also been found to be related to a higher satisfaction with travel, which in turn has a positive effect on overall life satisfaction and subjective wellbeing (e.g., Bergstad et al., 2011). For children, the right to independent mobility, typically active, was found to be directly associated to travel satisfaction and indirectly to life satisfaction (Waygood, Friman, Taniguchi, & Olsson, 2019).

Another beneficial aspect of active travel among children is that it can lead to improvement of social connections in the neighborhood. Having social connections in the neighborhood is important for the social capital and social cohesion in the neighborhood (Waygood, Friman, Olsson, & Taniguchi, 2017a), which in turn is beneficial for both physical and subjective wellbeing, for adults as well as children (Waygood et al., 2017a).

Finally, active travel is also important for the development of children. An important skill that children can gain from physical activity is motor skill or the ability of knowing how to move. It is essential for children's development towards adult life that they learn motor skills involved in different physical activities. Moreover, the increasing car-usage for school trips does not only result in less physical activity, but also increases traffic danger for others at the schools. As a result, parents react to these safety concerns by driving their children to school, leading to a vicious circle.

Children's active travel is decreasing and it is important to turn this trend around, which is why more insights in children's travel behavior are needed. The contexts of the Netherlands is different than much research that stems from countries such as the United States (e.g., McDonald, 2007; Omura et al., 2019; Rothman, Macpherson, Ross, & Buliung, 2018), Canada (e.g., Buliung et al., 2009), Australia (e.g., Babb, Olaru, Curtis, & Robertson, 2017; Carver et al., 2019; Carver, Timperio, & Crawford, 2013) and New Zealnad (Bhosale, Duncan, & Schofield, 2017). The Netherlands is seen as more bicycle-friendly (Pucher & Buehler, 2008) and cycling remains a common means of transportation across all population groups. Thus far however, surprisingly few studies have investigated children's active travel in the Netherlands. Existing literature has tended to focus on travel behavior of adults, whereas children's travel behavior has only recently come under increased focus due to decreases in active and independent travel (McMillan, 2007; Panter, Jones, Van Sluijs, & Griffin, 2010b; Van Goeverden & de Boer, 2013). Children's travel behavior should be investigated on its own, as the influential factors may be different between adults and children (McMillan, 2005; Mitra, 2013; Panter et al., 2010b; Sirard & Slater, 2008). Therefore, this chapter will first introduce the context of the Netherlands and then present findings from a study that looked into the potential influencing factors of active travel among Dutch children attending primary school, using a socio-ecological approach. The aim was to learn about the relationships between factors in the different layers of the child's environment (personal and household characteristics, school, social and physical environment and external environment) and active travel and subjective wellbeing, specifically satisfaction with travel.

2 Children's school travel in the Netherlands

In the Netherlands the bicycle is traditionally an important mode of transport. In 2016 the Netherlands counted 22.8 million bicycles, which is an average of 1.3 per inhabitant (CBS, 2019). The Netherlands is known for its strong cycling culture which has resulted in a built environment that is also favorable to cycling, with cycling-friendly infrastructure that makes cycling more convenient and safer than in most other countries (Bere, van der Horst, Oenema, Prins, & Brug, 2008). This strong cycling culture is related to the fact that Dutch children are required to theoretical and practical lessons in safe cycling when they are in 3rd or 4th grade. This reinforces the child's cycling skills from an early age, and makes them and their parents feel more comfortable to independently commute.

In contrast to many other countries studied, cycling has been the main transport mode to school among Dutch children in the modern era (Fig. 1). Overall, cycling rates have remained quite stable over the years. Fig. 2 shows

Fig. 1 The end of the school day sees many children and their parents on bicycles. *(Delft, 2011; photo credit E.O.D. Waygood.)*

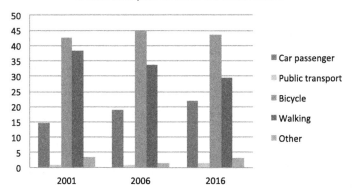

Fig. 2 Transport modes for school trips in the Netherlands in 2001, 2006 and 2016. *(Based on Kemperman & Timmermans, 2014; OViN, 2016; Van der Houwen, Goossen, & Veling, 2003.)*

the differences between 2001 (Van der Houwen et al., 2003), 2006 (Kemperman & Timmermans, 2014) and 2016 (OViN, 2016) in terms of transport modes to school. Note that all these studies are based on the Netherlands National Travel Survey data (OViN), that is collected yearly. The largest differences can be seen for walking and traveling to school as car passenger. While walking rates decreased by about 9 percentage points between 2001 and 2016, car passenger rates increased by over seven percentage points. Bicycling rates have remained almost the same.

There are several underlying trends that may have encouraged an increase in car use for school travel in the Netherlands. First, distances to primary schools have increased due to closing schools in small towns, as a result of a decreasing number of children living there. In 2006 the average distance to the nearest school was 600 m, while by 2016 this has increased to 700 m. The average number of primary schools within 3 km has decreased from 12.1 to 11.3 over the same period (CBS, 2019). Moreover, parents increasingly choose schools with specific educational programs, even if these schools are farther away from home. Previous research has repeatedly identified travel distance as one of the strongest determinants of school travel mode outcome (e.g., review by Carver et al., 2013; Rothman et al., 2018). In the Netherlands walking rates are high for the lowest travel distances; approximately 70% of school trips between 0.1 and 0.5 km occur by foot (OViN, 2016). As distance increases, the walking rate decrease quickly to only 10% for 1.0–2.5 km and close to zero at 2.5–5.0 km. Bicycle rates, on the other hand, start increasing and are highest at distances between 1.0 and 2.5 km (around 70% of trips). This is also the distance at which car travel starts rapidly increasing (OViN, 2016).

A second trend that may have resulted in an increase in car use for school travel, regards the increasing parental concerns around a child's safety. This development is remarkable, because traffic collision statistics indicate that the number of young people being killed in traffic collisions has significantly decreased, while roads have become more crowded (NOS, 2013). The fact that parents are driving their children to school as a reaction to safety concerns is part of a vicious circle (VVN, 2014). As more parents drive their children to school, there will be more cars, which results in more chaos and an increased perception of the area being unsafe.

3 Factors influencing school travel mode

The socio-ecological model is a framework that has been widely used by authors studying the multi-level factors influencing physical activity behavior. First introduced by Bronfenbrenner (1979), the socio-ecological approach proposes that behavior is influenced by factors from different levels including the personal level, the household level, the community level (or social environment), the physical built environment and the external environment. Several factors from these different levels have also been found to affect children's active travel behavior (see Chapter 5 for an in-depth discussion). This section will discuss how research from the Netherlands relates to various influences on children's travel in relation to other studies where relevant.

Personal factors of the child such as gender and age have been found to influence active travel. Several studies showed that boys are more likely to actively travel to school than girls (e.g., Panter, Jones, Van Sluijs, & Griffin, 2010a). Cervesato and Waygood (2019) and Waygood and Kitamura (2009) found no difference between boys and girls for independent travel during the week, while girls were more independent on the weekend. In the Netherlands, Kemperman and Timmermans (2014) found no association between travel behavior and gender. Regarding age, several studies have indicated that older age is associated with more participation in active travel (e.g., Carver et al., 2013). This was also found for the Netherlands (Kemperman & Timmermans, 2014). According to Trapp et al. (2012) and Carver et al. (2013) the age and gender differences in physical activity are mostly due to differences in what children of different genders and ages are allowed to do by their parents.

Regarding household characteristics such as ethnicity and socio-economic status, findings from different studies are inconclusive. For instance, lower household income was found to be associated with more active travel participation in Southern California by Sidharthan, Bhat, Pendyala, and Goulias (2011), while Van Goeverden and de Boer (2013) found lower income to be associated with less active travel participation in the Netherlands. Households with more children have been found to have higher bicycling rates in the Netherlands (Aarts, Mathijssen, van Oers, & Schuit, 2013). The influence of cars varies by context (Pont, Ziviani, Wadley, Bennett, & Abbott, 2009). Aarts et al. (2013) found that the number of cars in the household was negatively associated with active walking and cycling to school.

Several other social and ecological aspects have been investigated abroad, but were not studied in the Dutch context. Children have higher odds of participating in active school travel when their parents used active travel modes to get to their work (Panter et al., 2010a), which should be relevant for a country such as the Netherlands. Henne, Tandon, Frank, and Saelens (2014) found that more working hours of American parents led to their children participating less in active travel, but it is unclear whether this would be the case for Dutch children. Finally, parental safety perception has been found to influence the transport mode decision-making process by many researchers (e.g., Crawford et al., 2017; Guliani, Mitra, Buliung, Larsen, & Faulkner, 2015; Kerr et al., 2006; see also Chapters 5 and 11). In the contexts of the Netherlands with separate infrastructure for cycling (Fig. 3), the perception of danger may be different.

Next to personal and household characteristics, several social characteristics in the neighborhood are indicators of children's participation in physical activity, such as the degree of social cohesion (Kemperman & Timmermans, 2014), and the perception of safety of the neighborhood (Trapp et al., 2012). Waygood et al. (2017a) also suggest that having neighborhood connections decreases parental concern which leads to more children traveling independently. In the Netherlands, children living in neighborhoods with high social cohesion and more opportunities of meeting friends during travel are more likely to be allowed to travel unaccompanied by their parents (Aarts et al., 2013).

Regarding built environment factors, the most commonly found influencing factor of school travel behavior was, not surprisingly, distance

Fig. 3 Example of segregated bicycle infrastructure in the Netherlands. *(Delft, 2011; photo credit E.O.D. Waygood.)*

to school. Living closer to school was found to enable active travel internationally (e.g., McMillan, 2007; Panter et al., 2010a) as well as in the Netherlands (Aarts et al., 2013; Kemperman & Timmermans, 2014). Kemperman and Timmermans (2014) found that Dutch primary school children were more likely to walk in more urbanized neighborhoods. Moreover, street connectivity (Giles-Corti et al., 2011; Kerr et al., 2006), indicating walkability of a neighborhood, are positively related to active travel to school. De Vries, Hopman-Rock, Bakker, Hirasing, and van Mechelen (2010) found that cycling to school and cycling for transportation were significantly associated with higher numbers of recreational facilities in the neighborhood.

Finally, in the external layer, weather is considered. Buliung, Faulkner, Beesley, and Kennedy (2011) found that one of the reasons for Canadian parents to drive their children to school by car was the weather. How weather might affect children in the Netherlands has not previously been studied. The temperature extremes are less than in Canada, but wet conditions are common.

4 Active travel and wellbeing

As described in Chapter 1 of this book, children's wellbeing can be divided into the physical, psychological, cognitive, social, and economic domains, and active travel is likely related to each domain of a child's wellbeing. In their review of the relations between transport and child wellbeing, Waygood, Friman, Olsson, and Taniguchi (2017b) highlighted that research into the psychological domain relations are still limited. One such measure is subjective wellbeing (for more detail, see Chapter 3).

Subjective wellbeing is about emotion, happiness and the extent a person is satisfied with their life in general (Bergstad et al., 2011). According to Bergstad et al. (2011), daily travel likely has an influence on the overall satisfaction of an individual. Bergstad et al. (2011) argue that their results show the importance of daily travel satisfaction for subjective wellbeing. Ettema et al. (2011) reported that satisfaction with travel had a high reliability in predicting subjective wellbeing as a result of the trip. This is why it is believed that satisfaction with travel can be considered as an indicator of the (school) trip's contribution to subjective wellbeing of the traveler, which, conveniently, is more easily measured than wellbeing in general.

Although scarce, there are some studies that have already looked into the association between children's travel mode to school and their subjecting wellbeing. A Canadian study with a large sample found active travel as opposed to passive travel to school to be associated with positive emotions such as feeling happy or relaxed, for children as well as for parents (Ramanathan et al., 2014). Children and parents who travel with passive modes such as the car were found to be significantly more likely to feel negative emotions such as feeling tired or in a hurry. Waygood et al. (2017b) reported consistent findings of walking being related to positive emotions and to lowering stress. In Sweden, Westman, Olsson, Gärling, and Friman (2017) found travel mode to be associated with the degree of children's satisfaction with travel, active modes were associated with a higher rated quality of the trip than car travel. Similar results were found by

Waygood (2018) in Quebec, Canada where active modes were found to be rated higher for best (versus worst) trip and being alert (versus bored) during the trip.

5 Methods

To examine the relationships between factors discussed above, a survey was developed for primary school pupils and their parents. The explanatory factors for active travel considered were the personal and household characteristics, school, social and physical environment and external environment. As well, the relationships between measures of travel satisfaction and travel mode were investigated. The survey was distributed among 15 primary schools in and around the Dutch city Arnhem in the fall of 2018. The schools vary in number of pupils, education type, health attitude and they were located in areas with different urban density levels. All children in grades 5–8 (aged 7–12 years old) of the 15 participating schools received a questionnaire in class, which they were asked to immediately fill in. They were then asked to bring a related questionnaire home to be completed by their parents on a voluntary basis. All parents gave their informed consent for inclusion before they participated in the study. In the end, 676 completed (by the children and their parents) questionnaires were collected from 14 primary schools. Although 15 schools agreed to participate in the current study and distributed questionnaires among their students, one of the schools did not receive any completed questionnaires from the parents in their school. After removing some unsuitable responses, a final sample of 660 respondents remained. This is a response rate of 46%. For more information on the data collection we refer to Van de Craats (2019).

Children's travel mode to school was explored by asking the child's travel mode to school on the day of the survey. See Fig. 4 for the mode choice question specifically designed for children (the original was in Dutch).

In this study, satisfaction with travel was used as a proxy for a child's subjective wellbeing. The Satisfaction with Travel was explored using a scale that measures both affective and cognitive satisfaction (Ettema et al., 2011). The cognitive evaluation can be understood as a measure of enjoyment, difficulty and usefulness of the trip. The affective evaluation measures the extent to which the trip elicits valence and activation. This is measured by six items that distinguish positive activation versus negative deactivation and negative activation versus positive deactivation. The six affective items and three questions about cognitive evaluation were derived from scales

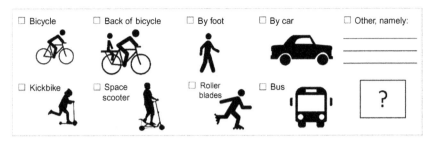

Fig. 4 Transport mode options child questionnaire.

used by Ettema et al. (2011) and Westman et al. (2017), the latter of which focused on children. The survey questions for the Satisfaction with Travel Scale for Children (STS-C; Westman et al., 2017) were translated to Dutch and described in words that are understandable to young children. The nine questions used to measure satisfaction with travel are described in Table 1. The children could answer these nine questions on a five point scale.

In addition, the survey included questions about personal and household characteristics, parental safety perception (traffic safety, social safety and perception of child's travel skills), school, social and physical environment and the external environment.

Table 1 Measurement of satisfaction with travel used in child-survey

Cognitive evaluation
What did you think of the trip to school this morning?

1. A lot of fun	Very lame
2. Very easy	Very difficult
3. I learnt a lot	I learnt nothing

Affective evaluation
How did you feel during your trip to school this morning?

Negative deactivation	*Positive activation*
4. Very bored	Very excited
5. Very indifferent	Very much looking forward to the day
6. Very tired	Very well rested
Positive deactivation	*Negative activation*
7. Very at ease	Very tense
8. I had a lot of time	I was in a big hurry
9. I was carefree	I was worried

6 Results

To test the relationships between different aspects of the child's environment and school transport mode, several bivariate analyses (crosstabs with chi-square tests and ANOVA's with F-tests) are performed. Subsequently, to test the relationship between travel mode and satisfaction with travel (SWT) ANOVA (F-test) is used.

6.1 Sample characteristics

Table 2 shows the characteristics of the sample. Age, grade and gender are quite equally distributed. Only the seven-year-olds and the twelve-year-olds are less common. In terms of household work status, most households reported to be two wage-earner households (69.2%). Only 8% reported that they were seeking employment or were in another situation such as

Table 2 Sample characteristics

Variables	n	% of sample
Age		
7	27	4.1
8	140	21.2
9	180	27.3
10	155	23.5
11	132	20.0
12	26	3.9
Gender ($N=656$)		
Boy	315	48
Girl	341	52
Household work status		
Two wage earner household	457	69.2
One wage earner household	150	22.7
Seeking employment or other	53	8.0
Household income		
More than average Dutch income	252	38.2
Equal to average Dutch income	286	43.3
Lower than average Dutch income	122	18.5
Car ownership		
No car	52	7.9
One car	292	44.2
Two or more cars	319	47.9

Continued

Table 2 Sample characteristics—cont'd

Variables	n	% of sample
Household composition		
One parent—only child	25	3.8
One parent—sibling(s)	75	11.4
Two parents—only child	61	9.2
Two parents—sibling(s)	499	75.6
Travel distance		
<500 m	145	22.0
500–1000 m	190	28.8
1–2 km	172	26.1
2–5 km	100	15.2
>5 km	53	8.0
School type		
Public school (5)	293	44.4
School with religious background (4)	145	22.0
Dalton school (2)	122	18.5
Jenaplan school (1)	22	3.3
Special education (2)	78	11.8

retirement or unpaid work. The largest share of respondents reported their household as having a yearly income similar to the average Dutch household (43.3%). A smaller percentage of respondents (38.2%) had a higher income than average and only 18.5% reported to have a lower income than average. Only 7.9% of the sample did not own a car, almost half (49.9%) had two or more cars, and 44.2% were single-car household. This is similar to the car ownership pattern in the Dutch population. The household composition distribution of the sample indicates that the largest group consists of households with two parents and at least two children (75.6%). After that, the single parent household with several children is the largest group (11.4%).

Half of the children in our sample have a school travel distance of 1 km or less, which is higher than 41%, which is reported in the national travel survey (OViN, 2016). Around a quarter of the respondents have a medium travel distance (1–2 km) and another quarter have a long travel distance (>2 km). The percentage of students with long travel distances is similar in the national travel survey (OViN, 2016). The majority of children in the sample attend public schools (44.4%) or schools with a religious focus (22%), which are in practice quite similar to a public school. Interestingly, also a fair share of children attend a school with a Dalton education vision (18.5%) and a special education school (11.8%). Special education schools are for children that need special attention because they face extra challenges in learning and developing. This last group is overrepresented in the sample, as only 2.4% of Dutch children attend special education schools.

6.2 School transport mode

The school transport mode is presented in Fig. 5, which represents the distribution of travel modes that children used on the day they completed the questionnaire. Almost half of the children (48%) used a bicycle to get to school. This percentage is somewhat higher than the percentage in the Netherlands presented in Fig. 2 (OViN, 2016). Around 20% used the car and about the same percentage of children walked to school. Car levels are similar to the national levels, though walking is roughly 5% lower (Fig. 2). Only a small amount of children came to school by public transport or on the back of a bicycle; and another 6% came by other modes, most of which can be assigned to the transport mode taxibus. The taxibus is a transport mode organized by the municipality, especially for children attending special education schools. These children generally live further away from school, not within cycling distance. For the analyses, public transport and the back of the bicycle were merged with the category 'other'.

6.3 Factors affecting transport mode to school

Several bivariate analyses were conducted to explore associations between a child's transport mode to school and different social and ecological factors. The results are summarized in Table 3.

First, regarding personal characteristics, Table 3 shows that age is significantly associated with travel mode. When children are older they are more likely to travel to school by bicycle, while the likelihood of traveling by car decreases with increasing age.

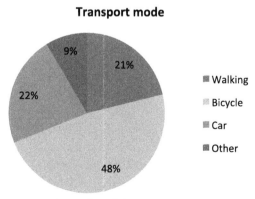

Fig. 5 School transport mode on day of the survey.

Table 3 Bivariate analyses of factors affecting transport mode to school

Variables	Walking	Bicycle	Car	Other	X^2 or F (sig.)
Age					
7	22%	26%	37%	15%	$X^2 = 39.226$
8	19%	44%	29%	8%	$(P = 0.001)$
9	27%	39%	26%	8%	
10	21%	50%	20%	9%	
11	17%	65%	12%	6%	
12	19%	50%	12%	19%	
Parents' active travel frequency					
Never	20%	44%	27%	9%	$X^2 = 16.252$
1–4 days	19%	51%	22%	8%	$(p = 0.012)$
>4 days	28%	53%	11%	9%	
Household income					
More than average Dutch income	22%	56%	20%	3%	$X^2 = 40.422$ $(P = 0.000)$
Equal to average Dutch income	23%	46%	23%	9%	
Lower than average Dutch income	16%	36%	27%	21%	
Household composition					
One parent—only child	16%	32%	28%	24%	$X^2 = 43.890$
One parent—sibling(s)	9%	37%	36%	17%	$(P - 0.000)$
Two parents—only child	10%	48%	31%	12%	
Two parents—sibling(s)	25%	50%	19%	6%	
Parental safety perception					F = 38.796
	3.70	3.80	3.46	3.10	$(P = 0.000)$
Travel distance					
<500 m	64%	26%	8%	1%	$X^2 = 408.181$
500–1000 m	21%	57%	20%	2%	$(P = 0.000)$
1–2 km	4%	69%	23%	5%	
2–5 km	1%	47%	38%	14%	
>5 km	2%	6%	40%	53%	
Weather					
Sunny	21%	44%	23%	12%	$X^2 = 32.374$
Partly clouded	23%	47%	22%	8%	$(P = 0.000)$
Very clouded	19%	56%	21%	5%	
Raining	24%	25%	31%	21%	

Regarding household characteristics, the results indicate that travel behavior of parents is significantly associated with the travel behavior of children. Children whose parents use active transport modes more often, tend to walk and cycle more, while children whose parents never use active modes are more likely to be transported by car. Next to travel behavior of parents, household income is found to be related to school transport mode. As can be seen, bicycle use increases with income, while car use decreases. This finding seems in line with the finding that in the Netherlands low income was associated with more car use (Van Goeverden & de Boer, 2013).

Household composition is also related to school transport mode choice. Walking and bicycling rates are higher for larger households (two parents and more than one child). This is in line with earlier findings. For example, Aarts et al. (2013) also found an association between the number of siblings and active travel participation.

In addition, we found that if the parental safety perception is higher, children are more likely to use active modes to school, especially the bicycle. This finding is also in line with existing international research on this topic (e.g., Ghekiere et al., 2017; Kerr et al., 2006; Wilson, Clark, & Gilliland, 2018).

Regarding the physical and social environment, we found that travel distance is significantly associated with school transport mode. This can be seen in Table 3 and Fig. 6. As expected, and in line with findings from the Dutch National Travel Survey (OViN, 2016), we found that walking is most common for short distances (<500 m), bicycling is highest for medium distances (1–2 km), and the use of car and other transport modes increase with longer distances. The association between higher odds of using active modes when the distance to school is smaller is in line with international research (e.g., McMillan, 2007; Rothman et al., 2018) as well as Dutch research (Aarts et al., 2013).

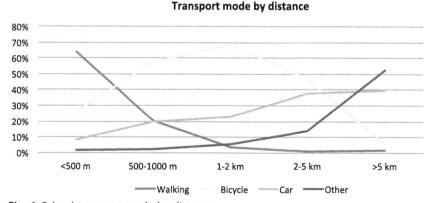

Fig. 6 School transport mode by distance.

Finally, regarding external factors, we found that bicycle use is lower when it is raining. When it is raining, bicycle trips are likely substituted by car and other modes. This finding is in line with Buliung et al. (2011) who found that the weather was one of the main reasons for Canadian parents to drive their children to school by car. Weather is not found to influence walking rates.

6.4 Satisfaction with travel

The satisfaction with travel (SWT) scale consists of nine statements, each scoring a value between one and five (see Table 1). Fig. 7 visualizes the answers that children have given to the nine satisfaction with travel questions. Note that for every chart the legend shows from which words the children could choose per question. Every time they were asked to choose which best described how they felt during their trip to school that morning.

Very few children (only 9%) said that their trip was lame or very lame, most were neutral about the trip (43%). More than half of the children (63%) said that their trip was very easy, only 2% indicated the trip was hard. About 20% of the children thinks that they learned something on the trip to school, 35% indicates not having learnt anything. A large share of the children found their trip to school fun (39%) or neutral (29%). The rest are mostly equally divided between being a little bored and finding the trip a lot of fun.

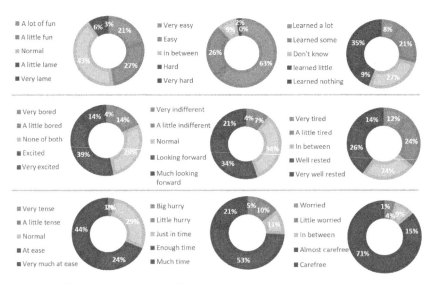

Fig. 7 Satisfaction with travel—children.

One third was looking forward to the day, one third was neutral and one third was either very much looking forward or (a little) indifferent. About a quarter was a little tired, a quarter was well rested and a quarter was something in between. The rest were either very tired or very well rested. Nearly half of the children were very much at ease during the trip, nearly nobody was worried. Around three quarters of the children had enough time or a lot of time on their way to school. The rest were mostly just in time or a little in a hurry. 71% of the children was completely carefree, 15% was almost carefree. Only 5% was (a little) worried.

In the analysis for the current study, one overall SWT variable will be used. A Cronbach's Alpha Reliability analysis was conducted to check for the internal consistency between the nine items. The results of the analysis indicated that it would be best to not include the second and third item (about difficulty level and learning). The combination of the remaining seven items resulted in a Cronbach's Alpha of 0.673, indicating moderate to good internal consistency. The final SWT variable will therefore represent the mean of the scores on items 1 and items 4–9 in Table 1.

6.5 Transport mode and satisfaction with travel

Finally, the relationship between the transport mode to school on the day of the survey and the satisfaction with travel was analyzed. The results of an ANOVA are presented in Fig. 8 and indicate that walking or cycling to school results in a higher satisfaction than traveling by car to school. This finding is in line with Westman et al. (2017) and Waygood (2018) who also found that children are more satisfied with their trips when they travel with an active mode.

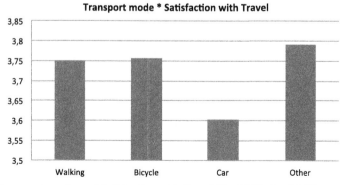

Fig. 8 Transport mode and Satisfaction with Travel (F = 2.730, P = 0.043).

7 Conclusions

This chapter has focused on the factors that are potentially influencing Dutch children's active travel to school and related travel satisfaction, which is explored here as a proxy for their subjective wellbeing. Based on data collected among 660 children in grades 5–8 of 14 elementary schools in and around the Dutch city of Arnhem, it was found that nearly half of all children traveled by bicycle to school, with a nearly equal portions going by car or by foot. Thus, a strong majority are still using active modes. This is in strong contrast to what is reported from English-speaking countries such as the USA, Australia, Canada, and New Zealand. As such, it is important to understand what is associated with such travel.

To examine what might explain children's transport mode outcomes, several bivariate analyses were performed. The results of the bivariate analyses indicate that school travel mode is strongly related to distance. Even in a country where cycling is very popular, for the shortest distances (<1 km) walking is still the preferred mode for many, while the bicycle is preferred for the medium distances (1–2 km). Perhaps it is the high quality bicycle infrastructure in the Netherlands that allows active travel to remain prevalent for medium-distance trips. Walking is often the dominant active mode for the school commute in other countries, so the extra mobility provided by the bicycle allows for a much larger percentage of children to take advantage of active travel. However, as the school distances increase, the use of motorized modes become more common. It is therefore advisable to retain (small) schools in local communities in order to keep distances limited to under 2 km. Another finding suggests that children's school travel mode is strongly related to travel mode choices of their parents. In order to promote active travel among children, their parents should be addressed as well. Possible interventions therefore include informing parents as well as children on the benefits of active travel. Improving the safety (perception) of walking and cycling infrastructure would be another possible intervention, as higher parental safety perception is related to higher walking and bicycling rates.

In addition to examining what explains such travel, this study also examined psychological measures of the trips. As previous findings have shown a link between active modes and more positive measures of trip quality, an ANOVA was conducted on the relationship between transport mode and satisfaction with travel. Results of the latter analysis show that children are least satisfied with their school travel when they travel by car.

Traveling by active mode (walking or bicycling) results in a higher satisfaction with travel, which in turn is likely to have a positive effect on their overall wellbeing. This further underlines the importance of stimulating active travel of school children.

This study has some limitations. First, the data were measured at one day in the year, in fall, while travel behavior may differ between seasons. In addition, more variables could be used to measure children's health and wellbeing. Finally, a more advanced modeling approach could be used to simultaneously estimate the factors influencing school travel mode and subjective wellbeing. Although the current study has some limitations, it adds new empirical evidence and draws attention to the understanding of children's active travel participation and wellbeing in the Netherlands.

Walking and cycling have many positive associations to children's wellbeing as has been shown in the various chapters of this book. As so many children in the Netherlands cycle, the argument that only those who really love to cycle are cycling and this might explain why it has higher satisfaction is harder to make. Thus, along with the physical activity benefits of these modes, we see again that active modes are associated with better psychological wellbeing measures. The challenge for many countries is how best to facilitate these trips. Along with smaller schools allowing for smaller catchment areas, the approach to bicycle infrastructure in the Netherlands is likely a key factor in their continued success at maintaining high cycling levels for children.

References

Aarts, M. -J., Mathijssen, J. J. P., van Oers, J. A. M., & Schuit, A. J. (2013). Associations between environmental characteristics and active commuting to school among children: A cross-sectional study. *International Journal of Behavioral Medicine, 20*(4), 538–555.

Babb, C., Olaru, D., Curtis, C., & Robertson, D. (2017). Children's active travel, local activity spaces and wellbeing: A case study in Perth, WA. *Travel Behaviour and Society, 9*, 81–94.

Bere, E., van der Horst, K., Oenema, A., Prins, R., & Brug, J. (2008). Socio-demographic factors as correlates of active commuting to school in Rotterdam, the Netherlands. *Preventive Medicine, 47*(4), 412–416.

Bergstad, C. J., Gamble, A., Gärling, T., Hagman, O., Polk, M., Ettema, D., et al. (2011). Subjective well-being related to satisfaction with daily travel. *Transportation, 38*, 1–15.

Bhosale, J., Duncan, S., & Schofield, G. (2017). Intergenerational change in children's independent mobility and active transport in New Zealand children and parents. *Journal of Transport & Health, 7*, 247–255.

Bronfenbrenner, U. (1979). *The ecology of human development. Experiments by nature and design.* Cambridge, Massachusetts and London: Harvard University Press.

Buliung, R., Faulkner, G., Beesley, T., & Kennedy, J. (2011). School travel planning: Mobilizing school and community resources to encourage active school transportation. *Journal of School Health, 81*(11), 704–712.

Buliung, R., Mitra, R., & Faulkner, G. (2009). Active school transportation in the Greater Toronto Area, Canada: An exploration of trends in space and time (1986–2006). *Preventive Medicine, 48*(6), 507–512.

Carver, A., Barr, A., Singh, A., Badland, H., Mavoa, S., & Bentley, R. (2019). How are the built environment and household travel characteristics associated with children's active transport in Melbourne, Australia? *Journal of Transport & Health, 12,* 115–129.

Carver, A., Timperio, A., & Crawford, D. (2013). Parental chauffeurs: What drives their transport choice? *Journal of Transport Geography, 26,* 72–77.

CBS (2019). *Nabijheid voorzieningen; afstand locatie, regionale cijfers.* Available from:https://statline.cbs.nl/Statweb/publication/?DM=SLNL&PA=80305NED&D1=55-58&D2=0&D3=a&HDR=G1,G2&STB=T&VW=T (Retrieved 03 March 2019).

Cervesato, A., & Waygood, E. O. D. (2019). Children's independent trips on weekdays and weekends: Case study of Québec City. *Transportation Research Record, 2673*(4), 907–916.

Crawford, S., Bennetts, S., Hackworth, N., Green, J., Graesser, H., Cooklin, A., et al. (2017). Worries, 'weirdos', neighborhoods and knowing people: A qualitative study with children and parents regarding children's independent mobility. *Health & Place, 45,* 131–139.

De Vries, S. I., Hopman-Rock, M., Bakker, I., Hirasing, R. A., & van Mechelen, W. (2010). Built environmental correlates of walking and cycling in Dutch urban children: Results from the SPACE study. *International Journal of Environmental Research and Public Health, 7* (5), 2309–2324.

Ettema, D., Gärling, T., Eriksson, L., Friman, M., Olsson, L. E., & Fujii, S. (2011). Satisfaction with travel and subjective well-being: Development and test of a measurement tool. *Transportation Research Part F: Traffic Psychology and Behaviour, 14*(3), 167–175.

Ghekiere, A., Deforche, B., Carver, A., Mertens, L., de Geus, B., Clarys, P., et al. (2017). Insights into children's independent mobility for transportation cycling—Which socio-ecological factors matter? *Journal of Science and Medicine in Sport, 20*(3), 267–272.

Giles-Corti, B., Wood, G., Pikora, T., Learnihan, V., Bulsara, M., Van Niel, K., et al. (2011). School site and the potential to walk to school: The impact of street connectivity and traffic exposure in school neighborhoods. *Health and Place, 17*(2), 545–550.

Guliani, A., Mitra, R., Buliung, R. N., Larsen, K., & Faulkner, G. E. (2015). Gender-based differences in school travel mode choice behaviour: Examining the relationship between the neighbourhood environment and perceived traffic safety. *Journal of Transport & Health, 2*(4), 502–511.

Henne, H. M., Tandon, P. S., Frank, L. D., & Saelens, B. E. (2014). Parental factors in children's active transport to school. *Public Health, 128*(7), 643–646.

Kemperman, A., & Timmermans, H. (2014). Environmental correlates of active travel behavior of children. *Environment and Behavior, 46*(5), 583–608.

Kerr, J., Rosenberg, D., Sallis, J. F., Saelens, B. E., Frank, L. D., & Conway, T. L. (2006). Active commuting to school: Associations with environment and parental concerns. *Medicine and Science in Sports and Exercise, 38*(4), 787–794.

McDonald, N. C. (2007). Active transportation to school: Trends among U.S. schoolchildren, 1969–2001. *American Journal of Preventive Medicine, 32*(6), 509–516.

McMillan, T. (2005). Urban form and a child's trip to school: The current literature and framework for future research. *Journal of Planning Literature, 19,* 440–456.

McMillan, T. E. (2007). The relative influence of urban form on a child's travel mode to school. *Transportation Research Part A: Policy and Practice, 41*(1), 69–79.

Mitra, R. (2013). Independent mobility and mode choice for school transportation: A review and framework for future research. *Transport Reviews, 33*(1), 21–43.

NOS (2013). *30% kinderen met auto naar school.* Available from:https://nos.nl/artikel/552504-30-kinderen-met-auto-naar-school.html (Retrieved 02 May 2018).

Omura, J. D., Hyde, E. T., Watson, K. B., Sliwa, S. A., Fulton, J. E., & Carlson, S. A. (2019). Prevalence of children walking to school and related barriers—United States, 2017. *Preventive Medicine*, *118*, 191–195.

OViN (2016). *Onderzoek Verplaatsingen in Nederland (OViN)*. .

Panter, J. R., Jones, A. P., Van Sluijs, E. M. F., & Griffin, S. J. (2010a). Attitudes, social support and environmental perceptions as predictors of active commuting behaviour in school children. *Journal of Epidemiology and Community Health*, *64*(1), 41–48.

Panter, J. R., Jones, A. P., Van Sluijs, E. M., & Griffin, S. J. (2010b). Neighbourhood, route and school environments and children's active commuting. *American Journal of Preventive Medicine*, *38*(3), 268–278.

Pont, K., Ziviani, J., Wadley, D., Bennett, S., & Abbott, R. (2009). Environmental correlates of children's active transportation: A systematic literature review. *Health & Place*, *15*(3), 849–862.

Pucher, J., & Buehler, R. (2008). Making cycling irresistible: Lessons from the Netherlands, Denmark and Germany. *Transport Reviews*, *28*(4), 495–528.

Ramanathan, S., O'Brien, C., Faulkner, G., & Stone, M. (2014). Happiness in motion: Emotions, well-being, and active school travel. *Journal of School Health*, *84*(8), 516–523.

Rothman, L., Macpherson, A. K., Ross, T., & Buliung, R. N. (2018). The decline in active school transportation (AST): A systematic review of the factors related to AST and changes in school transport over time in North America. *Preventive Medicine*, *111*, 314–322.

Sidharthan, R., Bhat, C., Pendyala, R., & Goulias, K. (2011). Model for children's school travel mode choice. Accounting for effects of spatial and social interaction. *Transportation Research Record: Journal of the Transportation Research Board*, *2213*, 78–86.

Sirard, J. R., & Slater, M. E. (2008). Walking and bicycling to school: A review. *American Journal of Lifestyle Medicine*, *2*(5), 372–396.

Telama, R. (2009). Tracking of physical activity from childhood to adulthood: A review. *Obesity Facts*, *2*(3), 187–195.

Trapp, G. S. A., Giles-Corti, B., Christian, H. E., Bulsara, M., Timperio, A. F., McCormack, G. R., et al. (2012). Increasing children's physical activity: Individual, social, and environmental factors associated with walking to and from school. *Health Education & Behavior*, *39*(2), 172–182.

Van de Craats, I. (2019). *Healthy school environments. Analysis of the factors influencing the travel mode to school of Dutch primary school children and its relation with parental safety perception and children's well-being and health.* Eindhoven: Eindhoven University of Technology.https://research.tue.nl/nl/studentTheses/healthy-school-environments.

Van der Houwen, K., Goossen, J., & Veling, I. (2003). *Reisgedrag kinderen basisschool. Veenendaal.*

Van Goeverden, C. D., & de Boer, E. (2013). School travel behaviour in the Netherlands and Flanders. *Transport Policy*, *26*, 73–84.

VVN (2014). *Samen veilig naar school. Utrecht.* Retrieved from:http://www.driepas.nl/file_popup.php?id=313188&aPop=1&popup=true.

Waygood, E. O. D. (2018). Transport and child well-being: Case study of Quebec City. In *Quality of Life and Daily Travel* (pp. 199–218): Springer.

Waygood, E. O. D., Friman, M., Olsson, L. E., & Taniguchi, A. (2017a). Children's incidental social interaction during travel international case studies from Canada, Japan, and Sweden. *Journal of Transport Geography*, *63*(March), 22–29.

Waygood, E. O. D., Friman, M., Olsson, L. E., & Taniguchi, A. (2017b). Transport and child well-being: An integrative review. *Travel Behaviour and Society*, *9*, 32–49.

Waygood, E. O. D., Friman, M., Taniguchi, A., & Olsson, L. E. (2019). Children's life satisfaction and travel satisfaction: Evidence from Canada, Japan, and Sweden. *Travel Behaviour and Society*, *16*, 214–223.

Waygood, E. O. D., & Kitamura, R. (2009). Children in a rail-based developed area of Japan travel patterns, independence, and exercise. *Transportation Research Record, 2125*, 36–43.

Westman, J., Olsson, L. E., Gärling, T., & Friman, M. (2017). Children's travel to school: Satisfaction, current mood, and cognitive performance. *Transportation, 44*(6), 1365–1382.

Wilson, K., Clark, A. F., & Gilliland, J. A. (2018). Understanding child and parent perceptions of barriers influencing children's active school travel. *BMC Public Health, 18*(1), 1053.

Further reading

Westman, J., Johansson, M., Olsson, L. E., Mårtensson, F., & Friman, M. (2013). Children's affective experience of every-day travel. *Journal of Transport Geography, 29*, 95–102.

CHAPTER EIGHTEEN

Active commuting to school by Chinese school-age children

Lin Lin[a] and Lingling He[b]

[a]Xi'an Jiaotong—Liverpool University, Suzhou, China
[b]Beijing Zhishu Consulting, Beijing, China

Contents

1 Background

1.1 Rising overweight and obesity and physical inactivity among school children in developing countries

Worldwide obesity has nearly tripled since 1975, and it is estimated that over 340 million children and adolescents aged 5–19 were overweight or obese in 2016 (WHO, 2018). The prevalence of overweight and obesity among schoolchildren and adolescents have also risen alarmingly in many developing countries (Gupta, Goel, Shah, & Misra, 2012). Lack of physical inactivity is identified as an important contributor to overweight and obesity problems (Popkin, 2001). A study that analyzed data from 105 countries showed that 80% of adolescents worldwide are not accumulating the minimum recommendation of 60 min of daily moderate- to vigorous-intensity physical activity (Hallal et al., 2012). Unfortunately, physical inactivity is pervasive in developed countries as well as in developing countries. For example, almost two thirds of Iranian adolescents aged 11–18 were physically inactive (Kelishadi et al., 2005). Only 14.2% of the school children were frequently participating in physical activity in the eight countries of the Sub-Saharan Africa (Muthuri et al., 2014; Peltzer, 2010). In Brazil, only 29% of the adolescents reached the recommended level of physical activity (de Rezende et al., 2014). In Latin America, only about 10–20% of adolescents are physical active (Hallal et al., 2012). In the Association of Southeast Asian Nations (ASEAN) member states, the prevalence of physical inactivity among students aged 13–15 was 80.4% (Peltzer & Pengpid, 2016).

Studies conducted in sub-Saharan Africa found that lower socioeconomic (SES) and rural children engaged in higher levels of active transportation (e.g., walking and running to school), spent more time in activities of daily living (e.g., house chores, work related, habitual activity), but spent less time engaged in organized sports or formal activities compared to their higher SES and urban peers (Muthuri et al., 2014). Another study that investigated the adolescents in the Association of Southeast Asian Nations identified that not walking or biking to school, not attending physical education classes, inadequate vegetable consumption with less than three servings a day and lack of protective factors such as peer and parental or guardian supports and supervisions were associated with physical inactivity (Peltzer & Pengpid, 2016). In Brazil, active commuting and physical education at school are found to contribute to be physical activity among adolescents (de Rezende et al., 2014).

Nonetheless, most research on active living has focused on children living in developed countries (Day, 2018), despite an acknowledgement that health interventions that are shown to be effective in the developed countries will not necessarily work in the developing world (Miranda & Zaman, 2010). For many emerging economies, a shift toward reduced habitual physical activity may relate to broad social changes and economic growth (González et al., 2018). Greater use of motorized transportation, rural to urban migration, and increased use of technology that coincide with economic growth may be contributing to decreased active transportation and leisure time physical activity and to increased sedentary recreational activities (Day, 2018). Scholars have pointed out that focusing on individual level determinants of health while ignoring more important macro-level determinants such as social, economic, and physical environment is like obtaining the right answer to the wrong question (Schwartz & Carpenter, 1999).

In this context, more research on physical activity among school children from developing countries, in particular research that explores social, economic, and physical environmental contexts within which children engage in physical activity, are warranted. A recent study that evaluated child and youth physical activity in 49 countries found that China is among the least successful countries in terms of community and environmental supports and government policies that relate to physical activity and sedentary behaviors at a population level (Aubert et al., 2018). As the largest developing country in the world with high prevalence of physical inactivity among children and youth, it is especially urgent to explore and understand not only individual factors, but also social and physical environmental factors associated with child and youth physical activity in China, so that effective interventions could be developed.

1.2 China's urbanization and physical activity

China's rapid urbanization, urban expansion, and motorization since the economic reform has led to major transformation of life style. Between 1980 and 2016, China's urbanization increased from 19.4% to 57.4% (The National Bureau of Statistics of China, 2017). The built-up areas of Chinese cities expanded rapidly from 12,253 km^2 in 1990 to 40,534 km^2 in 2010, a 131% increase (Wang et al., 2012). This rapid urbanization was accompanied by a growth in the interest and use of the automobiles. China, overtaking the US, has become the largest automobile market in the world since 2009 (Li, 2010). The private automobile ownership grew from 0.02 per 1000 people in 1985 to 107.7 in 2016 (the National Bureau of Statistics of China, 2017). In contrast, the levels of physical activity for adults in China fell by nearly half between 1991 and 2011 (Zang & Ng, 2016). Thirty percent of Chinese adults are currently overweight, and another 11.9% are obese (Xinhua Net, 2017).

The increased risk relating to physical inactivity, overweight, and obesity is affecting not only Chinese adults, but also Chinese children. Prevalence of overweight and obesity in children in China has a significant and continuous increase between 1985 and 2010 (Sun, Ma, Han, Pan, & Xu, 2014). At the same time, physical activity level of Chinese children has been declining (He & Lin, 2016). Recent research shows that few children have met the recommendation of 60 min/day of moderate-to-vigorous physical activity in Chinese cities, with only 9.4% of boys and 1.9% of girls accumulate sufficient physical activity on a daily basis (Wang, Chen, & Zhuang, 2013).

Active commuting to and from school, which can positively contribute to physical activity of children (Schoeppe, Duncan, Badland, Oliver, & Curtis, 2013; Tudor-Locke, Ainsworth, Adair, Du, & Popkin, 2003; van Sluijs et al., 2009) and can easily be incorporated into their daily life, has been identified as one of the common and widely accepted approaches for reversing the downward physical activity trends in children (Mori, Armada, & Willcox, 2012; Sirard & Slater, 2008). However, active commuting to school has also been decreasing in China. About 84% of Chinese youth were actively commuting to school in 1997 (Tudor-Locke et al., 2003), and the rate decreased to 55.8% by 2010 (Sun, Liu, & Tao, 2015).

1.3 Previous studies on active commute to school in China

Previous studies on children's active transport were conducted mostly in developed countries. Factors associated with active commuting to school, including home-to-school distance, household income, automobile ownership, and walk or bike paths (Pont, Ziviani, Wadley, Bennett, & Abbott, 2009), social interaction (Panter, Jones, & van Sluijs, 2008), traffic safety, and urban form measures such as residential density, land use mix, and street connectivity (McMillan, 2005; Panter et al., 2008) have been identified. Nonetheless, not all factors that were found to be associated with active commuting to school in developed countries might not be applicable in Chinese cities, due to unique urban, social and mobility characteristics of China. For instance, Chinese cities have much higher density compared with cities in the US or many other Western countries (Day, Alfonzo, Chen, Guo, & Lee, 2013), and previous research has reported a correlation between living in a higher residential density area and an increased likelihood of childhood overweight and obesity in China (An, Shen, Yang, & Yang, 2018). Furthermore, rapid urban urbanization has transformed urban landscape of Chinese cities (Wang et al., 2012), wherein the impact of these processes on children's wellbeing remains less explored.

Limited research on factors associated with school-age children's active commuting to school has been carried out in China. Shi, Lien, Kumar, and Holmboe-Ottesen (2006) investigated the association between socio-demographic factors and active commuting to school among adolescents in Jiangsu Province, China, and found that more girls went to school by bus than boys and that boys who were from high income households or had fathers with high levels of education had the lowest rates of walking to school. Another recent study (Cui, Bauman, & Dibley, 2011) found that driven trips to school has been increasing steadily in China, and in urban areas, mother's education level and attending school not in the local community were positively associated with children being driven to school. As a rapidly urbanizing country with fast changing urban landscape, up-to-date knowledge on factors that have direct impacts on promoting active commuting to school is particularly required in China. Furthermore, environmental factors associated with school-age children's active commuting to school remain understudied in the context of Chinese cities. In this chapter, we summarize results from a study that aims to systematically examine social-demographic as well as environmental factors of active commuting to school of Chinese school-age children, by investigating students and their parents from 32 public elementary schools in Shanghai, China.

2 Methods

2.1 Research design

A cross-sectional research design was used in this study to explore factors associated with active commuting to school of school-age children in Shanghai, the most populous city in China. Located in Yangtze River Delta, Shanghai has a population of 24 million (Shanghai Bureau of Statistics, 2015) and a total land area of $6340.5\,km^2$ (Shanghai Municipal Government, 2008). Thirty-two elementary schools, evenly chosen from four strata of residential building density and located in 16 districts of Shanghai were selected (Fig. 1). Detailed sampling strategy could be found elsewhere (Lin, 2018). Trained college student research assistants went to each school entrance in the afternoon of non-raining school days when school was over to conduct surveys between May 2015 and April 2016, as we previously observed that on average almost three quarters of school-age children would be picked up by an adult after school (Lin, 2018).

2.2 CLASS-C parent survey

The modified Chinese version of the Children's Leisure Activities Study Survey (CLASS-C) for parents, validated in China (Li, Chen, & Zhuang, 2011), was conducted. The CLASS-C for parents/caregivers collected information on physical activity of both school-age children and respondents, as well as respondent's socio-demographic information, home

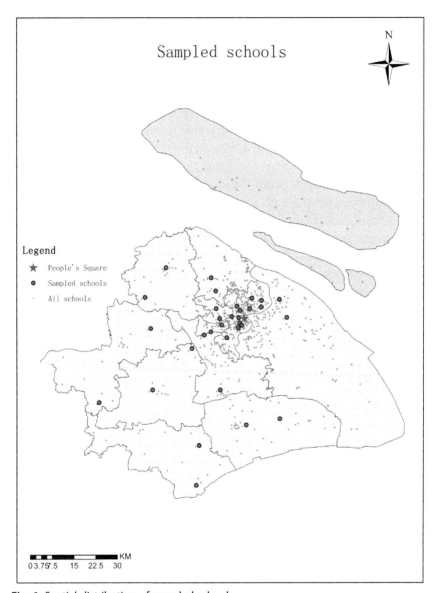

Fig. 1 Spatial distribution of sampled schools.

addresses, perceptions of their home neighborhoods, attitudes toward physical activity, etc. With a total of 72 questions, it took 25 min to complete one survey on average.

The active commuting to/from school was assessed by the survey question "How often does your child walk or cycle to/from school in a week?" School-age children who walked/cycled to school at least three times a week were identified as active travelers.

For each leisure-time physical activity (LTPA) that a school-age child participated in a week, the survey included individual questions on the frequency and the duration of the LTPA. Therefore, the total duration of all LTPAs in a week was computed based on those survey questions.

2.3 Respondent's home neighborhood built environment

With respondent's home address information collected in the survey, we were able to geocode their home locations using Baidu Maps. The built environment attributes such as residential density (counts of residential buildings), parks, restaurants, bus stops, metro stations, and street connectivity (measured in terms of street intersections density and total street network length), were measured within 200-m and 400-m buffers around a respondent's home were derived using APIs provide by Baidu Maps. Euclidian distance between home and school was also computed.

2.4 Data analysis

All data were analyzed using the software package SPSS 23.0. Principle component analysis (PCA) was performed for social support variables. Multivariate binomial logistic regression models were estimated to examine individual, social and built environmental factors associated with whether a school-age child was an active commuter.

3 Results
3.1 Descriptive statistics results

A total of 899 surveys were collected, and 719 of these were complete. Among those completed surveys, 649 (90.3%) parents/caregivers recorded valid values for those questions investigated in this study. About 62% of respondents reported to walk 150 min or more a week. On average, the majority of respondents thought one hour physical activity per day was appropriate for their children. The average age of school-age children was 9.03, ranging from 6 to 13 years old, and 53.9% school-age children were girls.

On average, 159 min a week of LTPA was reported for school-age children. 43.1% of school-age children were active travelers to school with three times and more walking or cycling to/from school in a week. There were about 31% of children attending schools with an enrollment fewer than 550 students, and 36% attending schools with an enrollment between 551 and 1100 students. About 29% of children attended a sports specialty school.

At the household level, 28% of households had a monthly income of 6000 RMB (USD$ 857) or less, and 35% with a monthly income between 6001 RMB and 10,000 RMB (USD$ 1429). Only 37% of households had Shanghai household registration status. Due to some records with incomplete home addresses, 61.5% of records (399 records) included in the study could be geocoded with objective built environmental attributes measured around respondent's home. Of those 399 households, 39.1% of school-age children were active travelers to school. Other variables such as school-age children's individual characteristics, respondent's characteristics, behaviors, preference of physical activity duration for their children and perception of home environment, social supports for physical activity, household characteristics, and school characteristics were not found to significantly differ from the larger sample of 649 records.

Objective built environmental attributes were measured in the 200-m and 400-m buffers around respondent's homes, respectively. For those geocoded records, more than half (52.4%) of school-age children lived within 1 km of their schools. Another 21.1% lived between 1 and 2 km away from their schools.

3.2 Social support toward children's physical activity

Thanks to the high correlations among social support variables, principle component analysis (PCA) was performed to reduce nine variables on family members' involvement in and support toward physical activities and sedentary activities into fewer clearly distinguishable factors (Table 1). Three factors were derived, which were defined as: (1) closely bonded family, where family members would do both physical activities and sedentary activities together; (2) active family, where family members would do physical activities together; and (3) sedentary family, where family members would do sedentary activities together.

Similarly, Table 2 summarizes the PCA results for four variables on family members' and community's encouragement toward children's

Table 1 Principal component analysis summarizing family members' direct involvement in physical activities and sedentary activities with children

	Factor 1 Closely bonded family	Factor 2 Active family	Factor 3 Sedentary family
The frequency of all family members involved in child's physical activity together	0.714	0.194	−0.068
The frequency of father involved in child's physical activity	0.731	0.169	−0.239
The frequency of mother involved in child's physical activity	0.693	0.237	−0.189
The frequency of grandparents involved in child's physical activity	0.284	0.391	−0.167
The frequency of siblings involved in child's physical activity	0.074	0.373	0.666
The frequency of friends involved in child's physical activity	0.180	0.254	0.569
Play games with family members	0.430	−0.641	0.082
Use the internet with family members	0.413	−0.666	0.154
Watch TV with family members	0.353	−0.172	0.430
Eigenvalue	2.122	1.362	1.108
Explained variance (%)	23.58%	15.13%	12.31%
Total explained variance (%)	51.02%		

Table 2 Principal component analysis result for family encouragement toward physical activities

	Factor 4 Encouraging parents	Factor 5 Encouraging community
Father's encouragement of children doing physical activities	0.84	−0.24
Mother's encouragement of children doing physical activities	0.87	−0.13
Grandparent's encouragement of children doing physical activities	0.44	0.40
Other people's encouragement of children doing physical activities	0.16	0.89
Eigenvalue	1.673	1.017
Explained variance (%)	41.83%	25.43%
Total explained variance (%)	67.26%	

physical activities. Two factors were derived: (1) family with highly encouraging parents and grandparents; and (2) family with encouraging community members.

3.3 Factors associated with active commuting to/from school

Table 3 summarizes the factors that potentially influence a child's active commuting to school, in the form of correlates of the logistic regression model that was estimated. The results highlight the importance of parent/caregiver behavior and preference of physical activity duration for their children on their likelihood of actively commuting to/from school (Table 3). If a parent/caregiver had reached the recommendation physical activity level

Table 3 Factors associated with active commuting to/from school ($n = 399$)

		Coefficient	Sig.	Odds ratio (Exp (B))
	Constant	−1.69	*0.09*	0.18
School-age children's individual characteristics	Age	0.01	0.87	1.01
	Sex (women vs. men[a])	0.01	0.97	1.01
	BMI (z-score)	0.16	0.20	0.85
Respondent's behavior and preference of physical activity duration for their children	Respondent's total minutes of walking in a week (greater than 150 min vs. fewer than 150 min[a])	1.38	**0.00**	3.96
	Respondent's duration preference of their children's physical activity per day	0.44	**0.02**	1.55
Household characteristics	Household income per month		0.29	
	Household income per month: less than 6000 RMB/month	0.39	0.22	1.48
	Household income per month: 6001–10,000 RMB/month	0.42	0.15	1.53
	Household income per month: 10001 and more RMB/month[a]			
	TV in child's bedroom (with TV vs. no TV[a])	−0.29	0.29	0.75

Table 3 Factors associated with active commuting to/from school ($n = 399$)—cont'd

		Coefficient	Sig.	Odds ratio (Exp (B))
Social supports	Factor 1: closely bonded family: family members doing both physical activities and sedentary activities together	0.29	**0.02**	1.34
	Factor 2: active family: family members doing physical activities together	−0.33	**0.01**	0.72
Home neighborhood perception	Perception of indoor gym within 20 min travel of respondent's home (yes vs. no[a])	−0.37	0.15	0.69
School characteristics	School enrollment		**0.00**	
	School enrollment: 551–1100 students	0.95	**0.00**	2.59
	School enrollment: 1101 and more students	0.25	0.44	1.28
	School enrollment: up to 550 students[a]			
	Sports specialty school (sports specialty school vs. regular school[a])	0.23	0.40	1.26
	Distance between home and school	−0.08	**0.02**	0.93
	Restaurants in 200 m buffer of a respondent's home		**0.03**	
	Restaurants in 200 m buffer of a respondent's home: 4–12 restaurants	0.679	**0.03**	1.973
	Restaurants in 200 m buffer of a respondent's home: 13 and more restaurants	0.729	**0.02**	2.074
	Restaurants in 200 m buffer of a respondent's home: 0–3 restaurants[a]			
	−2 log likelihood	435.68		
	AIC	463.68		
	BIC	519.53		

[a]Reference category. Coefficients in **bold** are statistically significant at $\alpha = 0.05$.

with more than 150 min of walking in a week, their children were more likely to active commute to/from school. A child was also more likely to be active commuter if their parent/caregiver had a longer duration preference for their children's physical activity per day. Two family/social support factors were significantly associated with whether a child was an active traveler. Specially, if a child was from a closely bonded family, the child was more likely to active commute to/from school. Meanwhile, the social support factor—active family—had a significant negative association with being an active traveler. The other factors identified in Tables 1 and 2 were not associated with a child's school commute mode choice.

School size was important- a child attending a school with an enrollment between 551 and 1100 students would be more likely to active commute to/from school than those children who attended schools with a smaller enrollment. Children's age, sex, and body mass index (BMI) were not associated with their school transport mode. Household income per month was also not statistically associated with child's active commute to/from school.

The objectively measured built environmental attributes, namely— distance between home and school and counts of restaurants in 200-m buffer of a respondent's home, were found to be significantly associated with school age children's active commute to/from school. Home-school distance was negatively associated with being an active traveler. A child who lived in a neighborhood with four and more restaurants within 200 m of their home was more likely to walk or cycle than others who lived in a neighborhood with three and fewer restaurants around their homes.

4 Discussion

4.1 Children's active commuting in China

This study identified several variables that were statistically associated with active commuting to/from school by school-age children in Shanghai, China. These factors included parents'/caregivers' physical activity level and duration preference of their children's physical activity per day, family support and encouragement, school type, home-to-school distance, and restaurant density (a proxy for land use mix) around children's home location. Some of these factors found to be important in Shanghai were consistent with the results in other studies conducted in developed countries. For instance, social support factor—closely bonded family which refers to family members doing both physical activities and sedentary activities together— was positively associated with active commuting to school. This finding was in accordance with the results from previous studies (Panter et al., 2008). Interestingly, a social support factor—active family—was negatively associated with active commuting to school. Compared with closely bonded family where family members engage in both physical activities and sedentary activities together, active family whose family members doing physical activities together might demonstrate a weaker social support. The reasons for this negative association is unclear, and further studies on social and family supports and active school transport in China might reveal more insights into these causalities. The importance of home-school distance has also been repeatedly emphasized in previous studies in the developed countries (Ikeda et al., 2018; Pont et al., 2009; Rothman, Macpherson, Ross, & Buliung, 2018).

In previous studies, perception of traffic safety was found to be associated with active commuting to school (McMillan, 2005; Panter et al., 2008). Our study did not include data on traffic safety. Instead, we found that school type was associated with active commuting to school. Schools with small school enrollment might have very different school layout, street design, and traffic volume with that of schools with median size school enrollment or large enrollment. The differences in terms of school layout, street design, and traffic volume might be related to traffic safety, and as a result, contributed to active commuting to school. Future studies should assess the impacts of traffic safety from the perspective of school layout, street design, and traffic volume on active commuting to school in Chinese cites.

It should be noted that none of residential density (counts of residential buildings in 200-m and 400 m buffers) or street connectivity (counts of street intersections and total length of street network in 200-m and 400-m buffers) measures were significant in the regression models, even though previous research has repeatedly found residential density and street connectivity to have associate with active commuting to school in developed countries (Curtis, Babb, & Olaru, 2015; McMillan, 2005; Panter et al., 2008). In fact, a previous review on impacts of built environment on physical activity in China concluded that higher residential density was associated with lower physical activity among children and adolescents (An et al., 2018). This might exemplify the unique characteristics of Chinese cities with regard to development density (Day et al., 2013), and that the impact of residential density on physical activity behavior may be different from what is typically expected in western societies with much lower average density. Instead of residential density or street connectivity, our study found that land use mix, which was measured in this study in terms of counts of restaurants within

200-m of school-age children's home, was associated with active commuting to/from school in Shanghai. Further study should explore measures of active transportation infrastructure, including sidewalks and separated bike lines, around children's home neighborhood.

In addition, our study did not find an association between household income and active commuting to/from school, contrary to the previous studies conducted elsewhere (Panter et al., 2008). In the CLASS-C for parent, we did not include questions on automobile ownership that was also found to be associated with travel mode choices to school in other studies (Li & Zhao, 2015; McMillan, 2007).

Recent research has indicated that children's behaviors, such as active commuting to school, may be influenced by their parents' and caregivers' attitudes and beliefs. As expected, both adult respondent's physical activity level and respondent's duration preference of their children's physical activity per day were positively associated with children being an active traveler. However, parent's/caregiver's education level was not associated with the likelihood of a child's active commuting to school in Shanghai. Our finding was different from the results reported in Jiangsu, China in 2005 (Shi et al., 2006), where boys with highly educated fathers had the lowest percentage walking to school, and a study using a national data between 1997 and 2006 also reported that mother's educational level was positively associated with being driven commuting to school (Cui et al., 2011).

Previous studies consistently showed that active travel positively contributed to a child's physical activity (Schoeppe et al., 2013). In this context, active school transport has been identified as an important source where children can accumulate light to moderate physical activity on a daily basis throughout the school year. Encouraging and promoting active school transport could play a positive role in reversing the current trend of children's physical inactivity in developed as well as developing countries.

4.2 Environmental measures and data issues in developing countries

This study used APIs provided by a web mapping service application to objectively measure neighborhood level built environmental attributes in a Chinese city. Very few active transport studies in China have used such detailed micro level built environmental data, which might be due to limited access to detailed GIS data. Li and Zhao (2015) who investigated potential determinants of travel modes to school in Beijing using travel survey data in 2005, only included a dummy variable indicating whether a neighborhood was in the core area (i.e., downtown) or not. Pan, Shen, and Zhang (2009) measured four neighborhoods in Shanghai using published transit maps. Feng (2016) measured built environmental attributes for traffic analysis zones in Nanjing, China. However, it was not clear where the built environmental data were obtained from or the format of the data. With online mapping services widely available in China, using APIs to derive micro level built environmental attributes could be a new and feasible approach to acquire data for research and practice focusing on children's transport.

To investigate physical environmental factors on physical activity and active travel in developing countries, subjective measures could be acquired via surveys. Objective data on the built environment attributes could also be collected by conducting systematic environmental audits such as Irvine–Minnesota Inventory-China (IMI-C) environmental audit (Alfonzo, Guo, Lin, & Day, 2014), or using satellite images to derive objective environmental measures (Stoler et al., 2012).

5 Conclusion

This study identified that parents'/caregivers' physical activity level and duration preference of their children's physical activity per day, family support and encouragement, and school type were associated with active travel to and from school in Shanghai, China. The findings showed some similarity with the results that were previously reported based on studies conducted in developed countries. Meanwhile, children's individual characteristics such as age, gender, and BMI was not associated with being an active school commuter, unlike what has been previously reported elsewhere. This study also used APIs to objectively measure detail built environmental attributes at neighborhood level in Shanghai, China. The method was an innovative solutions to address the rarity of GIS-based built environment data in the context of developing countries. Based on this data, this study confirmed that home-school distance was significantly associated with active commuting to/from school, consistent with findings from research conducted in the developed countries. It was not residential density or street connectivity, but land use mix (measured in terms of restaurant density) around children's home that was associated with active commuting to school. With different social, economic, and physical environments from those of developed countries, China's active travel to and from school exhibited some uniqueness with some difference in factors that might influence school transport outcomes. Effective interventions to encourage and promote active school transport in developing countries should be tailored to social, economic, and physical environments of the developing countries.

Acknowledgments

This research was supported by National Science Foundation of China (grand number: 41301153). The objective built environmental attributes were derived by Xiaoliu Wang at East China Normal University. The school addresses were collected by Dan Qin at. East China Normal University. The school addresses were geocoded by Jian Shi at East China Normal University. The CLASS-C survey was conducted by more than 20 students at East China Normal University.

References

Alfonzo, M., Guo, Z., Lin, L., & Day, K. (2014). Walking, obesity and urban design in Chinese neighborhoods. *Preventive Medicine, 69*(Supplement), S79–S85. https://doi.org/10.1016/j.ypmed.2014.10.002.

An, R., Shen, J., Yang, Q., & Yang, Y. (2018). Impact of built environment on physical activity and obesity among children and adolescents in China: A narrative systematic review. *Journal of Sport and Health Science.* https://doi.org/10.1016/j.jshs.2018.11.003.

Aubert, S., Barnes, J. D., Abdeta, C., Abi Nader, P., Adeniyi, A. F., Aguilar-Farias, N., et al. (2018). Global matrix 3.0 physical activity report card grades for children and youth: Results and analysis from 49 countries. *Journal of Physical Activity and Health, 15*(S2), S251–S273. https://doi.org/10.1123/jpah.2018-0472.

Cui, Z., Bauman, A., & Dibley, M. J. (2011). Temporal trends and correlates of passive commuting to and from school in children from 9 Provinces in China. *Preventive Medicine, 52* (6), 423–427. https://doi.org/10.1016/j.ypmed.2011.04.005.

Curtis, C., Babb, C., & Olaru, D. (2015). Built environment and children's travel to school. *Transport Policy, 42*(August), 21–33. https://doi.org/10.1016/j.tranpol.2015.04.003.

Day, K. (2018). Physical environment correlates of physical activity in developing countries: A review. *Journal of Physical Activity and Health, 15*(4), 303–314. https://doi.org/10.1123/jpah.2017-0184.

Day, K., Alfonzo, M., Chen, Y., Guo, Z., & Lee, K. K. (2013). Overweight, obesity, and inactivity and urban design in rapidly growing Chinese cities. *Health & Place, 21*(May), 29–38. https://doi.org/10.1016/j.healthplace.2012.12.009.

de Rezende, L. F. M., Azeredo, C. M., Canella, D. S., Claro, R. M., de Castro, I. R. R., Levy, R. B., et al. (2014). Sociodemographic and behavioral factors associated with physical activity in Brazilian adolescents. *BMC Public Health, 14*(1), 485. https://doi.org/10.1186/1471-2458-14-485.

Feng, J. (2016). The built environment and active travel: Evidence from Nanjing, China. *International Journal of Environmental Research and Public Health, 13*(3), 301. https://doi.org/10.3390/ijerph13030301.

González, S. A., Barnes, J. D., Abi Nader, P., Susana Andrade Tenesaca, D., Brazo-Sayavera, J., Galaviz, K. I., et al. (2018). Report card grades on the physical activity of children and youth from 10 countries with high human development index: Global Matrix 3.0. *Journal of Physical Activity and Health, 15*(S2), S284–S297. https://doi.org/10.1123/jpah.2018-0391.

Gupta, N., Goel, K., Shah, P., & Misra, A. (2012). Childhood obesity in developing countries: Epidemiology, determinants, and prevention. *Endocrine Reviews, 33*(1), 48–70. https://doi.org/10.1210/er.2010-0028.

Hallal, P. C., Andersen, L. B., Bull, F. C., Guthold, R., Haskell, W., & Ekelund, U. (2012). Global physical activity levels: Surveillance progress, pitfalls, and prospects. *The Lancet*, *380*(9838), 247–257. https://doi.org/10.1016/S0140-6736(12)60646-1.

He, L., & Lin, L. (2016). Zhongguo chengshi xueling ertong tili huodong bianhua qushi, the trends of physical activity levels of Chinese urban school-age children. *Chinese Journal of School Health*, *37*(4), 636–640. https://doi.org/10.16835/j.cnki.1000-9817.2016.04.049. [Chinese].

Ikeda, E., Stewart, T., Garrett, N., Egli, V., Mandic, S., Hosking, J., et al. (2018). Built environment associates of active school travel in New Zealand children and youth: A systematic meta-analysis using individual participant data. *Journal of Transport & Health*, *9*(June), 117–131. https://doi.org/10.1016/j.jth.2018.04.007.

Kelishadi, R., Sadri, G., Tavasoli, A. A., Kahbazi, M., Roohafza, H. R., Sadeghi, M., et al. (2005). Cumulative prevalence of risk factors for atherosclerotic cardiovascular diseases in Iranian adolescents: IHHP-HHPC. *Jornal de Pediatria*, *81*(6), 447–453. https://doi.org/10.2223/JPED.1418.

Li, F. (2010). Chinese auto market overtakes US as world's largest. *China Daily, January*, *9*, 2010.http://www.chinadaily.com.cn/business/2010-01/09/content_9292112.htm.

Li, H. -Y., Chen, P. -J., & Zhuang, J. (2011). Revision and reliability validity assessment of children's leisure activities study survey. *Chinese Journal of School Health*, *32*(3), 268–270 [Chinese].

Li, S., & Zhao, P. (2015). The determinants of commuting mode choice among school children in Beijing. *Journal of Transport Geography*, *46*(June), 112–121. https://doi.org/10.1016/j.jtrangeo.2015.06.010.

Lin, L. (2018). Leisure-time physical activity, objective urban neighborhood built environment, and overweight and obesity of Chinese school-age children. *Journal of Transport & Health*, *10*, 322–333. https://doi.org/10.1016/j.jth.2018.05.001.

McMillan, T. E. (2005). Urban form and a child's trip to school: The current literature and a framework for future research. *Journal of Planning Literature*, *19*(4), 440–456. https://doi.org/10.1177/0885412204274173.

McMillan, T. E. (2007). The relative influence of urban form on a child's travel mode to school. *Transportation Research Part A: Policy and Practice*, *41*(1), 69–79. https://doi.org/10.1016/j.tra.2006.05.011.

Miranda, J. J., & Zaman, M. J. (2010). Exporting "failure": Why research from rich countries may not benefit the developing world. *Revista De Saude Publica*, *44*(1), 185–189.

Mori, N., Armada, F., & Willcox, D. C. (2012). Walking to school in Japan and childhood obesity prevention: New lessons from an old policy. *American Journal of Public Health*, *102*(11), 2068–2073. https://doi.org/10.2105/AJPH.2012.300913.

Muthuri, S. K., Wachira, L. -J. M., Leblanc, A. G., Francis, C. E., Sampson, M., Onywera, V. O., et al. (2014). Temporal trends and correlates of physical activity, sedentary behaviour, and physical fitness among school-aged children in Sub-Saharan Africa: A systematic review. *International Journal of Environmental Research and Public Health*, *11*(3), 3327–3359. https://doi.org/10.3390/ijerph110303327.

Pan, H., Shen, Q., & Zhang, M. (2009). Influence of urban form on travel behaviour in four neighbourhoods of Shanghai. *Urban Studies*, *46*(2), 275–294. https://doi.org/10.1177/0042098008099355.

Panter, J. R., Jones, A. P., & van Sluijs, E. M. F. (2008). Environmental determinants of active travel in youth: A review and framework for future research. *International Journal of Behavioral Nutrition and Physical Activity*, *5*(1), 34. https://doi.org/10.1186/1479-5868-5-34.

Peltzer, K. (2010). Leisure time physical activity and sedentary behavior and substance use among in-school adolescents in eight African countries. *International Journal of Behavioral Medicine*, *17*(4), 271–278. https://doi.org/10.1007/s12529-009-9073-1.

Peltzer, K., & Pengpid, S. (2016). Leisure time physical inactivity and sedentary behaviour and lifestyle correlates among students aged 13–15 in the association of Southeast Asian Nations (ASEAN) member states, 2007–2013. *International Journal of Environmental Research and Public Health*, *13*(2), 217. https://doi.org/10.3390/ijerph13020217.

Pont, K., Ziviani, J., Wadley, D., Bennett, S., & Abbott, R. (2009). Environmental correlates of children's active transportation: A systematic literature review. *Health & Place*, *15*(3), 849–862. https://doi.org/10.1016/j.healthplace.2009.02.002.

Popkin, B. M. (2001). The nutrition transition and obesity in the developing world. *The Journal of Nutrition*, *131*(3), 871S–873S. https://doi.org/10.1093/jn/131.3.871S.

Rothman, L., Macpherson, A. K., Ross, T., & Buliung, R. N. (2018). The decline in active school transportation (AST): A systematic review of the factors related to AST and changes in school transport over time in North America. *Preventive Medicine*, *111*(June), 314–322. https://doi.org/10.1016/j.ypmed.2017.11.018.

Schoeppe, S., Duncan, M. J., Badland, H., Oliver, M., & Curtis, C. (2013). Associations of children's independent mobility and active travel with physical activity, sedentary behaviour and weight status: A systematic review. *Journal of Science and Medicine in Sport*, *16*(4), 312–319. https://doi.org/10.1016/j.jsams.2012.11.001.

Schwartz, S., & Carpenter, K. M. (1999). The right answer for the wrong question: Consequences of type III error for public health research. *American Journal of Public Health*, *89*(8), 1175–1180.

Shanghai Bureau of Statistics (2015). *Shanghai economic and social development statistical bulletin 2014*. http://www.stats-sh.gov.cn/sjfb/201502/277392.html.

Shanghai Municipal Government (2008). *Basic facts. Shanghai, China*. http://www.shanghai.gov.cn/images/2010english/shanghaifacts2008.pdf.

Shi, Z., Lien, N., Kumar, B. N., & Holmboe-Ottesen, G. (2006). Physical activity and associated socio-demographic factors among school adolescents in Jiangsu Province, China. *Preventive Medicine*, *43*(3), 218–221. https://doi.org/10.1016/j.ypmed.2006.04.017.

Sirard, J. R., & Slater, M. E. (2008). Walking and bicycling to school: A review. *American Journal of Lifestyle Medicine*, *2*(5), 372–396. https://doi.org/10.1177/1559827608320127.

Stoler, J., Daniels, D., Weeks, J. R., Stow, D. A., Coulter, L. L., & Finch, B. K. (2012). Assessing the utility of satellite imagery with differing spatial resolutions for deriving proxy measures of slum presence in Accra, Ghana. *GIScience & Remote Sensing*, *49*(1), 31–52. https://doi.org/10.2747/1548-1603.49.1.31.

Sun, Y., Liu, Y., & Tao, F. -B. (2015). Associations between active commuting to school, body fat, and mental well-being: Population-based, cross-sectional study in China. *Journal of Adolescent Health*, *57*(6), 679–685. https://doi.org/10.1016/j.jadohealth.2015.09.002.

Sun, H., Ma, Y., Han, D., Pan, C. -W., & Xu, Y. (2014). Prevalence and trends in obesity among China's children and adolescents, 1985–2010. *PLoS ONE*. *9*(8)e105469. https://doi.org/10.1371/journal.pone.0105469.

The National Bureau of Statistics of China (2017). *China Statistical Yearbook-2017. Available from:http://www.stats.gov.cn/tjsj/ndsj/2017/indexeh.htm Retrieved 20 March 2019.*

Tudor-Locke, C., Ainsworth, B. E., Adair, L. S., Du, S., & Popkin, B. M. (2003). Physical activity and inactivity in Chinese school-aged youth: The China health and nutrition survey. *International Journal of Obesity*, *27*(9), 1093–1099. https://doi.org/10.1038/sj.ijo.0802377.

van Sluijs, E. M. F., Fearne, V. A., Mattocks, C., Riddoch, C., Griffin, S. J., & Ness, A. (2009). The contribution of active travel to children's physical activity levels: Cross-sectional results from the ALSPAC study. *Preventive Medicine*, *48*(6), 519–524. https://doi.org/10.1016/j.ypmed.2009.03.002.

Wang, C., Chen, P., & Zhuang, J. (2013). A national survey of physical activity and sedentary behavior of Chinese City children and youth using accelerometers. *Research Quarterly for Exercise and Sport*, *84*(sup2), S12–S28. https://doi.org/10.1080/02701367.2013.850993.

Wang, L., Li, C., Ying, Q., Cheng, X., Wang, X., Li, X., et al. (2012). China's urban expansion from 1990 to 2010 determined with satellite remote sensing. *Chinese Science Bulletin*, *57*(22), 2802–2812. https://doi.org/10.1007/s11434-012-5235-7.

WHO (2018). *Obesity and overweight*. Available from: https://www.who.int/news-room/fact-sheets/detail/obesity-and-overweight [Retrieved 20 March 2019].

Xinhua Net. (May 25, 2017). 30 percent of Chinese adults overweight. Available from: http://www.xinhuanet.com/english/2017-05/25/c_136315042.htm.

Zang, J., & Ng, S. W. (2016). Age, period and cohort effects on adult physical activity levels from 1991 to 2011 in China. *International Journal of Behavioral Nutrition and Physical Activity*, *13*(April), 40. https://doi.org/10.1186/s12966-016-0364-z.

Further reading

Cheng, T. O. (2012). Childhood obesity in modern China. *International Journal of Cardiology*, *157*(3), 315–317. https://doi.org/10.1016/j.ijcard.2012.03.003.

Cole, T. J., Faith, M. S., Pietrobelli, A., & Heo, M. (2005). What is the best measure of adiposity change in growing children: BMI, BMI %, BMI Z-score or BMI centile? *European Journal of Clinical Nutrition*, *59*(3), 419–425. https://doi.org/10.1038/sj.ejcn.1602090.

Huang, G., Su, Z., Liu, J., Yan, Y., Meng, L., Cheng, H., et al. (2014). The current status of physical activity in urban school-aged children and its association with obesity. *Chinese Journal of Epidemiology*, *35*(4), 376–380. https://doi.org/10.3760/cma.j.issn.0254-6450.2014.04.007. [Chinese].

Laird, Y., Fawkner, S., Kelly, P., McNamee, L., & Niven, A. (2016). The role of social support on physical activity behaviour in adolescent girls: A systematic review and meta-analysis. *International Journal of Behavioral Nutrition and Physical Activity*. *13*(July). https://doi.org/10.1186/s12966-016-0405-7.

Lin, L., & Moudon, A. V. (2010). Objective versus subjective measures of the built environment, which are most effective in capturing associations with walking? *Health & Place*, *16*(2), 339–348. https://doi.org/10.1016/j.healthplace.2009.11.002.

Tucker, J. M., Welk, G. J., & Beyler, N. K. (2011). Physical activity in U.S. adults: Compliance with the physical activity guidelines for Americans. *American Journal of Preventive Medicine*, *40*(4), 454–461. https://doi.org/10.1016/j.amepre.2010.12.016.

Yao, C. A., & Rhodes, R. E. (2015). Parental correlates in child and adolescent physical activity: A meta-analysis. *International Journal of Behavioral Nutrition and Physical Activity*, *12*(February), 10. https://doi.org/10.1186/s12966-015-0163-y.

PART FIVE

Future directions

CHAPTER NINETEEN

Transport and children's wellbeing: Future directions

Margareta Friman[a], Lars E. Olsson[a], E. Owen D. Waygood[b] and Raktim Mitra[c]

[a]Service Research Center and Department of Social and Psychological Studies, Karlstad University, Karlstad, Sweden
[b]Department of Civil, Geological, and Mining Engineering, Polytechnique Montréal, Montreal, QC, Canada
[c]School of Urban and Regional Planning, Ryerson University, Toronto, ON, Canada

Contents

1 Introduction

This edited volume brings together leading scholars from around the world, scholars who have discussed various aspects of children's transport and wellbeing, as well as key theoretical, policy and community-based approaches that may improve child wellbeing in our societies. In this final chapter, it is our pleasure to discuss the key findings and proposals in these eighteen chapters, with the aim of providing some guidelines for the future. As a whole, this book reflects the sentiment of Waygood, Friman, Olsson, and Taniguchi (2017) that transport influences several different domains of a child's wellbeing. The different chapters included in this book show how children represent a uniquely vulnerable group that has received less of a research and policy focus than adults have. The developments of the past century show how children's travel has changed—with their independent mobility having been replaced by constant adult supervision, and with more children being driven between different locations than ever before. Many transport-related changes affect children's physical health and wellbeing, but may also lead to psychological and cognitive health consequences, albeit that these latter effects are less well-documented. We view this chapter as input into the ongoing discussion on how to integrate children's perspectives into transport research and practice.

The book shows how children's physical, psychological and cognitive wellbeing is related to transport issues (e.g., Larouche, Mitra, and Waygood in Chapter 2 and Westman, Olsson, and Friman in Chapter 3), and how transport can influence social interaction (Waygood, Chapter 4). The social and ecological context and the urban policy/regulations shaping the child's transport outcomes were also discussed (Mitra and Manaugh, Chapter 5). Several chapters of this book focus on the key aspects of modern transport systems affecting children's wellbeing, e.g. traffic speeds (Rothman, Buliung, Howard, Macarthur, and Macpherson, Chapter 6), home-school distance (Lin and He, Chapter 18), and emissions (Boothe and Baldauf, Chapter 7).

A section of the book is devoted to solutions and to understanding how children's travel might be improved (for instance, how disabled children's experiences and perspectives can be included by Ross in Chapter 15). Shaw presents various policies that have been introduced to counteract the enormous impact of private vehicles on children (Chapter 9). Witten and Field (Chapter 11) emphasize the importance of licensing children's independent mobility; in relation to this, Johansson, Mårtensson, Jansson, and Sternudd (Chapter 12) discuss four approaches to planning, designing and managing the built environment in order to enable independent and active mobility. Within this context, Raktim Mitra and Zainab Abbasi (Chapter 13) present a case study where a human-centric design approach was adopted in order to engage children in the redesigning of streets and greenways. How we shape our outdoor spaces and transport infrastructure has important economic implications as well. As Waygood and Manaugh (Chapter 14) discuss, capital investments in active and transport-friendly infrastructure may create multi-modal mobility options for children and adults alike, entailing reduced costs for families and school districts. Health Impact Assessment can also be another way of better integrating such considerations in our planning practices (Rojas-Rueda, Chapter 8).

In conclusion, evidence of the link between transport and children's wellbeing has been presented, showing that transport can impact children's wellbeing by facilitating or restricting their mobility (e.g., their access to locations and activities), by influencing their wellbeing when traveling (defined as intrinsic, e.g., physical activity, injuries due to negligence, or social interactions with other citizens), and impacting them through potential dangers resulted from other travelers' behavior (also called "extrinsic", a typical example being car crashes). This book has taken a broad approach to the subject but is in no way all-inclusive. Researchers contributing to this book have devoted their time and resources to studying the subject among children of different ages, among children traveling by different modes, and among children living in different contexts; in doing so, they have generated much-needed and valuable knowledge. However, far fewer researchers have systematically discussed policy implications as a means of counteracting potentially negative wellbeing consequences.

The following sections focus on the relationship between children's wellbeing and transport, on transport attributes affecting child wellbeing, on how to include children's voices in transport planning, and on how to change children's travel on the basis of a policy perspective. In the final section, Conclusions, we discuss important avenues for future research, and how to move forward.

2 The relationships between transport and children's wellbeing

As has been emphasized throughout this book, research on children's everyday travel and their wellbeing has increased in recent years. Existing research on children's travel focuses largely on mode choice and physical health (e.g., physical activity, injury); however, other domains of their wellbeing remain less discussed. A large amount of research has also explored the external impact of traffic in the form of emissions, traffic safety and traffic accidents; but again, in relation to physical health attributes rather than other domains of wellbeing.

In an effort to investigate the impact of transport on children's wellbeing, Waygood et al. (2017) compiled and analyzed 93 studies in the field. Their conclusion was that five domains of wellbeing (physical, psychological, cognitive, social and economic) are influenced by the transport practices of both children themselves and others. The introductory chapter of this book defines these domains, and further in-depth discussions were made in various chapters of this book. A key finding from Waygood et al.'s review was that a child receives positive wellbeing-related benefits from active and independent transport. In Chapter 2, Larouche et al. present a number of research reviews which convincingly show that children who travel actively by bike or on foot are more physically active than children who travel more passively (i.e., by motorized means). The hypothesis that children who travel actively compensate for this by being less active in their leisure time is not found to be true. These findings provide insights into a potential causal relationship; and in accordance with this, Larouche et al. conclude that active travel contributes to healthy habits, which are positively associated with children's long-term wellbeing. However, such evidence with regard to other aspects of a child's wellbeing is not as prevalent (see, for instance, the discussions in Chapters 3 and 4). Active and independent travel is in focus in Chapter 4, which discusses transport's ability to contribute to children's social wellbeing. Waygood shows how transport enables children to socially interact with other people in society (e.g., neighbors, friends, relatives, people working in the city). Children's independent travel, in particular, has shown itself to contribute to more social interaction, benefiting the child's social development. However, transport can also limit children by acting as a barrier to social interaction. A worrying example of this is the current trend wherein children are increasingly being driven by their parents. The car has effectively become a barrier to spontaneously meeting, or greeting, people along the way.

Wootman et al., in Chapter 3, take their starting point in children's psychological wellbeing. More specifically, this chapter focuses on research that tries to establish a link between children's means of travel and their experienced independence, as well as their confidence, mood, wellbeing, and satisfaction with travel. Two studies from the 1990s were identified, but the majority of studies identified were published in the latter part of the 21st century. Based on the empirical findings of these studies, the authors call for the careful use of, and clear definitions of, concepts and methods in order to be able to make comparisons and generalize research results, knowledge which is necessary if we are to be able to do meta-analyses in the future in this field of research.

Our knowledge of the relationship between everyday travel and children's wellbeing has improved thanks to the emerging literature on this topic. Current research also indicates that the relationship between travel behavior and children's wellbeing may not be a linear one, with the effects possibly varying across geographic locations and socio-demographic groups, for instance. Thus, improvements to transport infrastructure, for example, improved safety, can only produce limited benefits within some contexts and mobility cultures, where constant adult supervision is seen as a necessary element of childhood. However, children's independent mobility is becoming more restricted than that of previous generations in many cultures, generally in the name of safety (or the absence of it). In order for transport planning practice to enable a cultural shift, we need to better understand perceptions of children's safety, and the social and ecological forces influencing those perceptions. Mitra and Manaugh propose a theoretical model (the social-ecological framework) for exploring these relationships in Chapter 5. Their conceptualization builds on previous works that have emphasized the difference between adult travel behavior and children's mobility (Johansson, 2006; McMillan, 2005; Mitra, 2013; Panter, Jones, & van Sluijs, 2008), and provides a comprehensive framework for exploring children's mobility with regard to their travel destinations, independence and mode choice.

Overall, the contemporary research presented in this book shows that everyday travel influences all five domains of a child's wellbeing, as initially pointed out by Waygood et al. (2017). Existing research has mainly focused on one domain at a time; however, some have recognized that several domains are influenced by transport practices and experiences simultaneously. Important insights have been gained; however, as pointed out in various chapters of this book, important knowledge gaps still exist. In future studies, further focus needs to be placed on the relationship between children's travel and the consequences related to their wellbeing, above and beyond the impact on their physical activity levels, which still remains the key focus of much of the literature on children's travel.

Continued research can provide insights and guidance with regard to ways of including wellbeing data both in travel behavior models and transport project appraisals, using improved applications of existing planning and assessment tools such as the Health Impact Assessments (HIA: Chapter 8) and economic cost-benefit analysis (Chapter 14). Continued research is also needed in terms of exploring transport interventions and policies that can contribute to increased wellbeing among children; Mitra and Abbasi (Chapter 13) and McDonald, Palmer, and Steiner (Chapter 10) discuss some new approaches.

3 Transport attributes affecting children's wellbeing

Over the past century, transport engineering guidelines and practices (e.g., level of service) have typically focused on the maximization of motor vehicle movements, frequently emphasizing speed. The focus on individual mobility in motor vehicles was paired with Modern-era urban planning practices that highlight the separation of housing from other land uses (e.g., work, shopping, schools and recreational facilities) and a low-density urban form. Within this context, transport infrastructure were designed to have a primary emphasis on space-time convergence, supposedly allowing great accessibility to destinations, despite great distances. However, as outlined in Chapter 6 by Rothman et al., fast-moving traffic on urban roads creates dangerous conditions for children and adults alike. Not surprisingly as a result, traffic collisions are one of the primary causes of death in children and adolescents. The above is just one example of how a transport attribute, in this case speed, can have unintentional negative impact on a child's wellbeing.

The benefits of new transport infrastructure are often measured in terms of travel times savings. This approach assumes that a working adult can use the time gained (from an efficient transport system) to be more productive or, in simpler terms, to work. Travel times are also important for children, but can entail both positive and negative consequences depending on the contextual conditions. Long travel times can improve a child's health and wellbeing if they involve physical movement or social interaction. In contrast, long travel times can have a negative effect when a child is exposed to poor air quality or a greater risk of traffic danger. More broadly, and although not directly addressed in this book, we cannot ignore the long-term impact of climate change on health and wellbeing. A transport system designed for children's needs and their willingness to travel independently by more sustainable modes can make a difference in mitigating these impacts. Independent travel, as an alternative to parents' chauffeuring, may also help in reducing carbon dioxide emissions and traffic congestion, with co-benefits for children's physical and mental health.

Traveling with friends is generally seen as one major benefit of the active and independent modes of travel. This offers children an opportunity to discuss their world without worrying about adult censorship (parents, teachers, etc.). These active and independent journeys are also associated with greater community connections (see Chapter 4 for a detailed discussion). Walking may obviously be a better means of connecting with those living in the same area; however, it appears that traveling independently increases such instances. Conceivably, when children are traveling independently, they are probably more aware of their surroundings, and they may also be choosing routes where they know positive social interactions can occur. Putting adult accompaniment to one side, walking can benefit children as it offers the opportunity to reflect on and take control of their actions.

Although research is growing in this field, much remains to be learned. Other transport attributes may be important; transport attributes and different segments of children may be worth looking into, as well as different contextual factors determining or influencing the importance of various transport attributes (for instance, Lin and He in Chapter 18 discuss transport attributes in developed countries as well as in developing countries; similarly van de Craats, van den Berg, Kemperman, and Waygood in Chapter 17 discuss children's transport and wellbeing in the Netherlands, where the predominant mobility culture is different from what is commonly expected in other western societies).

4 How to include children's voices in transport planning

The innovation literature on product and service development has been showing for decades that user involvement is important and adds important value when new ideas are being generated, developed, assessed and implemented (Magnusson, Matthing, & Kristensson, 2003; Von Hippel, 1977). Although most research has been conducted with adults, children have also been acknowledged as both consumers and knowledgeable end-users, and have also been included successfully in the development of new ideas and products, e.g. building new models for LEGO or computer game features for computer games producers (Jeppesen & Molin, 2003). However, the involvement of children in the problem identification, idea generation and development processes is less common in the domains of urban and transport planning/engineering. Ross (Chapter 15) and Mitra and Abbasi (Chapter 13), in two different chapters this book, discuss this limitation in further detail and showcase the potential of including children in the process.

Ross proposes video-ethnography as a promising method to use among children with different forms of disabilities. In the case study, this method made it possible for the participating children to get their voices heard by allowing them to make films or take photos of the important situations and problems in their daily lives, e.g. traveling to school or doing other activities. Three approaches are suggested to assist in participatory methods considering the views by disabled children, namely using inclusive technologies, supporting their engagement, and using reflexivity in order to adequately understand their experiences and viewpoints.

Looking beyond (dis)ability, we would argue that cellular (mobile) phones, cameras and tablets should be seen as promising tools that easily allow any child, with or without a disability, to participate in the planning or design processes concerning transport and/or local environments. As an increasing number of children are becoming connected to different social media platforms and other information channels, digital techniques could be used for online communication, making these children's voices heard instantly and paving the way for easily-administered dialogues between children and city and transport planners. Although this is a promising way to go in the future, it is also important to recognize that, regardless of the type of method employed, the ethical aspects must always be considered when including children in such processes. Parental consent may be required, and data protection and privacy concerns must be considered. Within this context, inequity as regards both access to and the use of technology is something that should also be given much consideration. For example, a research or planning exercise that requires such tools to be available to children or families may exclude those who do not have such tools at their disposal.

In a similar vein, Mitra and Abbasi (Chapter 13) discuss a human-centric design approach to involving children in guiding the designing of interventions and the redesigning of local environments. The authors report on a case study where focus groups were engaged in order to understand how local residents, adults and children alike, move around their neighborhoods. The results from school-based focus groups, with respect to concerns about and the desire to change their local environments, was used during design-negotiation processes. The process produced positive results children felt safer crossing roads after taking part in the design intervention. Children's voices are not commonly heard in neighborhood and transport planning processes; this case study provides an example of the importance of including them in decision-making processes. In another chapter (Chapter 12), Johansson and colleagues discuss this topic more broadly, proposing four different approaches, i.e. place attachment, affordance, wayfinding and prospect-refuge, which may help us understand and address children's perspectives and experiences during the planning, design and management of urban spaces.

A third way of providing children with voices concerns surveys, diaries and interviews where the children themselves report on their experiences and thoughts in relation to travel, independence, social interaction, and wellbeing. These methods have indeed been the traditional means of capturing the voices of children, and should be seen as important problem-identification tools that can assist in transport planning. Westman et al. (Chapter 3) argue that it is important to apply methods that are adapted to the age of the child, whereby younger children should receive more focused and open-ended questions while older children should participate alone rather than with their peers in order to avoid social influences. A point of criticism has been raised in that, the absence of a universal set of methods and measures has made it difficult to provide conclusive answers related to the generalizability of current findings linking transport to a child's wellbeing. Although limiting the generalizability, the plethora of methods paves the way for a wider understanding of various phenomena that are of relevance.

Survey methods, video-ethnography, and focus groups are good at identifying the relevant problems and the important relationships. However, in order to more explicitly make children's voices heard, and acknowledged, during transport planning processes, other ways need to be explored. Taking a closer look at the innovation literature can give rise to new methods of including children's voices in transport planning in the future (Durl, Trischler, & Dietrich, 2017). New and interactive technologies are promising, e.g. virtual open innovation groups (Nambisan & Baron, 2009), where different stakeholders and citizens can meet online and innovate together, creating solutions to the relevant problems for the future.

5 How to change children's travel

One hundred and ninety-six countries are signatories to the United Nations Convention on the Rights of the Child (United Nations Treaty Collection, 1990), which emphasizes children's wellbeing through various articles. An example of this is Article 27, which underlines the importance of providing a quality of living that facilitates a "child's physical, mental, spiritual, moral and social development." Most countries have already committed to protecting their children and their wellbeing; however, this book has highlighted that children's rights and needs have mostly been neglected during the planning, design and management of urban spaces and transport infrastructure. Current policy and practice have contributed to a situation where children are dependent on their parents for their mobility needs. In order for our policies and planning practice to be just and equitable, children's right to independent mobility and a safe transport environment must be given more attention.

Decisions regarding capital investment in transport infrastructure are almost always based on assessments of cost versus benefit. Unfortunately, for most part of the past century, space-time convergence (i.e., mobility) was seen as a key benefit of transport systems with few other considerations; unsurprisingly, the design speed of roadways was a key indicator of the level of service. During recent decades, however, we have seen a shift in transport planning approaches. For example, the multi-modal level of service, which considers the efficient and desirable movement of pedestrians, cycles, public transit vehicles and cars, has become a popular concept when designing roadways. The Vision Zero concept (see Chapters 6 and 9), which emphasizes the value of traffic safety and fatality rates over any other benefits offered by transport systems, is becoming increasingly popular across the world after being successful in Sweden and some other European countries. Several chapters of this book focus on new methods and approaches that may advance this emerging emphasis on health and wellbeing during transport planning and design processes. For example, Rojas-Rueda (Chapter 8) discusses how to utilize and improve Health Impact Assessments (HIA) in order to emphasize transport-related impacts on children's wellbeing and to inform transport planning processes. Similarly, Waygood and Manaugh (Chapter 14) discuss the economic benefits of investment in transport infrastructure which makes active transport (e.g., walking, cycling) safe, reporting that several communities have used this approach to influencing transport planning processes.

An improved approach to infrastructure planning can help improve safety and thus also children's transport experiences and outcomes. For decades, the Netherlands has been building infrastructure that separates and protects cyclists from automobile traffic. It would appear, according to van de Craats et al. in Chapter 17, that this approach has been successful in protecting children who travel by bicycle, since the largest number of school journeys in that country are by bicycle. Japan has also succeeded in protecting journeys on foot through residential streets that are often narrow, which limits speed, as identified by Waygood and Taniguchi in Chapter 16. These streets would be termed shared spaces in the Western countries, where all modes can mingle and share the same space. Arterial roads that are meant to facilitate high-speed mobility do have pavements (or sidewalks), but the speeds on such road are still often limited to 40 km/h. The examples of the Netherlands and Japan show that vulnerable road users can be protected using context-appropriate solutions. The cost of such solutions should be understood as the cost of high mobility, not the cost of active travel.

Significant wellbeing benefits may also be gained by treating neighborhood streets as parts of the public domain, and not merely as roadways facilitating the movement of vehicles. Children have traditionally used the streets adjacent to their homes to gather and play; however, in many places around the world, they have been engineered out of their streets in order to facilitate unobstructed, high-speed vehicle movement. Somewhat ironically, children's health and safety is often cited as a reason for legally preventing them from using these important public spaces. However, community-led efforts to reverse this practice are becoming increasingly common (see also Chapter 9). As McDonald, Palmer, and Steiner discuss in Chapter 10, communities across the Western world have organized play streets so as to bring children back to their neighborhood streets, creating new opportunities for play and independent mobility. Programs that create local play areas, and also local events, will improve children's wellbeing by improving their independent travel and by reducing the negative impact of transport on them.

In urban planning, the siting of schools, parks, and other leisure and recreational destinations must take accessibility by foot or bicycle into account, not just access by high mobility modes such as cars. Primary schools should operate at the local level, ideally using catchment areas with a radius of 2 km at most, to allow walking and cycling. Middle and high schools should facilitate active travel, but should also be located where they are accessible by public transport. These policies can be critical in developing lifelong habits of mobility where the use of active and sustainable transport modes would be integral parts reducing their dependency on expensive private transport options at an young age and also later as adults.

Safe and convenient access to schools is a daily concern for millions of parents across the world. A vicious circle exists whereby some parents will cite traffic danger as a reason for driving their children to school, thus exacerbating the problem. Rothman, Buliung, Howard, Macarthur, and Macpherson (2017) have described the dangerous behaviors arising from parents dropping their children off at school. Countries with extremely low numbers of traffic deaths in school-going children, e.g. Japan, have national laws that restrict traffic within a 500 m radius of elementary schools (see Chapter 16). If restricting traffic at such a distance is impossible, creating a smaller no drop off radius could also help improve conditions as discussed by Shaw in Chapter 9. Parents could drop their children off roughly 100 m from the school, thus reducing the comings and goings right by the school, where the children will concentrate. One individual's desire to drive his/her child "right to the door" should not override the safety of the other children. If the roles were reversed, one assumes that that a specific parent would want the other parents to respect the life of his/her child. Simply put, one's convenience should not trump society's safety.

Related to this is the school-related policy of creating School Safety Zones, where traffic is limited and the advantage is given to active modes. Road crossing distances can be reduced using street design features such as curb extensions. Speeds should be limited as much as possible. Integrating the above-mentioned restriction on through-traffic with corridors would create conditions where parents would feel safe letting their children walk. In combination with that, school programs could work towards developing walking school buses. Due to its success, the Japanese model (see Chapter 16), which has existed for over half a century, should be looked to for inspiration. Seeing the journey to school as part of the school day would be one way of better incorporating this.

The social-ecological framework presented in Chapter 5, by Mitra and Manaugh, can support practitioners in identifying the right "market" for interventions, and the specific factors to be addressed. Additionally, the model emphasizes that the factors of influence may not be the same for every socio-demographic group, or every geographic location. Thus, interventions may need to specifically cater to local needs; a "one-size-fits-all" approach may not work that well. Another approach is to take a holistic perspective on transport planning, as discussed by Johansson et al. (Chapter 12). This implies that transport planners should consider the prerequisites of the physical and social environments that enable children to develop an attachment to their neighborhoods, to develop an understanding of what various places offer or afford them, and how this becomes part of their independent mobility, in order to facilitate their wayfinding and address how the environment supports how they experience safety.

6 Conclusion and how to move forwards

In the different chapters of this book, the impact of transport on children's wellbeing has been discussed with respect to the physical, psychological, cognitive, social and economic domains. A number of promising avenues have been identified, with future research directions being suggested. Great merit should be given to these specific suggestions; however, the most important message in this book might be to encourage academics, practitioners and policy makers to stop believing that providing for adults' mobility will necessarily provide for children's transport needs and wellbeing. As has been discussed, children's developmental and physical attributes are different to those of adults; so too are their daily travel needs. Great advantages in the transporting of adults, who are more capable, should not come at the expense of a vulnerable and marginalized group. We thus plead for a more dedicated and nuanced approach to transport planning and policy making, which not only takes such impacts into consideration, but which also includes children's voices during planning, design and management of infrastructure and public spaces. After all, they are citizens of our cities and nations, and they are the future that we are building our society for.

References

Durl, J., Trischler, J., & Dietrich, T. (2017). Co-designing with young consumers—reflections, challenges and benefits. *Young Consumers*, *18*(4), 439–455.

Jeppesen, L. B., & Molin, M. J. (2003). Consumers as co-developers: Learning and innovation outside the firm. *Technology Analysis & Strategic Management*, *15*, 363–384.

Johansson, M. (2006). Environmental and parental factors as determinants of mode for children's leisure travel. *Journal of Environmental Psychology*, *26*, 156–169.

Magnusson, P. R., Matthing, J., & Kristensson, P. (2003). Managing user involvement in service innovation: Experiments with innovating end users. *Journal of Service Research*, *6*(2), 111–124.

McMillan, T. E. (2005). Urban form and a child's trip to school: The current literature and a framework for future research. *Journal of Planning Literature*, *19*(4), 440–456.

Mitra, R. (2013). Independent mobility and mode choice for school transportation: A review and framework for future research. *Transport Reviews*, *33*(1), 21–43.

Nambisan, S., & Baron, R. A. (2009). Virtual customer environments: Testing a model of voluntary participation in value co-creation activities. *Journal of Product Innovation Management*, *26*(4), 388–406.

Panter, J. R., Jones, A. P., & van Sluijs, E. M. F. (2008). Environmental determinants of active travel in youth: A review and framework for future research. *International Journal of Behavioral Nutrition and Physical Activity*, *5*, 34.

Rothman, L., Buliung, R., Howard, A., Macarthur, C., & Macpherson, A. (2017). The school environment and student car drop-off at elementary schools. *Travel Behaviour and Society*, *9*, 50–57.

United Nations Treaty Collection (1990). *Convention on the rights of the child*. *Retrieved from: https://www.ohchr.org/en/professionalinterest/pages/crc.aspx*.

Von Hippel, E. (1977). Has a customer already developed your next product. *Sloan Management Review*, *18*(2), 63–74.

Waygood, E. O. D., Friman, M., Olsson, L. E., & Taniguchi, A. (2017). Transport and child well-being: An integrative review. *Travel Behaviour and Society*, *9*, 32–49.

Index

Note: Page numbers followed by *f* indicate figures and *t* indicate tables.

Printed in the United States
By Bookmasters